Sep

Dearest Paco

Many, many happy

day! Lots of love, Vinayak (VV)

THE COMPACT BOOK OF THE WORLD CUP

CHRIS HUNT

First published in Great Britain in 2010 by Hayden Media Limited

A CIP catalogue record for this title is available from the British Library

ISBN 978-0-9564976-0-4

Printed in the United Kingdom by Butler Tanner and Dennis

A 'MILE AWAY CLUB' PRODUCTION
Author: Chris Hunt
Contact: www.ChrisHunt.biz
Designed by David Houghton
Additional contributions: Steve Cresswell, James Eastham, Nick Gibbs, Tim Hartley, Kevin Hughes, Sara Hunt, Luke Nicoli, Mike Pattenden, Alistair Philips, John Plummer, Gary Tipp, Andrew Winter

A Hayden Media Book, Ashford, Middlesex, Great Britain

CONTENTS

ITALIA
FIFA
FIFA
FIFA
FIFA
FIFA
FIFA

THE HISTORY OF THE WORLD CUP

The World Cup

There is no other sporting event that captures the imagination across the globe quite like the World Cup. Ever since the first competition in Uruguay in 1930, the tournament has grown in popularity and prestige. That's not to say it hasn't been without its share of problems. Indeed, the origins of the tournament were so wrapped up in politics that it took 26 years for the idea of a World Cup to become a reality.

During its inaugural meeting in 1904, FIFA agreed that it had the sole right to organise a tournament that brought together the world's strongest national football teams. However, it wasn't until the 1920s that an idea nurtured by FIFA president Jules Rimet and French football administrator Henri Delaunay gained impetus.

In the interim the Olympic football tournament had begun to establish itself as a credible competition, and such was its success that a FIFA commission was established in 1927 to examine the creation of a football World Cup. The recommendations struck a chord with FIFA's Executive Committee, and at the 1928 congress, held at the Amsterdam Olympics, FIFA voted in favour of a world championship.

Pelé, 1970 World Cup

The Uruguayans beat Argentina in 1928 to retain the Olympic title and proved they were the country most determined to host the inaugural World Cup. Not only did the Uruguayan government offer to build a magnificent new stadium in Montevideo capable of staging a showcase event, but they offered to cover the travel and accommodation costs of the visiting teams. Rivals Italy, Holland, Hungary, Spain and Sweden were unprepared to match this offer and withdrew their bids, leaving Uruguay to stage the first World Cup.

On July 13, 1930 the first two World Cup games kicked-off simultaneously amid the snow of a southern hemisphere winter. The tournament was not without its problems. At one stage it seemed that no European sides would make the two-week journey by sea. Ultimately just four signed on for the competition, although they were hardly major football nations at the time: France, Romania, Belgium and Yugoslavia.

It was the only World Cup not to involve qualifying rounds, with 13 invited teams competing for the 12-and-a-half-inch solid silver and goldplated prize. The original World Cup trophy was designed by French sculptor Abel Lafleur and based upon one of the great surviving masterpieces of Greek sculpture, the Winged Victory of Samothrace.

Since 1934 the 18 tournaments have seen only seven different winners. However, the World Cup has still been punctuated by some dramatic upsets that have helped create football history: the USA's defeat of England in 1950; North Korea beating Italy in 1966; Cameroon's opening match defeat of reigning champions Argentina in 1990; and Senegal's shock victory against holders France in 2002.

Bobby Moore and the England team celebrate, 1966

The early years of the competition were dogged by controversy. In 1934 holders Uruguay, still upset by the stay-away attitude of the European sides four years earlier, boycotted the tournament in Italy. Rumours also circulated about the many biased refereeing decisions in favour of the hosts. Sadly, not for the last time, the shadow of world politics threatened to eclipse the event, as Italian dictator Benito Mussolini used the World Cup competition as a showcase for his Fascist regime.

In 1938 the tournament was played under the clouds of impending conflict and there were late withdrawals. Spain was in the middle of a bloody civil war, while Austria had been annexed by Germany, and many of the best Austrian players had been co-opted into a 'Greater Germany' side.

The World Cup was contested three times

Fabio Grosso, Italy, 2006 World Cup Final

Rummenigge of West Germany, 1982 World Cup Final

in the 1930s before the Second World War put a 12-year stop to the competition. The trophy was renamed the Jules Rimet Cup in 1946, having survived World War II hidden in a shoebox under the bed of Dr Ottorino Barassi, the Italian vice-president of FIFA.

In 1950 the World Cup made its comeback in Brazil. To host the event the country built the Maracanã, the largest stadium in the world. It was the first time England had entered the World Cup, although several other countries withdrew on the eve of the competition. This could have resulted in scheduling headaches, but the original draw was retained, leaving a decidedly uneven competition: two groups consisting of four teams, one of three teams, and one of two.

The World Cup format was rejigged again in 1954. Each group of four in the first round possessed two seeded teams who played only the two unseeded teams in their group. This increased the likelihood of sides ending up with the same number of points, and the need for play-offs meant that 26 games had to be played in just 19 days. It was a system that was never used again. But the constant evolution of the format has not deterred interest.

Throughout its history the number of teams entering has continued to rise: just 38 nations started the 1954 qualifying campaign, while 204 nations entered the 2010 competition.

In 1974 the World Cup had a new solid gold trophy, three-time winners Brazil having retained the Jules Rimet Cup in 1970. In 1982, FIFA president João Havelange expanded the field from 16 teams to 24, opening the World Cup to the less established football nations. His expansionist philosophy saw the USA given the tournament in 1994, while in 1998 it was expanded further to include 32 finalists.

The tournament continues to evolve. The 2002 competition in Japan and South Korea marked the first time the World Cup was held in Asia, and the first occasion it was staged by co-hosts, while in 2010 it visits yet another continent when the South Africans play host.

It's been a long journey for the World Cup since its first tentative steps in 1930. Despite its many changes in format, such as the introduction of a second group stage between 1974 and 1982, and the use of the 'golden goal' in 1998, it still remains the biggest sporting event in the world, with viewing figures to match. However, the focus still remains the same: to raise aloft that glorious golden trophy.

Uruguay 1930

STADIUM GUIDE

TOURNAMENT STATS

WINNER Uruguay

FINAL
Uruguay 4-2 Argentina

SEMI-FINALS
Argentina 6-1 USA
Uruguay 6-1 Yugoslavia

THIRD PLACE PLAY-OFF
Not held

TOP GOALSCORERS
8 goals: Guillermo Stábile (Argentina)
5 goals: Pedro Cea (Uruguay)
4 goals: Guillermo Subiabre (Chile)

FASTEST GOAL
1 minute: Adalbert Desu (Romania v Peru)

TOTAL GOALS
70

AVERAGE GOALS
3.88 per game

There were sound reasons why 1930 was the right time for Uruguay to host the World Cup. Not only were they the holders of the Olympic title, but 1930 marked the centenary of the country's independence. The decision hadn't been popular with the European nations. Coming as it did just eight months after the Wall Street Crash, they weren't comfortable with the expense and travelling time that a tournament in South America would entail.

As a consequence, the inaugural tournament was contested by only 13 countries out of the 41 that could claim FIFA membership, with nine of the competing nations hailing from the Americas: Brazil, Bolivia, Mexico, Argentina, Chile, Peru, Paraguay, Uruguay and the United States.

There was a disappointing turn-out from Europe, with only Yugoslavia, Belgium, France and Romania making the two-week journey by boat, the latter no doubt encouraged by royal approval as they were coached by the country's reigning monarch, King Carol. None of the British sides entered, as they had withdrawn from FIFA in 1928 following a row over the definition of 'amateurism', while the Italians didn't attend as they had wanted to stage the competition themselves.

The rather unwieldy number of teams was split into four pools – four teams in one, three in the rest – and the draw itself didn't take place until all the sides had arrived in Uruguay. The first two World Cup matches were staged simultaneously on July 13, 1930, but disappointingly neither game took place at the Centenary Stadium in Montevideo, because it would not be finished for five more days.

In one of the opening matches the French comfortably beat Mexico 4-1, their first – and the

Keeper Ballestrero watches Argentina's first goal hit the net in the World Cup final

tournament's first – goal scored by Lucien Laurent in the 19th minute. The victory was even more impressive considering they played most of the match with ten men, as their keeper left the pitch through injury after 20 minutes (no substitutes were allowed at the World Cup until 1970).

France were probably the European side most likely to win the tournament, but any such ambitions came grinding to a halt in their next match, a controversial encounter with Argentina. The South Americans were leading 1-0, but with the French slowly but surely gaining the upper hand it was an advantage that looked increasingly fragile. However, Brazilian referee Almeido Rego blew the whistle for full time with six minutes still left on the clock and with France on the attack, provoking angry scenes and many accusations of foul play. Such was the furore that the referee called the players back out to complete the final six minutes, but by that stage the French had lost their rhythm and the game ended 1-0.

The Argentinians went on to qualify for the semi-finals at a canter. They defeated Chile 3-1, but had been at their most impressive in a 6-3 win over Mexico that featured three penalties and a hat-trick from young striker Guillermo Stábile.

THE FINAL

URUGUAY (1) **4**
ARGENTINA (2) **2**

Date Wednesday July 30, 1930
Attendance 93,000
Venue Centenary Stadium, Montevideo
Referee John Langenus (Belgium)

Uruguay coach Alberto Suppicci

Argentina coaches Francisco Olazar & Juan José Tramutola

URUGUAY
ENRIQUE BALLESTRERO
JOSE NASAZZI (c)
ERNESTO MASCHERONI
JOSÉ ANDRADE
ALVARO GESTIDO
LORENZO FERNÁNDEZ
HECTOR SCARONE
PEDRO CEA *Goal: 57 mins*
PABLO DORADO *Goal: 12 mins*
HECTOR CASTRO *Goal: 89 mins*
SANTOS IRIARTE *Goal: 68 mins*

ARGENTINA
JUAN BOTASSO
JOSE DELLA TORRE
FERNANDO PATERNÓSTER
JUAN EVARISTO
LUÍS MONTI
PEDRO SUÁREZ
FRANCISCO VARALLO
MANUEL FERREIRA (c)
CARLOS PEUCELLE *Goal: 20 mins*
GUILLERMO STÀBILE *Goal: 37 mins*
MARIO EVARISTO

July 18, 1930: five days into the World Cup and the Centenary Stadium is ready for the inauguration ceremony.

The Yugoslavians headed Pool 2 after wins over Brazil and Bolivia. They were the only European entrants to reach the semi-finals, as Uruguay and the USA took the honours in Pools 3 and 4 respectively. Uruguay didn't concede a single goal as they despatched Peru and Romania, a feat matched by the Americans, who had little difficulty putting Belgium and Paraguay to the sword in two impressive 3-0 victories. The latter USA victory featured the first World Cup hat-trick from Bert Patenaude, although for 76 years the official match report attributed one of his goals to captain Thomas Florie and it wasn't until 2006 that FIFA considered new evidence and amended their records to confirm Patenaude as the scorer.

Argentina and Uruguay ran up high scores against lesser opposition in the semi-finals, Argentina battering the United States in every sense of the word in a 6-1 win. Uruguay, meanwhile, started their showdown with Yugoslavia slowly, falling behind after four minutes. The lead was short-lived as Pedro Cea equalised after 18 minutes. Pelegrin Anselmo also claimed a brace of goals before the interval to make it 3-1, although in the build up to his second goal the ball had appeared to go out of play, only to be kicked discretely back onto the pitch by a uniformed policeman. Iriarte made it 4-1 with half an hour to play, and Cea completed an extraordinary hat-trick with goals in the 67th and 72nd minutes to cap a crushing victory.

The stage was set for a fiercely contested World Cup final, as Argentina and Uruguay had met to decide Olympic gold two years earlier in

THE FIRST WORLD CUP GOAL

As the World Cup had been the idea of Frenchman Jules Rimet, it was fitting that the first goal should be scored by his compatriot, Lucien Laurent. With two games kicking off at the same time on the opening day, it took 19 minutes before France registered the competition's first goal against Mexico.

"Thépot, our keeper, launched the ball long for Augustin Chantrel, who in turn found Liberati on the wing," Laurent would much later recall. "He then played a cut-back cross to me. The cut-back is football's deadliest weapon and I volleyed it first time into the top corner. When I scored I just felt a simple joy, the joy of a goalscorer with his team-mates. At the time it never occurred to me that it was the first goal in World Cup history."

Amsterdam. Uruguay won the Olympic encounter after a replay and this created an intense rivalry between the two finalists that manifested itself in the hostile reaction of the home crowd. Argentina may have been the reigning South American champions, but in this environment they were unable to exact revenge on their great rivals.

It was perhaps fitting that the first hosts should also end up as its first winners. On top after 12 minutes through Pablo Dorado, Uruguay were nonetheless stunned when Carlos Peucelle brought the Argentinians level eight minutes later, firing a ferocious shot high to the keeper's left, leaving the stranded Ballestrero no option but to watch the ball hit the back of the net.

It was Argentina who took the lead in the 37th minute from close range through Stábile – the man who would finish the tournament as its highest scorer with eight goals – and they skilfully dominated the remainder of the half.

Uruguay rallied after the break, determinedly clawing their way back into the match. Pedro Cea equalised in the 57th minute, and Santos Iriarte snatched the lead with a shot from outside the area 11 minutes later. Argentina were unlucky when Francisco Varallo had a shot cleared off the line by Andrade, and their ill fortune was compounded a minute before the end when one-armed striker Hector Castro hit the winner.

Montevideo celebrated with a spontaneous street party, motor horns sounding and ships sirens wailing. The following day was declared a national holiday and each member of the winning team was gifted a house. In Buenos Aires the scenes couldn't have been more different, as thousands of despondent Argentines returned from Montevideo by boat. An angry mob stoned the Uruguayan Consulate and the two football associations broke off relations with each other.

THE BATTLE OF THE BALL

The first World Cup final didn't manage to kick off without incident. FIFA's competition rules hadn't anticipated that each team might want to use their own ball and a pre-match argument ensued. "The Uruguayans wanted to use their bigger ball and we were expecting to play with ours," recalled Argentina striker Francisco Varallo, nicknamed 'El Canonito' (the Little Canon) because of his powerful shot.

"A coin thrown into the air decided that it would be our ball and we could have won the match. I hit the post when we were leading 2-1, but as they were losing they disrespected the promise and used their ball in the second-half."

Playing with their own ball the Uruguayans fought their way back into the game and clinched the trophy.

Below left: Castro scores the winning goal in the final. Below: Uruguay start the celebrations.

Italy 1934

STADIUM GUIDE

TOURNAMENT STATS

WINNER Italy

FINAL
Italy 2-1 Czechoslovakia *(aet)*

SEMI-FINALS
Czechoslovakia 3-1 Germany
Italy 1-0 Austria

THIRD PLACE PLAY-OFF
Germany 3-2 Austria

TOP GOALSCORERS
5 goals: Oldrich Nejedly (Czechoslovakia)
4 goals: Angelo Schiavio (Italy), Edmund Conen (Germany)

FASTEST GOAL
30 seconds: Ernst Lehner (Germany v Austria)

TOTAL GOALS
70

AVERAGE GOALS
4.12 per game

Italian dictator Benito Mussolini hoped to use the first World Cup on European soil to further the cause of his Fascist regime, but while the tournament can claim to have been a success it was not without controversy. Following the widespread European boycott of the 1930 competition, the South American nations retaliated, with holders Uruguay not even sending a team and both Brazil and Argentina fielding understrength sides.

With 32 teams competing, qualification was required before 16 nations reached the finals in Italy. Unlike the 1930 tournament that had been staged solely in Montevideo, eight cities across Italy hosted matches, the first round kicking off simultaneously on May 27 in Genoa, Turin, Florence, Milan, Trieste, Rome, Naples and Bologna, though naturally it was to be Rome that would eventually stage the showpiece final.

Brazil, Argentina, USA and Egypt were the only non-European countries in the final 16 and all were making the long journey home after just one game, although the USA played one extra pre-tournament qualifier against Mexico in Rome. The Americans

The Italians lift their coach after victory in the final

had made a late application and, unfairly for the Mexicans who had qualified once already, FIFA insisted that the two teams play-off against each other. The Mexicans made an 8,000 mile round trip without even playing in the finals proper.

The Argentina team to arrive in Italy was very different to the one that had lost the final four years earlier in Uruguay. Many of the country's stars had moved abroad to play in the European leagues and a split in domestic football had left a breakaway professional league and an amateur league running in tandem. Not one member of their 1930 team appeared against Sweden in Bologna. However, despite their largely uncapped team, twice the Argentinians led before a late goal

THE FINAL

ITALY (0) 2
CZECHOSLOVAKIA (0) 1
(AET; 1-1 AT 90 MINS)

Date June 10, 1934
Attendance 55,000
Venue Stadio del PNF, Rome
Referee Ivan Eklind (Sweden)

Italy coach Vittorio Pozzo

Czechoslovakia coach Cornel Petru

ITALY

- GIANPIERO COMBI (c)
- ERALDO MONZEGLIO
- LUIGI ALLEMANDI
- ATTILIO FERRARIS
- LUÍS MONTI
- LUIGI BERTOLINI
- GIUSEPPE MEAZZA
- GIOVANNI FERRARI
- ENRIQUE GUAITA
- ANGELO SCHIAVIO — *Goal: 95 mins*
- RAIMUNDO ORSI — *Goal: 81 mins*

CZECHOSLOVAKIA

- FRANTISEK PLÁNICKA (c)
- LADISLAV ZENISEK
- JOSEF CTYROKY
- JOSEF KOSTÁLEK
- STEFAN CAMBAL
- RUDOLF KRCIL
- FRANTISEK SVOBODA
- OLDRICH NEJEDLY
- FRANTISEK JUNEK
- JIRI SOBOTKA
- ANTONIN PUC — *Goal: 71 mins*

from Knut Kroon sent the Swedes through 3-2.

Brazil were barely in the game in Genoa before the Spanish took total control, leading 2-0 by the break. The South Americans pulled one back but their fate was sealed by Isidro Langara's second goal of the match.

France took a shock lead against second-favourites Austria in Turin, and though the scores were levelled by centre-forward Matthias Sindelar, known as The Man Of Paper because of his slight build, it wasn't until extra-time that Austria's superiority showed. It took an offside strike from Toni Schall to unsettle the French before Josef Bican decided the match for Austria. A late penalty was nothing more than a consolation for France.

Germany turned around a 2-1 half-time deficit to beat Belgium 5-2 in Florence, the victory owing much to a hat-trick in less than 20 minutes from Edmund Conen. The Dutch, meanwhile, crashed out of the competition 3-2 to Switzerland in Milan.

There were no such problems for favourites Italy against the USA. Angelo Schiavio netted a hat-trick in Rome as the hosts won 7-1. In Naples the first African challenge on the world stage succumbed in the second-half as Egypt, who had put 11 goals past Palestine to qualify for the finals, went out of the competition with a 4-2 defeat to Hungary.

In Trieste, highly-fancied Czechoslovakia struggled past Romania. Stefan Dobay had given the Romanians the lead shortly before the break,

THE FASCIST WORLD CUP

Benito Mussolini was the first politician to acknowledge the power of football to unite a nation and he planned to use the 1934 World Cup as a propaganda tool for his Fascist regime in Italy. Mussolini even took personal control of planning and Jules Rimet is said to have felt the Italian dictator was acting more like FIFA president than he was himself.

The Italian team may have won the World Cup but victory was tarnished by accusations that Mussolini had handpicked the referees. After the semi-final the Austrians were convinced that their game with Italy had been fixed. "The referee even played for them," Austrian striker Josef Bican would later recall. "When I passed the ball out to the right wing one of our players ran for it and the referee headed it back to the Italians."

but the Czechs possessed the formidable forward pairing of Antonin Puc and Oldrich Nejedly, who both scored to line up a quarter-final with the Swiss.

Once again the Czechs did not have it all their own way, falling behind to an early Kielholz goal before Svoboda levelled the tie. Sobotka put the Czechs ahead early in the second-half, but Switzerland hit back and once again it needed Nejedly to find the target seven minutes from time to decide the see-saw match and put Czechoslovakia through to the semi-finals.

Germany and Austria disposed of Sweden and Hungary respectively, but the most remarkable contest of the quarter-finals saw Italy triumph over Spain in Florence a full 24 hours after the tie had kicked-off. The first encounter finished 1-1 and not even extra-time could separate the sides in a bruising fixture, so the first replay in World Cup history was arranged for the following day. The Spanish were forced to make seven changes and the Italians four, but it was another close encounter, that was ultimately settled in favour of the hosts by prolific Inter Milan marksman Giuseppe Meazza who threw himself at the ball to head the winner in the 12th minute.

There was little respite for Vittorio Pozzo's side and just 48 hours later, having moved on to Milan, they took on Austria's 'Wunderteam' in the semi-final. A first-half goal from Argentine-born winger Guaita was enough to take Italy through their fourth game in eight days.

The Czechs progressed through the other semi-final in Rome with a 3-1 victory over Germany and Nejedly took centre stage once again, scoring a hat-trick. Four days later the Germans did at least salvage some pride by winning the third place play-off with a 3-2 victory over Hugo Meisl's Austria.

Giuseppe Meazza heads into the net as Italy beat Spain in a quarter-final replay.

Mussolini's azzurri. Italy prepare to do battle before the final.

Mussolini and all of Italy had the dream they had longed for with the *azzurri* in the final. For the second tournament running the hosts had gone all the way and now only Czechoslovakia stood before Pozzo's men and glory at Mussolini's showcase stadium in Rome. The stage was set for the perfect finale, and for the first time a World Cup final would be transmitted live on the radio.

The Czechs were a strong side who played in a similar way to the Austrians, pushing the ball around the pitch with style, while the Italians defended well and attacked with pace. One thing they did have in common was that goalkeepers captained both teams.

It was eventually the Czechs that scored first, Antonin Puc firing them ahead in the 71st minute despite having just returned to the field after a bout of cramp. They kept up the pressure, Frantisek Svoboda hitting the post, but with eight minutes remaining Italy broke through and equalised. Raimondo Orsi ran through the Czech defence and dummied a shot with his left-foot, shooting instead with the outside of the right and curling the ball freakishly past the Czech keeper who appeared to have it covered. It looked like a fluke, and although afterwards Orsi insisted he could repeat the shot on demand, when asked to try the next day for the assembled press, he missed every one of his 20 attempts. Five minutes into extra-time Pozzo's men grabbed a deserved winner thanks to Angelo Schiavio's fourth goal of the competition.

THE FULL MONTI

The 1934 World Cup Final saw Italy's tough-tackling hardman Luís Monti set a unique record, appearing in his second consecutive final, but for different nations. Such was the desire for victory on home soil, Italian coach Vittorio Pozzo recruited several Argentinian *oriundi* - foreign players of Italian extraction - who were playing their club football in Italy.

Monti had represented Argentina in the previous World Cup final, but after receiving death threats from fans who blamed him for the final defeat, he had moved to Italy to play for Juventus. For Monti four years after finishing a runner-up with the country of his birth, he was finally celebrating World Cup success with his adopted home.

France 1938

Brazil's Martim and Szczepaniak of Poland

TOURNAMENT STATS

WINNER Italy

FINAL
Italy 4-2 Hungary

SEMI-FINALS
Italy 2-1 Brazil
Hungary 5-1 Sweden

THIRD PLACE PLAY-OFF
Brazil 4-2 Sweden

TOP GOALSCORERS
7 goals: Leônidas (Brazil)
6 goals: Gyula Zsengellér (Hungary)
5 goals: György Sárosi (Hungary), Silvio Piola (Italy)

FASTEST GOAL
35 seconds: Arne Nyberg (Sweden v Hungary)

TOTAL GOALS
84

AVERAGE GOALS
4.67 per match

The 1938 World Cup introduced football fans to Vittorio Pozzo's new Italy, one of the greatest teams of all time, and Leônidas, the Brazilian striker who emerged as the outstanding individual of the tournament. While nobody could argue with Italy's eventual triumph, thanks largely to an outstanding mix of tactical astuteness and pragmatic defending, it was hard luck on Leônidas that he finished without even a place in the final. As top scorer with seven goals, and with some magnificent performances, he was one of the earliest luminaries of the world game.

If there had been questions about the validity of Italy's World Cup victory on home soil four years earlier, the 1938 tournament proved that this time the Italians were unquestionably worthy winners. With just two survivors from the 1934 team, Giuseppe Meazza and Giovanni Ferrari, Pozzo's new side was peppered with the stars of the Italian gold medal winning team from the 1936 Berlin Olympics, most noticeably the fullbacks Pietro Rava and Alfredo Foni. It also had the undeniable talents of prolific striker Silvio Piola.

Italy's all-round mix of resilience and flair was enough for a second consecutive triumph and confirmed Vittorio Pozzo as the foremost coach of his era. Who knows how great the *azzurri* dynasty could have been but for World War II?

Impending conflict in Europe cast a shadow over the competition from the outset. Adolf Hitler's Germany had annexed Austria and insisted the country's best players join a 'Greater Germany' side. Several did, but others refused, notably striker Matthias Sindelar. Austria were forced to withdraw from the tournament, while Spain too pulled out, racked by civil war. Champions eight years earlier, Uruguay also stayed at home, while Argentina withdrew over the decision to give the tournament to France. They had wanted to hold it themselves and felt FIFA should have alternated the venue between Europe and South America.

When the tournament finally kicked off, the three outstanding sides, Italy, Brazil and Hungary, were joined in the 16-team format by lesser nations such as Cuba and the Dutch East Indies, but the competition was no less exciting for that. Italy

Coach Vittorio Pozzo raises the trophy, while goalscorer Silvio Piola lends him an arm

THE FINAL

ITALY	(3) 4
HUNGARY	(1) 2

Date Sunday June 19, 1938
Attendance 45,000
Venue Stade Olympique de Colombes, Paris
Referee George Capdeville (France)

Italy coach Vittorio Pozzo

Hungary coach Karoly Dietz

ITALY

- ALDO OLIVIERI
- ALFREDO FONI
- PIETRO RAVA
- PIETRO SERANTONI
- MICHELE ANDREOLO
- UGO LOCATELLI
- GIUSEPPE MEAZZA (c)
- GIOVANNI FERRARI
- AMEDEO BIAVATI
- SILVIO PIOLA — *Goal: 16 mins, 82 mins*
- GINO COLAUSSI — *Goal: 6 mins, 35 mins*

HUNGARY

- ANTAL SZABÓ
- GYULA POLGAR
- SANDOR BIRÓ
- ANTAL SZALAY
- GYORGY SZÜCS
- GYULA LÁZÁR
- JENO VINCZE
- GYULA ZSENGELLÉR
- FERENC SAS
- GYORGY SÁROSI (c) — *Goal: 70 mins*
- PAL TITKOS — *Goal: 8 mins*

Austrian keeper Rudi Raftl playing for the 'Greater Germany' as Swiss striker André Abegglen bears down.

needed a Silvio Piola goal in extra-time to win their opening match against Norway, while Cuba drew 3-3 with Romania and then stunned their opponents by winning 2-1 in the replay. France beat Belgium 3-1 while Czechoslovakia knocked out Holland with a 3-0 win.

Switzerland, in a memorable clash, drew 1-1 with Germany and fell two goals behind in the replay, but despite playing much of the game with only ten fit men after an injury to Georges Aeby, they shocked the Germans with four second-half goals to send their opponents home early.

The game of the first round saw Brazil beat Poland 6-5, thanks mainly to an inspirational performance from Leônidas. After 90 minutes the game was level at 4-4, but three minutes into extra-time the striker scored his second goal to put Brazil ahead and he completed his hat-trick in the 104th minute. Such was the exceptional nature of his performance that it is often overlooked that just minutes later Polish striker Ernest Wilimowski did, in fact, score four goals, the first player to do so in a World Cup game.

The Italians faced France at Stade Colombes in their quarter-final. Since both teams normally played in blue Italy were forced to change, but instead of wearing their usual away colour of white, Mussolini ordered them to play in fascist black. Piola added two more to his tally in the game and captain Giuseppe Meazza dominated in midfield as Italy beat the hosts 3-1. It meant that for the first time the hosts would not win the World Cup.

Following their attacking exploits in the previous round the Brazilians showed an uglier side to their game in the clash with Czechoslovakia. A brawl and the sending-off of three players blighted the first match, which ended 1-1, before Brazil won the replay through the goals of Leônidas and Roberto. Hungary impressed beating Switzerland, while

THE CLOUDS OF WAR

As war looked increasingly likely it was important to avoid the 1938 tournament being used for political ends. As a result, France was entrusted with the World Cup by 19 votes to four. If the delegates of the FIFA Congress needed any warnings about sporting events being used for propaganda purposes, the proof was all around them as the vote was taking place at the 1936 Berlin Olympics, that showcase for Hitler's National Socialist regime.

The tournament was not without political controversy. The games of Italy and Germany (pictured right) were accompanied by fascist salutes on the pitch and anti-fascist demonstrations off it, while political pressure resulted in Germany coach Sepp Herberger fielding a team to represent the 'Greater Germany' made up almost evenly of Germans and the annexed Austrians.

Sweden scored four times in the last ten minutes to crush Cuba 8-0 and complete the final quartet.

In the semi-finals the Brazilians faced Italy, but coach Adhemar Pimenta rested Leônidas, a decision that proved their undoing. Gino Colaussi scored shortly after half-time and Meazza added a penalty on the hour. Brazil managed only a consolation from Romeu three minutes from time.

In the other semi-final Hungary ended Sweden's run with a 5-1 triumph despite conceding within seconds of the kick-off. Sweden's lead lasted only 19 minutes before Hungary equalised, thanks to Gyula Zsengellér's header deflecting into the net off Sven Jacobsson, and strikes by Pal Titkos, Gyorgy Sárosi and two more from Zsengellér clinched the match. The forward partnership between Zsengellér and Sárosi was perhaps the most thrilling in the tournament.

Leônidas returned for the third place play-off and Brazil fell two goals behind to Sweden before fighting back to win 4-2. He scored twice to finish top-scorer with seven.

In the final the Italians confirmed their place as one of the greatest sides of all time. Pozzo's side were much stronger than Hungary and far more decisive in attack. Colaussi opened the scoring when he collected a Piola cross in the sixth minute and prodded home past Antal Szabó from close range. Titkos immediately equalised, but Hungarian hopes were dashed when Piola scored on 16 minutes, picking up a pass from Meazza to lash the ball high into the net. Colaussi added a third before half-time to put Italy in total control.

The reigning champions defended their lead in the second-half. Sárosi's goal put Hungary back in contention, but when Piola scored with eight minutes remaining, Italy were certain of a 4-2 win.

THE BLACK DIAMOND

The undoubted star of the 1938 World Cup was the distinctive-looking, pencil-moustached Brazil striker Leônidas, who had been dubbed 'The Rubber Man' at the finals four years earlier by the European press because of the array of tricks he could perform. Famed at home for pioneering the bicycle kick, his three goals in Brazil's 6-5 defeat of Poland helped the match to become the stuff of World Cup legend. He even scored one of his goals in his stockinged feet after a boot had come off in the mud.

'The Black Diamond', as Leônidas was nicknamed, finished the tournament as the highest goalscorer and he would return home as the most famous man in Brazil, inspiring a brand of cigarettes and causing confectionary company Lacta to launch the *Diamante Negro*, still one of Brazil's best-selling chocolate bars.

Captain Étienne Mattler, left, a veteran of the first World Cup, leads France onto the pitch alongside Belgium.

Brazil 1950

STADIUM GUIDE

TOURNAMENT STATS

WINNER Uruguay

FINAL POOL MATCH
Uruguay 2-1 Brazil

FINAL POOL

	P	W	D	L	Pts
Uruguay	3	2	1	0	5
Brazil	3	2	0	1	4
Sweden	3	1	0	2	2
Spain	3	0	1	2	1

THIRD PLACE PLAY-OFF
Not held

TOP GOALSCORERS
9 goals: Ademir Menezes (Brazil)
5 goals: Juan Schiaffino (Uruguay), Estanislao Basora (Spain)

FASTEST GOAL
2 minutes: Alfredo (Brazil v Switzerland)

TOTAL GOALS
88

AVERAGE GOALS
4.00 per game

Brazil had been pitching to stage the 1950 World Cup since FIFA first discussed the matter on the opening day of the World Cup in Paris 12 years earlier, but having finally secured a competition that meant so much to this football-mad country, in reality it turned out to be the strangest of tournaments, throwing up shocks and thrills in equal measure.

Withdrawals dominated the build-up as only 13 teams started the competition, and the idea of a winner-takes-all final had been rejected by the organisers, in favour of a second league phase. Even the new 200,000-capacity Maracanã stadium, built specifically for the tournament, wasn't ready when the first game kicked off. In the end, however, the competition produced moments of pure drama. The chaotic preparations eventually gave way to some excellent football and one of the greatest clashes the World Cup has ever seen, a game that will never be forgotten.

With only 13 teams in the draw the competition took on a rather lop-sided look, as the opening round consisted of two groups of four teams, one of three and one of two. Argentina were among the many teams to pull out before the qualifiers, while Scotland and Turkey withdrew after booking a place in the finals. India also refused to compete, according to some reports because FIFA insisted their players wore boots.

All eyes were on Pool 1, where the host nation and highly fancied outsiders Yugoslavia impressed immediately. With a wonderfully entertaining line-up, boasting a trio of attackers who ranked among the finest in the world – Ademir, Jair and Zizinho – Brazil played skilful and inventive football and were favourites to lift the trophy for the first time. They made a superb start beating Mexico 4-0 in their

Juan Schiaffino, far left, equalises for Uruguay in the final game

THE FINAL POOL MATCH

URUGUAY	(0) **2**
BRAZIL	(0) **1**

Date Sunday July 16, 1950
Attendance 199,854
Venue Maracanã, Rio de Janeiro
Referee George Reader (England)

Uruguay coach Juan Lopez

Brazil coach Flavio Costa

URUGUAY
ROQUE MÁSPOLI
MATÍAS GONZÁLES
VICTOR RODRÍGUEZ ANDRADE
EUSEBIO TEJERA
OBDULIO VARELA (c)
SCHUBERT GAMBETTA
JULIO PERÉZ
JUAN ALBERTO SCHIAFFINO *Goal: 66 mins*
ALCIDES GHIGGIA *Goal: 79 mins*
OSCAR MIGUEZ
RUBÉN MORÁN

BRAZIL
BARBOSA
AUGUSTO (c)
JUVENAL
BAUER
DANILO
BIGODE
ZIZINHO
JAIR
FRIAÇA *Goal: 47 mins*
ADEMIR
CHICO

opener, with Ademir scoring twice. Yugoslavia kept pace with an impressive 3-0 win over Switzerland, maintaining their stunning form with a 4-1 win over Mexico in their second match.

Switzerland surprisingly held Brazil 2-2, but when the two group leaders met in the Maracanã in front of 142,429 spectators, the hosts kicked off the game with a one-man advantage after Yugoslavia's star player, inside-right Rajko Mitic, injured his head walking out of the dressing rooms. Badly shaken, Mitic only returned to the pitch heavily bandaged later in the game, by which time Ademir's third minute opening goal had already put the hosts in front. A further strike from Zizinho ensured Brazil's safe passage to the final pool, and with only one team to go through, it was harsh on the talented Yugoslavs who went home early.

The English were the biggest attraction in Pool 2 and were taking part in their first World Cup. The team had lost star players such as keeper Frank Swift and Tommy Lawton since the war but still boasted Billy Wright, Tom Finney and Stan Mortensen in their ranks. It was an impressive line-up and goals from Mortensen and Wilf Mannion secured a 2-0 win over Chile. It looked as though they would cruise through to the next round but in their second game the USA inflicted on them one of the most embarrassing defeats in football

A crowd of 200,000 pack the Maracanã for the final game of the 1950 World Cup.

history. The USA, who had lost their opening game with Spain 3-1, recorded a 1-0 win in Belo Horizonte, with Joe Gaetjens scoring the 38th minute winner. It was a major shock for England, and despite shaking up the team for the decisive game against Spain, Zarra's single strike put the Spaniards through to the final pool with a 100 per cent record, the winning goal inspiring Spanish radio commentator Matías Prats to announce, "Zarra – the best head in Europe after Churchill". Walter Winterbottom's team returned home to England thoroughly humiliated.

In Pool 3 reigning champions Italy contested a place in the final with Sweden and Paraguay. It was the Swedes that earned an early advantage thanks to a 3-2 win over Italy, and a 2-2 draw with Paraguay in the next match was enough for the Scandinavians to clinch the top spot. In truth the reigning champions had been dealt a mighty blow the previous year, when ten Italian internationals were among the 18 members of the all-conquering Torino team killed as their plane crashed into Superga Basilica on the hills overlooking Turin.

In the absurd two-team Pool 4, Uruguay – who didn't even have to kick a ball to qualify for the tournament – thrashed Bolivia 8-0 to make the final pool, with Juan Schiaffino catching the eye and Omar Miguez grabbing a hat-trick.

In the Final Pool the World Cup trophy would go to whoever topped the group. It could have been an anti-climax if one team had clinched the trophy

THE GREATEST SHOCK OF ALL

Entering the World Cup for the first time, England could not have anticipated the scale of their humiliation at the hands of the United States. This was a USA team beaten 9-0 by Italy in a warm-up game, but on the rutted pitch of the tiny Estadío Independência in Belo Horizonte, England suffered one of the most embarrassing defeats in football history.

The US team contained three foreign-born players, including captain for the match Eddie McIlvenny, a Scot who had signed for Manchester United on the eve of the tournament. But it was Haitian-born Joseph 'Larry' Gaetjens who made all the difference when the US team finally managed to break out of their half for a 38th minute goal. The USA weathered the resulting onslaught and pulled off a victory that shocked world football.

early, but in the event it provided perhaps the most thrilling climax to any World Cup, with scorelines and scheduling throwing up an 'unofficial final' in front of the largest football crowd ever.

Certainly the hosts looked the best bet to win when the pool kicked-off, racking up a 7-1 win over Sweden, which included some of the finest attacking football ever seen. In a truly blistering display Ademir scored four goals as his understanding with Jair and Zizinho reached its peak. Next they thrashed Spain 6-1, all three strikers getting on the scoresheet, and Chico hitting the target twice. The hosts began to look unstoppable.

Uruguay kept pace with a 2-2 draw against Spain in a tough physical encounter. A 3-2 win over Sweden was enough to retain a slim chance of causing an upset, but it meant that the final group match, between Brazil and Uruguay, would decide exactly who would collect the Jules Rimet trophy. Uruguay needed to win the match, while Brazil needed only a draw.

As Brazil had played the better football and had home advantage, the result seemed a foregone conclusion, but the unimaginable happened. The hosts may have had 30 shots at goal and the will of a nation behind them, but the Uruguayans refused to read the script.

During a goalless first-half Uruguay weathered the storm, their defence doing everything to match the efforts of Brazil's famed attack until Friaça scored two minutes after the break, making victory for Brazil seem inevitable. Juan Schiaffino equalised from Ghiggia's cross in the 66th minute to give the vistors a lifeline and with 11 minutes remaining they caught Brazil on the break. Right-winger Ghiggia beat Bigode on the flank, just as he had done to set up the previous goal, but instead of crossing he caught keeper Barbosa off guard by shooting towards the near post and into the net.

Uruguay had achieved the impossible. In the most dramatic of circumstances, in front of 200,000 shell-shocked fans in the Maracanã, Brazil had lost the World Cup. The 'Fateful Final', as it came to be known, or 'Maracanazo', left a bitter feeling in Brazil that remains to this day.

THE LUCK OF BARBOSA

When Uruguay winger Alcides Ghiggia wrong-footed Moacir Barbosa at the near post, he didn't just win the World Cup for Uruguay, he blighted the reputation of Brazil's best ever keeper. After the World Cup defeat Barbosa's international career was all but over as the nation searched for a scapegoat. He only played once more for Brazil and later worked as a cleaner at the Maracanã. When the old World Cup goalposts were being replaced in 1963, he made a bonfire of them.

Not allowed to forget the 'fateful final', when he visited the Brazil training camp in 1993, he was turned away by a superstitious squad. "The maximum punishment in Brazil is 30 years imprisonment," he said just a before his death in 2000, "but for 50 years I have been paying for something I am not even responsible for."

Below left: Uruguay's Obdulio Varela drinks from the trophy. Below: Milburn heads at goal during England's defeat to Spain at the Maracanã.

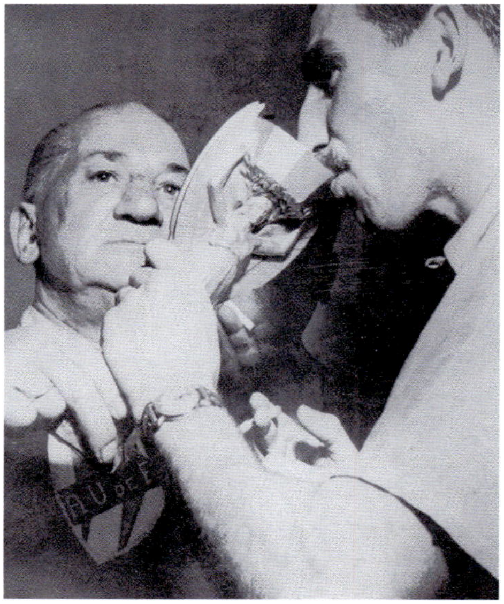

Switzerland 1954

TOURNAMENT STATS

WINNER West Germany

FINAL
West Germany 3-2 Hungary

SEMI-FINALS
West Germany 6-1 Austria
Hungary 4-2 Uruguay *(aet)*

THIRD PLACE PLAY-OFF
Austria 3-1 Uruguay

TOP GOALSCORERS
11 goals: Sándor Kocsis (Hungary)
6 goals: Max Morlock (West Germany), Josef Hügi (Switzerland), Erich Probst (Austria)

FASTEST GOAL
2 minutes: Mamat Suat (Turkey v West Germany)

TOTAL GOALS
140

AVERAGE GOALS
5.38 per game

Coming nearly ten years after the end of the Second World War, the 1954 World Cup may have been seen by a privileged few in flickering black and white television pictures for the first time, but it produced some of the most colourful attacking football in the competition's history, with 140 goals shared between 16 teams at an average of over five goals a game. The quarter-final between Austria and their Swiss hosts finished 7-5, still the highest aggregate for a game at the finals, and several other matches finished with scorelines that appear improbable today.

Switzerland was a logical choice to host the first European-based post-war tournament, and not simply because it had escaped the devastation sustained across the rest of the continent. FIFA's headquarters were situated in Zurich and 1954 represented the organisation's 50th anniversary.

The Swiss had been granted the tournament at FIFA's first post-war congress in 1946, and eight years were spent building new stadia for the competition. The finished football grounds had limited capacities and were not really up to the requirements of such a tournament, but it proved to be a financial success. The organisers even displayed early signs of grasping the World Cup's marketing potential by having special commemorative coins minted.

The qualifying rounds featured the highest number of nations yet, with 38 entries. Sweden and Spain failed to qualify, the latter beaten by Turkey who automatically became seeds in their place, a ruling that was to have particular significance as the competition unfolded. England and Scotland came through the Home Nations group, though the Scots were to lose both their games and make a rapid return. Once again the Soviet Union and Argentina were notable absentees.

Almost inevitably FIFA tampered with the format, reverting to a complicated pool phase

Max Morlock inspires West Germany's comeback, sliding the ball past Gyula Grosics

featuring 16 teams divided into four groups, with two seeded sides in each who would not play each other. At the end the four winners competed in a knock-out phase, as did the four runners-up, which meant the final would definitely be contested between a group winner and a group runner-up. But the system was open to exploitation and the West Germans did just that.

It was no surprise to find that Hungary, coached by Gusztáv Sebes, were favourites. This was the era of the 'Magical Magyars'. Two years previous they had been crowned Olympic champions and now their players were at their peak. The line-up was crammed with legends, including the 'Galloping Major' Ferenc Puskás, striker Sándor Kocsis, midfield dynamo József Bozsik and deep-lying centre-forward Nandor Hidegkuti.

This was the core of the side that destroyed English pretensions to superiority with a 6-3 win at Wembley in November 1953 (England's first home defeat to a continental side) and a 7-1 pasting in Budapest six months later. The Magyars hammered South Korea 9-0 in their opening game in Zurich and put eight past a deliberately weakened German side, eventually scoring a record 27 goals in the tournament. Sándor Kocsis raced to the Golden Boot with 11 goals, including two hat-tricks.

For all the talent in their ranks, Hungary's quarter-final against Brazil went down in football history for all the wrong reasons. The match degenerated into hand-to-hand combat, since dubbed the 'Battle Of Berne'. The bout was refereed by future British television personality Arthur Ellis, who sent-off three players, Hungary's Bozsik and

THE FINAL

WEST GERMANY (2) **3**
HUNGARY (2) **2**

Date Sunday July 4, 1954
Attendance 60,000
Venue Wankdorf Stadium, Berne
Referee Bill Ling (England)

West Germany coach Sepp Herberger

Hungary coach Gusztáv Sebes

WEST GERMANY
1 TONI TUREK
7 JUPP POSIPAL
3 WERNER KOHLMEYER
6 HORST ECKEL
10 WERNER LIEBRICH
8 KARL MAI
13 MAX MORLOCK (Goal: 11 mins)
16 FRITZ WALTER (c)
12 HELMUT RAHN (Goal: 18 mins, 84 mins)
15 OTTMAR WALTER
20 HANS SCHÄFER

HUNGARY
1 GYULA GROSICS
2 JENO BUZÁNSZKY
4 GYULA LANTOS
5 JOZSEF BOZSIK
3 GYULA LÓRÁNT
6 JOZSEF ZAKARIÁS
8 SANDOR KOCSIS
10 FERENC PUSKÁS (c) (Goal: 6 mins)
11 ZOLTAN CZIBOR (Goal: 9 mins)
9 NANDOR HIDEGKUTI
20 MIHALY TÓTH

FRITZ WALTER WEATHER

The star of German football was Fritz Walter, but he struggled to perform in hot weather, a result of catching malaria during the war. Imprisoned by the Soviets, he was only spared from the gulags of Siberia when a Hungarian guard recognised him as one of the stars of Germany's defeat of Hungary in 1942. After returning home, the worse the weather got, the better Fritz played.

On the day of the 1954 World Cup Final the rain fell and the German team grew in confidence, knowing their captain would be at his best on the muddy Berne pitch. Their performance improved as the rain got heavier, helped by the innovative Adidas screw-in studs that enabled them to adapt their boots to suit the conditions. Thanks to their World Cup win, wet weather is still called 'Fritz Walter weather' in Germany to this day.

Below right: Billy Wright of England and Jozef Mermans of Belgium swap pennants. Below: Tom Finney gets a header in against Uruguay seconds before scoring with a follow up shot.

Brazil's Humberto Tozzi and Nilton Santos, after trouble broke out over a disputed penalty. The game descended into violence that continued in the changing rooms after the match, embroiling both managers and even the official delegations.

England, under Walter Winterbottom, topped a group including Belgium, Italy and hosts Switzerland. The side, featuring Billy Wright, Nat Lofthouse, Stanley Matthews and Tom Finney, should have gone further but came unstuck against Uruguay, losing 4-2 with goalkeeper Gil Merrick at fault for three goals. In the end the feeling was that their shattering 7-1 defeat at the hands of Hungary just weeks earlier had destroyed the team's confidence.

West Germany were admitted after their banishment following World War II and rapidly made a mockery of their non-seeding, beating Turkey 4-1, while France, another seeded side, lost to Yugoslavia. German manager Sepp Herberger then exploited the play-off system by electing to send out a weakened side against Hungary in the knowledge that the group winners would play Brazil in the knock-out phase, while the runners-up would face Korea or Turkey in a play-off.

His plan worked and Germany duly thrashed Turkey 7-2 in the play-off and squeezed past the Yugoslavs 2-0, scoring early on and holding out until a late goal sealed the victory. A 6-1 semi-final victory over Austria sent out an ominous warning.

Hungary's semi-final against holders Uruguay was another memorable encounter that put paid to the South Americans' unbeaten record in the competition. Hungary won 4-2 in extra-time, but the celebrations would have a consequence. After the match the Hungary players were asked to go back onto the pitch and salute the home fans who

were refusing to leave the ground. This caused the squad to miss the train back to their hotel, where they eventually arrived by taxi in the early hours of the morning.

On paper the final looked to be a forgone conclusion. Unseeded West Germany faced the might of Hungary, who had not lost in 31 matches and who had scored 25 goals in four games on their way to the final, but the form book was discarded in a fascinating see-saw encounter.

Though carrying an injury picked up in the first game with West Germany, Puskás put his side ahead after only six minutes when he followed up a Kocsis shot. Two minutes later Czibor latched onto a weak back pass to put them two up, but Max Morlock reduced the arrears after 11 minutes and a mistake by the Hungarian keeper Gyula Grosics in the 18th minute allowed Rahn to equalise.

In the second-half Hungary threw themselves into the attack, Hidegkuti hitting the post, Kocsis the bar, Kohlmeyer clearing off the line and German keeper Turek making a succession of great saves. Six minutes from time, however, Helmut Rahn picked up a half-hearted clearance, raced to the edge of the box and struck a low shot past Grosics, who appeared to slip. There was more drama when Puskás had a goal disallowed, with the Hungarians still arguing after the final whistle.

The players of this mighty Hungarian team were stunned by the defeat, and when the Soviet Union crushed the country's uprising two years later, the squad broke up, effectively ending the country's football dominance forever.

Fritz Walter scores from the spot as West Germany beat Austria 6-1 in the semi-final. Behind him, Helmut Rahn takes a rest.

TECHNICOLOUR BRAZIL

The 1954 tournament was the first World Cup to see the most recognisable sports strip on the planet - the yellow and green shirt of Brazil. In a country where national pride had become inextricably linked with the fortunes of football, Brazil's traditional white kit had become so tainted by the defeat in the 1950 World Cup final that it needed replacing. Rio newspaper *Correio da Manhã* launched a competition to design a new strip using the colours of the Brazilian flag: blue, white, green and yellow.

The winner was 19-year-old Aldyr Schlee, who had entered the competition as a joke. Brazil wore his creation for the first time in March 1954 in preparation for the finals, but it wasn't until the 1970 World Cup, the first tournament transmitted in colour, that the strip was turned into an iconic symbol for the beauty of football.

Sweden 1958

STADIUM GUIDE

TOURNAMENT STATS

WINNER Brazil

FINAL
Brazil 5-2 Sweden

SEMI-FINALS
Brazil 5-2 France
Sweden 3-1 West Germany

THIRD PLACE PLAY-OFF
France 6-3 West Germany

TOP GOALSCORERS
13 goals: Just Fontaine (France)
6 goals: Pelé (Brazil), Helmut Rahn (West Germany)
5 goals: Vavá (Brazil), Peter McParland (Northern Ireland)

FASTEST GOAL
90 seconds: Vavá (Brazil v France)

TOTAL GOALS
126

AVERAGE GOALS
3.60 per game

For fans of the beautiful game, the 1958 World Cup will always be remembered for the birth of a football nation, the competition that introduced Pelé to the world stage. Brazil had not previously won the World Cup and it had been Uruguay that had forged a reputation as South America's finest side by twice lifting the trophy. In 1958 the balance of power shifted as the Brazilians won the competition for the first time. They did so by pioneering a style of play that had football writers everywhere purring at its grace and beauty, a feat made all the more special by the fact that it occurred in an era when defenders could – and did – get away with kicking the opposition's best players off the park.

'Samba football' was born in Sweden, where the Brazilians had perfected their own attack-minded 4-2-4 formation, reminiscent of the Hungarians of the early Fifties. It was the first time that a football formation would actually be referred to using a numbering system. Brazil would win the 1958 tournament with two dedicated centre-forwards, Vavá and Pelé, flanked by wingers Garrincha and Zagallo. With four across the back, the system depended on quick-moving outside fullbacks who could attack on the overlap, adding strength to the midfield and allowing Brazil to press forward with wild abandon.

"Where skill alone counted Brazil stood alone," reported *The Times* newspaper in England. "The way each daffodil shirt of theirs pulled the ball down out of the sky, tamed it with a touch of the foot, caressed it and stroked it away into an open space was a joy." Looking back, it is easy to over-romanticise about Brazil and to think that any team

World Cup winners at last. Brazil pose with the trophy after beating Sweden

with so much skill, and with arguably the greatest ever player, was bound to succeed, but there was nothing inevitable about it.

In the early decades of the World Cup, sides unfamiliar with foreign conditions did not travel well: until this tournament the winners had always been a team from the host continent. The Brazilians finished third in 1938 and spurned another great chance in 1950. This time they meant business and even brought along a psychiatrist.

As for Pelé, while everyone knew he was a bit special, at 17 no-one knew how special. His mere selection remained in doubt, partly because of a niggling injury and partly because some believed he wasn't up to it.

The tournament, though, was something of a watershed. Although the tackles could be tough, Sweden marked the last days of the more carefree, attack-minded post-war era of international football. In the 1960s World Cup matches became increasingly cynical and defensive.

The competition kicked off without some familiar names as Uruguay and fellow two-time winners Italy both failed to qualify. For British

THE FINAL

BRAZIL	(2) 5
SWEDEN	(1) 2

Date Sunday June 29, 1958
Attendance 51,800
Venue Råsunda Stadium, Solna, Stockholm
Referee Maurice Guigue (France)

Brazil coach Vicente Feola

Sweden coach George Raynor

BRAZIL
3 GILMAR
4 DJALMA SANTOS
2 BELLINI (c)
15 ORLANDO
12 NÍLTON SANTOS
6 DIDI
19 ZITO
11 GARRINCHA
20 VAVÁ ⚽⚽ *Goal: 9 mins, 32 mins*
10 PELÉ ⚽⚽ *Goal: 55 mins, 90 mins*
7 MARIO ZAGALLO ⚽ *Goal: 68 mins*

SWEDEN
1 KALLE SVENSSON
2 ORVAR BERGMARK
3 SVEN AXBOM
15 REINO BORJESSON
14 BENGT GUSTAVSSON
6 SIGGE PARLING
8 GUNNAR GREN
4 NILS LIEDHOLM (c) ⚽ *Goal: 4 mins*
7 KURT HAMRIN
9 AGNE SIMONSSON ⚽ *Goal: 80 mins*
11 LENNART SKOGLUND

Above: Lev Yashin fails to save from England's Derek Kevan.
Above right: Garrincha in full flight during the final.

football though, 1958 remains a high point with all four home nations reaching the finals for the only time. England, despite the Munich air disaster denying them such talents as Duncan Edwards, Tommy Taylor and Roger Byrne, were the favourites, having never lost to any of the teams in their group. But it was to prove a frustrating tournament for Walter Winterbottom's side.

Creditable draws against the Soviet Union and Brazil – the first goalless match in World Cup finals history – meant England only had to beat eliminated Austria to advance. However, the draws continued and it came down to a play-off with the Soviets, where England lost by a single goal.

Scotland also went out at the first hurdle, but Northern Ireland and Wales both advanced to the next round. The Irish, who had drawn 2-2 with West Germany in their group, beat Czechoslovakia in a play-off, a situation that Wales were also catapulted into after drawing all three group matches. Inspired by their one truly world-class player, Juventus striker John Charles, they came from behind to beat Hungary 2-1.

Charles was injured for the quarter-final meeting with Brazil and for 70 minutes the Welsh dream lived on as Garrincha, Didi, Mazzola and Zagallo were continually thwarted, but when Pelé scored the first of his 12 World Cup goals, it was all over.

The big guns were beginning to fire. In the quarter-finals France ended Northern Ireland's resistance with a 4-0 thumping. The West Germans sneaked past Yugoslavia, and Sweden put paid to the ambitions of the Soviet Union. Although the defending champions were still in the competition, Sweden and Brazil had emerged as favourites.

The Swedes were coached by Englishman George Raynor, who had helped them to Olympic gold in 1948. At previous World Cup tournaments their chances had been damaged by their strict amateur ethos and their refusal to call up many of their Italian-based stars. Swedish football's acceptance of professionalism meant that in 1958 they could field their strongest team possible.

THE PELÉ & GARRINCHA SHOW

If Brazil were the best side at the 1958 World Cup, then Pelé and Garrincha were the tournament's brightest stars, but the pairing didn't make their World Cup bow until Brazil's third game. Indeed, 17-year-old Pelé's selection remained in doubt until the last minute as an injury on a tour of Italy threatened his inclusion. Legend has it that in advance of the clash with the Soviet Union, Brazil's senior players made a deputation to coach Vicente Feola in an attempt to bring about the selection of Garrincha and Pelé.

He was convinced. They started the match and turned on the magic immediately, both hitting the post in the first minute. Brazil went on to win the tournament and until their final game together at the World Cup finals of 1966, the team never lost when Pelé and Garrincha played together.

Sweden underlined their credentials in front of 53,000 fans in Gothenburg when they eliminated West Germany 3-1 in the semi-final. The Germans had hung on until the last ten minutes when the hosts scored twice to trigger wild celebrations. It was one of West Germany's darkest World Cup moments. Erich Juskowiak was sent-off for kicking and they were reduced to nine men for a time when Fritz Walter left the pitch for treatment after a ferocious tackle by Sigvard Parling.

In the other semi-final in Stockholm, Brazil electrified the tournament with a 5-2 defeat of France, who had cruised through their quarter-final and were expected to pose a severe test. For half the match they did but after losing centre-half Jonquet in a collision with Vavá, France were left with ten men and they were blown away when Pelé netted a hat-trick in 23 unforgettable second-half minutes.

The dream final had arrived, matching the host nation with the magical Brazilians, wearing blue shirts because of the clash of colours with Sweden. Heavy rain suggested this wasn't a match for South American flair, and when Liedholm fired the hosts ahead after four minutes, it seemed the Brazilians might struggle. Five minutes later, however, Vavá equalised from Garrincha's cross, then Pelé struck the post and Vavá added a second. Suddenly Sweden were chasing the game.

The second-half belonged to Pelé. His first goal in the 55th minute combined individual trickery with a rasping volley. Zagallo made it 4-1 before Simonsson restored hope for Sweden. But Pelé had the game's final word, heading home for a 5-2 win. At the final whistle the Brazilians were overcome, weeping openly, and they sportingly paraded the Swedish flag around the pitch, bringing the stadium to its feet in acclaim.

FONTAINE OF GOALS

Just Fontaine scored 13 goals at the 1958 World Cup, a record that looks unlikely to be beaten. But going into the competition, he wasn't guaranteed his place in the team until an ankle injury to René Bliard gave him his chance to team up with Raymond Kopa, his former Reims strike partner. With 'Le Tandem Terrible' up front France hit 23 goals in just six games on the way to a third place finish.

Fontaine could have scored even more had he been his side's penalty taker and his tally is all the more remarkable given that it was achieved in boots borrowed from team-mate Stéphane Bruey after his own had fallen apart. "At the end of the tournament I gave them back," Fontaine would later joke, "but they didn't make him score more goals."

After winning the World Cup, Didi, left, comforts a weeping Pelé, as keeper Gilmar and Orlando offer support.

Chile 1962

STADIUM GUIDE

TOURNAMENT STATS

WINNER Brazil

FINAL
Brazil 3-1 Czechoslovakia

SEMI-FINALS
Brazil 4-2 Chile
Czechoslovakia 3-1 Yugoslavia

THIRD PLACE PLAY-OFF
Chile 1-0 Yugoslavia

TOP GOALSCORERS
4 goals: Garrincha (Brazil), Valentin Ivanov (Soviet Union), Leonel Sánchez (Chile), Flórián Albert (Hungary), Drazen Jerkovic (Yugoslavia), Vavá (Brazil)
** Garrincha awarded Top Scorer prize, drawn by lot*

FASTEST GOAL
15 seconds: Vaclav Masek (Czechoslovakia v Mexico)

TOTAL GOALS
89

AVERAGE GOALS
2.78 per game

"We have nothing, that is why we must have the World Cup," pleaded Carlos Dittborn, president of the Chilean football federation. FIFA had been looking for an alternative host following the devastating earthquake that caused serious damage and loss of life in Chile in May 1960, but Dittborn's pleas were heeded and Chile kept the World Cup, serving up a tournament of extremes, ranging from the appalling 'Battle Of Santiago' to the beautiful, crafted performances of the sublime Brazilians.

For holders Brazil, the 1962 competition was the perfect opportunity to build on their World Cup success. They arrived in Chile with a gifted and experienced team built around their established world champions of four years earlier. Gilmar, Djalma Santos, Nílton Santos, Didi, Vavá, Zagallo, Zito, Pelé and Garrincha were all in the running to add a second winners' medal to their collection, but there were changes too. Mauro, a reserve in 1958, joined the team as centre-half and captain in place of Bellini, while Zózimo replaced Orlando. The most significant change saw coach Vicente Feola ruled out through illness and replaced by Aymoré Moreira, brother of Zezé Moreira, the coach of the team at the 1954 World Cup.

When the tournament kicked off local Chilean interest wavered wildly, from disappointingly small attendances of under 6,000 at one extreme, to the crowds of over 60,000 who squeezed into the cauldron of Santiago. It was also a World Cup that witnessed the dawn of defensive football, partly due to one of the competition's rule changes. The format of the tournament had remained largely

Mauro lifts the Jules Rimet Trophy after Brazil's victory over Czechoslovakia

unaltered, but for the first time goal average was brought in as a means of separating teams with the same amount of points – it eliminated the need for play-offs but encouraged a more defensive mindset and the group stages were dominated by cagey play and excessive violence.

This largely dismal football showpiece reached its nadir with the infamous 'Battle Of Santiago' between Italy and Chile. It was a brawling affair that resulted in the dismissal of Italians Ferrini and David, but it wasn't the only example of rough play.

The tournament had been in progress for just three days when the Chilean press reported there had been 34 serious injuries. Among the casualties was 21-year-old Pelé, the result of a torn muscle from a groin injury sustained in a pre-tournament friendly – Pelé had refused to declare it because of trainer Paolo Amaral's 'don't train, don't play' policy.

The opening stages did feature the occasional thrilling encounter, the most amazing being the Group 1 clash between the Soviet Union and first time qualifiers Colombia in Arica, a match

THE FINAL

BRAZIL (1) 3
CZECHOSLOVAKIA (1) 1

Date Sunday June 17, 1962
Attendance 69,000
Venue Estadio Nacional, Santiago
Referee Nikolaj Latychev (Soviet Union)

Brazil coach Aymore Moreira

Czechoslovakia coach Rudolf Vytlacil

BRAZIL
1 GILMAR
2 DJALMA SANTOS
3 MAURO (c)
5 ZÓZIMO
6 NÍLTON SANTOS
4 ZITO *Goal: 69 mins*
8 DIDI
7 GARRINCHA
19 VAVÁ *Goal: 77 mins*
20 AMARILDO *Goal: 17 mins*
21 ZAGALLO

CZECHOSLOVAKIA
1 VILIAM SCHROJF
12 JIRI TICHY
5 SVATOPLUK PLUSKAL
3 JAN POPLUHAR
4 LADISLAV NOVÁK (c)
19 ANDREJ KVASNAK
6 JOSEF MASOPUST *Goal: 16 mins*
8 ADOLF SCHERER
17 TOMAS POSPICHAL
18 JOSEF KADRABA
11 JOSEF JELINEK

THE BATTLE OF SANTIAGO

When Italy faced Chile in 1962, it resulted in the most bruising encounter ever seen at the World Cup. Before the clash, anti-Italian feeling had been whipped-up as a result of the publication of derogatory articles about Chilean life in the Italian press.

Staged in front of a hostile crowd, the game descended into violence, which referee Ken Aston failed to control. He dismissed Italy's Giorgio Ferrini for retaliating but the player had to be removed by the police. A punch to Mario David by Leonel Sánchez was overlooked, but when the Italian kicked Sánchez in the head, he too was sent off. The disgraceful violence continued until the final whistle. The BBC's David Coleman described the game as "the most stupid, appalling, disgusting and disgraceful exhibition of football, possibly in the history of the game".

described by *L'Équipe* as "one of the greatest surprises of modern football". Three goals in three minutes gave the Soviets a commanding lead and the game looked over by the 11th minute. The Colombians pulled a goal back ten minutes later through Aceros, but Ponedelnik scored a fourth for the Soviets early in the second-half. Colombia then staged a magnificent comeback to secure an amazing 4-4 draw, with Coll, Rada and Klinger all scoring in a roller coaster match.

Outside of Santiago the games were poorly attended. The six Group 4 matches in Rancagua attracted an average crowd of just 7,000, the lowest being England's dull 0-0 draw against Bulgaria.

The quickest goal was scored after just 15 seconds when Czechoslovakia's Vaclav Masek put the ball past Mexico keeper Antonio Carbajal. The Mexicans went on to win the game 3-1. It was their first World Cup victory, but they were out of the tournament and Carbajal announced his retirement, having not kept a clean sheet in any of his four World Cups (he would later change his mind to play at the 1966 finals).

Despite the defeat, Czechoslovakia finished second in the group to Brazil and both nations would eventually contest the final. The Czechs had built a team around the players of the successful Dukla Prague, with a strategy reliant on defence. A cautious, counter-attacking team, they had held Brazil to a goalless draw and beaten a disharmonious Spain 1-0, reaching the quarter-

Italy keeper Renzo Buffon tries to beat West Germany's Uwe Seeler to the ball.

Above: Pelé, unable to play in the final because of injury, hugs replacement Amarildo. Above left: Johnny Haynes of England watches as Hungary keeper Grosics does his job.

finals on goal average by virtue of conceding fewer goals than Mexico. They could be thankful for the performances of Viliam Schrojf, the goalkeeper of the tournament. He was in splendid form, particularly in the knockout stages against Hungary and Yugoslavia, when a series of magnificent saves kept his opponents at bay.

For all the flair of their team, even the Brazilians combated the high altitude of Chile by playing a more defensive 4-3-3 system, employing Zagallo deeper and packing the central midfield, allowing the fullbacks to attack on the overlap. Brazil may have suffered the loss of Pelé after two games but they remained unfazed, having unearthed Tavares Amarildo, who was quickly dubbed 'the white Pelé'. It was Garrincha, though, who was Brazil's inspiration. The father of seven children, he was just as productive on the pitch when creating and scoring goals, and rarely would a single player have such an impact on the outcome of a World Cup.

Brazil breezed through their quarter-final in Vinã del Mar, outclassing England who had finished runners-up in Group 4. Garrincha, the smallest player on the field, opened the scoring with a header before setting up Vavá and finding the net again in a 3-1 win. The game would remain most notable for the crowd-amusing moment when Jimmy Greaves got onto all fours to apprehend a stray dog, which Garrincha ended up keeping.

The semi-final pitched Brazil against Chile in an open game that was streaked with spite. Inspired by Garrincha, who scored twice and set up the first of Vavá's two headed goals, the Brazilians left the pitch 4-2 winners, but minus Garrincha, who had harshly been expelled for a foul on Eladio Rojas.

Firm favourites Brazil had progressed to the final where they would face Czechoslovakia for the second time in the competition. They named an unchanged side that boasted eight of the players who had won the World Cup final in 1958, including Garrincha despite his sending-off.

Regardless of their talent the Brazilians trailed after 14 minutes to a low shot from Masopust. Amarildo equalised from an acute angle just two minutes later, and the match was closely fought until Zito headed home a high Amarildo pass in the 69th minute. Brazil wrapped up the contest when Czech keeper Schrojf allowed a Djalma Santos high ball to fall through his hands, enabling Vavá to stab home for an unassailable 3-1 lead. It was the best match of the tournament.

GARRINCHA MAKES THE FINAL

Garrincha was lucky to play in the final having been sent-off during Brazil's semi with Chile. Never a dirty player, he retaliated to one of many kicks by cheekily tapping Eladio Rojas on the backside with his knee. The Chilean's delayed reaction collapse was comical, but on the advice of the linesman, Garrincha was sent from the pitch.

Punishment was not automatic, but FIFA had suspended all the other players dismissed. Brazil lobbied hard and even the President of Peru asked the Peruvian referee to exonerate Garrincha. Mysteriously the linesman who had witnessed the incident was unable to provide testimony, having left Chile the following morning on a ticket to Montevideo - via Paris - that had been reportedly paid for by the Brazilian representative on the FIFA board. As a result, Garrincha was cleared to play in the final.

England 1966

TOURNAMENT STATS

WINNER England

FINAL
England 4-2 West Germany *(aet)*

SEMI-FINALS
West Germany 2-1 Soviet Union
England 2-1 Portugal

THIRD PLACE PLAY-OFF
Portugal 2-1 Soviet Union

TOP GOALSCORERS
9 goals: Eusébio (Portugal)
5 goals: Helmut Haller (West Germany)
4 goals: Geoff Hurst (England), Franz Beckenbauer (West Germany), Ferenc Bene (Hungary), Valeri Porkujan (Soviet Union)

FASTEST GOAL
1 minute: Park Seung-Zin (North Korea v Portugal)

TOTAL GOALS
89

AVERAGE GOALS
2.78 per game

In 1966 the English staged a tournament that saw the pragmatism of the European game finally outpace the flair of the South Americans. After back-to-back wins by the beautiful Brazilians, the 1966 World Cup was characterised by dour, often ugly defending, punctuated by flashes of brilliance and moments of high drama, but in the epic encounter between old adversaries England and West Germany, it was also a competition capable of springing the most fantastic of surprises, right up to the final whistle of the final match.

Hosts England could boast internationally revered players of the calibre of Bobby Moore, Bobby Charlton and Jimmy Greaves, while in Alf Ramsey they had a progressive manager who, shortly after his appointment in October 1962, promised the nation that his team would win the World Cup. In the intervening years he had developed a much-admired 4-3-3 system, played either with three dedicated strikers or two supported by a single winger. England went on an eight-month unbeaten run before the tournament, but while impressing the world game, it still left

critics at home cold because of its reliance on work rate over creativity. "It's not Alf's fault," TV pundit Jimmy Hill famously said at the time, "nobody could win the World Cup with those players."

England's opening game proved an anticlimax with the negative Uruguayans blotting out England's sterile attack. A less than convincing 2-0 win against Mexico followed, but England progressed to the second round after beating France. After the match the FA had asked Ramsey to drop Nobby Stiles because of his fierce tackle on Jacky Simon, but the coach stood by his man.

The England players lift their captain Bobby Moore as he lifts the Jules Rimet Cup

THE FINAL

ENGLAND (1) 4
WEST GERMANY (1) 2
(AET: 2-2 AT 90 MINS)

Date Saturday July 30, 1966
Attendance 93,000
Venue Wembley Stadium, London
Referee Gottfried Dienst (Switzerland)

England coach Alf Ramsey

West Germany coach Helmut Schön

ENGLAND
1 GORDON BANKS
2 GEORGE COHEN
5 JACK CHARLTON
6 BOBBY MOORE (C)
3 RAY WILSON
4 NOBBY STILES
9 BOBBY CHARLTON
16 MARTIN PETERS *Goal: 78 mins. Booked.*
10 ALAN BALL
21 ROGER HUNT
10 GEOFF HURST *Goal: 18 mins, 101 mins, 120 mins*

WEST GERMANY
1 HANS TILKOWSKI
2 HORST-DIETER HÖTTGES
5 WILLI SCHULZ
6 WOLFGANG WEBER *Goal: 90 mins*
3 KARL-HEINZ SCHNELLINGER
8 HELMUT HALLER *Goal: 12 mins*
4 FRANZ BECKENBAUER
12 WOLFGANG OVERATH
9 UWE SEELER (C)
10 SIGI HELD
11 LOTHAR EMMERICH

In Group 2 West Germany got off to a flying start with a crushing 5-0 win over a Swiss side depleted by internal suspensions. The first real surprise came when the physical Argentinians beat a Spain team built around the players of the mighty Real Madrid side. While the Spanish recovered to beat the Swiss, West Germany faced Argentina and were subjected to the kind of brutal tactics that saw the South Americans pick up a FIFA warning. It did not prevent them progressing though, Argentina clinching qualification against Switzerland in front of a hostile Hillsborough crowd. West Germany, meanwhile, qualified as group leaders after an Uwe Seeler goal put Spain out.

Group 3 favourites Brazil started well by beating Bulgaria 2-0 with two great strikes from Pelé and Garrincha, though the game was marred by a series of ugly challenges. Hungary, meanwhile, beat Portugal 3-1, who were without their first choice goalkeeper, before defeating a Brazil team minus the injured Pelé. It was a classic match with the Hungarians showing a flair and skill rarely seen in the finals. Bene gave them the lead after three minutes and Tostão equalised for Brazil against the

Wolfgang Overath gives chase as Geoff Hurst unleashes his third, and England's fourth, goal in the World Cup final.

run of play. The second-half saw Hungary step up a gear, with Flórián Albert at the heart of their 3-1 win. It was Brazil's first World Cup defeat since the 'Battle Of Berne' in 1954. Portugal finished top of the group after beating Bulgaria and Brazil, and Hungary joined them in the quarter-finals.

Group 4 opened with the Soviets overpowering outsiders North Korea 3-0 and Italy beating Chile by two goals. The English fans warmed to the energetic North Koreans and inspired them to a draw with Chile in their next game. The meeting of the group heavyweights saw a curiously unbalanced Italy run ragged by the Soviets, who were not flattered by their 1-0 win. Italy faced the Koreans expecting to qualify in second place, but the nippy Koreans exploited the fact that coach Fabbri had picked his slowest defenders. Pak Doo-Ik scored to eliminate Italy and pull off the biggest World Cup shock since the USA beat England in 1950.

England faced Argentina in the first quarter-final, with Geoff Hurst coming in for the country's best striker Jimmy Greaves, injured in the game with France. Ramsey's much trialled 4-3-3 system morphed into a wingless 4-4-2 formation, with Hunt and Hurst paired as twin strikers and midfielder Nobby Stiles sitting in front of the defence as a ball winner charged with feeding the creative players. It proved effective and although Argentina continued their cynical approach in a very physical game, it was Hurst's single headed goal that put England into the semi-finals.

The second quarter-final between West Germany and Uruguay was equally unpleasant. Uruguay had looked the better side in an open first-half, but after the interval the game descended into violence. The Germans reacted to provocation and Lothar Emmerich kicked Horacio Troche, only for the

AN INTERNATIONAL INCIDENT

Argentina's quarter-final against England was not so much a football match as an international incident. Captain Antonio Rattín became so incensed by what he saw as European bias towards Latin American football that he began a running argument with the referee. When he was sent-off it sparked chaos as he refused to leave and it seemed his team might walk off in protest.

England coach Alf Ramsey was so incensed that he tried to prevent his players exchanging shirts after the game, and in an ill-advised TV interview he expressed his desire to face teams who wanted "to play football and not to act as animals". In Argentina his comments caused such a furore that it was as if he had called the entire nation 'animals'. He withdrew the statement but it would be the cause of a rivalry that would last for years.

Uruguayan to respond with a kick to the stomach. Troche was sent-off and he slapped Uwe Seeler in the face as he left the field. Minutes later Uruguay were down to nine men and Germany scored four times in the last 20 minutes.

The Soviets pressed Hungary into mistakes, as twice keeper József Gelei blundered and his team went down 2-1. The most exciting game of the round, however, brought North Korea and Portugal together, with the Koreans 3-0 up in just 25 minutes. Eusébio scored twice before half-time as Portugal began their comeback and after the break he scored twice more, before Augusto added a fifth. Eusébio would finish as the tournament's most popular player and its top scorer with nine goals.

The first semi-final saw West Germany face the Soviet Union in another bruising encounter. Poor sportsmanship and violent conduct marred the game and the Soviets left the pitch with nine men, having lost 2-1. England's match with Portugal was altogether different. The Portuguese struggled to breach England's resolute defence and Bobby Charlton was outstanding going forward, scoring in each half to put England ahead. A penalty for Portugal was too little too late and England, who had controversially retained Hurst in the line-up over Greaves, were in the final to face the Germans.

Ramsey overlooked Greaves and fielded an unchanged line-up for the final, but got off to a poor start as Haller gave the Germans a 12th minute lead. It was short-lived, as a fine header from Hurst soon made it 1-1. Both sides continued to press forward until, with only 12 minutes remaining, Martin Peters latched on to a poor clearance to give England the advantage. In the final minute, however, West Germany won a free-kick and Wolfgang Weber scrambled in an equaliser.

England went into extra-time on the attack and had already gone close twice when Hurst thumped a shot against the underside of the bar, turning to celebrate as the ball bounced downwards towards the goal line. The referee awarding the goal after a discussion with his linesman and in the final minute any debate became academic when Hurst broke away to complete the only ever World Cup final hat-trick. Not even a first choice selection at the start of the tournament, Hurst had written himself into the football history books just five months after making his international debut.

THE RUSSIAN LINESMAN

When Geoff Hurst turned to celebrate as the ball bounced down from the underside of the bar for England's third World Cup final goal, he sparked a debate that would last for decades. Was it a goal or not? The Germans protested, but after consulting 'Russian linesman' Tofik Bakhramov, the referee awarded the goal.

Since that day Bakhramov's notoriety has grown. Legend has it he was presented with a golden whistle by the Queen "for services to England", and in 1992 Margaret Thatcher apparently requested to meet him on a visit to his hometown of Baku. So revered was he in Azerbaijan that the national stadium was named after him. An urban myth also has it that shortly before his death, Bakhramov was asked how he could have been so certain the ball had crossed the line. The former Red Army soldier simply replied: "Stalingrad".

Below left: Eusébio takes on the Hungarian defence. Below: The North Koreans celebrate beating Italy.

Mexico 1970

Pelé and Bobby Moore swap shirts

TOURNAMENT STATS

WINNER Brazil

FINAL
Brazil 4-1 Italy

SEMI-FINALS
Italy 4-3 West Germany *(aet)*
Brazil 3-1 Uruguay

THIRD PLACE PLAY-OFF
West Germany 1-0 Uruguay

TOP GOALSCORERS
10 goals: Gerd Müller (West Germany)
7 goals: Jairzinho (Brazil)
5 goals: Teófilo Cubillas (Peru)

FASTEST GOAL
3 minutes: Ladislav Petras (Czechoslovakia v Romania)

TOTAL GOALS
95

AVERAGE GOALS
2.97 per game

Against all the odds Mexico 70 turned out to be the most exciting tournament in World Cup history. Despite the extreme heat of the Mexican summer, the midday kick-off times scheduled to appease European broadcasters, the energy-sapping altitude that threatened to stifle attacking football, and pre-tournament fears of ultra-defensive and violent play, the 1970 World Cup proved a hit like no other. Thanks to the colourful flamboyance and daring excellence of the multi-skilled Brazilians, the beautiful game somehow managed to prosper like never before.

The format of the World Cup remained largely unaltered, although the tossing of a coin was introduced to settle a tie if teams were equal after extra-time in the knockout stages. Substitutes were allowed for the first time, two per team, and FIFA ruled that squad members did not have to wear the Number 13 shirt if they were superstitious. The first official World Cup ball was introduced too. With 32 black or white hexagonal panels, the Adidas-created Telstar was far more visible on TV and became the symbol of the tournament.

Hosts Mexico kicked off with a lifeless 0-0 draw against the Soviet Union at the Azteca, a glorious stadium completed four years earlier at a cost of £7 million. They went on to beat El Salvador 4-0 and sneaked past Belgium thanks to a disputed penalty, qualifying from Group 1 along with the Soviet Union, the two teams dropping only a point each. The ultra-cautious Italians qualified on top of Group 2 without conceding a goal and having scored just once, while Uruguay edged out Sweden to qualify for the quarter-finals in second place.

The outstanding match of the group stage was between twice-champions Brazil and holders England. In a wonderful end-to-end game, famed for an incredible Gordon Banks save from a downward, goal-bound Pelé header, Brazil stole the honours with the only goal courtesy of the powerful Jairzinho. Both teams progressed to the next stage.

In Group 4, despite an early struggle against a spirited Morocco side, the West Germans gained maximum points with 'Der Bomber', Gerd Müller, knocking in hat-tricks against Peru and Bulgaria. In the next round they faced England in a rematch

Carlos Alberto lifts the Jules Rimet Cup

THE FINAL

BRAZIL (1) 4
ITALY (1) 1

Date Sunday June 21, 1970
Attendance 107,412
Venue Azteca Stadium, Mexico City
Referee Rudi Glöckner (East Germany)

Brazil Coach Mario Zagalo

Italy Coach Ferruccio Valcareggi

BRAZIL
1 FÉLIX
4 CARLOS ALBERTO (c) — Goal: 87 mins
2 BRITO
3 WILSON PIAZZA
16 EVERALDO
7 JAIRZINHO — Goal: 71 mins
5 CLODOALDO
8 GÉRSON — Goal: 66 mins
9 TOSTÃO
10 PELÉ — Goal: 18 mins
11 RIVELINO — Booked

ITALY
1 ENRICO ALBERTOSI
2 TARCISIO BURGNICH — Booked
5 PIERLUIGI CERA
10 MARIO BERTINI — Subbed: 75 mins (Juliano)
3 GIACINTO FACCHETTI (c)
8 ROBERTO ROSATO
13 ANGELO DOMENGHINI
16 GIANCARLO DE SISTI
15 SANDRO MAZZOLA
20 ROBERTO BONINSEGNA — Goal: 38 mins. Subbed: 84 mins (Rivera)
11 GIGI RIVA
18 ANTONIO JULIANO Sub
14 GIANNI RIVERA Sub

THE BOGOTÁ INCIDENT

When England arrived in Mexico it was without captain Bobby Moore, who was being held by police in Colombia after being accused of stealing an emerald bracelet from the gift shop at the team's hotel in Bogotá. The initial accusation was against both Moore and Bobby Charlton, but it was dismissed as a set-up and the players released. Several days later, after the appearance of a mysterious 'witness', Moore was arrested and charged with theft.

There had been a fear that he would not be released for the World Cup, with British prime minister Harold Wilson becoming involved in negotiations, but Moore was finally able to rejoin the team just five days before their first game. Despite the lack of evidence, his case would not be formally dropped until 1972 and he didn't receive official notification until December 1975.

of the previous World Cup final. Five players from each team had played in the final four years earlier.

With goals from Alan Mullery and Martin Peters, England were 2-0 up and in control early in the second-half. However, a couple of rhythm-disturbing substitutions by Sir Alf Ramsey (Norman Hunter and Colin Bell on for Bobby Charlton and Martin Peters) gave the Germans the edge as they clawed themselves back into the game, and goals from Franz Beckenbauer and Uwe Seeler took the tie to extra-time. A close-range volley from Müller past second-choice keeper Peter Bonetti (Banks had been sidelined by illness) finally eliminated the holders.

In the other quarter-finals, Mexico lost 4-1 to an atypically free-scoring Italian side in Toluca, with the talented striker Gigi Riva scoring twice. In Guadalajara, Brazil continued their irrepressible form, getting the better of Peru in a six-goal thriller, while in Mexico City Uruguay narrowly defeated the Soviet Union with an extra-time goal by substitute Victor Esparrago.

Pelé celebrates scoring in the final as Tarcisio Burgnich lies beaten on the pitch.

The match of the tournament came at the Azteca, where European giants Italy and West Germany were pitted against each other in a thrilling semi-final. Italy scored first through Roberto Boninsegna before withdrawing to protect their lead. It was a tactic that nearly worked, but an equaliser in the third minute of injury-time from Karl-Heinz Schnellinger meant the game would not to be decided without extra-time.

Beckenbauer famously remained on the field even with a dislocated shoulder, his arm strapped to his body, and the goals kept coming in extra-time. Müller edged West Germany into the lead, while Burgnich and Riva gave Italy a 3-2 edge. Müller equalised for the Germans, before substitute Gianni Rivera finally clinched one of the World Cup's most epic struggles in favour of Italy.

The other semi-final pitted South American foes Uruguay against Brazil in Guadalajara. The Uruguayans took the early advantage through Cubilla and immediately tried to sit back on their lead. It was not the tactic to try against Mario Zagallo's thrilling Brazilians, as right-half Clodoaldo powered in an equaliser before half-time. Despite aggressive tackling from Uruguay, second-half goals from Jairzinho and Rivelino sealed a 3-1 victory for Brazil. Late on Pelé almost hit the goal of the tournament, outrageously dummying Mazurkiewicz in the Uruguayan goal before pulling his shot just wide.

The final was staged at the Azteca in front of a crowd of 107,000 and a global TV audience of millions. At stake was the permanent home of the cup itself. According to FIFA rules, the trophy that Jules Rimet had inspired in 1930 was to be kept by the first team to win it three times and both finalists had won it twice already.

Despite Italy's well-organised catenaccio defence, marshalled by veteran Giacinto Facchetti, Brazil could boast the kind of attacking flair that had them installed as the undoubted favourites. However, with their frail defence and goalkeeping deficiencies, they were vulnerable if the Italians

'Der Bomber' Gerd Müller bears down on England keeper Peter Bonetti.

chose to attack, but with Italian coach Valcareggi continuing to select Sandro Mazzola over European Player Of The Year Gianni Rivera, Italy had limited attacking options.

Pelé opened the scoring after 18 minutes, athletically getting his head on the end of Rivelino's cross. Against the run of play Boninsegna pounced on a careless mistake by Clodoaldo to level the score, but Italy were unable to match the Brazilians in terms of possession. In the 66th minute Gerson's left-footed cross-shot found the back of the net, followed by another strike from Jairzinho, making him the only player to have scored in all six rounds of the World Cup, including the final.

By the time that Rivera came on as an 84th minute substitute there was too little time, and two minutes later Brazil scored one of the most loved goals in football history. In a move that saw eight of the team's ten outfield players touch the ball, Jairzinho found Pelé who laid the ball into the stride of Carlos Alberto, the captain thundering it low into the corner of the net. The Jules Rimet Cup was Brazil's to keep.

The competition had been a personal victory for Pelé. Having threatened to quit football after his treatment at the 1966 finals, his performances in 1970 stood as a permanent testament to his genius.

The 1970 World Cup was a triumph, and thanks, ironically, to television, a triumph on a global scale. How fitting that Mexico 70 was the first tournament to be broadcast in colour, and because of the fantasy football of the Brazilians, it proved to be glorious technicolour.

SEEING RED AND YELLOW

The 1970 World Cup saw the first use of red and yellow cards to indicate a caution. Following the furore caused by Argentina's Antonio Rattín's refusal to leave the pitch at the 1966 World Cup, Ken Aston of FIFA's Referees' Committee decided that some kind of visual clarification was needed in case a player did not understand, or chose not to understand, that he had been sent-off.

Not only had Aston refereed the infamous 'Battle Of Santiago' at the 1962 World Cup, but he had also been called to the Wembley touchline in 1966 to resolve matters after Rattín's refusal to leave the pitch. His idea for red and yellow cards, inspired by traffic lights, was much debated by FIFA before its adoption in 1970.

West Germany 1974

STADIUM GUIDE

Gerd Müller takes on Yugoslavia

TOURNAMENT STATS

WINNER West Germany

FINAL
West Germany 2-1 Holland

SEMI-FINALS
Replaced by a second round group phase

THIRD PLACE PLAY-OFF
Poland 1-0 Brazil

TOP GOALSCORERS
7 goals: Gregorz Lato (Poland);
5 goals: Johan Neeskens (Holland), Andrzej Szarmach (Poland);
4 goals: Gerd Müller (West Germany), Ralf Edström (Sweden), Johnny Rep (Holland)

FASTEST GOAL
80 seconds: Johan Neeskens (Holland v West Germany)

TOTAL GOALS
97

AVERAGE GOALS
2.55 per game

When West Germany staged the 1974 World Cup they were expected to win. Twenty years earlier they had been the outsiders who had managed to snatch the Jules Rimet Cup against all the odds, but now they were among the true giants of the game, reigning European champions who had won that competition with an overwhelming display of elegance and power. With home advantage and a team marshalled by the magisterial attacking sweeper Franz Beckenbauer, the West Germans were brim full of confidence and had their eye on the main prize.

The 1970 finals in Mexico had ended somewhat ignobly for European football. Italy had been demolished by a seemingly unstoppable Brazil, but by 1974 the European game was once more in the ascendance. Not only were the West Germans a force to be reckoned with, but the Dutch also arrived at the tournament as genuine contenders. They may have struggled during the qualifying stages, but under Barcelona coach Rinus Michels, who had taken over the national side on a temporary basis just three months before the tournament, Holland could rely on an impressive array of world-class talent from Ajax, the all-conquering club side that had dominated European football for the previous three years.

The format of the competition changed in 1974, with a second group stage replacing the knockout phase. The top two teams in each group progressed to the second round, where they were split into two further groups of four, which replaced the drama of the quarter-finals and the semi-finals. The winners of each group would qualify directly for the final, a format aimed at guaranteeing half the participants at least six games each. To separate teams level on points, goal difference was introduced in place of goal average.

When the tournament kicked off, the Dutch cut a swathe through the group stages. Their unique brand of 'Total Football', in which players switched positions and roles with astonishing versatility, saw them score 14 goals in six games, conceding just once. They began the first group stage with a comfortable 2-0 win over Uruguay and bounced

'Der Kaiser' Franz Beckenbauer in his greatest moment

THE FINAL

WEST GERMANY	(2)	**2**
HOLLAND	(1)	**1**

Date Sunday July 7, 1974
Attendance 75,200
Venue Olympic Stadium, Munich
Referee Jack Taylor (England)

West Germany coach Helmut Schön

Holland coach Rinus Michels

WEST GERMANY

1 SEPP MAIER
2 BERTI VOGTS – *Booked: 3 mins*
4 HANS-GEORG SCHWARZENBECK
5 FRANZ BECKENBAUER (c)
3 PAUL BREITNER – *Goal: 25 mins (pen)*
16 RAINER BONHOF
14 ULI HOENESS
12 WOLGANG OVERATH
9 JÜRGEN GRABOWSKI
13 GERD MÜLLER – *Goal: 43 mins*
17 BERND HÖLZENBEIN

HOLLAND

8 JAN JONGBLOED
20 WIM SUURBIER
17 WIM RIJSBERGEN – *Subbed: 69 mins (De Jong)*
2 ARIE HAAN
12 RUUD KROL
6 WIM JANSEN
13 JOHAN NEESKENS – *Goal: 2 mins (pen). Booked: 39 mins*
3 WIM VAN HANEGEM – *Booked: 22 mins*
16 JOHNNY REP
14 JOHAN CRUYFF (c) – *Booked: 45 mins*
15 ROB RENSENBRINK – *Subbed: 46 mins (Van De Kerkhof, R)*
10 RENÉ VAN DE KERKHOF Sub
7 THEO DE JONG Sub

Above: East meets West as the two Germanys do battle. Above right: Joe Jordan in action for Scotland during the victory over Zaïre.

back from a goalless draw with Sweden to record an impressive 4-1 rout of Bulgaria. This was enough to clinch top spot and qualify for the last eight along with Sweden.

A pre-tournament defeat of West Germany had made Argentina a good outside bet, but after only just edging out Italy for a place in the last eight, they were effectively dismantled by the Dutch in their opening second group stage game. Goals from Johnny Rep, Ruud Krol and two from Johan Cruyff completed the 4-0 landslide. Holland's 2-0 win over East Germany, set up an all or nothing showdown with reigning world champions Brazil: the prize was a place in the final.

Without Pelé, who had by now retired, the Brazilians were clearly not the force they had once been. They scraped through the first stage thanks to goalless draws with Yugoslavia and Scotland, and a 3-0 win over a hapless Zaïre side that had conceded nine against Yugoslavia. However, Brazil started the second stage with something approaching their old swagger, beating East Germany 1-0, thanks to a second-half strike from Rivelino, and Argentina 2-1, with goals from Jairzinho and Rivelino again.

Despite improving form the Brazilians found it impossible to live with a Dutch side approaching the peak of its powers. A gorgeous 50th minute lob from Neeskens and a Cruyff strike 15 minutes later saw Holland run out 2-0 winners. The self-destructing Brazilians finished the match with ten men after the dismissal of Luís Pereira. Holland, many assumed, were well on their way to a first and hugely deserved world championship.

In contrast West Germany started the tournament slowly. After a narrow win over Chile and an unimpressive 3-0 victory against Australia, Helmut Schön's men had progressed to the last eight in second place after a shock 1-0 defeat to East Germany. Finishing second meant they avoided Brazil, Argentina and Holland in the next group stage and slowly but surely the West German team started to get into their stride.

The West Germans were relying ever more heavily on Franz Beckenbauer, their inspirational captain, who had become increasingly influential in team selection behind the scenes after the psychological blow dealt to coach Helmut Schön

PLAYER POWER AT THE CASH CUP

In 1974 the players fought for their share of the spoils in the face of headlines branding them 'greedy'. The West German federation went though heated negotiations after players learned their bonus was less than a third of that promised to the Italians and the Dutch. Coach Helmut Schön even threatened to send all 22 players home.

The Dutch similarly invoked the wrath of their coach, while so powerful was the Puma-sponsored Johan Cruyff that he was permitted to play in a bespoke kit featuring just two stripes rather that the three-striped Adidas shirt worn by his team-mates

The fiery Billy Bremner was in charge of Scottish negotiations and as a result they trained with the Adidas logo blacked out on their boots. Even Uruguay, who were no longer a football power, were refusing to give any interviews without payment.

by defeat to his former homeland, East Germany. His players were stung into action and started the second group stage impressively, beating Yugoslavia 2-0. In the following game they were deadlocked at 2-2 against Sweden with 15 minutes to play, but Jürgen Grabowski and Uli Hoeness put the tie beyond doubt, setting up a crucial group game with Poland, a match the Germans only needed to draw to reach their third World Cup final.

The Poles, who had eliminated England during the qualifiers, were unbeaten thus far in the tournament and in Grzegorz Lato had a striker who would become its highest scorer, two of his seven goals coming in a 3-2 first stage victory over Argentina. He also scored a crucial second-half winner in the 2-1 victory over Yugoslavia that effectively brought Poland face-to-face with the West Germans and a place in the final at stake.

When the two teams met, the tension mounted as the kick-off was delayed due to a severely waterlogged pitch. Poland's best chances came in the first-half, Robert Gadocha and the effervescent Lato forcing keeper Sepp Maier into a couple of excellent saves. Maier's opposite number, Jan Tomaszewski, saved a penalty from Uli Hoeness after the break, but the Germans snatched the winner 14 minutes from time when Müller clinically buried the ball in the back of the net after a shot from Hoeness had deflected into his path.

A 1-0 third place play-off victory over Brazil, the goal coming courtesy of Lato, was scant consolation for the Poles, who had been the tournament's biggest surprise package. The final, however, was now to be contested between West Germany, who hadn't won the tournament since 1954, and Holland, who hadn't even managed to qualify since 1938. It was the battle of efficiency, organisation and hard work against versatility, vision and precocious talent.

After the kick-off was delayed by English referee Jack Taylor, who had spotted that there were no corner flags, Holland got off to the best possible start. With less than a minute on the clock Johan Cruyff was up-ended in the West German penalty area by Uli Hoeness and Johan Neeskens calmly slotted the first World Cup final penalty past Maier. When the keeper picked the ball out of the net, he was the first German to have touched the ball.

The Dutch continued to dominate the early exchanges, but then surrendered their lead cheaply in the 25th minute when a surging Bernd Hölzenbein run was bought to an abrupt end by a trip in the Holland penalty area, although it looked very much like a dive. Paul Breitner duly converted the spot-kick, and the Germans went on to take a solid lead two minutes before half-time through Gerd Müller. For all their flair and guile, the Dutch could not claw themselves back into the game, despite laying seige to Maier's goal. In his third World Cup Franz Beckenbauer had finally led West Germany to the world championship, 20 years and three days after the 'Miracle Of Berne'.

THE NEW WORLD CUP TROPHY

After the Brazilians had won the World Cup for the third time in 1970, FIFA rules dictated that they keep the Jules Rimet Cup in perpetuity, so a new trophy was needed. The original may have been classical in fashion and made from gold plated sterling silver, but its replacement was far grander in scale and execution.

The new FIFA World Cup, as it was formally named, was a solid gold manifestation of world football depicting two human figures holding up the Earth. Designed by Italian sculptor Silvio Gazzaniga, at the opening ceremony of the 1974 finals Pelé and Uwe Seeler showed off both trophies side by side. However, the Jules Rimet Cup would only remain in the hands of the Brazilians until it was stolen in 1983, the wooden back of its bulletproof glass case having been prized open. It has never been recovered.

Italy's Giacinto Facchetti and Haiti's Wilner Nazaire meet in Munich.

Argentina 1978

STADIUM GUIDE

TOURNAMENT STATS

WINNER Argentina

FINAL
Argentina 3-1 Holland *(aet)*

SEMI-FINALS
Replaced by a second round group phase

THIRD PLACE PLAY-OFF
Brazil 2-1 Italy

TOP GOALSCORERS
6 goals: Mario Kempes (Argentina)
5 goals: Teófilo Cubillas (Peru), Rob Rensenbrink (Holland)
4 goals: Hans Krankl (Austria), Leopoldo Luque (Argentina)

FASTEST GOAL
31 seconds: Bernard Lacombe (France v Italy)

TOTAL GOALS
102

AVERAGE GOALS
2.68 per game

When Daniel Passarella hoisted the World Cup aloft in at the Monumental Stadium in Buenos Aires, it was one of the most romantic and tragic moments in football history. For Argentina, named as hosts back in 1966, just to have staged the event was an achievement given the political turmoil that had prompted several participants to talk of a boycott. To then win the trophy sent the nation ecstatic.

Yet for Holland, whose players endured the victory night celebrations cooped up in their hotel, defeat in the final for the second consecutive time was cruel beyond measure. The country that had illuminated Seventies football and had probably done more to create the modern game than any other, was destined to end the decade without a major honour.

Coming as it did in the wake of the great Brazil team performance of 1970 and the Beckenbauer/ Cruyff head-to-head of 1974, the tournament itself was not a vintage. Mario Kempes may have emerged as Argentina's hero, but it was not to the extent that Diego Maradona would eight years later.

While Argentina 78 lacked a true superstar or a great team, the extreme emotions it generated – not to mention the whiff of scandal – ensured its place in football folklore.

The threatened boycott in protest at General Videla's military regime never materialised and all 16 teams arrived as planned, although Holland's Johan Cruyff stayed at home, not prepared to leave his family for such a long period of time after a kidnap attempt the previous year. Once again there

'El Gran Capitan' Daniel Passarella celebrates with the World Cup trophy

was no knockout stage. The top two teams in four groups would progress into a second group stage with the winners of each group going into the final.

Most of the football superpowers had qualified, with the exception of Euro 76 winners Czechoslovakia, the Soviet Union and, for the second consecutive finals, England. British interest centred on Scotland, who assembled perhaps their greatest team, but their campaign degenerated into shambles and acrimony. Poor results, coupled with winger Willie Johnston failing a drugs test, ensured a shameful early exit for Scotland. Only then, when it was too late, did they show what they could do by beating Holland 3-2.

In the first group stage Peru had demonstrated they weren't the expected pushovers, while doubts persisted about whether Holland could mount a serious challenge without Cruyff. In the end, the Dutch scraped through to the second round behind the Peruvians.

THE FINAL

ARGENTINA	(1) **3**
HOLLAND	(1) **1**

(AET; 1-1 AT 90 MINS)

Date Sunday June 25, 1978
Attendance Attendance 71,483
Venue Estadio Monumental, Buenos Aires
Referee Sergio Gonella (Italy)

Argentina coach César Luis Menotti

Holland coach Ernst Happel

ARGENTINA
5 UBALDO FILLOL
15 JORGE OLGUIN
7 LUIS GALVAN
19 DANIEL PASSARELLA (c)
19 ALBERTO TARANTINI
2 OSVALDO ARDILES *Booked: 40 mins. Subbed: 66 mins (Larossa)*
6 AMERICO GALLEGO
16 OSCAR ORTIZ *Subbed: 75 mins (Houseman)*
4 DANIEL BERTONI *Goal: 115 mins*
14 LEOPOLDO LUQUE
10 MARIO KEMPES *Goal: 38, 105 mins*
12 OMAR LAROSSA Sub *Booked: 94 mins*
9 RENÉ HOUSEMAN Sub

HOLLAND
8 JAN JONGBLOED
2 JAN POORTVLIET *Booked: 96 mins*
5 RUUD KROL (c) *Booked: 15 mins*
22 ERNIE BRANDTS
6 WIM JANSEN *Subbed: 73 mins (Suurbier)*
13 JOHAN NEESKENS
9 ARIE HAAN
11 WILLY VAN DE KERKHOF
10 RENÉ VAN DE KERKHOF
16 JOHNNY REP *Subbed: 59 mins (Nanninga)*
12 ROB RENSENBRINK
18 DICK NANNINGA Sub *Goal: 82 mins*
20 WIM SUURBIER Sub *Booked: 94 mins*

Above: West German keeper Sepp Maier beats Italy's Franco Causio to the ball. Above right: Mario Kempes, the tournament's top scorer.

West Germany also qualified as runners-up to Poland in perhaps the weakest group, while Brazil, under coach Claudio Coutinho, had gone from poetic to pragmatic. They were far from convincing, managing only two goals in their three group games, but along with Austria they still squeezed through ahead of Spain and Sweden.

With so many big guns misfiring, the tournament appeared to be opening up. Italy, masters of the defensive approach that characterised football in this era, looked likely to prosper when they topped a group that also included Argentina, France and Hungary. The hosts had beaten France 2-1 and progressed as runners-up.

THE WORLD CUP 'FIX'

As Argentina kicked off against Peru they knew a victory by four goals would take them to the World Cup final. They had not beaten them by that margin since 1927, and when Peru conceded six goals there were immediate suspicions of a fix. Conspiracy theories developed: it was pointed out that Peru's keeper, Ramon Quiroga, was born in Argentina, while his reserve keeper Manzo reportedly admitted to the fix while drunk before retracting his words.

In 1986 *The Sunday Times* published an article alleging a deal struck by Argentina's ruling military junta - the shipping of 35,000 tons of free grain to Peru, possibly arms too, and that the Argentine central bank had unfrozen $50 million in credits. The journalist responsible for the story was put on trial in Argentina but acquitted. The story has never gone away.

Despite their indifferent showings, all of the favourites had spluttered their way into a second round that fizzed with exciting match-ups. Group A featured European superpowers West Germany, Holland and Italy, plus a useful Austria side gorging itself on the goals of Hans Krankl. Group B included the less fancied Poles and Peru, plus arguably the fiercest rivals in world football, Argentina and Brazil.

When the two met in Rosario, the weight of history and the fear of defeat were too much for either side to bear and the match petered out into an ill-tempered 0-0 draw. With both sides having already recorded victories (Brazil had beaten Peru 3-0 and Argentina defeated Poland 2-0), providing both could win their last matches the finalist would be decided on goal difference.

When Brazil overcame Poland 3-1, the balance of power appeared to have swung their way. But owing to some unfair scheduling, Argentina didn't kick-off their final game against Peru in Rosario until 45 minutes after Brazil's game had finished. César Luis Menotti's side had the advantage of knowing they had to win by four clear goals to reach the final.

Peru, who had looked so accomplished early in the tournament, at first seemed prepared for the challenge, even hitting the post. Then, in one of the most talked about matches in World Cup history, they rolled over and lost 6-0. Rumours had already circulated about some controversial decisions in Argentina's favour against France in the first round, and it was soon alleged that the match with Peru had been fixed by the country's ruling military junta. When the dust settled, however, it was Argentina – 48 years after they had lost the first World Cup to Uruguay – who had booked their ticket to the final.

Holland exploded into life with a 5-1 destruction of Austria to take an early stranglehold on the other group, while Italy and West Germany played out a scoreless draw. Holland strengthened their hand when, in a rematch of the 1974 finalists, goals from Arie Haan and Rene van der Kerkhof earned them a useful 2-2 draw with West Germany.

With Italy beating Austria, the Dutch knew that unless the West Germans could manage a landslide against Austria, a draw with Italy would be sufficient. West Germany, a shadow of their 1974 side, were put out of their misery when they lost 3-2 to the already-eliminated Austrians. Holland did all that was required and more by beating Italy 2-1.

In the third place play-off, Brazil overcame Enzo Bearzot's Italy 2-1 to maintain the only unbeaten record of the tournament. However, the victory only upset the Brazilians even more, as for the first time in the competition they had shed their inhibitions and played in the great Brazil tradition, leaving many to wonder why they left it so late.

The 1978 World Cup Final began with mind games as Argentina attempted to unnerve the Dutch by keeping them waiting on the pitch for five minutes before their arrival to a sea of sky blue and white ticker tape. They then objected to a lightweight cast on René van der Kerkhof's arm, which he had worn in the five previous matches. The game was delayed while the referee insisted that yet another bandage was applied over the top.

When play began, high skill mingled with barely restrained violence. Johnny Rep wasted a great chance for Holland before Kempes put Argentina ahead on 37 minutes. The Dutch were growing feverish with frustration when, in the 81st minute, substitute Dick Nanninga headed the ball into the net. Then with a minute to go, Rob Rensenbrink tantalisingly struck the foot of the post.

Kempes, the tournament's top scorer, scrambled Argentina back into the lead a minute before the first period of extra-time ended and, with four minutes to go, Bertoni made the game safe and Argentina were finally world champions.

THE DUTCH STAND FIRM

A military junta seized power in Argentina two years before the World Cup and was responsible for the illegal arrest, torture and forced disappearance of thousands of Argentinians. Several European teams, most notably Holland, had threatened to pull out of the World Cup in protest. While a campaign by Amnesty International had persuaded stars like Paolo Rossi and Sepp Maier to sign petitions, the threatened boycott never materialised.

In advance of the final the Dutch team decided to refuse to accept the trophy from General Jorge Videla should they win. Events conspired against them, but the players stood firm and declined to accept their runners-up medals. They also passed on the tournament's closing dinner, but the full impact of their courageous snub had been undermined by defeat.

Below left: Scotland's Archie Gemmill scores his wonder goal against Holland.
Below: Argentina get a ticker tape welcome before the final at the Monumental Stadium.

Spain 1982

STADIUM GUIDE

TOURNAMENT STATS

WINNER Italy

FINAL
Italy 3-1 West Germany

SEMI-FINALS
West Germany 3-3 France
(aet: West Germany won 5-4 on penalties)
Italy 2-0 Poland

THIRD PLACE PLAY-OFF
Poland 3-2 France

TOP GOALSCORERS
6 goals: Paolo Rossi (Italy)
5 goals: Karl-Heinz Rummenigge (West Germany)
4 goals: Zbigniew Boniek (Poland), Zico (Brazil)

FASTEST GOAL
27 seconds: Bryan Robson (England v France)

TOTAL GOALS
146

AVERAGE GOALS
2.81 per game

There was a real sense of trepidation ahead of the 1982 World Cup Finals. Many doubted Spain's ability to host such a spectacular global event and those fears were heightened as the draw descended into chaos. To begin with the balls representing Peru and Chile were accidentally left in the draw when it was FIFA policy to keep them out initially, in order to ensure the teams were kept apart from their more illustrious neighbours, Argentina and Brazil.

Scotland, meanwhile, found themselves mistakenly in Argentina's group instead of Belgium, before being moved into the correct grouping with Brazil. The confusion led to a halt in proceedings, then to compound the situation, the cage containing the balls jammed and one split in half. Just a week before the opening game, and with the organisational infrastructure still in a chaotic state, Spain's leading newspaper *El Pais* called the tournament "the great national disaster".

The critics were given further ammunition with the tournament's expansion to 24 teams and there was a genuine fear that the likes of Kuwait, Honduras and El Salvador would amount to little more than cannon fodder for the major footballing nations. Thankfully, the inspirational opening ceremony, and Belgium's subsequent 1-0 victory against champions Argentina, allayed the fears and set the tone for a tournament that would promote the World Cup as a truly thrilling global occasion.

Brazil were clear favourites to win. The flair and breathtaking skill – so absent four years earlier – had returned, while in Zico, Socrates, Falcão and Junior, they had a prowess that few could match. Their 4-1 victory against Scotland, in which David

Gaetano Scirea takes his turn with the World Cup trophy on Italy's lap of honour

THE FINAL

ITALY (0) 3
WEST GERMANY (0) 1

Date Sunday July 11, 1982
Attendance 90,000
Venue Santiago Bernabéu, Madrid
Referee Arnaldo Coelho (Mexico)

Italy coach Enzo Bearzot

West Germany coach Jupp Derwall

ITALY
1 DINO ZOFF (c)
6 CLAUDIO GENTILE
7 GAETANO SCIREA
5 FULVIO COLLOVATI
3 GIUSEPPE BERGOMI
4 ANTONIO CABRINI *Missed pen: 25 mins*
13 GABRIELE ORIALI *Booked: 73 mins*
14 MARCO TARDELLI *Goal: 69 mins*
16 BRUNO CONTI *Booked: 31 mins*
19 FRANCESCO GRAZIANI *Subbed: 8 mins (Altobelli)*
20 PAOLO ROSSI *Goal: 57 mins*
18 ALESSANDRO ALTOBELLI Sub *Goal: 81 mins. Subbed: 88 mins (Causio)*
15 FRANCO CAUSIO Sub

WEST GERMANY
1 HARALD SCHUMACHER
20 MANFRED KALTZ
15 ULI STIELIKE *Booked: 73 mins*
4 KARL-HEINZ FÖRSTER
5 BERND FÖRSTER
7 PIERRE LITTBARSKI *Booked: 88 mins*
6 WOLFGANG DREMMLER *Booked: 61 mins. Subbed 63 mins (Hrubesch)*
3 PAUL BREITNER *Goal: 83 mins*
2 HANS-PETER BRIEGEL
8 KLAUS FISCHER
11 KARL-HEINZ RUMMENIGGE (c) *Subbed: 70 mins (Müller, H)*
9 HORST HRUBESCH Sub
10 HANSI MÜLLER Sub

Narey had the audacity to score first, and a 4-0 win over New Zealand demonstrated their abilities.

Their rivals did not have it so easy. Italy made a less than auspicious start, drawing against Poland and Peru, and their progression was only confirmed in a winner-takes-all game against Cameroon. A Graziani header ensured another draw but, although he had secured a safe passage on goal difference, the Italian team were being ridiculed at home.

West Germany progressed to the second round after an uncompetitive victory over Austria assured the progress of both teams at the expense of Algeria, whose complaint to FIFA fell on deaf ears. As a consequence of the match, however, at all subsequent tournaments the final group games have always been played at the same time, so as not to give any team the unfair advantage of knowing what result would be needed.

Spain were another country left sweating on their progression as a Gerry Armstrong goal for Northern Ireland stunned the home support, but the 1-0 defeat ensured both teams progressed, with Billy Bingham's side heading the group. The Irish

ROSSI FIXES IT FOR ITALY

He was the biggest star of the 1982 World Cup, but Paolo Rossi nearly missed out. His reputation had suffered following his alleged involvement in an Italian match-fixing scandal. He was accused of taking a bribe while playing on loan for Perugia against Avellino in December 1979, a match that saw him score both of Perugia's goals in a 2-2 draw. Rossi claimed that his reply to a question asked by an opposition player - "2-2? If you want!" - was entirely innocent, but he was banned for two years.

His suspension ended on April 29, 1982, allowing him to play just three games for Juventus before the end of the season. Enzo Bearzot caused a sensation when he called Rossi up to the Italian World Cup squad, but despite his complete lack of match fitness Rossi ended up as the tournament's highest scorer.

also created history when their winger, Norman Whiteside, became the youngest player to appear in the finals, aged 17 years and 41 days.

Europe's other leading lights, France and England, were left to battle it out in Group Four. Aggrieved at England's seeding, the French were left to lick their wounds as Ron Greenwood's side put them to the sword with an emphatic 3-1 victory, kicked-off by a Bryan Robson goal in 27 seconds. Further wins against Czechoslovakia and Kuwait served to enhance England's reputation. The French limped through to the next round, helped by a 4-1 defeat of Kuwait, although the game would be more remembered for coach Michel Hidalgo's clash with police when a goal was disallowed because the Kuwaitis claimed they had stopped playing on hearing a whistle from the crowd.

With the second phase split into four groups of three, and with only the top side guaranteed a semi-final place, victory was imperative in the opening game, certainly in Group C which contained Brazil, Argentina and Italy. The latter's flaccid displays had them installed as elimination fodder, yet goals from Marco Tardelli and Antonio Cabrini ensured a 2-1 win against Argentina. With Brazil defeating their South American counterparts – a game that saw Maradona red-carded – the fixture between Brazil and Italy was billed as the clash of the tournament. The pendulum swung back and forth, yet it was the superlative finishing of Paolo Rossi that ensured Italy's 3-2 victory. His hat-trick, completed 15 minutes from time, created a new national hero.

England's progress, meanwhile, was halted by a lack of firepower. A sterile 0-0 draw against West Germany meant they had to beat Spain by two goals, but with the creativity of Kevin Keegan and Trevor Brooking still absent through injury, another scoreless draw prevailed. Both players were desperately plunged into action with 27 minutes remaining, but a clearly unfit Keegan fluffed a simple header that could have provided the impetus so desperately needed.

In the semi-final Poland sorely missed striker Zbigniew Boniek in a 2-0 defeat to Italy, while Rossi enhanced his credentials with a goal in each half.

Below left: Northern Ireland's Martin O'Neill is shadowed by Gerard Janvion of France. Below: Zico opens the scoring against New Zealand.

The other semi-final proved more competitive. With Platini in sparkling form for France, the game against West Germany finished 1-1 after 90 minutes. Further goals from Alain Giresse and Marius Trésor had the French dreaming of the final, yet Germany refused to quit. Coach Jupp Derwall gambled by introducing half-fit captain Karl-Heinz Rummenigge, who pulled a goal back in the 106th minute. Fischer then equalised with an overhead kick. The resulting penalty shoot-out went to sudden death and Hrubesch saw the Germans home.

The hero of the shoot-out was German keeper Harald 'Toni' Schumacher, yet he should not have been on the pitch following an appalling challenge on French substitute Patrick Battiston, which left the Frenchman unconscious for three minutes. Battiston lost two teeth, had his vertebrae broken and was put out of the game for months, but no penalty was awarded and Schumacher appeared unconcerned.

The incident won the Germans few admirers but they had reached the World Cup final. Italy were installed as clear favourites, but with midfielder Antognoni injured, anxieties were heightened even further for the Italians when Francesco Graziani left the field with an injured shoulder inside the first ten minutes. Things then got even worse when Cabrini became the first player to miss a penalty in a World Cup final. Yet Italy shaded a first-half dominated by fouls. The game finally came to life after 57 minutes when Rossi rose highest to connect with Gentile's pin-point cross.

Victory was secured 11 minutes later when Marco Tardelli hit a superb left-foot shot from the edge of the area, and by the time Altobelli hammered home a Conti cross, the game was safely in Italy's control. Paul Breitner scored a late consolation but the West Germans were left to pay a heavy price for their epic semi-final. The Italians claimed their third World Cup and toasted overnight sensation Paolo Rossi.

Above: Paolo Rossi beats Antonio Cabrini to score Italy's first goal of the final. Above left: Bryan Robson celebrates scoring a goal in 27 seconds against France.

THE SHAME OF GIJON

The West Germans may have reached the 1982 World Cup Final, but in doing so the team contributed to one of the most distasteful moments in the competition's history. After losing to Algeria, a win was needed against Austria in the final group game. After taking an early lead, and knowing a 1-0 score would ensure the progress of both sides, neither team made any further attempt to score as the second-half descended into farce at the expense of Algeria.

The crowd waved white handkerchiefs to suggest a truce had been agreed, while West Germany's largest tabloid ran with the headline, 'Shame On You'. "We have gone through, that's all that counts," argued Lothar Matthäus, and in a show of disregard for their public, the West German players dropped water-filled balloons on fans who had gathered outside the team's hotel.

Mexico 1986

STADIUM GUIDE

TOURNAMENT STATS

WINNER Argentina

FINAL
Argentina 3-2 West Germany

SEMI-FINALS
Argentina 2-0 Belgium
West Germany 2-0 France

THIRD PLACE PLAY-OFF
France 4-2 Belgium *(aet)*

TOP GOALSCORERS
6 goals: Gary Lineker (England)
5 goals: Emilio Butragueño (Spain), Careca (Brazil), Diego Maradona (Argentina)

FASTEST GOAL
63 seconds: Emilio Butragueño (Spain v Northern Ireland)

TOTAL GOALS
132

AVERAGE GOALS
2.54 per game

When Colombia decided they no longer had the financial muscle to host the 1986 World Cup, Mexico stepped into the breach to become FIFA's saviour in what proved to be another troubled episode for the game's governing body. The Mexicans may have hosted an exemplary tournament in 1970, but with their own financial crisis and Mexican unemployment at record levels, the decision looked dubious given the stability provided by the rival USA bid. To compound the problems, some 25,000 people were killed in a huge earthquake prior to the tournament.

Mexico simply had to deliver, yet little did they realise that a pint-sized genius from Argentina would play the trump card. Diego Maradona enlightened fans everywhere while exorcising the ghosts of Spain 82, when a red card for a lunge at Brazilian defender João Batista had ended his participation in the second round.

Going into the competition Argentina coach Carlos Bilardo had constructed his team to accommodate Maradona's extraordinary talent, making up for his lack of wide players by fielding a revolutionary 3-5-2 formation, with a sweeper in front of two central markers, five across the midfield and with two strikers. With a world record transfer fee of £6.9 million hanging over him, Maradona had a lot to live up to in his opening game, and the succession of fouls inflicted by South Korea gave an indication of the fear he instilled. Yet he destroyed his opponents, setting up goals for Jorge Valdano and Oscar Ruggeri in a 3-1 victory.

A truer test came against champions Italy. No team knew the diminutive Napoli midfielder better than the Italians, yet he shone in a game of

Maradona uses "the hand of God" to lift the trophy

THE FINAL

ARGENTINA	(1) **3**
WEST GERMANY	(0) **2**

Date Sunday June 29, 1986
Attendance 114,600
Venue Estadio Azteca, Mexico City
Referee Romualdo Arppi Filho (Brazil)

Argentina coach Carlos Bilardo

West Germany coach Franz Beckenbauer

ARGENTINA	
18 NERY PUMPIDO Booked: 85 mins	Booked
5 JOSÉ LUIS BROWN Goal: 23 mins	Goal
9 JOSÉ LUIS CUCIUFFO	
19 OSCAR RUGGERI	
16 JULIO OLARTICOECHEA Booked: 77 mins	Booked
14 RICARDO GIUSTI	
2 SERGIO BATISTA	
7 JORGE BURRUCHAGA Goal: 83 mins. Subbed: 90 mins (Trobbiani)	Goal, Subbed
12 HECTOR ENRIQUE Booked: 81 mins	
10 DIEGO MARADONA (c) Booked: 17 mins	Booked
11 JORGE VALDANO Goal: 56 mins	Goal
21 MARCELO TROBBIANI Sub	Sub

WEST GERMANY	
1 HARALD SCHUMACHER	
17 DITMAR JAKOBS	
14 THOMAS BERTHOLD	
4 KARL-HEINZ FÖRSTER	
2 HANS-PETER BRIEGEL Booked: 62 mins	Booked
8 LOTHAR MATTHÄUS Booked: 21 mins	Booked
3 ANDREAS BREHME	
10 FELIX MAGATH Subbed: 63 mins (Hoeness, D)	Subbed
6 NORBERT EDER	
11 KARL-HEINZ RUMMENIGGE (c) Goal: 74 mins	Goal
19 KLAUS ALLOFS Subbed: 46 mins (Völler)	Subbed
20 DIETER HOENESS Sub	Sub
9 RUDI VÖLLER Sub Goal: 80 mins	Sub, Goal

intrigue. In the 34th minute he eluded club team-mate Salvatore Bagni, his low centre of gravity enabling him to score from an acute angle. The goal cancelled out Alessandro Altobelli's penalty but both teams progressed to the next round.

Maradona may have created headlines with his exploits on the pitch, but in the stands it was the enthusiasm of the Mexican fans that proved so unprecedented, catching the imagination of the world with the 'Mexican Wave' phenomenon.

A crowd of 110,000 filled the Azteca to see the hosts beat Belgium in their opening game. Hero of the hour was Mexico's Hugo Sanchez, whose feats were rivalling those of Maradona. Having scored against Belgium, he was equally impressive against Paraguay and the consensus grew that the hosts could go far.

With the high altitude, European nations were given little chance. France were deemed a threat with Michel Platini, Patrick Battiston and Max Bossis providing experience and guile, but a 1-0 win against Canada was less than convincing, while a 1-1 draw with an impressive Soviet Union side left the European champions sweating on their progress. Their eventual qualification, in second place to the Soviets on goal difference, had more

Germany's Lothar Matthäus chases Patrick Battiston of France in the semi-final.

to do with the ineptitude of Canada and Hungary than their own creativity.

England also made heavy work of ensuring qualification for the second round, as a 1-0 defeat against Portugal was followed by a sorry draw with Morocco. The 0-0 scoreline created a furore, and with captain Bryan Robson dislocating his shoulder and fellow midfielder Ray Wilkins being sent-off, victory against Poland was imperative. In a shake up of the team Peter Beardsley was given his first start of the tournament and struck up a fantastic relationship with Gary Lineker, whose hat-trick not only saved the team but kept manager Bobby Robson in a job and England in the competition.

Denmark appeared the European side best equipped to succeed in the tournament. An opening 1-0 win against Scotland was just an aperitif for the Michael Laudrup-inspired 6-1 demolition of Uruguay and a shock 2-0 victory over West Germany.

The second phase reverted to a knockout format for the first time since 1970, with Brazil looking dangerous. Having cruised through their group against Spain, Algeria and Northern Ireland, a 4-0 demolition of Poland saw a return to the flamboyance of earlier Brazil sides. Edinho's third goal had the Guadalajara crowd mesmerised.

The expected nations progressed, with the exception of Denmark and Italy. The Danes had peaked and their 5-1 defeat at the hands of Spain is best remembered for Emilio Butragueño's four goals. The Italians, meanwhile, succumbed to the much-improved French. Platini confirmed his class

THE KAISER TAKES CHARGE

Franz Beckenbauer was a reluctant replacement for the unpopular Jupp Derwall as West Germany's coach. The DFB wanted Beckenbauer, but 'the Kaiser' was not interested. Before an approach could be made to rival Helmut Benthaus, a newspaper ran with the headline: 'Franz: I'm Ready'. The story was a fabrication by Beckenbauer's agent, but it led 'the Kaiser' to accept the job on a temporary basis.

It was a steep learning curve. He took West Germany to the 1986 World Cup Final, but often lost his temper with the press and failed to gain the respect of players, sending home keeper Uli Stein for calling him a clown. The night before the final he even offered his resignation. He may have lost in 1986, but Beckenbauer's day as coach would come.

with a casual chip over Galli to set up a 2-0 win.

The French, playing as potential champions, would have to overcome Brazil in the quarter-finals if they had realistic ambitions, and with so much riding on the outcome, a game of cat and mouse ensued. Substitute Zico missed with a crucial late spot-kick and the match was ultimately decided by a penalty shoot-out, France winning 4-3 thanks to Luis Fernandez's decider.

Shoot-outs decided three of the four quarter-final ties, with West Germany edging past Mexico and Belgium overcoming Spain. The process of elimination led to calls for sudden death football. Yet if this was knee-jerk anger on the part of the losers, their pain was nothing compared to that felt by England following their exit against Argentina.

With the scores level at 0-0, a harmless backpass from Steve Hodge was lobbed towards keeper Peter Shilton only for Maradona to seemingly head home. It appeared that the altitude had helped his elevation, but replays proved he had punched the ball. "A little of the hand of God and a little of the head of Maradona", was how he would refer to it, but his first goal only served to inspire his second, a fantastic solo effort six minutes later which put the game beyond doubt. Lineker's sixth goal of the tournament gave England nothing but hope, and the 'hand of God' goal would be the source of dispute between the two countries for many years.

A virtuoso semi-final performance against Belgium, which included two breathtaking second-half goals, restored faith in Maradona, and, although West Germany eased past France 2-0, there was little stopping the Argentina captain. His hands were one step away from the cup.

In the final the Argentinians proved they were no one man team, as their superior skill and creativity came to the fore. The Germans, who had so successfully stifled their opposition en route to the final, had no answer this time and the South American's were already dreaming of another ticker tape celebration back home.

Yet even when trailing 2-0 the Germans could never be written off. As the game limped to its conclusion, two headers inside six minutes, from Karl-Heinz Rummenigge and Rudi Völler, brought the tie level with just ten minutes to play. But cometh the hour, cometh the man. Maradona's inch-perfect pass found Jorge Burruchaga, who beat the offside trap to power the ball past Schumacher, winning the World Cup for Argentina.

IT'S MEXICO'S WORLD CUP AGAIN

When Colombian authorities declared they could no longer stage the 1986 World Cup Finals there wasn't a shortage of alternative candidates, with Brazil, Canada and the USA all prepared to take on the challenge. But when the FIFA World Cup committee met in Stockholm on May 20, 1983, Mexico was selected without even the formal consideration of a USA bid, despite the heavyweight presence of diplomat and longtime football fan Henry Kissinger among the American delegation.

When it was revealed that the tournament would be staged in Mexico by TV network Televisa, whose president was a close friend of FIFA president João Havelange, the decision drew outrage. "My conscience is clear," Havelange would say, having given Mexico the World Cup for the second time in 16 years.

Below left: Denmark's Michael Laudrup makes a dash for it, but Spain win 5-1.
Below: England's Gary Lineker salutes the crowd after his hat-trick against Poland.

Italy 1990

TOURNAMENT STATS

WINNER West Germany

FINAL
West Germany 1-0 Argentina

SEMI-FINALS
Argentina 1-1 Italy
(aet: Argentina won 4-3 on penalties)
West Germany 1-1 England
(aet: West Germany won 4-3 on penalties)

THIRD PLACE PLAY-OFF
Italy 2-1 England

TOP GOALSCORERS
6 goals: Salvatore Schillaci (Italy)
5 goals: Tomás Skuhravy (Czechoslovakia)

FASTEST GOAL
4 minutes: Safet Susic (Yugoslavia v UAE)

TOTAL GOALS
115

AVERAGE GOALS
2.21 per game

In many ways the 1990 World Cup failed to live up to its own hype, as FIFA stepped up its campaign to transform the World Cup into a global marketing phenomenon. The football was often dour and negative, while the final itself was an unattractive display of foul play that was overshadowed by two red cards and settled by the most dubious of penalties. But while not a tournament for the purists, somehow Italia 90 contained enough moments of high drama to capture the imagination, enshrining operatic aria 'Nessun Dorma' in the football psyche. Legends were created out of players such as Totò Schillaci, Paul Gascoigne and Roger Milla, while a combined TV audience of 26 billion watched the 52 matches, twice the viewing figures achieved by Mexico 86.

The format remained the same as four years previous, with 24 teams competing in six groups of four, the top two teams and the four best third placed teams progressing through to a knock-out second round. In an attempt to improve the quality of the football, FIFA tinkered with the laws of the game, and with very little planning, outlawed the 'professional foul'. Strict instructions were given to referees to issue draconian sanctions for foul play, and the tournament's opening game, a shock defeat of world champions Argentina by outsiders Cameroon, saw the first two of a stream of red cards. It set the tone for Italia 90. By the end of the tournament, 16 players had been sent-off – double the highest number previously seen.

Inevitably the hosts, under Azeglio Vicini, were hot favourites and their smooth progress only emphasised the feeling that their name was already

Maradona may have left in tears, but the Germans hung around for the celebrations

on the trophy. Sharing a group with Austria, USA and Czechoslovakia, they won all of their group games without conceding a goal, playing solid, attacking football.

The nation also discovered a new hero in the shape of Palermo-born Salvatore 'Totò' Schillaci, a diminutive Juventus striker who rose from the substitute's bench to win the Golden Boot with six goals. While Walter Zenga also kept a clean sheet for a record 517 minutes, aided by a watertight defence superbly marshalled by Franco Baresi, the *azzurri* dream died against Argentina at the semi-final stage in Naples – not for the last time in a penalty shoot-out. The hosts finished the tournament unbeaten, but still had to settle for third place while the nation mourned.

Of the other possible contenders, both Brazil and Holland went out tamely in the second round. European champions Holland could boast a talented team featuring Ruud Gullit, Frank Rijkaard and Marco van Basten, but they proved to be the biggest disappointments. Their encounter with

THE FINAL

WEST GERMANY (0) 1
ARGENTINA (0) 0

Date Sunday July 8, 1990
Attendance 73,603
Venue Olympic Stadium, Rome
Referee Edgardo Codesal (Mexico)

West Germany coach Franz Beckenbauer

Argentina coach Carlos Bilardo

WEST GERMANY

- 1 BODO ILLGNER
- 5 KLAUS AUGENTHALER
- 14 THOMAS BERTHOLD — *Subbed: 75 mins (Reuter)*
- 4 JÜRGEN KOHLER
- 6 GUIDO BUCHWALD
- 3 ANDREAS BREHME — *Goal: 85 mins (pen)*
- 8 THOMAS HÄSSLER
- 10 LOTHAR MATTHÄUS (c)
- 7 PIERRE LITTBARSKI
- 18 JÜRGEN KLINSMANN
- 9 RUDI VÖLLER — *Booked: 52 mins*
- 2 STEFAN REUTER Sub

ARGENTINA

- 12 SERGIO GOYCOECHEA
- 20 JUAN SIMÓN
- 18 JOSÉ SERRIZUELA
- 19 OSCAR RUGGERI — *Subbed: 46 mins (Monzon)*
- 21 PEDRO TROGLIO — *Booked: 84 mins*
- 17 ROBERTO SENSINI
- 7 JORGE BURRUCHAGA — *Subbed: 54 mins (Calderon)*
- 4 JOSÉ BASUALDO
- 13 NESTOR LORENZO
- 9 GUSTAVO DEZOTTI — *Sent-off: 65 mins*
- 10 DIEGO MARADONA (c) — *Booked: 87 mins*
- 15 PEDRO MONZON Sub — *Sent-off: 87 mins*
- 6 GABRIEL CALDERON Sub

Above: Dave Platt's volley against Belgium – one of the goals of the tournament. Above right: Paul McGrath on the ball as the Irish take on Italy in the quarter-final.

old enemy West Germany is best remembered for Rijkaard's rather too literal spat with Rudi Völler. Brazil topped a weak group featuring Sweden, Scotland and Costa Rica, but lacked the firepower to finish off Argentina when they had a chance.

For a while it seemed Cameroon might make history by winning the tournament. Despite being reduced to nine men, the 'Indomitable Lions' beat holders Argentina in a memorable opening encounter and became the first African nation to reach the quarter-finals when they beat Colombia in extra-time. Mixing some vibrant skills with a fairly strong physical presence, their unquenchable spirit was embodied by Roger Milla.

THE MAGICAL NIGHTS OF SCHILLACI

The surprise star of Italia 90 was Salvatore 'Totò' Schillaci. A late blossoming 26-year-old from a mafia-ridden part of Sicily, he had been playing in the lower leagues before Juventus plucked him from Serie B a year earlier. Receiving his first call-up two months earlier, he slipped into the World Cup squad with little fanfare, gaining his third cap as a substitute in Italy's first game of Italia 90.

As he waited to come on, Stefano Tacconi urged him to "score a header like John Charles", that other great Juventus forward of years gone by. That's exactly what Schillaci did after just four minutes on the pitch. He would hit six goals in Italia 90, winning the Golden Boot, and although he would score just once more for his country, Italian football fans still recall *le notti magiche di Totò Schillaci*, the magical nights of Totò Schillaci.

A goal-scoring talisman who danced around the corner flag after each of his four strikes scored as a substitute, Milla was then 38 years old and playing for JS Saint-Pierroise on Reunion Island. Even with the inspiration of Milla, it was Cameroon's recklessness in the tackle that eventually proved their undoing against England in the quarter-final.

The English had travelled to the World Cup more in hope than expectation, having just scraped through qualification as second best of the second-placed teams in the European groups. Bobby Robson's tenure as national coach had already involved the disastrous European Championship two years earlier and he was vilified by the British tabloid press for his team selections and tactics. However, in Gary Lineker England had a proven goalscorer, there was real creativity in a midfield that featured Chris Waddle and Paul Gascoigne. There was also defender Mark Wright, who could switch to sweeper, and in Peter Shilton the English had a keeper who had not conceded a goal in 540 minutes during qualification.

Nevertheless they made hard work of their group, progressing via two draws and a win, before stumbling past Belgium thanks to David Platt's memorable last minute volley. Their defeat of Cameroon was a tense affair and after trailing 2-1 it took a goal from Platt and two penalties from Lineker to see them into the semi-final.

England's finest performance was in a pulsating encounter with West Germany, a match that remains one of the great World Cup semi-finals, but their failure in the subsequent penalty shoot-out was to leave some deep psychological scars, and inspire at least one successful stage play.

West Germany were led to the final by Franz Beckenbauer, now the model of respectability compared to the bad tempered coach of 1986 who had demonstrated such little faith in his players. His team were strong in all departments and had Lothar Matthäus and Jurgen Klinsmann both at their peak. However, for all their strengths, they did nothing to help Italia 90 finish on a high. Regarded as the worst final in World Cup history, the game was characterised by negativity and poor sportsmanship.

Argentina arrived at Rome's Olympic Stadium with a tournament record of a foul every four minutes and as a consequence were missing four players through suspension. In the final, however, both teams were guilty of deeply cynical play. West Germany held the upper hand for much of the game but as the contest degenerated Pedro Monzon became the first player to be sent-off in a World Cup final following a wild lunge at Klinsmann.

It was no surprise when the match was settled by an Andreas Brehme spot-kick, after Völler had dramatically thrown himself over a challenge from Roberto Sensini. Argentina lost control and two minutes later Gustavo Dezotti was also sent-off. Maradona conducted his side's protests and the enduring image of the game is not Matthäus holding aloft the cup but the Argentinian captain's tear-stained face.

MARADONA DIVIDES ITALY

Maradona arrived at the World Cup as no stranger to the hosts, having spent six years as the hero of southern Italy with reigning champions Napoli. Helping his club challenge the dominance of Milan, Inter and Juventus, he had become a figure of hate in the north and was jeered in Milan during Argentina's first game.

In the semi-finals Argentina were drawn to face Italy on his home ground, giving Maradona the chance to exact revenge. He exploited the north-south divide by appealing to the people of Naples to back him rather than their own country. "For 364 days a year you are treated like dirt," he said, "and then they ask you to support them." Unsettled by Maradona's gamesmanship Italy put in a tense performance and ultimately lost to ten-man Argentina on penalties. Maradona had reached his second World Cup final.

Below left: Paul Gascoigne's tears after defeat in Turin. Below: Andreas Brehme is mobbed after scoring the World Cup winning penalty.

USA 1994

TOURNAMENT STATS

WINNER Brazil

FINAL
Brazil 0-0 Italy
(aet: Brazil won 3-2 on penalties)

SEMI-FINALS
Brazil 1-0 Sweden
Italy 2-1 Bulgaria

THIRD PLACE PLAY-OFF
Sweden 4-0 Bulgaria

TOP GOALSCORERS
6 goals: Oleg Salenko (Russia), Hristo Stoichkov (Bulgaria)
5 goals: Kennet Andersson (Sweden), Roberto Baggio (Italy), Jürgen Klinsmann (Germany), Romário (Brazil)

FASTEST GOAL
2 minutes: Gabriel Batistuta (Argentina v Greece)

TOTAL GOALS
141

AVERAGE GOALS
2.71 per game

The decision to award the 1994 World Cup to the United States was somewhat inevitable, as FIFA had long wanted to conquer football's one remaining frontier. With bidding rivals Morocco and Brazil unable to match the superior infrastructure of the USA, a lack of tradition was no barrier as FIFA used the competition to reach out to the untapped audiences of North America.

There were concerns that the World Cup would fail to capture the imagination, and the excruciating opening ceremony penalty miss by singer Diana Ross cemented the apprehension. Yet the tournament would prove a success. Three points for victory ended those lifeless group games, while the introduction of motorised carts for 'injured' players saw a decrease in the feigning of injuries. Stadiums were full to capacity and only the actions of one player managed to blight this festival of football.

Diego Maradona came to America looking to reach his third final, and on current form there was every chance that the dream could become reality.

Dunga leads the charge as the Brazilians enjoy their moment in Rose Bowl

However, after testing positive for five variants of the stimulant ephedrine, his aspirations – and his career – were brought to an end.

The tournament began with Germany taking on Bolivia in Group C, and a solitary goal from Jürgen Klinsmann spared his team from embarrassment, although it was overshadowed by the red-carding of Marco Etcheverry just four minutes after coming on as substitute.

The dismissal of defender Nadal would prove similarly costly for Spain in the same group. Having taken a 2-0 lead against South Korea, the

THE FINAL

BRAZIL (0) 0
ITALY (0) 0
(AET: BRAZIL WON 3-2 ON PENALTIES)

Date Sunday July 17, 1994
Attendance 94,194
Venue Pasadena Rose Bowl, Los Angeles
Referee Sándor Puhl (Hungary)

Brazil coach Carlos Parreira

Italy coach Arrigo Sacchi

BRAZIL
1 TAFFAREL
2 JORGINHO *Subbed: 22 mins (Cafu)*
13 ALDAIR
15 MARCIO SANTOS
6 BRANCO
17 MAZINHO *Booked: 4 mins*
5 MAURO SILVA
8 DUNGA (c)
9 ZINHO *Subbed: 106 mins (Viola)*
7 BEBETO
11 ROMÁRIO
14 CAFU Sub *Booked: 87 mins*
21 VIOLA Sub

ITALY
1 GIANLUCA PAGLIUCA
8 ROBERTO MUSSI *Subbed: 34 mins (Apolloni)*
6 FRANCO BARESI (c)
5 PAOLO MALDINI
3 ANTONIO BENARRIVO
14 NICOLA BERTI
13 DINO BAGGIO *Subbed: 95 mins (Evani)*
11 DEMETRIO ALBERTINI *Booked: 42 mins*
16 ROBERTO DONADONI
10 ROBERTO BAGGIO
19 DANIELE MASSARO
2 LUIGI APOLLONI Sub *Booked: 41 mins*
17 ALBERIGO EVANI Sub

Spanish conceded twice late on, and with their match against Germany also ending in stalemate, both superpowers teetered on the brink. However, normality was restored by Caminero, who hit a brace for Spain against Bolivia, while Klinsmann scored twice for the Germans in a 3-2 win against South Korea, taking his personal tally to four goals in three games.

Group A proved equally fascinating as the Colombians were ranked as a good bet following an impressive qualification campaign. Yet internal bickering and poor preparation caused their downfall. After losing 3-1 to Romania, a subsequent defeat to the hosts sealed their fate. Romania and Switzerland progressed at the top of the group and USA scraped into the second round as one of the best third placed teams.

Despite their tepid qualification form, Brazil opened with a 2-0 victory against Russia, while Romário and Bebeto proved the catalysts in a 3-0 defeat of Cameroon. The Africans came with high expectations following their powerful displays at the 1990 World Cup, yet they took their football association to the brink of a crisis two days before

A WORLD CUP FOR THE PEOPLE

Not every American wanted the World Cup in the USA, some seeing it as a threat to domestic sporting interests. In 1986 Jack Kemp, a former American Football quarterback and Republican politician, took to the floor of the United States Congress to announce that his own sport was "democratic capitalism, whereas soccer is a European socialist [sport]".

However, grounds were full throughout the World Cup, and contradicting all advance predictions, the average attendance of nearly 69,000 smashed the competition record that had stood since 1950. With 3,587,538 fans passing through the turnstiles, USA 94 remains the best-attended World Cup, even despite the expansion of the competition to 32 teams four years later.

the game with Brazil as their players refused to play without the payment of outstanding bonuses. After a 6-1 mauling by Russia the Cameroon squad were on their way home. During the game Oleg Salenko celebrated becoming the first player in World Cup history to score five goals, but Russia were already out of the tournament and it was the Swedes that booked a place in the second round with a 1-1 draw against Brazil.

Prior to Maradona's positive drugs test, Argentina had the look of champions. An emphatic 4-0 defeat of Greece was achieved courtesy of a hat-trick from Gabriel Batistuta and a manically celebrated goal from Maradona, while two strikes from Claudio Caniggia put paid to Nigeria. The Africans hailed their own hero, Rashidi Yekini, whose opener against Bulgaria was his country's first World Cup goal. With both Nigeria and Bulgaria beating Greece, Bulgaria went on to defeat an Argentina team clearly demoralised after the loss of Maradona. Nigeria and Bulgaria progressed as of right and Argentina limped into the second round as one of the best third placed teams.

The Italians could boast the guile of Roberto Baggio and they were regarded as certainties in Group E, yet when they conceded Ray Houghton's solitary strike for the Republic Of Ireland it meant that victory against Norway was imperative. The sending-off of goalkeeper Pagliuca and injury to Franco Baresi further troubled the *azzurri*, yet a goal from Dino Baggio ensured progress.

Bickering threatened Holland's chances in Group F. A spat between Ruud Gullit and coach Dick Advocaat led to the 32-year-old walking out the squad before the World Cup, and a less than convincing 2-1 win against Saudi Arabia confirmed their troubles. The Saudis became the surprise package, beating Morocco 2-1 before Saeed Owairan, the 'Maradona of the Arabs', ran 60 yards through the Belgian rearguard to secure victory and qualification to the second round.

The Germans continued their ominous march in the knockout phase as Rudi Völler inspired a 3-2 win over Belgium, while Spain's defeat of Switzerland was closer than the 3-0 scoreline would suggest. Two goals from Kennet Andersson enhanced his reputation as Sweden edged Saudi Arabia 3-1, while the tie of the round saw Argentina paired with Romania. Ariel Ortega did his best to fill Maradona's void, but it was the opposition playmaker, Gheorghe Hagi, who ran the midfield in a 3-2 victory.

Ireland's chances ended in the heat of Orlando when errors by Terry Phelan and Pat Bonner sealed the team's fate against Holland. USA's progress ended against Brazil, who had Leonardo sent-off for elbowing midfielder Tab Ramos, who was later diagnosed with a fractured skull.

A red card for substitute Gianfranco Zola meant that Italy made hard work of their tie with Nigeria, and it took a last-minute equaliser and an extra-time penalty – both courtesy of Robert Baggio – to progress to the second round. Bulgaria joined them after a penalty shoot-out victory over Mexico.

Bulgaria's Yordan Letchkov celebrates his quarter-final winning goal against Germany.

Robert Baggio ends Italy's dreams as he fires over in the final penalty shoot-out.

Seven European sides from eight made the quarter-finals, where Italy edged a thrilling contest against Spain thanks to goals from Dino and Roberto Baggio. Brazil and Holland dished up a similarly scintillating show, as Romário's drive and Bebeto's cool finish appeared to have won the game, but Dennis Bergkamp and Aron Winter replied to set up a grandstand finish, which Brazil won thanks to a free-kick from Branco. Bulgaria provided the biggest shock, beating Germany 2-1 with Hristo Stoichkov's free-kick and a header from Yordan Letchkov, the tournament's star midfielder.

Sweden's tussle with Romania went to extra-time. Stefan Schwarz's sending-off at 1-2 hindered the Scandinavians, but Andersson's goal took the game to penalties, where Thomas Ravelli saved from Miodrag Belodedici to win. Ravelli was once again in inspired form against Brazil in the semi-finals, but it would be the South Americans facing Italy in the final, who had two goals from Roberto Baggio to thank for their defeat of Bulgaria.

Although much was expected of the 1994 World Cup Final, the game proved a disappointment as defensive play killed off any excitement. Franco Baresi, just three weeks after cartilage surgery following injury in the second game against Norway, returned to shore up the Italian defence, and the first 90 minutes saw just one clear chance, when Pagliuca pushed Silva's effort onto a post. Bebeto and Roberto Baggio spurned chances in extra-time and the game went to penalties.

Baresi's opening shoot-out miss set the trend for the drama to follow. Santos missed for Brazil, but after successful spot-kicks from Albertini and Evani for Italy and Romário and Branco for Brazil, the scores were level. Massaro saw his effort stopped by Brazil keeper Taffarel, before Dunga converted. This left Roberto Baggio needing to score but he shot over before bowing his head in despair.

A MATTER OF LIFE AND DEATH

The Colombians were predicted to do well at USA 94. With a squad boasting stars such as Carlos Valderrama and Faustino Asprilla they had defeated Argentina 5-0 away in qualifying, yet the team did not live up to its reputation at the World Cup.

After losing 3-1 to Romania, a 2-1 defeat to the hosts sealed their fate at the finals, but the USA result had particularly tragic consequences for defender Andrés Escobar. Blamed for the defeat after scoring an own goal, he was murdered shortly after his return to Colombia. After an altercation with a group of men outside a restaurant in Medellin, he was shot 12 times, the accomplices reputedly yelling 'Goal' each time the trigger was pulled. Escobar's funeral was attended by 120,000 people and a statue was built in his honour.

France 1998

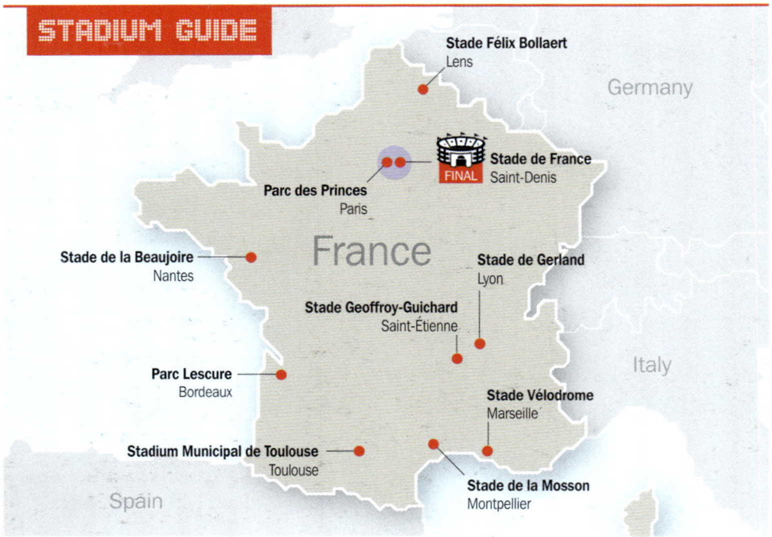

England's Michael Owen takes on Argentina

TOURNAMENT STATS

WINNER France

FINAL
France 3-0 Brazil

SEMI-FINALS
Brazil 1-1 Holland
(aet: Brazil won 4-2 on penalties)
France 2-1 Croatia

THIRD PLACE PLAY-OFF
Croatia 2-1 Holland

TOP GOALSCORERS
6 goals: Davor Suker (Croatia)
5 goals: Gabriel Batistuta (Argentina)

FASTEST GOAL
53 seconds: Celso Ayala (Paraguay v Nigeria)

TOTAL GOALS
171

AVERAGE GOALS
2.67 per game

After the sterile final of 1994, and a tournament which failed to grip the imagination, France 98 came like a breath of fresh air, providing excitement, passion, drama and controversy. While it was the world's best footballer, Ronaldo, who would inflame the passions of the conspiracy theorists in the final, there was also plenty of classic action throughout.

The competition featured 32 teams, more than ever before, and among those making a debut at the finals were Japan, Jamaica, South Africa and Croatia. There was also the introduction of the 'golden goal': if a game went into extra-time, the first goal scored would decide the match.

The hosts came into the tournament under pressure. They had failed to qualify for USA 94 and many claimed they had no strikers, but at this tournament they were driven by a fabulous midfield, as well as a fanatical home support in the later stages, and goals didn't seem to be a problem in their group as they dispatched South Africa 3-0, Saudi Arabia 4-0, and Denmark 2-1. The only problem they encountered was losing their most skilled player, Zinédine Zidane, who was sent-off during the Saudi Arabia match after stamping on Amin Fuad-Anwar, but by then the team had already qualified for the second round. After the game, Saudi Arabia sacked their manager, the reigning World Cup winning coach Carlos Alberto Parreira, with one game still to play.

It had been eight years since the Scots had graced the finals, but they kept up their tradition of giving the good teams a run for their money and flopping against the weaker sides. A narrow defeat to Brazil in the opening match, with the winner coming from a Tom Boyd own-goal, was followed by a draw with Norway and a 3-0 defeat to Morocco.

England went through the group stage with victories over Tunisia and Colombia, and a defeat to Romania after conceding Dan Petrescu's last-minute goal. In the other groups the major football nations emerged relatively unscathed, with one major exception. Always a favourite 'outsider' for any title given the exceptional talent within their domestic league, Spain again promised much but delivered very little. They lost a thriller

Didier Deschamps in the moment that all of France had waited for

THE FINAL

FRANCE (2) 3
BRAZIL (0) 0

Date Sunday July 12, 1998
Attendance 75,000
Venue Stade de France, Paris
Referee Said Belqola (Morocco)

France coach Aime Jacquet

Brazil coach Mario Zagallo

FRANCE

- 16 **FABIEN BARTHEZ**
- 15 **LILIAN THURAM**
- 8 **MARCEL DESAILLY**
  Booked: 48 mins. Sent-off (second booking) 68 mins
- 18 **FRANK LEBOEUF**
- 3 **BIXENTE LIZARAZU**
- 7 **DIDIER DESCHAMPS** (c)
  Booked: 39 mins
- 10 **ZINÉDINE ZIDANE**
  Goal: 27 mins, 45 mins
- 17 **EMMANUEL PETIT**
  Goal: 90 mins
- 19 **CHRISTIAN KAREMBEU**
  Booked: 56 mins. Subbed: 56 mins (Boghossian)
- 6 **YOURI DJORKAEFF**
  Subbed: 74 mins (Vieira)
- 9 **STEPHANE GUIVARC'H**
  Subbed: 66 mins (Dugarry)
- 14 **ALAIN BOGHOSSIAN** Sub
- 21 **CHRISTOPHE DUGARRY** Sub
- 4 **PATRICK VIEIRA** Sub

BRAZIL

- 1 **TAFFAREL**
- 2 **CAFU**
- 4 **JUNIOR BAIANO**
  Booked: 33 mins
- 3 **ALDAIR**
- 6 **ROBERTO CARLOS**
- 5 **CESAR SAMPAIO**
  Subbed: 57 mins (Edmundo)
- 18 **LEONARDO**
  Subbed: 46 mins (Denilson)
- 8 **DUNGA** (c)
- 10 **RIVALDO**
- 9 **RONALDO**
- 20 **BEBETO**
- 19 **DENILSON** Sub
- 21 **EDMUNDO** Sub

The Brazilians celebrate Tom Boyd's own goal as they beat Scotland in the opening game.

against Nigeria 3-2, drew with Paraguay, and made a desperate effort in the match with Bulgaria, winning 6-1 to no avail.

In the second round Brazil and Denmark were impressive, Italy and Croatia crept through by a single goal, Germany edged Mexico, and the Dutch beat Yugoslavia in a thriller. France struggled without the suspended Zidane but made it through to the quarter-finals after Laurent Blanc scored with the first World Cup 'golden goal' to pip Paraguay.

JACQUET WINS UNDER PRESSURE

France were led to their first World Cup final by coach Aimé Jacquet, who spent much of the build up to the tournament under fire from the media in his own country. In his first two years in the job Jacquet had dropped flair players such as Eric Cantona and David Ginola in favour of a team ethic, but after his team lost on penalties in the semi-final of Euro 96 the French media became critical of his every decision.

On the eve of the World Cup, newspaper *L'Équipe* claimed that Jacquet was ill-prepared to lead the national side. In return he promised that he would never forgive, and after proving his critics wrong by winning the World Cup, he walked away from the job of French national team coach and launched an embittered attack on the French press that had caused him so much misery.

The match of the round brought together two old foes: England and Argentina. The first-half was simply brilliant, Gabriel Batistuta giving the South Americans an early lead through a penalty before Alan Shearer converted a spot-kick for England. Then came one of those moments that build a reputation, as 18-year-old striker Michael Owen controlled a long pass, raced towards the Argentine goal leaving defenders floundering, and beat Carlos Roa with an unstoppable shot. England stayed ahead until just before the interval, when a clever free-kick routine saw Zanetti equalise.

The second-half saw drama of a different kind. Within minutes of the restart, Diego Simeone brought down David Beckham, and while on the ground the Englishman kicked Simeone on the leg. Beckham was sent-off and England had to play the rest of the second-half, and 30 minutes of extra-time, with ten men, even having an effort from Sol Campbell disallowed and a penalty appeal refused. In the deciding penalty shoot-out David Batty saw Roa save his spot-kick and England's dream was over, the fans blaming Beckham rather than Batty.

In the quarter-final Brazil and Denmark shared a thrilling duel, with Martin Jorgensen opening the scoring for the Danes in just the second minute, but the South Americans played with confidence, winning 3-2 thanks to a second goal from Rivaldo.

When Holland came up against Argentina both teams were reduced to ten men in the final 15 minutes, with Ariel Ortega red-carded in the 87th minute for head-butting goalkeeper Edwin van der Sar. From the resulting free-kick the ball was played to Dennis Bergkamp, who finished with aplomb.

Croatia caused the upset of the round with a late goal from Davor Suker sealing a 3-0 win over Germany, who had played the entire second-half with only ten men. Italy and France failed to register a goal in their own encounter and the game went to penalties. When Luigi di Biagio's effort hit the bar, the hosts were through.

The first semi-final saw Croatia come up against France. Suker opened the scoring but then the team with no strikers once again relied on a defender to score. Lilian Thuram equalised with his first international goal, before going on to score his second to seal the win. The other semi-final was also pure drama as Ronaldo's second-half goal looked enough to secure a place in the final until Kluivert scored a late equaliser for the Dutch. Neither side could grab the winner and the match went to penalties, Brazil winning the shoot-out 4-2.

The dream World Cup final was on: champions versus hosts. But with Brazil seemingly still dazed by the pre-match controversy surrounding Ronaldo, the French were able to dominate the first 20 minutes. Shortly before the half-hour mark Zidane headed home a corner supplied by Emmanuel Petit, forcing the Brazilians to push forward, but in response Zidane scored a carbon copy goal to put the hosts further in front.

Marcel Desailly was sent-off in the 68th minute, but the Brazilians were unable to capitalise. Petit confirmed the win for France in the 90th minute, picking up the ball from his Arsenal team-mate Patrick Vieira and firing a low left-footed shot past keeper Claudio Taffarel. The nation that had given us the World Cup had finally won it.

THE MYSTERY OF RONALDO

The 1998 World Cup Final was engulfed by a mystery when World Player Of The Year Ronaldo was initially omitted from the Brazil teamsheet, only to be reinstated just half an hour before kick-off. There were rumours of a dispute, which were fuelled when the team failed to take to the pitch for their pre-match warm-up.

A team doctor later revealed that Ronaldo had been rushed to hospital after suffering a convulsion in his sleep on the afternoon of the game, possibly brought on by stress. Hotel staff would paint a more graphic picture, the 21-year-old striker reportedly having swallowed his tongue. His place was given to Edmundo, but when Ronaldo arrived at the stadium he declared himself fit enough to play. A pale performance from both Ronaldo and his demoralised team-mates resulted in a multitude of conspiracy theories.

Below left: Denmark's Brian Laudrup after scoring against Nigeria.
Below: David Beckham is sent-off against Argentina.

Korea/Japan 2002

TOURNAMENT STATS

WINNER Brazil

FINAL
Brazil 2-0 Germany

SEMI-FINALS
Germany 1-0 South Korea
Brazil 1-0 Turkey

THIRD PLACE PLAY-OFF
Turkey 3-2 South Korea

TOP GOALSCORERS
8 goals: Ronaldo (Brazil)
5 goals: Miroslav Klose (Germany); Rivaldo (Brazil)

FASTEST GOAL
10.8 seconds: Hakan Sükür (Turkey v South Korea)

TOTAL GOALS
161

AVERAGE GOALS
2.51 per game

The 17th World Cup finals in Japan and Korea were not only the first to be played in Asia, but also the first to be staged outside of Europe or the Americas. As if to signify a shift in the balance of global football dominance, from the very first game it was a competition full of shocks and surprise results. It was a tournament that saw many of the established nations and the biggest stars of the world game catching an early flight home, while it was also notable for the emergence of several overlooked football nations, such as Senegal, Turkey and South Korea. Nevertheless, the final would ultimately be played out between the World Cup's two most successful sides.

It was debutantes Senegal who provided the biggest shock in the opening game, with a goal from Pape Bouba Diop defeating the holders and pre-tournament favourites France. In a physical game, the Africans over-powered the jaded looking French team, who were clearly missing the talismanic but injured Zinédine Zidane. France failed to score a goal in three qualifying games and were out of the tournament earlier than anyone could have expected, the first reigning champions to exit at the first group stage since Brazil in 1966.

Joint favourites Argentina also suffered the ignominy of early elimination. After a narrow win in their opening game against Nigeria, courtesy of a Gabriel Batistuta header, defeat to England and a draw against Sweden meant the hugely talented Argentine squad were to play no further part in the tournament. The clash with England was one of the most eagerly anticipated games of the competition, and saw David Beckham convert the match-winning penalty to gain revenge for his

Rivaldo takes his turn with the trophy

THE FINAL

BRAZIL (0) **2**
GERMANY (0) **0**

Date Sunday June 30, 2002
Attendance 69,029
Venue International Stadium, Yokohama
Referee Pierluigi Collina (Italy)

Brazil coach Luiz Felipe Scolari

Germany coach Rudi Völler

BRAZIL
1 MARCOS
3 LUCIO
5 EDMILSON
4 ROQUE JUNIOR *Booked: 6 mins*
2 CAFU (c)
15 KLEBERSON
8 GILBERTO SILVA
6 ROBERTO CARLOS
11 RONALDINHO *Subbed: 85 mins (Juninho Paulista)*
10 RIVALDO
9 RONALDO *Goal: 67 mins, 79 mins.* *Subbed: 90 mins (Denilson)*
18 JUNINHO PAULISTA Sub
15 DENILSON Sub

GERMANY
1 OLIVER KAHN (c)
2 THOMAS LINKE
5 CARSTEN RAMELOW
21 CHRISTOPH METZELDER
22 TORSTEN FRINGS
16 JENS JEREMIES *Subbed: 77 mins (Asamoah)*
8 DIETMAR HAMANN
19 BERND SCHNEIDER
17 MARCO BODE *Subbed: 84 mins (Ziege)*
7 OLIVER NEUVILLE
11 MIROSLAV KLOSE *Booked: 9 mins. Subbed: 74 mins (Bierhoff)*
20 OLIVER BIERHOFF Sub
14 GERALD ASAMOAH Sub
6 CHRISTIAN ZIEGE Sub

dismissal in the same fixture four years previous.

The much-fancied Portuguese side were the other high-profile casualties, losing out to both USA and co-hosts South Korea, who topped their group after having never before won a match at the finals. The South Koreans proved a revelation and were particularly well drilled for the competition by experienced coach Guus Hiddink. In preparation for the tournament Hiddink had persuaded the Korean football authorities to suspend their league championship in order to give him five months to transform the side for the World Cup.

An impressive looking Brazil, more assured and confident with every game, and perennial underachievers Spain were the only two countries to qualify from their respective groups with maximum points, while Slovenia, China and Saudi Arabia went home without a point. Germany's 8-0 demolition of the Saudis was, by quite a margin, the most one-sided of all the games of the tournament, while Miroslav Klose's hat-trick in the game was scored entirely with his head.

The other group winners were Denmark, Germany, Sweden, Mexico and Japan, much to

THE KOREAN CONSPIRACY

By the time the South Koreans were knocked out in the semi-final, they had stunned world football more than once. However, they also benefited from a series of fortuitous refereeing decisions.

In the second round the Italians complained that a goal had been disallowed and their star had been unnecessarily red-carded, while the Spanish also had two goals cancelled in the quarter-final. The president of the Spanish football federation resigned from the referee's committee and the match sparked a diplomatic row.

The Spanish media, like the Italians before them, suggested that the match had been fixed, but overlooked was the fact that under coach Guus Hiddink, South Korea had proved a revelation, and immediately after the tournament, the Gwangju World Cup Stadium was renamed the Guus Hiddink Stadium.

the delight of an enthusiastic co-host nation. The Japanese topped their group above Belgium, as Russia were knocked out.

In the opening games of the second round Germany and England secured routine wins against Paraguay and Denmark respectively, while South Korea were to provide the major upset of this stage. However, some controversial refereeing marred their 2-1 'golden goal' victory over the Italians, which saw Francesco Totti sent-off for diving, and an apparently good Italy goal ruled out.

The Republic Of Ireland did well against the odds. Despite the loss of influential captain Roy Keane, who walked out on the squad after criticising coach Mick McCarthy before they had even arrived at the World Cup, the Irish qualified for the knockout rounds, only to be eliminated by Spain on penalties.

The other games at this stage saw wins for the USA over Mexico, Senegal over Sweden, and Brazil over Belgium, while a headed goal from Turkey's Umit Davala ended the dreams of Japan.

The quarter-final stage consisted of four established football nations (Brazil, Germany, England, Spain), and four countries relatively inexperienced at this level of competition (USA, South Korea, Turkey and Senegal). Brazil beat England 2-1, countering an opportunistic Michael Owen strike with a defence-splitting goal from Rivaldo and a freak long-range shot from Ronaldinho, who was red-carded for a crass foul on Danny Mills shortly after scoring.

Germany were fortunate to get past USA 1-0, especially after a blatant handball by Torsten Frings in their own penalty area had gone unnoticed. Turkey secured a 'golden goal' victory over an unlucky Senegal, and South Korea were giant-killers once again. This time Gus Hiddink's superbly conditioned and disciplined team got the better of Spain, but again the victory was not without controversy, the Spanish side furious that two perfectly good goals had been disallowed.

The semi-finals saw the established powers

Below right: Japan's number 11, Suzuki, celebrates scoring against Belgium.
Below: Senegal enjoy the moment after Pape Bouba Diop's goal beats France.

assert some dominance. Brazil eased past a spirited Turkey 1-0 with a memorable goal from a rejuvenated Ronaldo, eager to atone for his pale performance in the 1998 World Cup Final. Germany narrowly got the better of the South Koreans with a solitary goal from Michael Ballack, but a booking during the game meant that Germany's match-winner would miss the final through suspension.

Despite sharing seven world titles between them, Brazil and Germany had never met in the final stages of the tournament. Going into the competition both nations had been considered to be fielding their weakest teams in living memory. Indeed, both had stumbled through the qualification process. At one point it had seemed highly possible that Brazil would fail to reach the finals for the first time in their history, and the Germans only made it through the backdoor of the play-offs. But against all expectations, in Yokohama the two football giants faced each other to contest the championship of the world.

The Brazilians started the final as clear favourites but to win they would have to beat Oliver Kahn, who had conceded just one goal in the competition. A largely uneventful first-half saw Kleberson hit the bar for Brazil and a couple of half-chances fell to Ronaldo. In the 67th minute, however, Kahn spilt Rivaldo's shot into the path of the grateful Ronaldo, who pounced on the ball to score. The Brazilian was on the scoresheet again 12 minutes later, curling the ball past Kahn to make it 2-0.

Shortly after the final whistle, skipper Cafu, in his third World Cup final, lifted the trophy to mark Brazil's record-breaking and wholly deserved fifth title win. Despite complaints over poor organisation in respect of ticket allocation, the first World Cup outside of Europe and the Americas was superbly staged. The wide-eyed enthusiasm of the supporters of both host nations was one of the lasting memories of a successful tournament.

No respecter of reputations, the 2002 World Cup will also be remembered as one when the smaller football nations fought back and nearly succeeded in overthrowing the existing global power base.

Above: Ronaldo scores the first of his two goals in the World Cup final.
Above left: David Beckham takes his spot-kick against Argentina.

THE GERMANS COME GOOD

Germany expected little from the 2002 World Cup. Booking their place via the play-offs, for the first time they travelled as outsiders. The German media had written off the team's chances, but this had a bonding effect on the players and brought the fans behind the team in a way not experienced for years.

At best it was thought that Germany would qualify from a weak group and reach the quarter-finals before being knocked out by Italy, and without the weight of expectations, the further the team went, the more the fans celebrated.

Back at home German flag factories struggled to keep up with the insatiable and unexpected demand that World Cup fever provoked. Reaching the final was an added bonus for the Germans, who allowed themselves to really enjoy this World Cup.

Germany 2006

STADIUM GUIDE

Argentina's Lionel Messi

TOURNAMENT STATS

WINNER Italy

FINAL
Italy 1-1 France
(aet: Italy won 5-3 on penalties)

SEMI-FINALS
Germany 0-2 Italy
Portugal 0-1 France

THIRD PLACE PLAY-OFF
Germany 3-1 Portugal

TOP GOALSCORERS
5 goals: Klose (Germany)
3 goals: Crespo (Argentina), Henry (France), Podolski (Germany), Rodriguez (Argentina), Ronaldo (Brazil), Torres (Spain), Villa (Spain), Zidane (France)

FASTEST GOAL
1 min 10 seconds: Asamoah Gyan (Ghana v Czech Republic)

TOTAL GOALS
147

AVERAGE GOALS
2.29 per game

After the shocks of the 2002 World Cup that saw outsiders South Korea and Turkey reach the semi-finals, Germany 2006 went some way to restoring the balance of power in favour of the established football nations. Only two of eight quarter-finalists had not previously won the competition, and even the hosts found they were a nation newly invigorated by this tournament after some years in relative decline.

Finding themselves paired in Group A with Ecuador, bitter rivals Poland, and opening game opponents Costa Rica, the Germans surprised the doubters, proving an unstoppable force in attack. Lahm scored their opening goal just five minutes after the tournament had kicked-off, and by the time the group stages were over the Germans had racked up eight goals, progressing to the second round with a 100 per cent record.

In a break with tradition the defending champions did not qualify for the finals automatically, yet Brazil reached the tournament with ease. On arriving in Germany they cruised through the group stage, but World Footballer Of The Year Ronaldinho seemed a shadow of his best, not benefiting from the defensive play dictated by coach Carlos Alberto Parreira. Ronaldo also appeared out of shape and his weight was even questioned by the president of Brazil.

Under the guidance of the 2002 World Cup winning coach Luiz Filipe Scolari, Portugal qualified for the second round without dropping a point. In doing so Scolari broke Vittorio Pozzo's 68-year-old record, becoming the first coach to win eight World Cup games in succession (the first seven he achieved with Brazil in 2002). Scolari would ultimately stretch this record to 11 games before the tournament was over.

Spain won all of their games and qualified ahead of Ukraine, while Argentina appeared to be in unstoppable form. A 6-0 demolition of Serbia and Montenegro demonstrated their pace and class, with players as talented as Lionel Messi and Carlos Tevez having to settle for substitute appearances. But not all of the seeded nations had it their own way. England topped their group despite some lacklustre performances that even drew criticism

Italy captain Fabio Cannavaro prepares for lift off

THE FINAL

ITALY	(1)	**1**
FRANCE	(1)	**1**

(AET: ITALY WON 5-3 ON PENALTIES)

Date Sunday June 9, 2006
Attendance 69,000
Venue Olympic Stadium, Berlin
Referee Horacio Elizondo (Argentina)

Italy coach Marcello Lippi

France coach Raymond Domenech

ITALY

- 1 **GIANLUIGI BUFFON**
- 3 **FABIO GROSSO**
- 23 **MARCO MATERAZZI**
  Goal: 23 mins
- 5 **FABIO CANNAVARO** (c)
- 19 **GIANLUCA ZAMBROTTA**
  Booked: 5 mins
- 20 **SIMONE PERROTTA**
  Subbed: 60 mins (De Rossi)
- 8 **GENNARO GATTUSO**
- 21 **ANDREA PIRLO**
- 16 **MAURO CAMORANESI**
  Subbed: 86 mins (Del Pierro)
- 10 **FRANCESCO TOTTI**
- 9 **LUCA TONI**
  Subbed: 60 mins (Iaquinta)
- 15 **VINCENZO IAQUINTA** Sub
- 4 **DANIELE DE ROSSI** Sub
- 7 **ALLESANDRO DEL PIERRO** Sub

FRANCE

- 16 **FABIEN BARTHEZ**
- 3 **ERIC ABIDAL**
- 5 **WILLIAM GALLAS**
- 15 **LILIAN THURAM**
- 19 **WILLY SAGNOL**
  Booked: 12 mins
- 6 **CLAUDE MAKELELE**
  Booked: 76 mins
- 7 **FLORENT MALOUDA**
  Booked: 111 mins
- 4 **PATRICK VIEIRA**
  Subbed: 56 mins (Diarra)
- 22 **FRANCK RIBÉRY**
  Subbed: 99 mins (Trezeguet)
- 10 **ZINÉDINE ZIDANE** (c)
  Goal: 7 mins (pen). Sent-off: 110 mins
- 12 **THIERRY HENRY**
  Subbed: 106 mins (Wiltord)
- 18 **ALOU DIARRA** Sub
  Booked: 75 mins
- 20 **DAVID TREZEGUET** Sub
- 11 **SYLVAIN WILTORD** Sub

Above: Ghana are delighted after beating the Czechs 2-0. Above right: Wayne Rooney of England is chased by Portugal's Ricardo Carvalho.

from FIFA president Sepp Blatter. Italy's progress looked uncertain after a draw with the USA that saw the Italians lose one man to a red card and the Americans two. An early exit was prevented by victory over the Czechs.

French fans had called for coach Raymond Domenech to drop his ageing stars in favour of youngsters like Franck Ribéry, the 23-year-old Marseille midfielder with just three international substitute appearances to his name. The coach stayed loyal to his stars but found a way to accomodate Ribéry, as France stumbled through as runners-up to the Swiss after coming alive in their final group game against Togo.

While the first round had thrown up plenty of exciting ties, the sudden death football of the second round brought a cautious approach. Argentina's clash with Mexico was an exception. The Mexicans took a sixth minute lead through Marquez, only to see Crespo equalise four minutes later, but a thunderous left-foot volley from Maxi Rodriguez eight minutes into extra-time secured the win for Argentina.

After a limp display in Cologne the Swiss lost on penalties to Ukraine, and in doing so became the first team to exit a World Cup without conceding a goal. A Beckham free-kick made all the difference in a pallid encounter between England and Ecuador, while Italy needed a controversial penalty to beat Australia with the last kick of the game. The hosts put in a workmanlike performance to see off Sweden, while Brazil brushed aside Ghana with little effort, Ronaldo becoming the World Cup's all-time leading goalscorer, with his 15th goal.

In the 700th World Cup finals game, France needed a bit of self-made luck against Spain to be certain of a place in the last eight. Portugal edged through with a Maniche goal against Holland, but it was a fraught encounter that equalled the World Cup record for bookings (there were 16) and broke the record for red cards: Portugal had Deco and Costinha dismissed, while Holland's Boulahrouz and Van Bronkhorst were sent-off.

The Germans were the first team to qualify for the semi-finals. They stunned Argentina with an 80th minute equaliser from Klose, before winning 4-2 in a penalty shoot-out. Portugal also needed

AND THE WINNER IS... GERMANY

The decision to allow Germany to host the 2006 World Cup was accompanied by a moment of controversy and high drama. Going into the final round of the voting process it seemed that South Africa would secure the tournament, but when Germany won a close competition by 12 votes to 11, the poll sparked fury among the losers and gave rise to allegations of foul play.

At the centre of the voting controversy was New Zealand's FIFA delegate, 78-year-old Charlie Dempsey, representing the Oceania federation. At the last moment Dempsey had decided to abstain rather than support South Africa, as his federation had instructed him. Later he claimed to have received death threats, "unsustainable pressure" and even offers of bribes. His abstention handed victory to a delighted but surprised Germany.

penalties to beat ten-man England, who had Wayne Rooney sent-off early in the second-half. Italy stepped up a gear to defeat Ukraine 3-0, and in the biggest surprise of the round, Zinédine Zidane – who had retired from international football two years earlier – proved the inspiration his team needed to achieve victory over Brazil.

The first semi-final provided a greater shock. Under the shrewd tactical stewardship of Marcello Lippi, the Italians ended German hopes of winning the trophy in the best game of the tournament. Late in extra-time, with penalties just a minute away, defender Fabio Grosso hammered a magnificent first time shot into the back of the net. Just two minutes later, Gilardino played a sublime reverse pass into the path of Del Piero, who had run the length of the field to fire past Lehman with the last kick of the game.

A Zidane penalty was enough to send France into the final at the expense of Portugal, giving their World Cup winning veterans – Thuram, Barthez, Vieira and Zidane – one more chance to shine on the biggest stage. Both France and Italy had started the competition slowly, but with both teams approaching top form at just the right time, the 2006 final would prove a dramatic encounter.

The day was always destined to belong to Zinédine Zidane, playing in what he said would be his last game, but by the time the Italians lifted the trophy it was their defender Marco Materazzi who had made the most decisive impact. France took the lead with a seventh minute penalty after Materazzi fouled Malouda in the box, Zidane's chipped spot-kick ricocheting into the net from the underside of the bar. Just 12 minutes later Materazzi made amends when he rose to head home Pirlo's corner. Italy remained the more threatening side, but in extra-time the best chance came to Zidane, his header pushed over the bar by Buffon.

When the end came for Zidane it wasn't as expected: he received a red card for an off-the-ball assault on Materazzi, having knocked the Italian to the floor with a butt to the chest. David Trezeguet struck the only failed penalty of the shoot-out and the trophy was lifted by Italy's Fabio Cannavaro.

THE END OF THE ROAD FOR ZIDANE

When Zinédine Zidane floored Italy's Marco Materazzi with a head-butt in an off-the-ball altercation during the 2006 World Cup Final it became the most talked about incident in world sport. It would be many months before either player would discuss the altercation, leading to fevered speculation about what had been said to provoke such an unexpected reaction.

Materazzi would later claim that the incident had been sparked by a tug at Zidane's shirt. "If you want my shirt that badly I'll give it to you at the end of the match," the Frenchman had said. Materazzi responded with an insult aimed at Zidane's sister. The head-butt that followed reduced France to ten men and damaged their chances of winning the World Cup. It would prove to be an unfortunate finale to a glorious career for Zidane.

Below left: Brazil's Juninho after scoring against Japan. Below: Germany after beating Argentina on penalties.

World cup results

1930

GROUP 1

July 13: Pocitos, Montevideo
France **4-1** Mexico

July 15: Parque Central, Montevideo
Argentina **1-0** France

July 16: Parque Central, Montevideo
Chile **3-0** Mexico

July 19: Estadio Centenario, Montevideo
Chile **1-0** France

July 19: Estadio Centenario, Montevideo
Argentina **6-3** Mexico

July 22: Estadio Centenario, Montevideo
Argentina **3-1** Chile

	P	W	D	L	F	A	Pts
Argentina	3	3	0	0	10	4	6
Chile	3	2	0	1	5	3	4
France	3	1	0	2	4	3	2
Mexico	3	0	0	3	4	13	0

GROUP 2

July 14: Parque Central, Montevideo
Yugoslavia **2-1** Brazil

July 17: Parque Central, Montevideo
Yugoslavia **4-0** Bolivia

July 20: Estadio Centenario, Montevideo
Brazil **4-0** Bolivia

	P	W	D	L	F	A	Pts
Yugoslavia	2	2	0	0	6	1	4
Brazil	2	1	0	1	5	2	2
Bolivia	2	0	0	2	0	8	0

GROUP 3

July 14: Pocitos, Montevideo
Romania **3-1** Peru

July 18: Estadio Centenario, Montevideo
Uruguay **1-0** Peru

July 21: Estadio Centenario, Montevideo
Uruguay **4-0** Romania

	P	W	D	L	F	A	Pts
Uruguay	2	2	0	0	5	0	4
Romania	2	1	0	1	3	5	2
Peru	2	0	0	2	1	4	0

GROUP 4

July 13: Parque Central, Montevideo
USA **3-0** Belgium

July 17: Parque Central, Montevideo
USA **3-0** Paraguay

July 20: Estadio Centenario, Montevideo
Paraguay **1-0** Belgium

	P	W	D	L	F	A	Pts
USA	2	2	0	0	6	0	4
Paraguay	2	1	0	1	1	3	2
Belgium	2	0	0	2	0	4	0

SEMI-FINALS

July 26: Estadio Centenario, Montevideo
Argentina **6-1** USA

July 27: Estadio Centenario, Montevideo
Uruguay **6-1** Yugoslavia

FINAL

July 30: Estadio Centenario, Montevideo
Uruguay **4-2** Argentina

1934

FIRST ROUND

May 27: Stadio Nazionale PNF, Rome
Italy **7-1** USA

May 27: Stadio Littorio, Trieste
Czechoslovakia **2-1** Romania

May 27: Stadio Giovanni Berta, Florence
Germany **5-2** Belgium

May 27: Stadio Benito Mussolini, Turin
Austria **3-2** France
(aet)

May 27: Stadio Luigi Ferraris, Genoa
Spain **3-1** Brazil

May 27: Stadio San Siro, Milan
Switzerland **3-2** Holland

May 27: Stadio Littoriale, Bologna
Sweden **3-2** Argentina

May 27: Stadio Ascarelli, Naples
Hungary **4-2** Egypt

QUARTER-FINALS

May 31: Stadio San Siro, Milan
Germany **2-1** Sweden

May 31: Stadio Littoriale, Bologna
Austria **2-1** Hungary

May 31: Stadio Giovanni Berta, Florence
Italy **1-1** Spain
(aet)

June 1: Stadio Giovanni Berta, Florence
Italy **1-0** Spain
(replay)

May 31: Stadio Benito Mussolini, Turin
Czechoslovakia **3-2** Switzerland

SEMI-FINALS

June 3: Stadio Nazionale PNF, Rome
Czechoslovakia **3-1** Germany

June 3: Stadio San Siro, Milan
Italy **1-0** Austria

THIRD PLACE PLAY-OFF

June 7: Stadio Asarelli, Naples
Germany **3-2** Austria

FINAL

June 10: Stadio Nazionale PNF, Rome
Italy **2-1** Czechoslovakia
(aet)

Argentina, 1930 World Cup Final

England v Chile, 1950

1938

FIRST ROUND

June 4: Parc des Princes, Paris
Switzerland **1-1** Germany
(aet)

June 9: Parc des Princes, Paris
Switzerland **4-2** Germany
(replay)

June 5: Stade Chapou, Toulouse
Cuba **3-3** Romania
(aet)

June 9: Stade Chapou, Toulouse
Cuba **2-1** Romania
(replay)

June 5: Stade Vélodrome Municipal, Reims
Hungary **6-0** Dutch E. Indies

June 5: Colombes, Paris
France **3-1** Belgium

June 5: Stade Cavée Verte, Le Havre
Czechoslovakia **3-0** Holland
(aet)

June 5: Stade de La Meinau, Strasbourg
Brazil **6-5** Poland
(aet)

June 5: Stade Velódrome, Marseilles
Italy **2-1** Norway
(aet)

Game not played
Sweden **w/o** Austria

QUARTER-FINALS

June 12: Stade du Fort Carré, Antibes
Sweden **8-0** Cuba

June 12: Stade Victor Boucquey, Lille
Hungary **2-0** Switzerland

June 12: Colombes, Paris
Italy **3-1** France

June 12: Parc Lescure, Bordeaux
Brazil **1-1** Czechoslovakia
(aet)

June 14: Parc Lescure, Bordeaux
Brazil **2-1** Czechoslovakia
(replay)

SEMI-FINALS

June 16: Stade Velódrome, Marseilles
Italy **2-1** Brazil

June 16: Parc des Princes, Paris
Hungary **5-1** Sweden

THIRD PLACE PLAY-OFF

June 19: Parc Lescure, Bordeaux
Brazil **4-2** Sweden

FINAL

June 19: Colombes, Paris
Italy **4-2** Hungary

1950

POOL 1

June 24: Maracanã, Rio de Janeiro
Brazil **4-0** Mexico

June 25: Independência, Belo Horizonte
Yugoslavia **3-0** Switzerland

June 28: Eucaliptos, Pôrto Alegre
Yugoslavia **4-1** Mexico

June 28: Estádio do Pacaembu, São Paulo
Brazil **2-2** Switzerland

July 1: Maracanã, Rio de Janeiro
Brazil **2-0** Yugoslavia

July 2: Eucaliptos, Pôrto Alegre
Switzerland **2-1** Mexico

	P	W	D	L	F	A	Pts
Brazil	3	2	1	0	8	2	5
Yugoslavia	3	2	0	1	7	3	4
Switzerland	3	1	1	1	4	6	3
Mexico	3	0	0	3	2	10	0

POOL 2

June 25: Estádio Durival de Brito, Curitiba
Spain **3-1** USA

June 25: Maracanã, Rio de Janeiro
England **2-0** Chile

June 29: Estádio Independencia, Belo Horizonte
USA **1-0** England

June 29: Maracanã, Rio de Janeiro
Spain **2-0** Chile

July 2: Maracanã, Rio de Janeiro
Spain **1-0** England

July 2: Estádio Ilha do Retiro, Recife
Chile **5-2** USA

	P	W	D	L	F	A	Pts
Spain	3	3	0	0	6	1	6
England	3	1	0	2	2	2	2
Chile	3	1	0	2	5	6	2
USA	3	1	0	2	4	8	2

POOL 3

June 25: Estádio do Pacaembu, São Paulo
Sweden **3-2** Italy

June 29: Estádio Durival de Brito, Curitiba
Sweden **2-2** Paraguay

July 2: Estádio do Pacaembu, São Paulo
Italy **2-0** Paraguay

	P	W	D	L	F	A	Pts
Sweden	2	1	1	0	5	4	3
Italy	2	1	0	1	4	3	2
Paraguay	2	0	1	1	2	4	1

POOL 4

July 2: Estádio Independencia, Belo Horizonte
Uruguay **8-0** Bolivia

	P	W	D	L	F	A	Pts
Uruguay	1	1	0	0	8	0	2
Bolivia	1	0	0	1	0	8	0

FINAL POOL

July 9: Estádio do Pacaembu, São Paulo
Uruguay **2-2** Spain

July 9: Maracanã, Rio de Janeiro
Brazil **7-1** Sweden

July 13: Estádio do Pacaembu, São Paulo
Uruguay **3-2** Sweden

July 13: Maracanã, Rio de Janeiro
Brazil **6-1** Spain

July 16: Estádio do Pacaembu, São Paulo
Sweden **3-1** Spain

July 16: Maracanã, Rio de Janeiro
Uruguay **2-1** Brazil*

The last game of the Final Pool decided the tournament and is regarded as the 1950 World Cup final.

	P	W	D	L	F	A	Pts
Uruguay	3	2	1	0	7	5	5
Brazil	3	2	0	1	14	4	4
Sweden	3	1	0	2	6	11	2
Spain	3	0	1	2	4	11	1

1954

POOL 1

June 16: La Pontaise Stadium, Lausanne
Yugoslavia **1-0** France

June 16: Charmilles Stadium, Geneva
Brazil **5-0** Mexico

June 19: Charmilles Stadium, Geneva
France **3-2** Mexico

June 19: La Pontaise Stadium, Lausanne
Brazil **1-1** Yugoslavia
(aet)

	P	W	D	L	F	A	Pts
Brazil	2	1	1	0	6	1	3
Yugoslavia	2	1	1	0	2	1	3
France	2	1	0	1	3	3	2
Mexico	2	0	0	2	2	8	0

POOL 2

June 17: Hardturm Stadium, Zurich
Hungary **9-0** South Korea

June 17: Wankdorf Stadium, Berne
West Germany **4-1** Turkey

June 20: St Jakob Stadium, Basle
Hungary **8-3** West Germany

June 20: Charmilles Stadium, Geneva
Turkey **7-0** South Korea

	P	W	D	L	F	A	Pts
Hungary	2	2	0	0	17	3	4
West Germany	2	1	0	1	7	9	2
Turkey	2	1	0	1	8	4	2
South Korea	2	0	0	2	0	16	0

PLAY OFF FOR 2ND GROUP PLACE

June 23: Hardturm Stadium, Zurich
West Germany **7-2** Turkey

POOL 3

June 16: Hardturm Stadium, Zurich
Austria **1-0** Scotland

June 16: Wankdorf Stadium, Berne
Uruguay **2-0** Czechoslovakia

June 19: Hardturm Stadium, Zurich
Austria **5-0** Czechoslovakia

June 19: St Jakob Stadium, Basle
Uruguay **7-0** Scotland

	P	W	D	L	F	A	Pts
Uruguay	2	2	0	0	9	0	4
Austria	2	2	0	0	6	0	4
Czechoslovakia	2	0	0	2	0	7	0
Scotland	2	0	0	2	0	8	0

POOL 4

June 17: St Jakob Stadium, Basle
England **4-4** Belgium
(aet)

June 17: La Pontaise Stadium, Lausanne
Switzerland **2-1** Italy

June 20: Wankdorf Stadium, Berne
England **2-0** Switzerland

June 20: Cornaredo Stadium, Lugano
Italy **4-1** Belgium

	P	W	D	L	F	A	Pts
England	2	1	1	0	6	4	3
Switzerland	2	1	0	1	2	3	2
Italy	2	1	0	1	5	3	2
Belgium	2	0	1	1	5	8	1

PLAY-OFF FOR 2ND GROUP PLACE

June 23: St Jakob Stadium, Basle
Switzerland **4-1** Italy

QUARTER- FINALS

June 26: La Pontaise Stadium, Lausanne
Austria **7-5** Switzerland

June 26: St Jakob Stadium, Basle
Uruguay **4-2** England

June 27: Charmilles Stadium, Geneva
West Germany **2-0** Yugoslavia

June 27: Wankdorf Stadium, Berne
Hungary **4-2** Brazil

SEMI-FINALS

June 30: St Jakob Stadium, Basle
West Germany **6-1** Austria

June 30: La Pontaise Stadium, Lausanne
Hungary **4-2** Uruguay
(aet)

THIRD PLACE PLAY-OFF

July 3: Hardturm Stadium, Zurich
Austria **3-1** Uruguay

FINAL

July 4: Wankdorf Stadium, Berne
West Germany **3-2** Hungary

1958

POOL 1

June 8: Malmö Stadium, Malmö
West Germany **3-1** Argentina

June 8: Örjans Vall, Halmstad
N. Ireland **1-0** Czechoslovakia

June 11: Olympia, Halsingborg
West Germany **2-2** Czechoslovakia

June 11: Örjans Vall, Halmstad
Argentina **3-1** N. Ireland

June 15: Malmö Stadium, Malmö
West Germany **2-2** N. Ireland

June 15: Olympia, Halsingborg
Czechoslovakia **6-1** Argentina

	P	W	D	L	F	A	Pts
West Germany	3	1	2	0	7	5	4
N. Ireland	3	1	1	1	4	5	3
Czechoslovakia	3	1	1	1	8	4	3
Argentina	3	1	0	2	5	10	2

PLAY-OFF FOR 2ND GROUP PLACE

June 17: Malmö Stadium, Malmö
N. Ireland **2-1** Czechoslovakia
(aet)

POOL 2

June 8: Idrottsparken, Norrköping
France **7-3** Paraguay

June 8: Arosvallen, Västerås
Yugoslavia **1-1** Scotland

June 11: Arosvallen, Västerås
Yugoslavia **3-2** France

Gilmar of Brazil, 1962 World Cup Final

June 11: Idrottsparken, Norrköping
Paraguay **3-2** Scotland

June 15: Eyravallen, Örebro
France **2-1** Scotland

June 15: Tunavallen, Eskilstuna
Yugoslavia **3-3** Paraguay

	P	W	D	L	F	A	Pts
France	3	2	0	1	11	7	4
Yugoslavia	3	1	2	0	7	6	4
Paraguay	3	1	1	1	9	12	3
Scotland	3	0	1	2	4	6	1

POOL 3

June 8: Råsunda Stadium, Solna, Stockholm
Sweden **3-0** Mexico

June 8: Jernvallen, Sandviken
Hungary **1-1** Wales

June 11: Råsunda Stadium, Solna, Stockholm
Wales **1-1** Mexico

June 12: Råsunda Stadium, Solna, Stockholm
Sweden **2-1** Hungary

June 15: Råsunda Stadium, Solna, Stockholm
Sweden **0-0** Wales

June 15: Jernvallen, Sandviken
Hungary **4-0** Mexico

	P	W	D	L	F	A	Pts
Sweden	3	2	1	0	5	1	5
Wales	3	0	3	0	2	2	3
Hungary	3	1	1	1	6	3	3
Mexico	3	0	1	2	1	8	1

PLAY-OFF FOR 2ND GROUP PLACE

June 17: Råsunda Stadium, Solna, Stockholm
Wales **2-1** Hungary

POOL 4

June 8: Nya Ullevi Stadium, Gothenburg
England **2-2** Soviet Union

June 8: Rimnersvallen, Uddevalla
Brazil **3-0** Austria

June 11: Nya Ullevi Stadium, Gothenburg
England **0-0** Brazil

June 11: Ryavallen, Borås
Soviet Union **2-0** Austria

June 15: Nya Ullevi Stadium, Gothenburg
Brazil **2-0** Soviet Union

June 15: Ryavallen, Borås
England **2-2** Austria

	P	W	D	L	F	A	Pts
Brazil	3	2	1	0	5	0	5
Soviet Union	3	1	1	1	4	4	3
England	3	0	3	0	4	4	3
Austria	3	0	1	2	2	7	1

PLAY-OFF FOR 2ND GROUP PLACE

June 17: Nya Ullevi Stadium, Gothenburg
Soviet Union **1-0** England

QUARTER-FINALS

June 19: Idrottsparken, Norrköping
France **4-0** N. Ireland

June 19: Malmö Stadium, Malmö
West Germany **1-0** Yugoslavia

June 19: Råsunda Stadium, Solna, Stockholm
Sweden **2-0** Soviet Union

June 19: Nya Ullevi Stadium, Gothenburg
Brazil **1-0** Wales

SEMI-FINALS

June 24: Råsunda Stadium, Solna, Stockholm
Brazil **5-2** France

June 24: Nya Ullevi Stadium, Gothenburg
Sweden **3-1** West Germany

THIRD PLACE PLAY-OFF

June 28: Nya Ullevi Stadium, Gothenburg
France **6-3** West Germany

FINAL

June 29: Råsunda Stadium, Solna, Stockholm
Brazil **5-2** Sweeden

1962

GROUP 1

May 30: Estadio Carlos Dittborn, Arica
Uruguay **2-1** Colombia

May 31: Estadio Carlos Dittborn, Arica
Soviet Union **2-0** Yugoslavia

June 2: Estadio Carlos Dittborn, Arica
Yugoslavia **3-1** Uruguay

June 3: Estadio Carlos Dittborn, Arica
Soviet Union **4-4** Colombia

June 6: Estadio Carlos Dittborn, Arica
Soviet Union **2-1** Uruguay

June 7: Estadio Carlos Dittborn, Arica
Yugoslavia **5-0** Colombia

	P	W	D	L	F	A	Pts
Soviet Union	3	2	1	0	8	5	5
Yugoslavia	3	2	0	1	8	3	4
Uruguay	3	1	0	2	4	6	2
Colombia	3	0	1	2	5	11	1

GROUP 2

May 30: Estadio Nacional, Santiago
Chile **3-1** Switzerland

May 31: Estadio Nacional, Santiago
West Germany **0-0** Italy

June 2: Estadio Nacional, Santiago
Chile **2-0** Italy

June 3: Estadio Nacional, Santiago
West Germany **2-1** Switzerland

June 6: Estadio Nacional, Santiago
West Germany **2-0** Chile

June 7: Estadio Nacional, Santiago
Italy **3-0** Switzerland

	P	W	D	L	F	A	Pts
West Germany	3	2	1	0	4	1	5
Chile	3	2	0	1	5	3	4
Italy	3	1	1	1	3	2	3
Switzerland	3	0	0	3	2	8	0

GROUP 3

May 30: Estadio Sausalito, Viña del Mar
Brazil **2-0** Mexico

May 31: Estadio Sausalito, Viña del Mar
Czechoslovakia **1-0** Spain

June 2: Estadio Sausalito, Viña del Mar
Brazil **0-0** Czechoslovakia

June 3: Estadio Sausalito, Viña del Mar
Spain **1-0** Mexico

June 6: Estadio Sausalito, Viña del Mar
Brazil **2-1** Spain

June 7: Estadio Sausalito, Viña del Mar
Mexico **3-1** Czechoslovakia

	P	W	D	L	F	A	Pts
Brazil	3	2	1	0	4	1	5
Czechoslovakia	3	1	1	1	2	3	3
Mexico	3	1	0	2	3	4	2
Spain	3	1	0	2	2	3	2

GROUP 4

May 30: Estadio Braden Copper, Rancagua
Argentina **1-0** Bulgaria

May 31, Estadio Braden Copper, Rancagua
Hungary **2-1** England

June 2: Estadio Braden Copper, Rancagua
England **3-1** Argentina

June 3: Estadio Braden Copper, Rancagua
Hungary **6-1** Bulgaria

June 6: Estadio Braden Copper, Rancagua
Argentina **0-0** Hungary

June 7: Estadio Braden Copper, Rancagua
England **0-0** Bulgaria

	P	W	D	L	F	A	Pts
Hungary	3	2	1	0	8	2	5
England	3	1	1	1	4	3	3
Argentina	3	1	1	1	2	3	3
Bulgaria	3	0	1	2	1	7	1

QUARTER-FINALS

June 10: Estadio Nacional, Santiago
Yugoslavia **1-0** West Germany

June 10: Estadio Sausalito, Viña del Mar
Brazil **3-1** England

June 10: Estadio Carlos Dittborn, Arica
Chile **2-1** Soviet Union

June 10: Estadio Braden Copper, Rancagua
Czechoslovakia **1-0** Hungary

SEMI-FINALS

June 13: Estadio Nacional, Santiago
Brazil **4-2** Chile

June 13: Estadio Sausalito, Viña del Mar
Czechoslovakia **3-1** Yugoslavia

THIRD PLACE PLAY-OFF

June 16: Estadio Nacional, Santiago
Chile **1-0** Yugoslavia

FINAL

June 17: Estadio Nacional, Santiago
Brazil **3-1** Czechoslovakia

1966

GROUP 1

July 11: Wembley Stadium, London
England **0-0** Uruguay

July 13: Wembley Stadium, London
France **1-1** Mexico

July 15: White City, London
Uruguay **2-1** France

July 16: Wembley Stadium, London
England **2-0** Mexico

July 19: Wembley Stadium, London
Uruguay **0-0** Mexico

July 20: Wembley Stadium, London
England **2-0** France

	P	W	D	L	F	A	Pts
England	3	2	1	0	4	0	5
Uruguay	3	1	2	0	2	1	4
Mexico	3	0	2	1	1	3	2
France	3	0	1	2	2	5	1

GROUP 2

July 12: Hillsborough, Sheffield
West Germany **5-0** Switzerland

July 13: Villa Park, Birmingham
Argentina **2-1** Spain

July 15: Hillsborough, Sheffield
Spain **2-1** Switzerland

July 16: Villa Park, Birmingham
Argentina **0-0** West Germany

July 19: Hillsborough, Sheffield
Argentina **2-0** Switzerland

July 20: Villa Park, Birmingham
West Germany **2-1** Spain

	P	W	D	L	F	A	Pts
West Germany	3	2	1	0	7	1	5
Argentina	3	2	1	0	4	1	5
Spain	3	1	0	2	4	5	2
Switzerland	3	0	0	3	1	9	0

Eusébio and Bobby Charlton, 1966

GROUP 3

July 12: Goodison Park, Liverpool
Brazil **2-0** Bulgaria

July 13: Old Trafford, Manchester
Portugal **3-1** Hungary

July 15: Goodison Park, Liverpool
Hungary **3-1** Brazil

July 16: Old Trafford, Manchester
Portugal **3-0** Bulgaria

July 19: Goodison Park, Liverpool
Portugal **3-1** Brazil

July 20: Old Trafford, Manchester
Hungary **3-1** Bulgaria

	P	W	D	L	F	A	Pts
Portugal	3	3	0	0	9	2	6
Hungary	3	2	0	1	7	5	4
Brazil	3	1	0	2	4	6	2
Bulgaria	3	0	0	3	1	8	0

GROUP 4

July 12: Ayresome Park, Middlesbrough
Soviet Union **3-0** North Korea

July 13: Roker Park, Sunderland
Italy **2-0** Chile

July 15: Ayresome Park, Middlesbrough
Chile **1-1** North Korea

July 16: Roker Park, Sunderland
Soviet Union **1-0** Italy

July 19: Ayresome Park, Middlesbrough
North Korea **1-0** Italy

July 20: Roker Park, Sunderland
Soviet Union **2-1** Chile

	P	W	D	L	F	A	Pts
Soviet Union	3	3	0	0	6	1	6
North Korea	3	1	1	1	2	4	3
Italy	3	1	0	2	2	2	2
Chile	3	0	1	2	2	5	1

QUARTER-FINALS

July 23: Wembley Stadium, London
England **1-0** Argentina

July 23: Hillsborough, Sheffield
West Germany **4-0** Uruguay

July 23: Goodison Park, Liverpool
Portugal **5-3** North Korea

July 23: Roker Park, Sunderland
Soviet Union **2-1** Hungary

SEMI-FINALS

July 25: Goodison Park, Liverpool
West Germany **2-1** Soviet Union

July 26: Wembley Stadium, London
England **2-1** Portugal

THIRD PLACE PLAY-OFF

July 28: Wembley Stadium, London
Portugal **2-1** Soviet Union

FINAL

July 30: Wembley Stadium, London
England **4-2** West Germany
(aet)

1970

GROUP 1

May 31: Estadio Azteca, Mexico City
Mexico **0-0** Soviet Union

June 3: Estadio Azteca, Mexico City
Belgium **3-0** El Salvador

June 6: Estadio Azteca, Mexico City
Soviet Union **4-1** Belgium

June 7: Estadio Azteca, Mexico City
Mexico **4-0** El Salvador

June 10: Estadio Azteca, Mexico City
Soviet Union **2-0** El Salvador

June 11: Estadio Azteca, Mexico City
Mexico **1-0** Belgium

England v Romania, 1970

	P	W	D	L	F	A	Pts
Soviet Union	3	2	1	0	6	1	5
Mexico	3	2	1	0	5	0	5
Belgium	3	1	0	2	4	5	2
El Salvador	3	0	0	3	0	9	0

GROUP 2

June 2: Estadio Cuauhtémoc, Puebla
Uruguay **2-0** Israel

June 3: Estadio Luis Dosal, Toluca
Italy **1-0** Sweden

June 6: Estadio Cuauhtémoc, Puebla
Uruguay **0-0** Italy

June 7: Estadio Luis Dosal, Toluca
Sweden **1-1** Israel

June 10: Estadio Cuauhtémoc, Puebla
Sweden **1-0** Uruguay

June 11: Estadio Luis Dosal, Toluca
Italy **0-0** Israel

	P	W	D	L	F	A	Pts
Italy	3	1	2	0	1	0	4
Uruguay	3	1	1	1	2	1	3
Sweden	3	1	1	1	2	2	3
Israel	3	0	2	1	1	3	2

GROUP 3

June 2: Estadio Jalisco, Guadalajara
England **1-0** Romania

June 3: Estadio Jalisco, Guadalajara
Brazil **4-1** Czechoslovakia

June 6: Estadio Jalisco, Guadalajara
Romania **2-1** Czechoslovakia

June 7: Estadio Jalisco, Guadalajara
Brazil **1-0** England

June 10: Estadio Jalisco, Guadalajara
Brazil **3-2** Romania

June 11: Estadio Jalisco, Guadalajara
England **1-0** Czechoslovakia

	P	W	D	L	F	A	Pts
Brazil	3	3	0	0	8	3	6
England	3	2	0	1	2	1	4
Romania	3	1	0	2	4	5	2
Czechoslovakia	3	0	0	3	2	7	0

GROUP 4

June 2: Estadio Guanajuato, León
Peru **3-2** Bulgaria

June 3: Estadio Guanajuato, León
West Germany **2-1** Morocco

June 6: Estadio Guanajuato, León
Peru **3-0** Morocco

June 7: Estadio Guanajuato, León
West Germany **5-2** Bulgaria

June 10: Estadio Guanajuato, León
West Germany **3-1** Peru

June 11: Estadio Guanajuato, León
Morocco **1-1** Bulgaria

	P	W	D	L	F	A	Pts
West Germany	3	3	0	0	10	4	6
Peru	3	2	0	1	7	5	4
Bulgaria	3	0	1	2	5	9	1
Morocco	3	0	1	2	2	6	1

QUARTER-FINALS

June 14: Estadio Guanajuato, León
West Germany **3-2** England
(aet)

June 14: Estadio Jalisco, Guadalajara
Brazil **4-2** Peru

June 14: Estadio Luis Dosal, Toluca
Italy **4-1** Mexico

June 14: Estadio Azteca, Mexico City
Uruguay **1-0** Soviet Union
(aet)

SEMI-FINALS

June 17: Estadio Azteca, Mexico City
Italy **4-3** West Germany
(aet)

June 17: Estadio Jalisco, Guadalajara
Brazil **3-1** Uruguay

THIRD PLACE PLAY-OFF

June 20: Estadio Azteca, Mexico City
West Germany **1-0** Uruguay

FINAL

June 21: Estadio Azteca, Mexico City
Brazil **4-1** Italy

1974

GROUP 1

June 14: Olympiastadion, Berlin
West Germany **1-0** Chile

June 14: Volksparkstadion, Hamburg
East Germany **2-0** Australia

June 18: Volksparkstadion, Hamburg
West Germany **3-0** Australia

June 18: Olympiastadion, Berlin
East Germany **1-1** Chile

June 22: Olympiastadion, Berlin
Australia **0-0** Chile

June 22: Volksparkstadion, Hamburg
East Germany **1-0** West Germany

	P	W	D	L	F	A	Pts
East Germany	3	2	1	0	4	1	5
West Germany	3	2	0	1	4	1	4
Chile	3	0	2	1	1	2	2
Australia	3	0	1	2	0	5	1

GROUP 2

June 13: Waldstadion, Frankfurt
Brazil **0-0** Yugoslavia

June 14: Westfalenstadion, Dortmund
Scotland **2-0** Zaïre

June 18: Waldstadion, Frankfurt
Brazil **0-0** Scotland

June 18: Parkstadion, Gelsenkirchen
Yugoslavia **9-0** Zaïre

June 22: Waldstadion, Frankfurt
Yugoslavia **1-1** Scotland

June 22: Parkstadion, Gelsenkirchen
Brazil **3-0** Zaïre

	P	W	D	L	F	A	Pts
Yugoslavia	3	1	2	0	10	1	4
Brazil	3	1	2	0	3	0	4
Scotland	3	1	2	0	3	1	4
Zaïre	3	0	0	3	0	14	0

GROUP 3

June 15: Niedersachsenstadion, Hanover
Holland **2-0** Uruguay

June 15: Rheinstadion, Düsseldorf
Bulgaria **0-0** Sweden

June 19: Westfalenstadion, Dortmund
Holland **0-0** Sweden

June 19: Niedersachsenstadion, Hanover
Bulgaria **1-1** Uruguay

June 23: Westfalenstadion, Dortmund
Holland **4-1** Bulgaria

June 23: Rheinstadion, Düsseldorf
Sweden **3-0** Uruguay

	P	W	D	L	F	A	Pts
Holland	3	2	1	0	6	1	5
Sweden	3	1	2	0	3	0	4
Bulgaria	3	0	2	1	2	5	2
Uruguay	3	0	1	2	1	6	1

GROUP 4

June 15: Olympiastadion, Munich
Italy **3-1** Haiti

June 15: Neckarstadion, Stuttgart
Poland **3-2** Argentina

June 19: Neckarstadion, Stuttgart
Argentina **1-1** Italy

June 19: Olympiastadion, Munich
Poland **7-0** Haiti

June 23: Olympiastadion, Munich
Argentina **4-1** Haiti

June 23: Neckarstadion, Stuttgart
Poland **2-1** Italy

	P	W	D	L	F	A	Pts
Poland	3	3	0	0	12	3	6
Argentina	3	1	1	1	7	5	3
Italy	3	1	1	1	5	4	3
Haiti	3	0	0	3	2	14	0

SECOND ROUND GROUP A

June 26: Niedersachsenstadion, Hanover
Brazil **1-0** East Germany

June 26: Parkstadion, Gelsenkirchen
Holland **4-0** Argentina

June 30: Parkstadion, Gelsenkirchen
Holland **2-0** East Germany

June 30: Niedersachsenstadion, Hanover
Brazil **2-1** Argentina

July 3: Parkstadion, Gelsenkirchen
East Germany **1-1** Argentina

July 3: Westfalenstadion, Dortmund
Holland **2-0** Brazil

	P	W	D	L	F	A	Pts
Holland	3	3	0	0	8	0	6
Brazil	3	2	0	1	3	3	4
East Germany	3	0	1	2	1	4	1
Argentina	3	0	1	2	2	7	1

SECOND ROUND GROUP B

June 26: Neckarstadion, Stuttgart
Poland **1-0** Sweden

June 26: Rheinstadion, Düsseldorf
West Germany **2-0** Yugoslavia

June 30: Waldstadion, Frankfurt
Poland **2-1** Yugoslavia

June 30: Rheinstadion, Düsseldorf
West Germany **4-2** Sweden

July 3: Rheinstadion, Düsseldorf
Sweden **2-1** Yugoslavia

July 3: Waldstadion, Frankfurt
West Germany **1-0** Poland

	P	W	D	L	F	A	Pts
West Germany	3	3	0	0	7	2	6
Poland	3	2	0	1	3	2	4
Sweden	3	1	0	2	4	6	2
Yugoslavia	3	0	0	3	2	6	0

East Germany v Holland, 1974

Mario Kempes, 1978 World Cup Final

THIRD PLACE PLAY-OFF

July 6: Olympiastadion, Munich
Poland **1-0** Brazil

FINAL

July 7: Olympiastadion, Munich
West Germany **2-1** Holland

1978

GROUP 1

June 2: Estadio Monumental, Buenos Aires
Argentina **2-1** Hungary

June 2: Estadio Mar del Plata, Mar del Plata
Italy **2-1** France

June 6: Estadio Monumental, Buenos Aires
Argentina **2-1** France

June 6: Estadio Mar del Plata, Mar del Plata
Italy **3-1** Hungary

June 10: Estadio Monumental, Buenos Aires
Italy **1-0** Argentina

June 10: Estadio Mar del Plata, Mar del Plata
France **3-1** Hungary

	P	W	D	L	F	A	Pts
Italy	3	3	0	0	6	2	6
Argentina	3	2	0	1	4	3	4
France	3	1	0	2	5	5	2
Hungary	3	0	0	3	3	8	0

GROUP 2

June 1: Estadio Monumental, Buenos Aires
West Germany **0-0** Poland

June 2: Gigante de Arroyito, Rosario
Tunisia **3-1** Mexico

June 6: Gigante de Arroyito, Rosario
Poland **1-0** Tunisia

June 6: Estadio Córdoba, Córdoba
West Germany **6-0** Mexico

June 10: Gigante de Arroyito, Rosario
Poland **3-1** Mexico

June 10: Estadio Córdoba, Córdoba
West Germany **0-0** Tunisia

	P	W	D	L	F	A	Pts
Poland	3	2	1	0	4	1	5
West Germany	3	1	2	0	6	0	4
Tunisia	3	1	1	1	3	2	3
Mexico	3	0	0	3	2	12	0

GROUP 3

June 3: Estadio José Amalfitani, Buenos Aires
Austria **2-1** Spain

June 3: Estadio Mar del Plata, Mar del Plata
Sweden **1-1** Brazil

June 7: Estadio José Amalfitani, Buenos Aires
Austria **1-0** Sweden

June 7: Estadio Mar del Plata, Mar del Plata
Brazil **0-0** Spain

June 11: Estadio José Amalfitani, Buenos Aires
Spain **1-0** Sweden

June 11: Estadio Mar del Plata, Mar del Plata
Brazil **1-0** Austria

	P	W	D	L	F	A	Pts
Austria	3	2	0	1	3	2	4
Brazil	3	1	2	0	2	1	4
Spain	3	1	1	1	2	2	3
Sweden	3	0	1	2	1	3	1

GROUP 4

June 3: Estadio Córdoba, Córdoba
Peru **3-1** Scotland

June 3: Estadio Mendoza, Mendoza
Holland **3-0** Iran

June 7: Estadio Córdoba, Córdoba
Scotland **1-1** Iran

June 7: Estadio Mendoza, Mendoza
Holland **0-0** Peru

June 11: Estadio Córdoba, Córdoba
Peru **4-1** Iran

June 11: Estadio Mendoza, Mendoza
Scotland **3-2** Holland

	P	W	D	L	F	A	Pts
Peru	3	2	1	0	7	2	5
Holland	3	1	1	1	5	3	3
Scotland	3	1	1	1	5	6	3
Iran	3	0	1	2	2	8	1

SECOND ROUND GROUP A

June 14: Estadio Monumental, Buenos Aires
Italy **0-0** West Germany

June 14: Estadio Córdoba, Córdoba
Holland **5-1** Austria

June 18: Estadio Monumental, Buenos Aires
Italy **1-0** Austria

June 18: Estadio Córdoba, Córdoba
Holland **2-2** West Germany

June 21: Estadio Monumental, Buenos Aires
Holland **2-1** Italy

June 21: Estadio Córdoba, Córdoba
Austria **3-2** West Germany

	P	W	D	L	F	A	Pts
Holland	3	2	1	0	9	4	5
Italy	3	1	1	1	2	2	3
West Germany	3	0	2	1	4	5	2
Austria	3	1	0	2	4	8	2

SECOND ROUND GROUP B

June 14: Gigante de Arroyito, Rosario
Argentina **2-0** Poland

June 14: Estadio Mendoza, Mendoza
Brazil **3-0** Peru

June 18: Gigante de Arroyito, Rosario
Argentina **0-0** Brazil

June 18: Estadio Mendoza, Mendoza
Poland **1-0** Peru

June 21: Estadio Mendoza, Mendoza
Brazil **3-1** Poland

June 21: Gigante de Arroyito, Rosario
Argentina **6-0** Peru

	P	W	D	L	F	A	Pts
Argentina	3	2	1	0	8	0	5
Brazil	3	2	1	0	6	1	5
Poland	3	1	0	2	2	5	2
Peru	3	0	0	3	0	10	0

THIRD PLACE PLAY-OFF

June 24: Estadio Monumental, Buenos Aires
Brazil **2-1** Italy

FINAL

June 24: Estadio Monumental, Buenos Aires
Argentina **3-1** Holland
(aet)

1982

GROUP 1

June 14: Estadio Balaidos, Vigo
Italy **0-0** Poland

June 15: Estadio Riazor, La Coruña
Peru **0-0** Cameroon

June 18: Estadio Balaidos, Vigo
Italy **1-1** Peru

June 19: Estadio Riazor, La Coruña
Poland **0-0** Cameroon

June 22: Estadio Riazor, La Coruña
Poland **5-1** Peru

June 23: Estadio Balaidos, Vigo
Italy **1-1** Cameroon

	P	W	D	L	F	A	Pts
Poland	3	1	2	0	5	1	4
Italy	3	0	3	0	2	2	3
Cameroon	3	0	3	0	1	1	3
Peru	3	0	2	1	2	6	2

GROUP 2

June 16: Estadio El Molinón, Gijón
Algeria **2-1** West Germany

June 17: Estadio Carlos Tartiere, Oviedo
Austria **1-0** Chile

June 20: Estadio El Molinón, Gijón
West Germany **4-1** Chile

June 21: Estadio Carlos Tartiere, Oviedo
Austria **2-0** Algeria

June 24: Estadio Carlos Tartiere, Oviedo
Algeria **3-2** Chile

June 25: El Molinóln Stadium, Gijón
West Germany **1-0** Austria

	P	W	D	L	F	A	Pts
West Germany	3	2	0	1	6	3	4
Austria	3	2	0	1	3	1	4
Algeria	3	2	0	1	5	5	4
Chile	3	0	0	3	3	8	0

GROUP 3

June 13: Camp Nou, Barcelona
Belgium **1-0** Argentina

June 15: Nuevo Estadio, Elche
Hungary **10-1** El Salvador

June 18: Estadio José Rico Perez, Alicante
Argentina **4-1** Hungary

June 19: Nuevo Estadio, Elche
Belgium **1-0** El Salvador

June 22: Nuevo Estadio, Elche
Belgium **1-1** Hungary

June 23: Estadio José Rico Perez, Alicante
Argentina **2-0** El Salvador

	P	W	D	L	F	A	Pts
Belgium	3	2	1	0	3	1	5
Argentina	3	2	0	1	6	2	4
Hungary	3	1	1	1	12	6	3
El Salvador	3	0	0	3	1	13	0

GROUP 4

June 16: Estadio San Mamés, Bilbao
England **3-1** France

June 17: Estadio José Zorrilla, Valladolid
Czechoslovakia **1-1** Kuwait

June 20: Estadio San Mamés, Bilbao
England **2-0** Czechoslovakia

June 21: Estadio José Zorrilla, Valladolid
France **4-1** Kuwait

June 24: Estadio José Zorrilla, Valladolid
France **1-1** Czechoslovakia

June 25: Estadio San Mamés, Bilbao
England **1-0** Kuwait

	P	W	D	L	F	A	Pts
England	3	3	0	0	6	1	6
France	3	1	1	1	6	5	3
Czechoslovakia	3	0	2	1	2	4	2
Kuwait	3	0	1	2	2	6	1

Italy v West Germany, 1982 World Cup Final

Northern Ireland v France, 1982

GROUP 5

June 16: Estadio Luis Casanova, Valencia
Spain **1-1** Honduras

June 17: Estadio La Romereda, Zaragoza
N. Ireland **0-0** Yugoslavia

June 20: Estadio Luis Casanova, Valencia
Spain **2-1** Yugoslavia

June 21: Estadio La Romereda, Zaragoza
N. Ireland **1-1** Honduras

June 24: Estadio La Romereda, Zaragoza
Yugoslavia **1-0** Honduras

June 25: Estadio Luis Casanova, Valencia
N. Ireland **1-0** Spain

	P	W	D	L	F	A	Pts
N. Ireland	3	1	2	0	2	1	4
Spain	3	1	1	1	3	3	3
Yugoslavia	3	1	1	1	2	2	3
Honduras	3	0	2	1	2	3	2

GROUP 6

June 14: Estadio Sánchez Pizjuán, Seville
Brazil **2-1** Soviet Union

June 15: Estadio La Rosaleda, Málaga
Scotland **5-2** New Zealand

June 18: Estadio Benito Villamarin, Seville
Brazil **4-1** Scotland

June 19: Estadio La Rosaleda, Málaga
Soviet Union **3-0** New Zealand

June 22: Estadio La Rosaleda, Málaga
Scotland **2-2** Soviet Union

June 23: Estadio Benito Villamarin, Seville
Brazil **4-0** New Zealand

	P	W	D	L	F	A	Pts
Brazil	3	3	0	0	10	2	6
Soviet Union	3	1	1	1	6	4	3
Scotland	3	1	1	1	8	8	3
New Zealand	3	0	0	3	2	12	0

SECOND ROUND GROUP A

June 28: Camp Nou, Barcelona
Poland **3-0** Belgium

July 1: Camp Nou, Barcelona
Soviet Union **1-0** Belgium

July 4: Camp Nou, Barcelona
Soviet Union **0-0** Poland

	P	W	D	L	F	A	Pts
Poland	2	1	1	0	3	0	3
Soviet Union	2	1	1	0	1	0	3
Belgium	2	0	0	2	0	4	0

SECOND ROUND GROUP B

June 29: Bernabéu, Madrid
West Germany **0-0** England

July 2: Bernabéu, Madrid
West Germany **2-1** Spain

July 5: Bernabéu, Madrid
England **0-0** Spain

	P	W	D	L	F	A	Pts
West Germany	2	1	1	0	2	1	3
England	2	0	2	0	0	0	2
Spain	2	0	1	1	1	2	1

Maradona, Argentina v England, 1986

SECOND ROUND GROUP C

June 29: Estadio Sarriá, Barcelona
Italy **2-1** Argentina

July 2: Estadio Sarriá, Barcelona
Brazil **3-1** Argentina

July 5: Estadio Sarriá, Barcelona
Italy **3-2** Brazil

	P	W	D	L	F	A	Pts
Italy	2	2	0	0	5	3	4
Brazil	2	1	0	1	5	4	2
Argentina	2	0	0	2	2	5	0

SECOND ROUND GROUP D

June 28: Estadio Vicente Calderón, Madrid
France **1-0** Austria

July 1: Estadio Vicente Calderón, Madrid
N. Ireland **2-2** Austria

July 4: Estadio Vicente Calderón, Madrid
France **4-1** N. Ireland

	P	W	D	L	F	A	Pts
France	2	2	0	0	5	1	4
Austria	2	0	1	1	2	3	1
N. Ireland	2	0	1	1	3	6	1

SEMI-FINALS

July 8: Camp Nou, Barcelona
Italy **2-0** Poland

July 8: Estadio Sánchez Pizjuán, Seville
West Germany **3-3** France
(aet)
West Germany won 5-4 on penalties

THIRD PLACE PLAY-OFF

July 10: Estadio José Rico Perez, Alicante
Poland **3-2** France

FINAL

July 11: Bernabéu, Madrid
Italy **3-1** West Germany

1986

GROUP A

May 31: Estadio Azteca, Mexico City
Bulgaria **1-1** Italy

June 2: Estadio Olimpico, Mexico City
Argentina **3-1** South Korea

June 5: Estadio Cuauhtémoc, Puebla
Italy **1-1** Argentina

June 5: Estadio Olimpico, Mexico City
Bulgaria **1-1** South Korea

June 10: Estadio Olimpico, Mexico City
Argentina **2-0** Bulgaria

June 10: Estadio Cuauhtémoc, Puebla
Italy **3-2** South Korea

	P	W	D	L	F	A	Pts
Argentina	3	2	1	0	6	2	5
Italy	3	1	2	0	5	4	4
Bulgaria	3	0	2	1	2	4	2
South Korea	3	0	1	2	4	7	1

GROUP B

June 3: Estadio Azteca, Mexico City
Mexico **2-1** Belgium

June 4: La Bombonera, Toluca
Paraguay **1-0** Iraq

June 7: Estadio Azteca, Mexico City
Mexico **1-1** Paraguay

June 8: La Bombonera, Toluca
Belgium **2-1** Iraq

June 11: La Bombonera, Toluca
Paraguay **2-2** Belgium

June 11: Estadio Azteca, Mexico City
Mexico **1-0** Iraq

	P	W	D	L	F	A	Pts
Mexico	3	2	1	0	4	2	5
Paraguay	3	1	2	0	4	3	4
Belgium	3	1	1	1	5	5	3
Iraq	3	0	0	3	1	4	0

GROUP C

June 2: Estadio Irapuato, Irapuato
Soviet Union **6-0** Hungary

June 1: Nou Camp, León
France **1-0** Canada

June 5: Nou Camp, León
Soviet Union **1-1** France

June 6: Estadio Irapuato, Irapuato
Hungary **2-0** Canada

June 9: Nou Camp, León
France **3-0** Hungary

June 9: Estadio Irapuato, Irapuato
Soviet Union **2-0** Canada

	P	W	D	L	F	A	Pts
Soviet Union	3	2	1	0	9	1	5
France	3	2	1	0	5	1	5
Hungary	3	1	0	2	2	9	2
Canada	3	0	0	3	0	5	0

GROUP D

June 1: Estadio Jalisco, Guadalajara
Brazil **1-0** Spain

June 3: Estadio Trez de Marzo, Guadalajara
N. Ireland **1-1** Algeria

June 6: Estadio Jalisco, Guadalajara
Brazil **1-0** Algeria

June 7: Estadio Trez de Marzo, Guadalajara
Spain **2-1** N. Ireland

June 12: Estadio Tecnológico, Monterrey
Spain **3-0** Algeria

June 12: Estadio Jalisco, Guadalajara
Brazil **3-0** N. Ireland

	P	W	D	L	F	A	Pts
Brazil	3	3	0	0	5	0	6
Spain	3	2	0	1	5	2	4
N. Ireland	3	0	1	2	2	6	1
Algeria	3	0	1	2	1	5	1

GROUP E

June 4: Estadio La Corregidora, Querétaro
West Germany **1-1** Uruguay

June 4: Estadio Neza 86, Nezahualcoyotl
Denmark **1-0** Scotland

June 8: Estadio Neza 86, Nezahualcoyotl
Denmark **6-1** Uruguay

June 8: Estadio La Corregidora, Querétaro
West Germany **2-1** Scotland

June 13: Estadio Neza 86, Nezahualcoyotl
Scotland **0-0** Uruguay

June 13: Estadio La Corregidora, Querétaro
Denmark **2-0** West Germany

	P	W	D	L	F	A	Pts
Denmark	3	3	0	0	9	1	6
West Germany	3	1	1	1	3	4	3
Uruguay	3	0	2	1	2	7	2
Scotland	3	0	1	2	1	3	1

GROUP F

June 2: Estadio Universitario, Monterrey
Morocco **0-0** Poland

June 3: Estadio Tecnológico, Monterrey
Portugal **1-0** England

June 6: Estadio Tecnológico, Monterrey
England **0-0** Morocco

June 7: Estadio Universitario, Monterrey
Poland **1-0** Portugal

June 11: Estadio Universitario, Monterrey
England **3-0** Poland

June 11: Estadio Jalisco, Guadalajara
Morocco **3-1** Portugal

	P	W	D	L	F	A	Pts
Morocco	3	1	2	0	3	1	4
England	3	1	1	1	3	1	3
Poland	3	1	1	1	1	3	3
Portugal	3	1	0	2	2	4	2

SECOND ROUND

June 15: Estadio Azteca, Mexico City
Mexico **2-0** Bulgaria

June 15: Nou Camp, León
Belgium **4-3** Soviet Union
(aet)

June 16: Estadio Jalisco, Guadalajara
Brazil **4-0** Poland

June 16: Estadio Cuauhtémoc, Puebla
Argentina **1-0** Uruguay

June 17: Estadio Olimpico, Mexico City
France **2-0** Italy

June 17: Estadio Universitario, Monterrey
West Germany **1-0** Morocco

June 18: Estadio Azteca, Mexico City
England **3-0** Paraguay

June 18: Estadio La Corregidora, Querétaro
Spain **5-1** Denmark

QUARTER-FINALS

June 21: Estadio Jalisco, Guadalajara
France **1-1** Brazil
(aet)
France won 4-3 on penalties

June 21: Estadio Universitario, Monterrey
West Germany **0-0** Mexico
(aet)
West Germany won 4-1 on penalties

June 22: Estadio Azteca, Mexico City
Argentina **2-1** England

June 22: Estadio Cuauhtémoc, Puebla
Spain **1-1** Belgium
(aet)
Belgium won 5-4 on penalties

SEMI-FINALS

June 25: Estadio Azteca, Mexico City
Argentina **2-0** Belgium

June 25: Estadio Jalisco, Guadalajara
West Germany **2-0** France

THIRD PLACE PLAY-OFF

June 28: Estadio Cuauhtémoc, Puebla
France **4-2** Belgium

FINAL

June 29: Estadio Azteca, Mexico City
Argentina **3-2** West Germany

1990

GROUP A

June 9: Stadio Olimpico, Rome
Italy **1-0** Austria

June 10: Stadio Comunale, Florence
Czechoslovakia **5-1** USA

June 14: Stadio Olimpico, Rome
Italy **1-0** USA

June 15: Stadio Comunale, Florence
Czechoslovakia **1-0** Austria

June 19: Stadio Olimpico, Rome
Italy **2-0** Czechoslovakia

June 19: Stadio Comunale, Florence
Austria **2-1** USA

	P	W	D	L	F	A	Pts
Italy	3	3	0	0	4	0	6
Czechoslovakia	3	2	0	1	6	3	4
Austria	3	1	0	2	2	3	2
USA	3	0	0	3	2	8	0

GROUP B

June 8: Stadio San Siro, Milan
Cameroon **1-0** Argentina

June 9: Stadio Sant Nicola, Bari
Romania **2-0** Soviet Union

June 13: Stadio San Paolo, Naples
Argentina **2-0** Soviet Union

June 14: Stadio Sant Nicola, Bari
Cameroon **2-1** Romania

June 18: Stadio San Paolo, Naples
Argentina **1-1** Romania

June 18: Stadio Sant Nicola, Bari
Soviet Union **4-0** Cameroon

	P	W	D	L	F	A	Pts
Cameroon	3	2	0	1	3	5	4
Romania	3	1	1	1	4	3	3
Argentina	3	1	1	1	3	2	3
Soviet Union	3	1	0	2	4	4	2

GROUP C

June 10: Stadio Delle Alpi, Turin
Brazil **2-1** Sweden

June 11: Stadio Luigi Ferraris, Genoa
Costa Rica **1-0** Scotland

June 16: Stadio Delle Alpi, Turin
Brazil **1-0** Costa Rica

June 16: Stadio Luigi Ferraris, Genoa
Scotland **2-1** Sweden

June 20: Stadio Delle Alpi, Turin
Brazil **1-0** Scotland

June 20: Stadio Luigi Ferraris, Genoa
Costa Rica **2-1** Sweden

Paul Gascoigne, 1990

Klinsmann and Buchwald, West Germany v Holland, 1990

	P	W	D	L	F	A	Pts
Brazil	3	3	0	0	4	1	6
Costa Rica	3	2	0	1	3	2	4
Scotland	3	1	0	2	2	3	2
Sweden	3	0	0	3	3	6	0

GROUP D

June 9: Stadio Renato Dall'Ara, Bologna
Colombia **2-0** UAE

June 10: Stadio San Siro, Milan
West Germany **4-1** Yugoslavia

June 14: Stadio Renato Dall'Ara, Bologna
Yugoslavia **1-0** Colombia

June 15: Stadio San Siro, Milan
West Germany **5-1** UAE

June 19: Stadio San Siro, Milan
West Germany **1-1** Colombia

June 19: Stadio Renato Dall'Ara, Bologna
Yugoslavia **4-1** UAE

	P	W	D	L	F	A	Pts
West Germany	3	2	1	0	10	3	5
Yugoslavia	3	2	0	1	6	5	4
Colombia	3	1	1	1	3	2	3
UAE	3	0	0	3	2	11	0

GROUP E

June 12: Marc'Antonio Bentegodi, Verona
Belgium **2-0** South Korea

June 13: Stadio Friuli, Udine
Uruguay **0-0** Spain

June 17, Marc 'Antonio Bentegodi, Verona
Belgium **3-1** Uruguay

June 17: Stadio Friuli, Udine
Spain **3-1** South Korea

June 21: Marc'Antonio Bentegodi, Verona
Spain **2-1** Belgium

June 21: Stadio Friuli, Udine
Uruguay **1-0** South Korea

	P	W	D	L	F	A	Pts
Spain	3	2	1	0	5	2	5
Belgium	3	2	0	1	6	3	4
Uruguay	3	1	1	1	2	3	3
South Korea	3	0	0	3	1	6	0

GROUP F

June 11: Stadio Sant 'Elia, Cagliari
England **1-1** Rep. Of Ireland

June 12: Stadio La Favorita, Palermo
Holland **1-1** Egypt

June 16: Stadio Sant 'Elia, Cagliari
England **0-0** Holland

June 17: Stadio La Favorita, Palermo
Egypt **0-0** Rep. Of Ireland

June 21: Stadio Sant 'Elia, Cagliari
England **1-0** Egypt

June 21: Stadio La Favorita, Palermo
Holland **1-1** Rep. Of Ireland

	P	W	D	L	F	A	Pts
England	3	1	2	0	2	1	4
Rep. Of Ireland	3	0	3	0	2	2	3
Holland	3	0	3	0	2	2	3
Egypt	3	0	2	1	1	2	2

SECOND ROUND

June 23: Stadio San Paolo, Naples
Cameroon **2-1** Colombia
(aet)

June 23: Stadio Sant Nicola, Bari
Czechoslovakia **4-1** Costa Rica

June 24: Stadio Delle Alpi, Turin
Argentina **1-0** Brazil

June 24: Stadio San Siro, Milan
West Germany **2-1** Holland

June 25: Stadio Luigi Ferraris, Genoa
Rep. Of Ireland **0-0** Romania
(aet)
Rep. Of Ireland won 5-4 on penalties

June 25: Stadio Olimpico, Rome
Italy **2-0** Uruguay

June 26: Marc'Antonio Bentegodi, Verona
Yugoslavia **2-1** Spain
(aet)

June 26: Stadio Dall'Ara, Bologna
England **1-0** Belgium
(aet)

QUARTER-FINALS

June 30: Stadio Comunale, Florence
Argentina **0-0** Yugoslavia
(aet)
Argentina won 3-2 on penalties

June 30: Stadio Olimpico, Rome
Italy **1-0** Rep. Of Ireland

July 1: Stadio San Siro, Milan
West Germany **1-0** Czechoslovakia

July 1: Stadio San Paolo, Naples
England **3-2** Cameroon
(aet)

SEMI-FINALS

July 3: Stadio San Paolo, Naples
Argentina **1-1** Italy
(aet)
Argentina won 4-3 on penalties

July 4: Stadio Delle Alpi, Turin
West Germany **1-1** England
(aet)
West Germany won 4-3 on penalties

THIRD PLACE PLAY-OFF

July 7: Stadio Sant Nicola, Bari
Italy **2-1** England

FINAL

July 8: Stadio Olimpico, Rome
West Germany **1-0** Argentina

1994

GROUP A

June 18: Pontiac Silverdome, Detroit
USA **1-1** Switzerland

June 18: Rose Bowl, Pasadena
Colombia **1-3** Romania

June 22: Rose Bowl, Pasadena
USA **2-1** Colombia

June 22: Pontiac Silverdome, Detroit
Romania **1-4** Switzerland

June 26: Rose Bowl, Pasadena
USA **0-1** Romania

June 26: Stanford Stadium, San Francisco
Switzerland **0-2** Colombia

	P	W	D	L	F	A	Pts
Romania	3	2	0	1	5	5	6
Switzerland	3	1	1	1	5	4	4
USA	3	1	1	1	3	3	4
Colombia	3	1	0	2	4	5	3

GROUP B

June 19: Rose Bowl, Pasadena
Cameroon **2-2** Sweden

June 20: Stanford Stadium, San Francisco
Brazil **2-0** Russia

June 24: Stanford Stadium, San Francisco
Brazil **3-0** Cameroon

June 24: Pontiac Silverdome, Detroit
Sweden **3-1** Russia

June 28: Stanford Stadium, San Francisco
Russia **6-1** Cameroon

June 28: Pontiac Silverdome, Detroit
Brazil **1-1** Sweden

	P	W	D	L	F	A	Pts
Brazil	3	2	1	0	6	1	7
Sweden	3	1	2	0	6	4	5
Russia	3	1	0	2	7	6	3
Cameroon	3	0	1	2	3	11	1

GROUP C

June 17: Soldier Field, Chicago
Germany **1-0** Bolivia

June 17: Cotton Bowl, Dallas
Spain **2-2** South Korea

June 21: Soldier Field, Chicago
Germany **1-1** Spain

June 23: Foxboro, Boston
South Korea **0-0** Bolivia

June 27: Soldier Field, Chicago
Bolivia **1-3** Spain

June 27: Cotton Bowl, Dallas
Germany **3-2** South Korea

	P	W	D	L	F	A	Pts
Germany	3	2	1	0	5	3	7
Spain	3	1	2	0	6	4	5
South Korea	3	0	2	1	4	5	2
Bolivia	3	0	1	2	1	4	1

GROUP D

June 21: Foxboro, Boston
Argentina **4-0** Greece

June 21: Cotton Bowl, Dallas
Nigeria **3-0** Bulgaria

June 25: Foxboro, Boston
Argentina **2-1** Nigeria

June 26: Soldier Field, Chicago
Bulgaria **4-0** Greece

June 30: Foxboro, Boston
Greece **0-2** Nigeria

June 30: Cotton Bowl, Dallas
Argentina **0-2** Bulgaria

	P	W	D	L	F	A	Pts
Nigeria	3	2	0	1	6	2	6
Bulgaria	3	2	0	1	6	3	6
Argentina	3	2	0	1	6	3	6
Greece	3	0	0	3	0	10	0

GROUP E

June 18: Giants Stadium, New Jersey
Italy **0-1** Rep. Of Ireland

June 19: RFK Stadium, Washington DC
Norway **1-0** Mexico

June 23: Giants Stadium, New Jersey
Italy **1-0** Norway

June 24: Citrus Bowl, Orlando
Mexico **2-1** Rep. Of Ireland

June 28: Giants Stadium, New Jersey
Rep. Of Ireland **0-0** Norway

June 28: RFK Stadium, Washington DC
Italy **1-1** Mexico

	P	W	D	L	F	A	Pts
Mexico	3	1	1	1	3	3	4
Rep. Of Ireland	3	1	1	1	2	2	4
Italy	3	1	1	1	2	2	4
Norway	3	1	1	1	1	1	4

GROUP F

June 19: Citrus Bowl, Orlando
Belgium **1-0** Morocco

June 20: RFK Stadium, Washington DC
Holland **2-1** Saudi Arabia

June 25: Citrus Bowl, Orlando
Belgium **1-0** Holland

June 25: Giants Stadium, New Jersey
Saudi Arabia **2-1** Morocco

June 29: Citrus Bowl, Orlando
Morocco **1-2** Holland

June 29: RFK Stadium, Washington DC
Belgium **0-1** Saudi Arabia

USA v Brazil, 1994

	P	W	D	L	F	A	Pts
Holland	3	2	0	1	4	3	6
Saudi Arabia	3	2	0	1	4	3	6
Belgium	3	2	0	1	2	1	6
Morocco	3	0	0	3	2	5	0

SECOND ROUND

July 2: Soldier Field, Chicago
Germany **3-2** Belgium

July 2: RFK Stadium, Washington DC
Spain **3-0** Switzerland

July 3: Cotton Bowl, Dallas
Saudi Arabia **1-3** Sweden

July 3: Rose Bowl, Pasadena
Romania **3-2** Argentina

July 4: Citrus Bowl, Orlando
Holland **2-0** Rep. Of Ireland

July 4: Stanford, Palo, Alto
Brazil **1-0** USA

July 5: Foxboro, Boston
Nigeria **1-2** Italy
(aet)

July 5: Giants Stadium, New Jersey
Bulgaria **1-1** Mexico
(aet)
Bulgaria won 3-1 on penalties

QUARTER-FINALS

July 9: Foxboro, Boston
Italy **2-1** Spain

July 9: Cotton Bowl, Dallas
Holland **2-3** Brazil

July 10: Giants Stadium, New Jersey
Germany **1-2** Bulgaria

July 10: Stanford Stadium, San Francisco
Sweden **2-2** Romania
(aet)
Sweden won 5-4 on penalties

SEMI-FINALS

July 13: Rose Bowl, Pasadena
Brazil **1-0** Sweden

July 13: Giants Stadium, New Jersey
Italy **2-1** Bulgaria

THIRD PLACE PLAY-OFF

July 16: Rose Bowl, Pasadena
Sweden **4-0** Bulgaria

FINAL

July 17: Rose Bowl, Pasadena
Brazil **0-0** Italy
(aet)
Brazil won 3-2 on penalties

1998

GROUP A

June 10: Stade de France, Saint-Denis
Brazil **2-1** Scotland

June 10: Stade de la Mosson, Montepellier
Morocco **2-2** Norway

June 16: Stade de la Beaujoire, Nantes
Brazil **3-0** Morocco

June 16: Parc Lescure, Bordeaux
Scotland **1-1** Norway

June 23: Stade Vélodrome, Marseilles
Brazil **1-2** Norway

June 23: Geoffroy-Guichard, St Etienne
Scotland **0-3** Morocco

	P	W	D	L	F	A	Pts
Brazil	3	2	0	1	6	3	6
Norway	3	1	2	0	5	4	5
Morocco	3	1	1	1	5	5	4
Scotland	3	0	1	2	2	6	1

GROUP B

June 11: Parc Lescure, Bordeaux
Italy **2-2** Chile

June 11: Municipal, Toulouse
Austria **1-1** Cameroon

June 17: Geoffroy-Guichard, St Etienne
Chile **1-1** Austria

June 17: La Mosson, Montpellier
Italy **3-0** Cameroon

June 23: Stade de la Beaujoire, Nantes
Chile **1-1** Cameroon

June 23: Stade de France, Saint-Denis
Italy **2-1** Austria

	P	W	D	L	F	A	Pts
Italy	3	2	1	0	7	3	7
Chile	3	0	3	0	4	4	3
Austria	3	0	2	1	3	4	2
Cameroon	3	0	2	1	2	5	2

GROUP C

June 12: Stade Felix Bollaert, Lens
Saudi Arabia **0-1** Denmark

June 12: Stade Vélodrome, Marseilles
France **3-0** South Africa

June 18: Stade de France, Saint-Denis
France **4-0** Saudi Arabia

June 18: Municipal, Toulouse
South Africa **1-1** Denmark

June 24: Stade de Gerland, Lyon
France **2-1** Denmark

June 24: Parc Lescure, Bordeaux
South Africa **2-2** Saudi Arabia

	P	W	D	L	F	A	Pts
France	3	3	0	0	9	1	9
Denmark	3	1	1	1	3	3	4
South Africa	3	0	2	1	3	6	2
Saudi Arabia	3	0	1	2	2	7	1

GROUP D

June 12: Stade de la Mosson, Montepellier
Paraguay **0-0** Bulgaria

June 13: Stade de la Beaujoire, Nantes
Spain **2-3** Nigeria

June 19: Parc des Princes, Paris
Nigeria **1-0** Bulgaria

June 19: Geoffroy-Guichard, St Etienne
Spain **0-0** Paraguay

June 24: Municipal, Toulouse
Nigeria **1-3** Paraguay

June 24: Stade Felix Bollaert, Lens
Spain **6-1** Bulgaria

	P	W	D	L	F	A	Pts
Nigeria	3	2	0	1	5	5	6
Paraguay	3	1	2	0	3	1	5
Spain	3	1	1	1	8	4	4
Bulgaria	3	0	1	2	1	7	1

GROUP E

June 13: Stade de Gerland, Lyon
South Korea **1-3** Mexico

June 13: Stade de France, Saint-Denis
Holland **0-0** Belgium

June 20: Parc Lescure, Bordeaux
Belgium **2-2** Mexico

June 20: Stade Vélodrome, Marseilles
Holland **5-0** South Korea

June 25: Parc des Princes, Paris
Belgium **1-1** South Korea

June 25: Geoffroy-Guichard, St Etienne
Holland **2-2** Mexico

	P	W	D	L	F	A	Pts
Holland	3	1	2	0	7	2	5
Mexico	3	1	2	0	7	5	5
Belgium	3	0	3	0	3	3	3
South Korea	3	0	1	2	2	9	1

GROUP F

June 15: Parc des Princes, Paris
Germany **2-0** USA

June 14: Geoffroy-Guichard, St Etienne
Yugoslavia **1-0** Iran

June 21: Stade Felix Bollaert, Lens
Germany **2-2** Yugoslavia

June 21: Stade de Gerland, Lyon
USA **1-2** Iran

June 25: Stade de la Mosson, Montepellier
Germany **2-0** Iran

June 25: Stade de la Beaujoire, Nantes
USA **0-1** Yugoslavia

	P	W	D	L	F	A	Pts
Germany	3	2	1	0	6	2	7
Yugoslavia	3	2	1	0	4	2	7
Iran	3	1	0	2	2	4	3
USA	3	0	0	3	1	5	0

GROUP G

June 15: Stade Vélodrome, Marseilles
England **2-0** Tunisia

June 15: Stade de Gerland, Lyon
Romania **1-0** Colombia

June 22: Stade de la Mosson, Montepellier
Colombia **1-0** Tunisia

June 22: Municipal, Toulouse
Romania **2-1** England

June 26: Stade de France, Saint-Denis
Romania **1-1** Tunisia

26 June: Stade Felix Bollaert, Lens
Colombia **0-2** England

	P	W	D	L	F	A	Pts
Romania	3	2	1	0	4	2	7
England	3	2	0	1	5	2	6
Colombia	3	1	0	2	1	3	3
Tunisia	3	0	1	2	1	4	1

Germany v Croatia, 1998

GROUP H

June 14: Municipal, Toulouse
Argentina **1-0** Japan

June 14: Stade Felix Bollaert, Lens
Jamaica **1-3** Croatia

June 20: Stade de la Beaujoire, Nantes
Japan **0-1** Croatia

June 21: Parc des Princes, Paris
Argentina **5-0** Jamaica

June 26: Parc Lescure, Bordeaux
Argentina **1-0** Croatia

June 26: Stade de Gerland, Lyon
Japan **1-2** Jamaica

	P	W	D	L	F	A	Pts
Argentina	3	3	0	0	7	0	9
Croatia	3	2	0	1	4	2	6
Jamaica	3	1	0	2	3	9	3
Japan	3	0	0	3	1	4	0

SECOND ROUND

June 27: Stade Vélodrome, Marseilles
Italy **1-0** Norway

June 27: Parc des Princes, Paris
Brazil **4-1** Chile

June 28: Stade Felix Bollaert, Lens
France **1-0** Paraguay
(aet)
France won with golden goal

June 28: Stade de France, Saint-Denis
Nigeria **1-4** Denmark

June 29: La Mosson, Montpellier
Germany **2-1** Mexico

June 29: Municipal, Toulouse
Holland **2-1** Yugoslavia

June 30: Parc Lescure, Bordeaux
Romania **0-1** Croatia

June 30: Geoffroy-Guichard, St Etienne
Argentina **2-2** England
(aet)
Argentina won 4-3 on penalties

QUARTER-FINALS

July 3: Stade de France, Saint-Denis
Italy **0-0** France
(aet)
France won 4-3 on penalties

July 3: Stade de la Beaujoire, Nantes
Brazil **3-2** Denmark

July 4: Stade Vélodrome, Marseilles
Holland **2-1** Argentina

July 4: Stade de Gerland, Lyon
Germany **0-3** Croatia

SEMI-FINALS

July 7: Stade Vélodrome, Marseilles
Brazil **1-1** Holland
(aet)
Brazil won 4-2 on penalties

July 8: Stade de France, Saint-Denis
France **2-1** Croatia

THIRD PLACE PLAY-OFF

July 11: Parc des Princes, Paris
Holland **1-2** Croatia

FINAL

July 12: Stade de France, Saint-Denis
France **3-0** Brazil

Zinédine Zidane, 1998 World Cup Final

2002

GROUP A

May 31: World Cup Stadium, Seoul
France **0-1** Senegal

June 1: Munsu Football Stadium, Ulsan
Uruguay **1-2** Denmark

June 6: World Cup Stadium, Daegu
Denmark **1-1** Senegal

June 6: Busan Asiad Main Stadium, Busan
France **0-0** Uruguay

June 11: World Cup Stadium, Suwon
Senegal **3-3** Uruguay

June 11: Incheon Munhak Stadium, Incheon
Denmark **2-0** France

	P	W	D	L	F	A	Pts
Denmark	3	2	1	0	5	2	7
Senegal	3	1	2	0	5	4	5
Uruguay	3	0	2	1	4	5	2
France	3	0	1	2	0	3	1

GROUP B

June 2: Busan Asiad Main Stadium, Busan
Paraguay **2-2** South Africa

June 2: World Cup Stadium, Gwangju
Spain **3-1** Slovenia

June 7: World Cup Stadium, Jeonju
Spain **3-1** Paraguay

June 8: World Cup Stadium, Daegu
South Africa **1-0** Slovenia

June 12: World Cup Stadium, Daejeon
South Africa **2-3** Spain

June 12: Jeju World Cup Stadium, Seogwipo
Slovenia **1-3** Paraguay

	P	W	D	L	F	A	Pts
Spain	3	3	0	0	9	4	9
Paraguay	3	1	1	1	6	6	4
South Africa	3	1	1	1	5	5	4
Slovenia	3	0	0	3	2	7	0

GROUP C

June 3: Munsu Football Stadium, Ulsan
Brazil **2-1** Turkey

June 4: World Cup Stadium, Gwangju
China **0-2** Costa Rica

June 8: Jeju World Cup Stadium, Seogwipo
Brazil **4-0** China

June 9: Incheon Munhak Stadium, Incheon
Costa Rica **1-1** Turkey

June 13: World Cup Stadium, Suwon
Costa Rica **2-5** Brazil

June 13: World Cup Stadium, Seoul
Turkey **3-0** China

	P	W	D	L	F	A	Pts
Brazil	3	3	0	0	11	3	9
Turkey	3	1	1	1	5	3	4
Costa Rica	3	1	1	1	5	6	4
China	3	0	0	3	0	9	0

GROUP D

June 4: Busan Asiad Main Stadium, Busan
South Korea **2-0** Poland

June 5: World Cup Stadium, Suwon
USA **3-2** Portugal

June 10: World Cup Stadium, Daegu
South Korea **1-1** USA

June 10: World Cup Stadium, Jeonju
Portugal **4-0** Poland

June 14: Incheon Munhak Stadium, Incheon
Portugal **0-1** South Korea

June 14: World Cup Stadium, Daejeon
Poland **3-1** USA

	P	W	D	L	F	A	Pts
South Korea	3	2	1	0	4	1	7
USA	3	1	1	1	5	6	4
Portugal	3	1	0	2	6	4	3
Poland	3	1	0	2	3	7	3

GROUP E

June 1: Niigata Big Swan Stadium, Niigata
Rep. Of Ireland **1-1** Cameroon

June 1: Sapporo Dome, Sapporo
Germany **8-0** Saudi Arabia

June 5: Kashima Stadium, Ibaraki
Germany **1-1** Rep. Of Ireland

June 6: Saitama Stadium 2002, Saitama
Cameroon **1-0** Saudi Arabia

June 11: Shizuoka Stadium Ecopa, Shizuoka
Cameroon **0-2** Germany

June 11: International Stadium, Yokohama
Saudi Arabia **0-3** Rep. Of Ireland

	P	W	D	L	F	A	Pts
Germany	3	2	1	0	11	1	7
Rep. Of Ireland	3	1	2	0	5	2	5
Cameroon	3	1	1	1	2	3	4
Saudi Arabia	3	0	0	3	0	12	0

GROUP F

June 2: Kashima Stadium, Ibaraki
Argentina **1-0** Nigeria

June 2: Saitama Stadium 2002, Saitama
England **1-1** Sweden

June 7: Kobe Wing Stadium, Kobe
Sweden **2-1** Nigeria

June 7: Sapporo Dome, Sapporo
Argentina **0-1** England

June 12: Miyagi Stadium, Miyagi
Sweden **1-1** Argentina

June 12: Osaka Nagai Stadium, Osaka
Nigeria **0-0** England

	P	W	D	L	F	A	Pts
Sweden	3	1	2	0	4	3	5
England	3	1	2	0	2	1	5
Argentina	3	1	1	1	2	2	4
Nigeria	3	0	1	2	1	3	1

GROUP G

June 3: Niigata Big Swan Stadium, Niigata
Croatia **0-1** Mexico

June 3: Sapporo Dome, Sapporo
Italy **2-0** Ecuador

June 8: Kashima Stadium, Ibaraki
Italy **1-2** Croatia

June 9: Miyagi Stadium, Miyagi
Mexico **2-1** Ecuador

June 13: Oita Big Eye Stadium, Oita
Mexico **1-1** Italy

June 13: International Stadium, Yokohama
Ecuador **1-0** Croatia

	P	W	D	L	F	A	Pts
Mexico	3	2	1	0	4	2	7
Italy	3	1	1	1	4	3	4
Croatia	3	1	0	2	2	3	3
Ecuador	3	1	0	2	2	4	3

GROUP H

June 4: Saitama Stadium 2002, Saitama
Japan **2-2** Belgium

June 5: Kobe Wing Stadium, Kobe
Russia **2-0** Tunisia

June 9: International Stadium, Yokohama
Japan **1-0** Russia

June 10: Oita Big Eye Stadium, Oita
Tunisia **1-1** Belgium

June 14: Osaka Nagai Stadium, Osaka
Tunisia **0-2** Japan

June 14: Shizuoka Stadium Ecopa, Shizuoka
Belgium **3-2** Russia

	P	W	D	L	F	A	Pts
Japan	3	2	1	0	5	2	7
Belgium	3	1	2	0	6	5	5
Russia	3	1	0	2	4	4	3
Tunisia	3	0	1	2	1	5	1

SECOND ROUND

June 15: Jeju World Cup Stadium, Seogwipo
Germany **1-0** Paraguay

June 15: Niigata Big Swan Stadium, Niigata
Denmark **0-3** England

June 16: Oita Big Eye Stadium, Oita
Sweden **1-2** Senegal
(aet)
Senegal won with golden goal

June 16: World Cup Stadium, Suwon
Spain **1-1** Rep. Of Ireland
(aet)
Spain won 3-2 on penalties

June 17: World Cup Stadium, Jeonju
Mexico **0-2** USA

June 17: Kobe Wing Stadium, Kobe
Brazil **2-0** Belgium

Japan v Russia, 2002

Italy v France, 2006 World Cup Final

June 18: Miyagi Stadium, Miyagi
Japan **0-1** Turkey

June 18: World Cup Stadium, Daejeon
South Korea **2-1** Italy
(aet)
South Korea won with golden goal

QUARTER-FINALS

June 21: Shizuoka Stadium Ecopa, Shizuoka
England **1-2** Brazil

June 21: Munsu Football Stadium, Ulsan
Germany **1-0** USA

June 22: World Cup Stadium, Gwangju
Spain **0-0** South Korea
(aet)
South Korea won 5-3 on penalties

June 22: Osaka Nagai Stadium, Osaka
Senegal **0-1** Turkey
(aet)
Turkey won with golden goal

SEMI-FINALS

June 25: World Cup Stadium, Seoul
Germany **1-0** South Korea

June 26: Saitama Stadium, Saitama
Brazil **1-0** Turkey

THIRD PLACE PLAY-OFF

June 29: World Cup Stadium, Daegu
South Korea **2-3** Turkey

FINAL

June 30: International Stadium, Yokohama
Brazil **2-0** Germany

2006

GROUP A

June 9: Allianz Stadium, Munich
Germany **4-2** Costa Rica

June 9: Arena AufSchalke, Gelsenkirchen
Poland **0-2** Ecuador

June 14: Westfalenstadion, Dortmund
Germany **1-0** Poland

June 15: AOL Arena, Hamburg
Ecuador **3-0** Costa Rica

June 20: Olympiastadion, Berlin
Ecuador **0-3** Germany

June 20: AWD-Arena, Hanover
Costa Rica **1-2** Poland

	P	W	D	L	F	A	Pts
Germany	3	3	0	0	8	2	9
Ecuador	3	2	0	1	5	3	6
Poland	3	1	0	2	2	4	3
Costa Rica	3	0	0	3	3	9	0

GROUP B

June 10: Waldstadion, Frankfurt
England **1-0** Paraguay

June 10: Westfalenstadion, Dortmund
Trinidad & T. **0-0** Sweden

June 15: Frankenstadion, Nuremberg
England **2-0** Trinidad & T.

June 15: Olympiastadion, Berlin
Sweden **1-0** Paraguay

June 20: Fritz-Walter-Stadion, Kaiserslautern
Paraguay **2-0** Trinidad & T.

June 20: Rhein-Energie Stadium, Cologne
Sweden **2-2** England

	P	W	D	L	F	A	Pts
England	3	2	1	0	5	2	7
Sweden	3	1	2	0	3	2	5
Paraguay	3	1	0	2	2	2	3
Trinidad & T.	3	0	1	2	0	4	1

GROUP C

June 10: AOL Arena, Hamburg
Argentina **2-1** Ivory Coast

June 11: Zentralstadion, Leipzig
Serbia & Mont. **0-1** Holland

June 16: Arena AufSchalke, Gelsenkirchen
Argentina **6-0** Serbia & Mont.

June 16: Gottleib-Daimler, Stuttgart
Holland **2-1** Ivory Coast

June 21: Waldstadion, Frankfurt
Holland **0-0** Argentina

June 21: Allianz Stadium, Munich
Ivory Coast **3-2** Serbia & Mont.

	P	W	D	L	F	A	Pts
Argentina	3	2	1	0	8	1	7
Holland	3	2	1	0	3	1	7
Ivory Coast	3	1	0	2	5	6	3
Serbia & Mont.	3	0	0	3	2	10	0

GROUP D

June 11: Frankenstadion, Nuremberg
Mexico **3-1** Iran

June 11: Rhein-Energie Stadium, Cologne
Angola **0-1** Portugal

June 16: AWD-Arena, Hanover
Mexico **0-0** Angola

June 17: Waldstadion, Frankfurt
Portugal **2-0** Iran

June 21: Arena AufSchalke, Gelsenkirchen
Portuga **2-1** Mexico

June 21: Zentralstadion, Leipzig
Iran **1-1** Angola

	P	W	D	L	F	A	Pts
Portugal	3	3	0	0	5	1	9
Mexico	3	1	1	1	4	3	4
Angola	3	0	2	1	1	2	2
Iran	3	0	1	2	2	6	1

GROUP E

June 12: Arena AufSchalke, Gelsenkirchen
United States **0-3** Czech Republic

June 12: AWD-Arena, Hanover
Italy **2-0** Ghana

June 17: Fritz-Walter-Stadion, Kaiserslautern
Italy **1-1** United States

June 17: Rhein-Energie Stadium, Cologne
Czech Republic **0-2** Ghana

June 22: AOL Arena, Hamburg
Czech Republic **0-2** Italy

June 22: Frankenstadion, Nuremberg
Ghana **2-1** United States

	P	W	D	L	F	A	Pts
Italy	3	2	1	0	5	1	7
Ghana	3	2	0	1	4	3	6
Czech Republic	3	1	0	2	3	4	3
USA	3	0	1	2	2	6	1

GROUP F

June 12: Fritz-Walter-Stadion, Kaiserslautern
Australia **3-1** Japan

June 13: Olympiastadion, Berlin
Brazil **1-0** Croatia

June 18: Frankenstadion, Nuremberg
Japan **0-0** Croatia

June 18: Allianz Stadium, Munich
Brazil **2-0** Australia

June 22: Westfalenstadion, Dortmund
Japan **1-4** Brazil

June 22: Gottleib-Daimler, Stuttgart
Croatia **2-2** Australia

	P	W	D	L	F	A	Pts
Brazil	3	3	0	0	7	1	9
Australia	3	1	1	1	5	5	4
Croatia	3	0	2	1	2	3	2
Japan	3	0	1	2	2	7	1

GROUP G

June 13: Waldstadion, Frankfurt
South Korea **2-1** Togo

June 13: Gottleib-Daimler, Stuttgart
France **0-0** Switzerland

June 18: Zentralstadion, Leipzig
France **1-1** South Korea

June 19: Westfalenstadion, Dortmund
Togo **0-2** Switzerland

June 23: Rhein-Energie Stadium, Cologne
Togo **0-2** France

June 23: AWD-Arena, Hanover
Switzerland **2-0** South Korea

	P	W	D	L	F	A	Pts
Switzerland	3	2	1	0	4	0	7
France	3	1	2	0	3	1	5
South Korea	3	1	1	1	3	4	4
Togo	3	0	0	3	1	6	0

GROUP H

June 14: Zentralstadion, Leipzig
Spain **4-0** Ukraine

June 14: Allianz Stadium, Munich
Tunisia **2-2** Saudi Arabia

June 19: Gottleib-Daimler, Stuttgart
Spain **3-1** Tunisia

June 19: AOL Arena, Hamburg
Saudi Arabia **0-4** Ukraine

June 23: Fritz-Walter-Stadion, Kaiserslautern
Saudi Arabia **0-1** Spain

June 23: Olympiastadion, Berlin
Ukraine **1-0** Tunisia

	P	W	D	L	F	A	Pts
Spain	3	3	0	0	8	1	9
Ukraine	3	2	0	1	5	4	6
Tunisia	3	0	1	2	3	6	1
Saudi Arabia	3	0	1	2	2	7	1

2ND ROUND

June 24: Allianz Stadium, Munich
Germany **2-0** Sweden

June 24: Zentralstadion, Leipzig
Argentina **2-1** Mexico
(aet)

June 25: Gottleib-Daimler, Stuttgart
England **1-0** Ecuador

June 25: Frankenstadion, Nuremberg
Portugal **1-0** Holland

June 26: Fritz-Walter-Stadion, Kaiserslautern
Italy **1-0** Australia

June 26: Rhein-Energie Stadium, Cologne
Switzerland **0-0** Ukraine
(aet)
Ukraine won 3-0 on penalties

June 27: Westfalenstadion, Dortmund
Brazil **3-0** Ghana

June 27: AWD-Arena, Hanover
Spain **1-3** France

QUARTER-FINALS

June 30: Olympiastadion, Berlin
Germany **1-1** Argentina
(aet)
Germany won 4-2 on penalties

June 30: AOL Arena, Hamburg
Italy **3-0** Ukraine

July 1: Arena AufSchalke, Gelsenkirchen
England **0-0** Portugal
(aet)
Portugal won 3-1 on penalties

July 1: Waldstadion, Frankfurt
Brazil **0-1** France

SEMI-FINALS

July 4: Westfalenstadion, Dortmund
Germany **0-2** Italy

July 5: Allianz Stadium, Munich
Portugal **0-1** France

THIRD PLACE PLAY-OFF

July 8: Gottleib-Daimler, Stuttgart
Germany **3-1** Portugal

FINAL

July 9: Olympiastadion, Berlin
Italy **1-1** France
(aet)
Italy won 5-3 on penalties

THE FINALISTS

How each finalist has fared in qualification and at the tournament...

	1930	1934	1938	1950	1954	1958	1962	1966	1970	1974	1978	1982	1986	1990	1994	1998	2002	2006	2010
ALGERIA												R1 13th	R1 22nd						●
ANGOLA																		R1 23rd	
ARGENTINA	2nd	R1 =9th				R1 13th	R1 10th	QF 5th		QF 8th	1st	R2 11th	1st	2nd	R2 10th	QF 6th	R1 18th	QF 6th	●
AUSTRALIA										R1 14th								R2 16th	●
AUSTRIA		4th	X		3rd	R1 15th					QF 7th	R2 8th		R1 =18th		R1 23rd			
BELGIUM	R1 11th	R1 15th	R1 13th		R1 12th				R1 =10th			R2 10th	4th	R2 11th	R2 11th	R1 19th	R2 14th		
BOLIVIA	R1 12th			R1 13th											R1 21st				
BRAZIL	R1 6th	R1 14th	3rd	2nd	QF 5th	1st	1st	R1 11th	1st	4th	3rd	R2 5th	QF 5th	R2 9th	1st	2nd	1st	QF 5th	●
BULGARIA							R1 15th	R1 15th	R1 13th	R1 12th			R2 15th		4th	R1 29th			
CAMEROON												R1 17th		QF 7th	R1 22nd	R1 25th	R1 20th		●
CANADA													R1 24th						
CHILE	R1 5th			R1 9th			3rd	R1 =13th		R1 11th		R1 22nd				R2 16th			●
CHINA																	R1 31st		
COLOMBIA							R1 14th							R2 14th	R1 19th	R1 21st			
CONGO DR										R1 16th									
COSTA RICA														R2 13th			R1 19th	R1 31st	
COTE D'IVOIRE																		R1 19th	●
CROATIA	Part of Yugoslavia until 1991															3rd	R1 23rd	R1 22nd	
CUBA			QF 8th																
CZECHOSLOVAKIA		2nd	QF 5th		R1 14th	R1 9th	2nd		R1 15th			R1 19th		QF 6th	See Czech Republic & Slovakia				
CZECH REPUBLIC	Part of Czechoslovakia until 1993																	R1 20th	
DENMARK													R2 9th			QF 8th	R2 10th		●
DUTCH EAST INDIES	See Indonisia (competed as Dutch East Indies 1930-1938)																		
EAST GERMANY	Part of Germany									QF 6th					Part of Germany				
ECUADOR																	R1 24th	R2 12th	
EGYPT		R1 13th												R1 20th					
EL SALVADOR									R1 16th			R1 24th							
ENGLAND				R1 8th	QF 6th	R1 11th	QF 8th	1st	QF 8th			R2 6th	QF 8th	4th		R2 9th	QF 6th	QF 7th	●
FRANCE	R1 7th	R1 =9th	QF 6th		R1 11th	3rd		R1 =13th			R1 12th	4th	3rd			1st	R1 28th	2nd	●
GERMANY		3rd	R1 10th		1st	4th	QF 7th	2nd	3rd	1st	QF 6th	2nd	2nd	1st	QF 5th	QF 7th	2nd	3rd	●
GHANA																		R2 13th	●
GREECE															R1 24th				●
HAITI										R1 15th									
HONDURAS												R1 18th							●
HUNGARY		QF 6th	2nd		2nd	R1 10th	QF 5th	QF 6th			R1 15th	R1 14th	R1 18th						
INDONESIA			R1 15th																
IRAN											R1 14th					R1 20th		R1 =25th	
IRAQ													R1 23rd						
ISRAEL									R1 12th										
ITALY		1st	1st	R1 7th	R1 10th		R1 9th	R1 9th	2nd	R1 10th	4th	1st	R2 12th	3rd	2nd	QF 5th	R2 15th	1st	●
JAMAICA																R1 22nd			
JAPAN																R1 31st	R2 9th	R1 =2[illegible]th	●

- **1st** Winner
- **2nd** Runner-up
- **3rd** Third place
- **4th** Fourth place
- **SF** Semi-finals (1930 only, when no third-place match was held)
- **QF** Quarter-finals (knockout round of eight teams, except 1974-78 when replaced by second group stage of eight teams)
- **R1** Round 1
- **R2** Round 2 (second group stage of 12 teams in 1982; a knockout round of 16 from 1986)
- ● 2010 finalist
- Did not qualify
- X Qualified but withdrew
- Did not enter/withdrew
- Hosts

	1930	1934	1938	1950	1954	1958	1962	1966	1970	1974	1978	1982	1986	1990	1994	1998	2002	2006	2010
KOREA DPR	North Korea							QF 8th											●
KOREA REPUBLIC	South Korea				R1 16th								R1 20th	R1 22nd	R1 20th	R1 30th	4th (hosts)	R1 17th	●
KUWAIT												R1 21st							
MEXICO	R1 13th			R1 12th	R1 13th	R1 16th	R1 11th	R1 12th	QF 6th (hosts)		R1 16th		QF 6th (hosts)		R2 13th	R2 13th	R2 11th	R2 15th	●
MOROCCO									R1 14th				R2 11th		R1 23rd	R1 18th			
NETHERLANDS		R1 =9th	R1 14th							2nd	2nd			R2 15th	QF 7th	4th		R2 15th	●
NEW ZEALAND												R1 23rd							●
NIGERIA															R2 9th	R2 12th	R1 27th		●
NORTHERN IRELAND						QF 8th						R2 9th	R1 21st						
NORWAY			R1 12th												R1 17th	R2 15th			
PARAGUAY	R1 9th			R1 11th		R1 12th							R2 13th			R2 14th	R2 16th	R1 18th	●
PERU	R1 10th								QF 7th		QF 8th	R1 20th							
POLAND			R1 11th							3rd	QF 5th	3rd	R2 14th				R1 25th	R1 21st	
PORTUGAL								3rd					R1 17th				R1 21st	4th	●
REPUBLIC OF IRELAND														QF 8th	R2 16th		R2 12th		
ROMANIA	R1 8th	R1 12th	R1 9th						R1 =10th					R2 12th	QF 6th	R2 11th			
RUSSIA						QF 7th	QF 6th	4th	QF 5th			R2 7th	R2 10th	R1 17th	R1 18th		R1 22nd		
SAUDI ARABIA															R2 12th	R1 28th	R1 32nd	R1 =28th	
SCOTLAND				X	R1 15th	R1 14th				R1 9th	R1 11th	R1 15th	R1 19th	R1 =18th		R1 27th			
SENEGAL																	QF 7th		
SERBIA	SF 4th			R1 5th	QF 7th	QF 5th	4th			QF 7th		R1 16th		QF 5th		R2 10th		R1 32nd	●
SERBIA & MONTENEGRO	See Serbia (competed as Serbia & Montenegro 2003-2006)																		
SLOVAKIA	Part of Czechoslovakia until 1993																		●
SLOVENIA	Part of Yugoslavia until 1991																R1 30th		●
SOUTH AFRICA																R1 24th	R1 17th		● (hosts)
SOVIET UNION	See Russia (competed as Soviet Union until 1991)																		
SPAIN		QF 5th		4th			R1 12th	R1 10th			R1 10th	R2 12th	QF 7th	R2 10th	QF 8th	R1 17th	QF 5th	R2 9th	●
SWEDEN		QF 8th	4th	3rd		2nd (hosts)			R1 9th	QF 5th	R1 13th			R1 21st	3rd		R2 13th	R2 14th	
SWITZERLAND		QF 7th	QF 7th	R1 6th	QF 8th (hosts)		R1 16th	R1 16th							R2 15th			R2 10th	●
TOGO																		R1 30th	
TRINIDAD & TOBAGO																		R1 27th	
TUNISIA											R1 9th					R1 26th	R1 29th	R1 24th	
TURKEY				X	R1 9th												3rd		
UKRAINE	Part of the Soviet Union until 1990																	QF 8th	
UNITED ARAB EMIRATES														R1 24th					
UNITED STATES	SF 3rd	R1 16th		R1 10th										R1 23rd	R2 14th (hosts)	R1 32nd	QF 8th	R1 =25th	●
URUGUAY	1st (hosts)			1st	4th		R1 13th	QF 7th	4th	R1 12th			R2 16th	R2 16th			R1 26th		●
WALES						QF 6th													
WEST GERMANY	See Germany (competed as West Germany 1954-1990)																		
YUGOSLAVIA	See Serbia (competed as Yugoslavia until 2003)																		
ZAÏRE	See Congo DR (competed as Zaïre until 1974)																		

PLAYER RECORDS

MOST APPEARANCES IN A WORLD CUP FINAL
3 Cafu (Brazil)

MOST APPEARANCES AS CAPTAIN
16 **Diego Maradona** (Argentina)

MOST APPEARANCES AS SUBSTITUTE
11 **Denílson** (Brazil)

YOUNGEST PLAYER
17 years and 41 days **Norman Whiteside** (Northern Ireland, 1982)

YOUNGEST PLAYER IN A FINAL
17 years and 249 days **Pelé** (Brazil, 1958)

YOUNGEST CAPTAIN
21 years and 109 days **Tony Meola** (USA, 1990)

OLDEST PLAYER
42 years and 39 days **Roger Milla** (Cameroon, 1994)

OLDEST PLAYER IN A FINAL
40 years and 133 days **Dino Zoff** (Italy, 1982)

OLDEST CAPTAIN
40 years and 292 days **Peter Shilton** (England, 1990)

MOST GOALS SCORED IN A MATCH
5 **Oleg Salenko** (Russia v Cameroon, 1994)

MOST GOALS SCORED IN A LOST MATCH
4 **Ernest Wilimowski** (Poland, v Brazil, 1938)

MOST GOALS SCORED IN A FINAL
3 **Geoff Hurst** (England, v West Germany, 1966)

RECORD GOALSCORER

1	**Ronaldo** (Brazil)	15
2	**Gerd Müller** (Germany)	14
3	**Just Fontaine** (France)	13
4	**Pelé** (Brazil)	12
5	**Sandor Kocsis** (Hungary)	11
=	**Jürgen Klinsmann** (Germany)	11
7	**Helmut Rahn** (Germany)	10
=	**Teófilio Cubillas** (Peru)	10
=	**Gary Lineker** (England)	10
=	**Grzegorz Lato** (Poland)	10
=	**Gabriel Batistuta** (Argentina)	10
=	**Miroslav Klose** (Germany)	10
13	**Roberto Baggio** (Italy)	9
=	**Paolo Rossi** (Italy)	9
=	**Uwe Seeler** (Germany)	9
=	**Jairzinho** (Brazil)	9
=	**Eusébio** (Portugal)	9
=	**Karl-Heinz Rummenigge** (Germany)	9
=	**Ademir** (Brazil)	9
=	**Vavá** (Brazil)	9
=	**Christian Vieri** (Italy)	9

MOST GOALS SCORED IN A TOURNAMENT

1	**Just Fontaine** (France, 1958)	13
2	**Sandor Kocsis** (Hungary, 1954)	11
3	**Gerd Müller** (Germany, 1970)	10
4	**Ademir** (Brazil, 1950)	9
=	**Eusébio** (Portugal, 1966)	9
6	**Guillermo Stábile** (Argentina, 1930)	8
=	**Ronaldo** (Brazil, 2002)	8
8	**Leônidas** (Brazil, 1938)	7
=	**Jairzinho** (Brazil, 1970)	7
=	**Gregorz Lato** (Poland, 1974)	7

MOST TOURNAMENTS
5 **Lothar Matthäus** (Germany) 1982, 1986, 1990, 1994, 1998

5 **Antonio Carbajal** (Mexico) 1950, 1954, 1958, 1962, 1966

PLAYERS WHO HAVE WON TWO WORLD CUP FINALS

Giovanni Ferrari (Italy) 1934, 1938
Giuseppe Meazza (Italy) 1934, 1938
Pelé (Brazil) 1958, 1970
Didi (Brazil) 1958, 1962
Djalma Santos (Brazil) 1958, 1962
Garrincha (Brazil) 1958, 1962
Gilmar (Brazil) 1958, 1962
Nílton Santos (Brazil) 1958, 1962
Vavá (Brazil) 1958, 1962
Zagallo (Brazil) 1958, 1962
Zito (Brazil) 1958, 1962
Cafu (Brazil) 1994, 2002

includes only players who appeared in the final

RECORD APPEARANCES

1	**Lothar Matthäus** (Germany)	25
2	**Paolo Maldini** (Italy)	23
3	**Diego Maradona** (Argentina)	21
=	**Wladislaw Zmuda** (Poland)	21
=	**Uwe Seeler** (Germany)	21
6	**Grzegorz Lato** (Poland)	20
=	**Cafu** (Brazil)	20
8	**Berti Vogts** (Germany)	19
=	**Karl-Heinz Rummenigge** (Germany)	19
=	**Wolfgang Overath** (Germany)	19
=	**Ronaldo** (Brazil)	19
12	**Claudio Taffarel** (Brazil)	18
=	**Franz Beckenbauer** (Germany)	18
=	**Pierre Littbarski** (Germany)	18
=	**Gaetano Scirea** (Italy)	18
=	**Antonio Cabrini** (Italy)	18
=	**Thomas Berthold** (Germany)	18
=	**Mario Kempes** (Argentina)	18
=	**Sepp Maier** (Germany)	18
=	**Carlos Dunga** (Brazil)	18

TEAM RECORDS

MOST WORLD CHAMPIONSHIPS
5 Brazil

MOST APPEARANCES IN A WORLD CUP FINAL
7 Brazil and Germany

MOST APPEARANCES IN SEMI-FINAL/LAST FOUR
11 Germany

MOST MATCHES
92 Germany and Brazil

FEWEST MATCHES
1 Indonesia (as Dutch East Indies)

MOST WINS
64 Brazil

MOST DEFEATS
22 Mexico

MOST DRAWS
19 Germany and Italy

MOST GOALS SCORED
201 Brazil

MOST GOALS CONCEDED
112 Germany

FEWEST GOALS SCORED
0 Canada, China, Congo DR (as Zaïre), Greece, Indonesia (as Dutch East Indies), Trinidad & Tobago

FEWEST GOALS CONCEDED
2 Angola

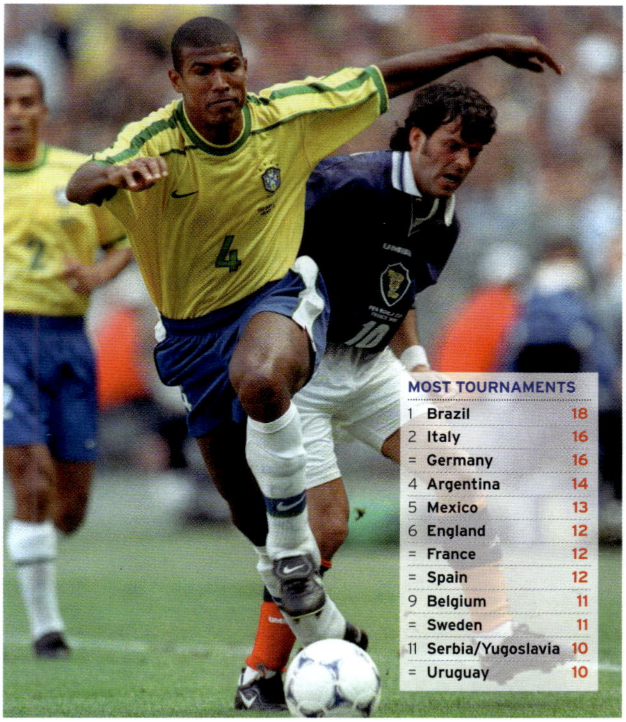

MOST TOURNAMENTS

1	Brazil	18
2	Italy	16
=	Germany	16
4	Argentina	14
5	Mexico	13
6	England	12
=	France	12
=	Spain	12
9	Belgium	11
=	Sweden	11
11	Serbia/Yugoslavia	10
=	Uruguay	10

BIGGEST VICTORIES

1	Hungary v El Salvador, 1982	10-1
2	Hungary v South Korea, 1954	9-0
=	Yugoslavia v Zaïre, 1974	9-0
4	Sweden v Cuba, 1938	8-0
=	Uruguay v Bolivia, 1950	8-0
=	Germany v Saudi Arabia, 2002	8-0

MOST GOALS IN ONE MATCH

1	Austria v Switzerland, 1954 (7-5)	12
2	Brazil v Poland, 1938 (6-5)	11
=	Hungary v West Germany, 1954 (8-3)	11
=	Hungary v El Salvador, 1982 (10-1)	11
5	France v Paraguay 1958 (7-3)	10

PENALTY SHOOT-OUT TABLE

		W	L	F	A
1	Germany	4	0	17	10
2	Argentina	3	1	13	12
3	Brazil	2	1	10	8
4	France	2	2	15	16
5	Ukraine	1	0	3	0
6	South Korea	1	0	5	3
7	Bulgaria	1	0	3	1
=	Portugal	1	0	3	1
9	Belgium	1	0	5	4
=	Sweden	1	0	5	4
11	Rep. of Ireland	1	1	7	7
12	Spain	1	2	10	12
13	Italy	1	3	13	14
14	Yugoslavia	0	1	2	3
15	Holland	0	1	2	4
16	Switzerland	0	1	0	3
17	Romania	0	2	8	10
18	Mexico	0	2	2	7
19	England	0	3	7	11

PENALTY SHOOT-OUT SUCCESS RATE

		Penalties	Scored	Success Rate
1	Belgium	5	5	100.0%
=	South Korea	5	5	100.0%
3	Germany	18	17	94.4%
4	Sweden	6	5	83.3%
5	Brazil	13	10	76.9%
6	France	20	15	75.0%
=	Bulgaria	4	3	75.0%
=	Ukraine	4	3	75.0%
9	Romania	11	8	72.7%
10	Argentina	18	13	72.2%
11	Spain	14	10	71.4%
12	Rep of Ireland	10	7	70.0%
13	Italy	20	13	65.0%
14	Portugal	5	3	60.0%
15	England	14	7	50.0%
=	Holland	4	2	50.0%
16	Yugoslavia	5	2	40.0%
17	Mexico	7	2	28.6%
18	Switzerland	3	0	0.0%

MOST WINS IN A TOURNAMENT
7 Brazil (2002)

MOST GOALS SCORED IN A TOURNAMENT
27 Hungary (1954)

FEWEST GOALS CONCEDED IN A TOURNAMENT
0 Switzerland (2006)

MOST GOALS CONCEDED IN A TOURNAMENT
16 South Korea (1954)

MOST MINUTES WITHOUT CONCEDING A GOAL
517 minutes Italy (1990)

MOST GOALS SCORED BECOMING CHAMPIONS
25 Germany (1954)

FEWEST GOALS SCORED BECOMING CHAMPIONS
11 Italy (1938), England (1966) and Brazil (1994)

FEWEST GOALS CONCEDED BECOMING CHAMPIONS
2 France (1998) and Italy (2006)

MOST GOALS CONCEDED BECOMING CHAMPIONS
14 Germany (1954)

MOST GOALS SCORED IN A TOURNAMENT
171 goals 1998

FEWEST GOALS SCORED IN A TOURNAMENT
70 goals 1930 and 1934

MOST GOALS PER MATCH IN A TOURNAMENT
5.38 goals per match 1954

MOST GOALS PER MATCH IN A TOURNAMENT
5.38 goals per match 1954

FEWEST GOALS PER MATCH IN A TOURNAMENT
2.21 goals per match 1990

MOST TOURNAMENTS WITHOUT REACHING SECOND ROUND
8 Scotland

RITZ
la galleta
BASF Magnetic

NATIONS OF THE WORLD CUP

KEY ★/☆ - *World Cup winner/runner-up*
[2010] - *2010 World Cup qualifier*
2006 - *Host nation*

Every World Cup finalist, 1930-2010

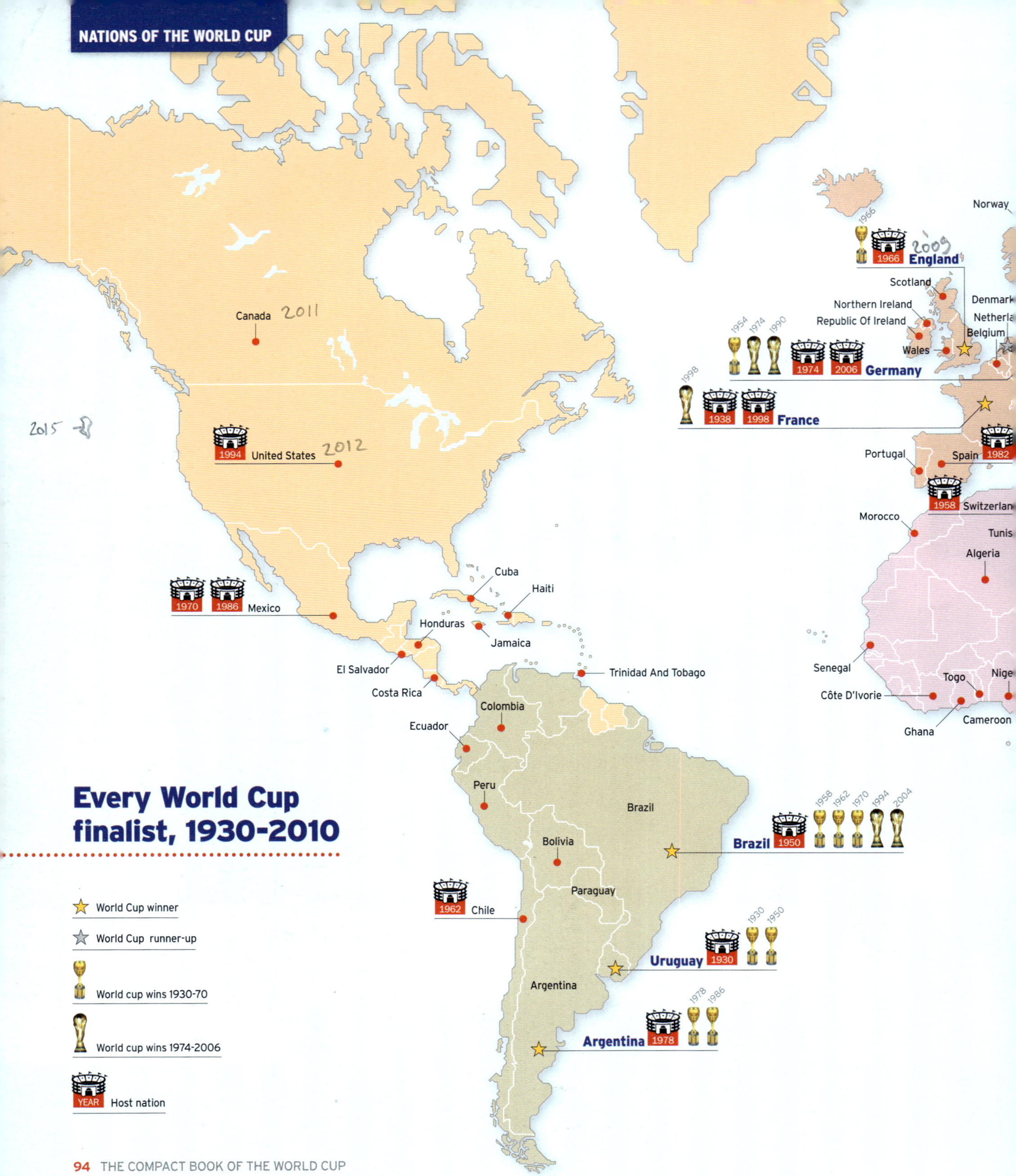

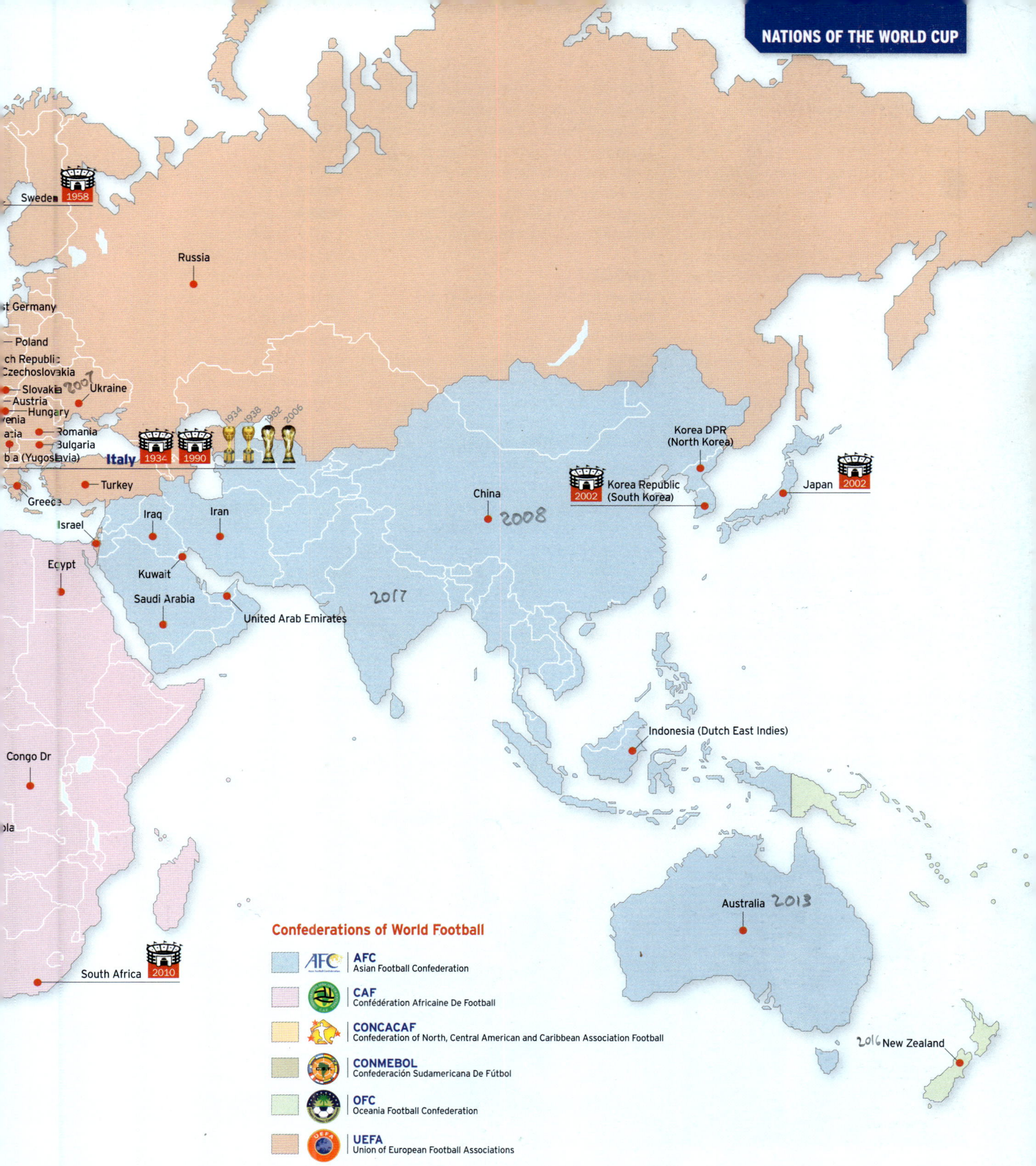
Sweden 1958
Russia
Germany
Poland
Czech Republic
Czechoslovakia
Slovakia
Ukraine
2007
Austria
Hungary
Romania
Bulgaria
(Yugoslavia)
Italy 1934 1990
1934 1938 1982 2006
Turkey
Greece
Israel
Iraq
Iran
Kuwait
Egypt
Saudi Arabia
United Arab Emirates
China
2008
2017
Korea DPR
(North Korea)
Korea Republic
(South Korea) 2002
Japan 2002
Indonesia (Dutch East Indies)
Congo Dr
Australia
2013
2016
New Zealand
South Africa 2010
Confederations of World Football
AFC
Asian Football Confederation
CAF
Confédération Africaine De Football
CONCACAF
Confederation of North, Central American and Caribbean Association Football
CONMEBOL
Confederación Sudamericana De Fútbol
OFC
Oceania Football Confederation
UEFA
Union of European Football Associations

ALGERIA

Joined FIFA: 1963 **Confederation:** CAF

Finals: 1982, 86, [2010]

Record: P6/W2/D1/L3/F6/A10

The greatest moment in Algerian football history was the shock 2-1 defeat of West Germany at the 1982 World Cup. Coach Mahieddine Khalef's team gave a resolute defensive performance against the attacking Germans, with goals from Rabah Madjer and Lakhdar Belloumi earning the landmark victory.

Despite another group win over Chile, the Algerians were cheated out of a second round place by 'The Great Gijón Swindle'. With West Germany playing Austria the day after Algeria's final group game, both teams knew what was needed and a convenient 1-0 win for the Germans at Gijón's Estadio El Molinón sent Austria and West Germany through at Algeria's expense. The crowd waved white handkerchiefs at the players to suggest that a truce had been agreed.

By the following tournament in Mexico the consequences of this match resulted in a change to World Cup rules, ensuring that deciding group games would always be played at the same time to prevent one team having an advantage. It proved little consolation to the Algerians, who failed to win a game at the 1986 World Cup when grouped with Brazil, Northern Ireland and Spain. The Algerians were obviously a team in decline by this time, gaining just a point from the opening fixture with Northern Ireland and losing to both Brazil and Spain.

Algeria would not reach the World Cup again until the 2010 tournament, when qualification went down to the wire. Having finished the group with an identical record to Egypt, the teams had to be separated with a tiebreaking play-off, which Algeria duly won.

Lakhdar Belloumi, Algeria v West Germany, 1982

ANGOLA

Joined FIFA: 1980 **Confederation:** CAF

Finals: 2006

Record: P3/W0/D2/L1/F/A2

For a country that has been blighted by over 30 years of bloody civil war, Angola's first World Cup qualification in 2006, under coach Luís Oliveira Gonçalves, was nothing short of incredible. The 'Palancas Negras' (Black Impalas) had only previously appeared in three African Nations Cup tournaments, and at the 2006 finals they proved that they could mix it with the best.

Narrowly losing their opening game to Portugal, the Angolans went on to earn their first World Cup point after a goalless draw with Mexico. They finished the tie with ten men following the red carding of Andre Macanga, but the result inspired wild celebrations from their fans. A 1-1 draw with Iran signalled the end of their tournament.

Historically many Angolan-born players have been raised in Portugal and the national team does its best to recruit from the European leagues.

Flavio Amado, Angola v Iran, 2006

ARGENTINA★★

Joined FIFA: 1912 **Confederation:** CONMEBOL

Finals: 1930★, 34, 58, 62, 66, 74, **78**★, 82, 86★, 90★, 94, 98, 2002, 06, [2010]

Record: P65/W33/D13/L19/F113/A74

Argentina's football history can be traced back to 1867, when immigrant English and Italian rail workers and sailors introduced the game to the South American country. By the time of the first World Cup tournament in 1930, Argentina had a fiercely competitive team, the most notorious of whom was defender Luis Monti, the most aggressive player of his time.

Winning all three of their group games, the Argentinians left a trail of injuries wherever they played. However, after a 6-1 victory over USA in the semi-finals, Monti was strangely anonymous in the final as Argentina lost 4-2 to hosts and old foes Uruguay. At least Guillermo Stábille ended the tournament as top scorer, his eight goals in four games achieved despite making his international debut in Argentina's second game. It would take 48 more years for Argentina to come that close to winning the trophy again.

Although the country's domestic football had turned professional in 1931, a team of amateurs was sent to the finals in 1934, only one of whom had been capped previously. A 3-2 defeat to Sweden in the first round saw them eliminated and none of the players would gain another cap. Indeed, Argentina would not enter the tournament again until the 1958 competition, conceding six goals to Czechoslovakia at the finals when they needed only to draw to force a play-off.

Chastened by the experience, they took a much more cynical approach to their campaign in 1962, selecting a team capable of aggressive tackling and defensive play. Yet they were taken apart by England and drew with a Hungarian team who were already through, and as a consequence they failed to reach the second round yet again.

At the 1966 tournament the continued foul play of the Argentina team and the sending-off of captain Antonio Rattín in the quarter-final against England created worldwide headlines for the wrong reasons, but the following year a league restructuring

Daniel Passarella, Argentina captain, 1978 World Cup Final

programme had a positive effect on domestic football and sowed the seeds for an era of international success.

In West Germany in 1974 Argentina reached the second group stage after a tremendous strike from René Houseman earned a draw with Italy. However, the young star of Argentinian football, Mario Kempes, was not yet fulfilling his potential, and a 4-0 defeat to Holland didn't auger well. After losing 2-1 to Brazil, they took just a point from East Germany and finished bottom of the table in their group.

Argentina capitalised on staging the World Cup in 1978 by winning the trophy, although the manner of the victory wasn't always straightforward. After an impressive victory over a skilful French side that saw the Argentinians attack with speed and pace, the hosts were rocked by defeat to Italy. However, having drawn with rivals Brazil in the second group stage, they had the advantage of playing 45 minutes after their rivals, knowing that to reach the final they needed to score four goals against Peru. They had not beaten the Peruvians by this margin since their very first meeting in 1927 but after the initial exchanges Peru rolled over and Argentina hit them for six, although the match would remain the focus of allegations and conspiracy theories for years to come.

Coach César Luis Menotti had taken Argentina to their first World Cup final in 48 years. His team received a ticker tape welcome in the Monumental Stadium, Buenos Aires, before beating pre-tournament favourites Holland 3-1 in extra-time. Two goals from player of the tournament Mario Kempes made him more popular than the country's president.

While Kempes had secured his place in Argentinian football history, his star would eventually be cast into the shadows by the emerging talent of Diego Maradona, first thrust onto the world stage at the 1982 finals in Spain.

Although Maradona made an impression at the tournament with his silky skills, unrivalled ball control and wonderful dribbling, in the second round he was effectively silenced by Italy's Claudio Gentile, who gave a master class in man marking, his niggling pulls and pushes taming Maradona as Argentina lost 2-1.

In the deciding group game against Brazil, Maradona showed his suspect temperament with a rash kick at Brazil substitute Batista. Awarded a red card for the foul, he left the pitch with Argentina only three minutes away from elimination.

Bowing out in round two proved to be a temporary blip. Four years later in Mexico, Argentina were more cautious at the back and far more dangerous going forward. Coach Carlos Bilardo had gambled on naming Maradona captain, and inspired by their mercurial genius, the Argentinians powered to the final.

In the quarter-final against England, Maradona scored both goals in a 2-1 win. The first he pushed past Peter Shilton with his hand ("a little of the hand of God, a little of the head of Maradona," is how he impishly described the goal at the time) but the second saw him run from the halfway line, weaving the ball through the English defence before rounding the keeper and stroking it into the net. He scored twice more in the semi-final victory over Belgium, the second every bit as good as his wonder goal against England.

In the final against West Germany it was time for the rest of the team to perform, as Maradona was shadowed by Lothar Matthäus for much of the game. Goals from José Luis Brown and Jorge Valdano gave the Argentinians the lead, but instead of killing off the game, they allowed their opponents back on level terms, and it took a goal from Jorge Burruchaga, five minutes from time, to clinch their second world title.

Argentina again reached the final in 1990, but their unsightly mix of roughhouse tactics and a safety-first approach won them few friends. The West Germans gained revenge in a final that was settled by a questionable penalty and that saw the sending-off of Argentinians Pedro Monzón and Gustavo Dezotti, the first players to be red carded in a World Cup final. Diego Maradona's positive drugs test at the 1994 World Cup further blemished the country's reputation.

At France 98 Argentina pipped Croatia to the top of the group after a Gabriel Batistuta hat-trick contributed towards a 5-0 victory over Jamaica, but the run was ended by Holland in the quarter-finals when both teams were reduced to ten men in the last 15 minutes. Ariel Ortega's red card was for head-butting goalkeeper Edwin van der Sar, and from the resulting free-kick the Dutch scored the deciding goal.

The new century has seen a fresh generation of world-class talent grace the national team, but this has not translated into further success at the World Cup. Argentina went to the 2002 finals as second favourites, but defeat to England and a draw with Sweden resulted in a shock first round exit.

Winning the 2004 Olympic title kick-started a fresh wave of optimism, and with an exciting and hugely talented team featuring players of the calibre of Lionel Messi and Carlos Tevez, who was voted South American Player Of The Year three years running, they reached the quarter-finals of the 2006 World Cup, only to lose on penalties to Germany.

Argentina only just reached the 2010 World Cup under coach Diego Maradona, coming perilously close to failure after an unexpected 6-1 hammering by Bolivia and successive defeats to Ecuador, Brazil and Paraguay. It took an 84th minute winner away to Uruguay in the last game of the campaign to qualify for the finals.

Mark Viduka and Gennaro Gattuso Australia v Italy, 2006

AUSTRALIA 2013

Joined FIFA: 1963 **Confederation:** AFC

Finals: 1974, 2006, [2010]

Record: P7/W1/D2/L4/F5/A11

The Australians qualified for the World Cup for the first time in 1974. It was only their third attempt, but they were definitely cast as overwhelming underdogs at the finals in West Germany. Drawn in a group with the hosts, East Germany and Chile, they managed only a point from their final game against the South Americans before returning home, having failed to score a goal.

It would be 32 years before Australia reached the finals again, by which time the country's domestic football structure had been completely overhauled. A 2005 revamp of their governing body saw the word 'soccer' dropped in favour of 'football', helping to rebrand the sport in Australia.

The switch from the Oceania Football Confederation to its Asian equivalent in 2006 was aimed at improving the standard of the national team and to give them more chance of reaching to the finals on a regular basis. Australia's last role as a member of the OFC was to represent the region at the World Cup in Germany.

In 2006 Australia fielded a squad of mostly European-based players. Of the 23-man squad for the 2006 finals only two were with Australian clubs, a stark contrast with the exclusively home-based 1974 squad

The Australians were unbeaten in the qualifying campaign for the 2010 World Cup, finishing ahead of Japan in their group.

AUSTRIA

Joined FIFA: 1905 **Confederation:** UEFA

Finals: 1934, 54, 58, 78, 82, 90, 98

Record: P29/W12/D4/L13/F43/A47

Austria's best years in the World Cup were in the earliest days of the competition, when the team was ranked among the strongest nations in Europe. By that time the Austrians already had a long heritage in the game, having staged the first international football match between European nations outside of Britain in 1902.

In the early years of the century Vienna was viewed as a centre of football excellence, and by the 1930s the country could boast a talented 'Wunderteam'. Under the direction of renowned coach Hugo Meisl, Austria reached the semi-finals of the 1934 World Cup, before losing to Italy 1-0 on a sticky, rain-soaked pitch that didn't suit their neat passing style of football.

Austria looked set to dominate the European game under Meisl but after qualifying for the finals of the 1938 World Cup they had to withdraw when the country was annexed by Germany in the *Anschluss* of March 1938. Hitler's Nazi regime incorporated Austria into a 'Greater Germany' and several of the country's best players were co-opted into the German side for the competition, while others refused, most notably star striker Matthias Sindelar.

After the war the Austrian game experienced a brief renaissance when the team was coached by Walter Nausch, reaching the semi-finals of the World Cup in 1954. The side included Ernst Ocwirk and Gerhard Hanappi and will be remembered for the incredible 7-5 quarter-final victory over hosts Switzerland in the heat of Lausanne.

They had already beaten Czechoslovakia by five goals in the group stages, but they came undone in the semi-finals, defeated 6-1 by West Germany. In that game the Austrians were forced to field Walter Zeman in goal, as Kurt Schmied had not recovered from the sunstroke he suffered in the quarter-final.

Austrian footballing influence began to fade and the national team did not qualify for the World Cup again until 1978, when they reached the last eight after topping their first round group. However, they exited the competition bottom of the table in the second group stage. They got just as far in 1982, but defeat to France and a draw with Northern Ireland ended their campaign. They failed to get further than the first round at both Italia 90 and France 98 and they have not reached the World Cup since.

BELGIUM

Joined FIFA: 1904 **Confederation:** UEFA

Finals: 1930, 34, 38, 54, 70, 82, 86, 90, 94, 98, 2002

Record: P36/W10/D9/L17/F46/A63

Belgium's first international game was against France in 1904 and the country's association was among the founder members of FIFA. Championing the World Cup from an early stage, the Belgians were one of only four European sides to travel to Uruguay in 1930 for the first tournament. Indeed, the referee of the first World Cup final was a Belgian.

Along with France's victory over Mexico, Belgium's opening day defeat to the USA shares the honour of being the first World Cup game, but it wasn't a successful tournament for the team. After losing to Paraguay they returned home bottom of the table, without a point to their name.

In their opening game of the 1934 tournament, the Belgians held a 2-1 half-time lead over Germany in the first round, but were undone by a hat-trick in less than 20 minutes from centre-forward Edmund Conen and exited the competition after the 5-2 defeat. In 1938 they were again dispatched in the first round, this time after a 3-1 defeat to France. In 1954 they fared slightly better against England, overturning a 3-1 deficit to finish the tie 4-4 after extra-time, but defeat in their next group game against Italy saw them on their way home.

At the 1970 finals the Belgians beat lowly El Salvador 3-0, but their captain and star Paul Van Himst struggled to find his best form and the team failed to gain another point out of the Soviet Union and Mexico, although in the latter game they suffered from some poor refereeing decisions, including the questionable penalty they conceded.

It was not until 1972 that club football turned fully professional in Belgium and as a consequence, between 1982 and 2002 the national team qualified for every World Cup. In 1982 they pulled off a shock in the tournament's opening game, beating an Argentina side that kicked off with nine of their reigning world champions plus Maradona, but although they progressed to the second group stage, they lost to both Poland and the Soviet Union.

Reaching the 1986 World Cup with a team boasting the talents of Jan Ceulemans, Eric Gerets and Enzo Scifo, a penalty shoot-out victory over Spain in the quarter-finals pitted Belgium against Argentina in the semis, but the run was ended by a virtuoso performance by Maradona, who scored two breathtaking second-half goals. After losing the third place play-off to France, the Belgians finished with their best ever World Cup showing.

Badjou punches away for Belgium v France, 1938

Reaching the knockout stages in both 1990 and 1994 only to be eliminated by England and Germany respectively, they failed to match the achievement at France 98, drawing all three of their group games. In 2002 they reached the second round along with Japan after a rollercoaster 3-2 victory over Russia, but when they came up against Brazil in the round of 16, goals from Rivaldo and Ronaldo sent them packing. They have not managed to qualify for the finals since.

BOLIVIA

Joined FIFA: 1926 **Confederation:** CONMEBOL

Finals: 1930, 50, 94

WC record: P6/W0/D1/L5/F1/A20

Bolivia is a modest football nation that has never progressed further than the first round of the World Cup, but in qualification its players can often count on a significant home advantage due to the altitude of capital city La Paz, which is 12,000 feet above sea level. Unfortunately it is their away record that has consistently let them down and limited their chances on the international stage.

The Bolivians have reached the World Cup finals on just three occasions: in 1930 when invited, in 1950 with a walk-over, and in 1994, when they successfully qualified in second place to Brazil in their group. They have only managed one goal at the finals – a solitary strike scored against Spain in 1994 by the future national team manager Erwin Sánchez. They also came close in 1930 when Renato Sáenz had a penalty saved in a 4-0 defeat to Brazil.

At the 1930 tournament their players famously paid tribute to the hosts by playing in individually lettered shirts that spelt out the message 'Viva Uruguay' when the team lined up.

BRAZIL★★★★★

Joined FIFA: 1923 **Confederation:** CONMEBOL

Finals: 1930, 34, 38, **50**★, 54, 58★, 62★, 66, 70★, 74, 78, 82, 86, 90, 94★, 98★, 2002★, 06, [2010]

Record: P92/W64/D14/L14/F201/A84

The most successful nation in World Cup history, Brazil is also the only country to have made an appearance at every tournament. However, success didn't come quickly and its teams didn't make it past the opening round in either of the first two World Cups. This was largely due to sending under-strength squads, a consequence of the internal political battle between amateurism and professionalism in Brazilian football.

Fielding ten international debutants in the country's first ever match at the finals, a defeat to Yugoslavia dented Brazil's chances of making it out of the group stage, and even a 4-0 win over Bolivia couldn't prevent elimination.

Four years later the Brazilians were one of only four non-European teams to compete but the players barely got a foothold in the competition. Trailing 2-0 to Spain in their only game, the Brazilians pulled a goal back through Leônidas, who had been dubbed 'The Rubber Man' by the European press because of the array of tricks he could perform, but their fate was sealed by Isidoro Langara's second strike of the match.

The tournament had been an unhappy experience for several members of the squad. On the 12-day sea voyage to Italy, their black players had not been allowed to mix with the other passengers or to train.

In 1938 Brazil were the only South American side to take part in the competition, but it proved a more rewarding experience, one that ended with a third place finish. Leônidas also emerged as the outstanding player of the tournament and its leading scorer. At the finals the Brazilians took part in one of the great games in World Cup history, a 6-5 win over Poland. The victory was in part due to the outstanding performance of Leônidas, who scored a hat-trick. However, when coach Adhemar Pimenta rested his star striker for the semi-final, Brazil faltered against the Italians and lost 2-1.

Brazil hosted the 1950 World Cup and en route to the final game the team looked unstoppable. Uniquely the 1950 competition was decided with a Final Pool of four teams rather than a one-off match, and Brazil brushed aside their first two opponents, putting seven goals past Sweden and six past Spain. As a result the final match of the group, against Uruguay, would decide the fate of the trophy. The Brazilians only needed a draw to be crowned world champions,

Roque Junior and Ronaldinho, Brazil v Germany, 2002 World Cup Final

1930: Eliminated from the first World Cup in Uruguay after only two matches.

1934: Beaten in the first round by Spain.

1938: Leônidas is top scorer as the Brazilians go out in the semi-finals and finish third.

1950: Hosts Brazil build the Maracanã and have top scorer Ademir, but lose the World Cup to Uruguay.

1954: Nîlton Santos and Humberto are sent-off in the disgraceful 'Battle Of Berne' against Hungary.

1958: Bellini lifts the World Cup for the first time after Brazil beat hosts Sweden. Didi is the Best Player Of The Tournament.

1962: Garrincha is the star turn in Chile as the Brazilians win the World Cup for a second time.

1966: Pelé considers international retirement after being consistently fouled as Brazil go out.

1970: Brazil takes home the Jules Rimet Cup for good after winning it for a third time. Jairzinho scores in every round and Pelé is voted best player.

1974: Defeat to Poland in the third place play-off sees Brazil finish fourth.

1930 · 1934 · 1938 · 1950 · 1954 · 1958 · 1962 · 1966 · 1970 · 1974

Amarildo, Brazil v Czechoslovakia, 1962 World Cup final

whereas their near neighbours needed to win, but in front of a partisan crowd of 199,854 at the Maracanã Stadium, the hosts surrendered a lead in the last half hour and lost the game 2-1.

Defeat in the 'Fateful Final' would haunt Brazilian football for years to come and as a consequence their traditional all white playing strip was abandoned in favour of the more inspiring and patriotic yellow, blue and green that they are known for today. They also attempted to add a little steel to their defence and in the quarter-finals of the 1954 tournament they uncharacteristically became involved in one of the ugliest matches in World Cup history, losing 4-2 to Hungary in a game dubbed the 'Battle Of Berne'.

Hungary's József Bózsik and Brazil's Nílton Santos were sent-off for brawling in the game, and late on Brazil were reduced to nine men when Humberto Tozzi was given his marching orders for a foul on Gyula Lorant. After the final whistle there was a pitch invasion by the Brazilian entourage and the violence even continued in the changing rooms, involving both managers and even the official delegations.

It would be a different story at the 1958 World Cup, as 17-year-old Pelé graced the tournament for the first time, playing in a team that also included an array of talent, such as Garrincha, Didi, Zagallo and Gilmar. To ensure the players had the mental toughness to avoid the kind of surrender witnessed in the 'Fateful Final' of 1950, the squad also travelled to Sweden with a psychologist, although coach Vicente Feola didn't hit upon the magical team selection until the final group game.

It was after Feola gave Pelé and Garrincha their first appearances of the tournament in the crucial clash with the Soviet Union that the team took on the look of champions. Both players hit the woodwork in the first two minutes and after that the Brazilians didn't hesitate, carving a path all the way to the World Cup final.

Pelé scored a hat-trick in the semi-final defeat of France and another two against hosts Sweden in the final, winning both games 5-2. In victory the Brazilians were completely overcome, Pelé weeping openly on the pitch, and in one of the most famous moments in World Cup history, they carried the Swedish flag around the ground in a gesture of sportsmanship that brought the home crowd to its feet.

1978: Brazil beat Italy to third but feel cheated out of a place in the final.

1982: The brilliant team of Sócrates, Falcão and Zico crashes out after a defeat to Italy in the 'Disaster of Sarrià'.

1986: Beaten on penalties in the quarter-finals by France, Sócrates and Júlio César fail with their spot-kicks.

1990: Brazil are knocked out in the second round by Argentina.

1994: A new generation of stars, including Romario, win the World Cup for Brazil for the first time in 24 years.

1998: The tournament's best player, Ronaldo is struck by illness but makes the team as Brazil lose the final to France.

2002: Brazil wins the World Cup for a record fifth time, beating Germany to set a tournament record of seven wins out of seven matches.

2006: Ronaldo scores his 15th World Cup goal to set a new record.

2006: Cafu sets a record in his 16th World Cu win.

2014: Brazil to host the World Cup for a second time.

1978 | 1982 | 1986 | 1990 | 1994 | 1998 | 2002 | 2006 | 2010 | 2014

Gérson of Brazil after the 1970 World Cup Final

In 1962, with the majority of the team still in place, Brazil lifted the World Cup again. Pelé had been injured in the second game and took no further part, allowing Garrincha to become the outstanding star of this tournament. He would score twice in each of the quarter-final and semi-final games against England and Chile, but with his play inhibited by a fever, Garrincha made little impact on Czechoslovakia in the final. After conceding an early goal Brazil retaliated with strikes from Amarildo, Zito and Vavá to lift the trophy for a second time.

Elimination from the group stage blighted Brazil's tournament in 1966, when both the style of play and the refereeing policy favoured the European teams, but by the 1970 World Cup they had a formidable squad that was talented enough to overcome the late change of manager, with Mario Zagallo taking over as coach from the eccentric João Saldanha during the build-up.

Regarded by many as the greatest team in the history of the sport, Brazil's World Cup winning side of 1970 showcased Pelé at his peak, alongside Rivelino, Tostão, Gérson, Jairzinho and Carlos Alberto. Their route to the final included a group victory over England in a match that many had predicted would be a dress rehearsal for the final. It also featured a cathartic defeat of their 1950 conquerors Uruguay in the semi-finals.

This was the first tournament to be televised in colour, bringing another dimension to the samba flair of the Brazilians, and because of that, Carlos Alberto's emphatic strike in the 4-1 final win against Italy remains an enduring image of the World Cup.

In the immediate aftermath of Pelé's retirement from international football Brazil struggled to make an impact at the World Cup, despite yielding talent such as Paulo Cesar, Zico, Falção, Socrates and Cerezo. There were high points, including the impressive team knocked out of the 1986 quarter-finals on penalties by France, but the real signs of a renaissance came as Brazil won silver medals at both the 1984 and 1988 Olympics, and this provided the foundation for the 1994 World Cup winning team.

Goalkeeper Taffarel, captain Dunga and star striker Romario formed the backbone of the Olympic sides and their potential finally came to fruition with victory over Italy in the final of USA 94, a game that was settled on penalties.

Following that triumph a new belief was instilled in the national team, and with the emergence of players such as Ronaldo, Denilson and Rivaldo, the Brazilians made their impact felt at the 1998 World Cup. However, a mysterious illness to Ronaldo on the morning of the final left the team demoralised and ended any chances of victory against France.

Four years later Brazil were once again in the ascendance, their thrilling brand of attacking football making them worthy champions as they beat Germany in the 2002 World Cup Final. An inspired Ronaldo, who scored eight goals in the competition, helped to restore their standing as the world's leading football nation, and in 2006, despite Brazil's surprise exit in the quarter-finals, he became the World Cup's all-time top goalscorer.

WORLD CUP WONDERS

The Brazilian stars who have racked up the most appearances at the World Cup finals...

Cafu
20 games

Ronaldo
19 games

Dunga
18 games

Taffarel
18 games

Roberto Carlos
17 games

Jairzinho
16 games

Bebeto
15 games

Rivelino
15 games

BULGARIA

Joined FIFA: 1924 **Confederation:** UEFA
Finals: 1962, 66, 70, 74, 86, 94, 98
Record: P26/W3/D8/L15/F22/A53

If it was good for nothing else, communism was good for the development of domestic football in Bulgaria. Although the sport was played, it was not well-organised, but the formation of the People's Republic of Bulgaria after World War II brought wholesale changes to Bulgarian life, and football was completely overhauled, immeasurably improving the effectiveness of the domestic game.

As a consequence the Bulgarians were regarded as one of Europe's top football nations, becoming World Cup regulars through the Sixties and early Seventies, although it would not be until the Nineties that they realised their full potential at the finals, ironically after the collapse of communism.

Although they failed to win a single game at the 1962 tournament and conceded six goals to Hungary, the Bulgarians earned a goalless draw with England before heading home. They lost all three of their games in 1966, including a heated encounter with Brazil that left Pelé bruised and complaining, and four years later they managed to rack up just one point before they were eliminated, in part thanks to a 5-2 defeat by West Germany.

At the 1974 tournament the Bulgarians drew with Sweden and Uruguay and were comprehensively defeated by the total football of the Dutch. In 1986 they finally managed to progress to the knockout stages for the first time, albeit without winning a game, but they were eliminated by Mexico.

The fall of communism led to many of the country's top players moving abroad, where they gained experience that would benefit the national team. As a result, the Bulgarians reached the World Cup semi-finals in 1994, with Barcelona's Hristo Stoichkov the tournament's joint top scorer with six goals. Beating Argentina in the group stages, they also knocked Germany out of the competition in the quarter-finals, with goals from Stoichkov and Yordan Lechkov. Italy proved too strong in the semis, but defeat to Sweden in the third place play-off match still gave them their best World Cup finish.

In 1998 the ageing 'Golden Generation' of Bulgarian footballers had just one more World Cup in them, but a single point from three group games concluded with a 6-1 hammering at the hands of Spain. Bulgaria have failed to qualify for any of the 21st century World Cups.

CAMEROON

Joined FIFA: 1962 **Confederation:** CAF
Finals: 1982, 90, 94, 98, 2002, [2010]
Record: P17/W4/D7/L6/F15/A29

The Cameroon national team are known as the 'Indomitable Lions' and their roar was first heard at the World Cup in 1982, when they boosted African football with an unbeaten appearance at the finals in Spain, drawing their three group games against Peru, Poland and Italy. The undoubted star of the team was Roger Milla, while their coach was Jean Vincent, a member of France's World Cup teams of the Fifties.

It was eight years later that Cameroon took African football to the next level. In a bruising encounter that saw both André Kana-Biyik and Benjamin Massing sent-off, Cameroon beat world champions Argentina 1-0 in a headline grabbing tournament-opener. Inspired by 38-year-old Roger Milla, who made a series of decisive interventions from the bench, Cameroon topped a group containing Argentina, Romania and the Soviets and went on a run that took them to within ten minutes of a semi-final place before they were defeated 3-2 by England.

Their success in 1990 resulted in an increase in African places at subsequent World Cups and they were joined by Morocco and Nigeria at USA 94. With 42-year-old Milla still in the squad, Cameroon arrived in the USA with high expectations, yet they took their football association to the brink of a crisis two days before their game with Brazil, as the players refused to play without receiving their outstanding bonuses.

It was rumoured that a suitcase packed with $450,000 arrived secretly, allowing the 'Indomitable Lions' to continue. However, after losing 3-0 to Brazil they finished their campaign with a poor display against Russia, defeated 6-1 in San Francisco.

In the game against Brazil, Cameroon broke two World Cup records, with Roger Milla becoming the competition's oldest ever player and Rigobert Song the youngest to be sent-off. Milla's goal in the final group game against Russia also made him the oldest player to have scored at the World Cup.

A series of poor performances at the finals of 1998 saw Cameroon flying home after a 3-0 defeat to Italy in the final group game. Four years later, despite a squad peppered

Roger Milla, Cameroon v Colombia, 1990

with the stars of the 2000 Olympic gold medal-winning team, such as Samuel Eto'o, they were unlucky to be edged out of the qualifying spots by the Republic Of Ireland after defeat to Germany.

Cameroon reached for the 2010 World Cup under coach Paul Le Guen following the sacking of Otto Pfister, who had made a poor start to the campaign. Qualification went down to the last game when a win over Morocco put them out of reach of Gabon.

CANADA 2011

Joined FIFA: 1913 **Confederation:** CONCACAF

Finals: 1986

Record: P3/W0/D0/L3/F0/A5

In a land where the sport of ice hockey dominates, football has struggled to make any kind of impact and the Canadians have only graced the World Cup finals on one occasion.

When Colombia pulled out of staging the 1986 tournament Canada expressed an interest, but after Mexico got the vote the Canadians sought consolation in an easier run through the qualification group and won the remaining CONCACAF spot at the finals.

With a largely part-time squad coached by former England keeper Tony Waiters, who had taken them to the quarter-finals of the Olympics two years earlier, they struggled at the World Cup. Drawn against France, Hungary and the Soviet Union, they failed to win a game, although they held the French for 79 minutes before a late strike from Jean-Pierre Papin finished them off.

CHILE

Joined FIFA: 1912 **Confederation:** CONMEBOL

Finals: 1930, 50, 62, 66, 74, 82, 98, [2010]

Record: P25/W7/D6/L12/F31/A40

Chile played its first international in 1910, although it did not win a game until 1926 and has gone on to make little impact at the World Cup, save for the 1962 competition, when as hosts the team reached the semi-finals, only to be outplayed by an awesome Brazil side. However, in one of the most passionately supported third place play-off matches in World Cup history, Eladio Rojas became a national hero by beating Yugoslavia with the last kick of the game.

Outside of Chile that performance was overshadowed by the appalling spectacle against Italy in the group stages, known as the 'Battle Of Santiago', which was reported on British television by commentator David Coleman as "the most stupid, appalling, disgusting and disgraceful exhibition of football, possibly in the history of the game".

Chile qualified for the 1974 World Cup after the Soviet Union refused to fulfil the second leg of a play-off fixture at the Estadio Nacional in Santiago, citing the stadium's use as a home for the political prisoners of General Pinochet's recent coup d'etat, during which some 3,000 Chileans were killed, or just simply 'disappeared'. FIFA declared that the match should go ahead and the Chileans took to the field to complete the fixture regardless of the fact that the Soviet Union had not made the journey. Chile had Brazilian club side Santos on hand ready for a friendly and played that game instead. At the finals they didn't progress beyond the group stage, losing to West Germany and drawing with East Germany and Australia.

After a disappointing showing at the 1986 tournament when they failed to win a point, the Chileans were banned from entering the two subsequent competitions, punished after keeper Roberto Rojas faked injury from a firework in a ham-fisted attempt to have a World Cup qualifier abandoned in 1989. When they finally made it back to the finals in 1998 they were helped beyond the group stage by the impressive strikeforce of Marcelo Salas and Iván Zamorano, but unfortunately they came up against Brazil in the first knockout round and were soundly beaten 4-1.

After 12 years away from biggest stage in football, Chile qualified for the 2010 World Cup Finals coming second in the South American group to Brazil.

Eladio Rojas, Chile v Yugoslavia, third place play-off, 1962

CHINA 2008

Joined FIFA: 1931-58, 1976 **Confederation:** AFC

WC: 2002

WC record: P3/W0/D0/L3/F0/A9

China played in the first international match in Asia at the Far Eastern Games in Manila in February 1913, losing 2-1 to the Philippines. Joining FIFA in 1931, the Chinese took part at the Olympics of 1936 and 1948, but they did not enter the World Cup until the qualification campaign for the 1958 tournament, when they played just once before again withdrawing from FIFA in protest at the membership of Taiwan.

This self-imposed exile did little for the development of the domestic game, and it was not until 1976 that China rejoined FIFA.

Having entered every World Cup tournament since 1982, the Chinese first qualified for the finals of 2002 in Japan, where they were followed by thousands of travelling fans. Coached by World Cup veteran Bora Milutinović, they failed to either win a game or score a goal, conceding four times to Brazil. They have not managed to qualify for the finals since.

Wu Chengying, China v Turkey, 2002

COLOMBIA

Joined Fifa: 1936-50, 1954 **Confederation:** CONMEBOL

Finals: 1962, 90, 94, 98

Record: P13/W3/D2/L8/F14/A23

Colombia has had a controversial football history, but it has also been able to claim flamboyant players who have produced moments of breathtaking skill on the pitch, ranging from the spectacular goals of Carlos Valderrama to the astonishing 'scorpion' saves of goalkeeper Rene Higuita.

First taking part in World Cup qualification for the 1958 tournament, the Colombians made it to the finals at their second attempt when they travelled to Chile for the 1962 competition. After a rugged defeat to Uruguay, they stunned the tournament by clinching a 4-4 draw against the Soviet Union, having trailed by three goals with just over 30 minutes remaining. The feat was even more remarkable given that Soviet keeper Lev Yashin was viewed as the best in the world at the time. A 5-0 crushing by Yugoslavia in their final game brought them back to earth with a jolt.

They did not qualify for the finals again until 1990, but with a team including Valderrama, Higuita and Freddy Rincon they achieved a place in the last 16 after Rincon's 90th minute goal earned a surprise 1-1 draw with West Germany. They progressed to the second round as one of the best third placed teams, but two extra-time errors from Rene Higuita allowed Cameroon substitute Roger Milla to score, and even a consolation goal from Bernardo Redin could not save Colombia's tournament.

During this period Colombia's domestic game was dogged by allegations of money laundering involving drug cartels and of high stake bets and bribes. Players, officials and investigators have all been brutally murdered, but in one of the more notorious incidents defender Andrés Escobar was shot dead after returning from the 1994 World Cup, having inadvertently scored an own-goal against the USA. The Colombians had been ranked among the favourites for the competition, having beaten Argentina 5-0 in qualification, but after losing their first two games they were eliminated. With many of the same players they fared little better in 1998, losing to England and Romania and registering their single win against Tunisia.

Colombia had been expected to host the 1986 World Cup but was forced to withdraw after being unable to provide sufficient facilities and communications.

Carlos Valderrama, Colombia v England, 1998

CONGO DR

Joined FIFA: 1962 **Confederation:** CAF

Finals: 1974

Record: P3/W0/D0/L3/F0/A14

In 1974, when known as Zaïre, the Democratic Republic of Congo became the first sub-Saharan (and black African) team to qualify for the World Cup finals, doing so at their first attempt. Heavily influenced by European football – and the Belgians in particular, who had introduced the game to the country – Zaïre was a major force in African football from the mid-Sixties to the mid-Seventies.

Their players did not show this kind of form during the tournament in West Germany in 1974, when they found themselves in a group with Scotland, Yugoslavia and Brazil. They equalled a World Cup record when they conceded nine goals to Yugoslavia (only El Salvador's 10-1 defeat in 1982 has seen more goals against), forcing coach Miljan Miljanic to substitute keeper Kazadi Mwamba after just 21 minutes and with the score at 3-0. His replacement, Tubilandu Dimbi, fared little better and his first action of the game was to pick the ball out of the net.

'The Leopards' have failed to qualify for every World Cup since 1974, although they did not enter in 1986.

COSTA RICA

Joined FIFA: 1927 **Confederation:** CONCACAF

Finals: 1990, 2002, 06

Record: P10/W3/D1/L6/F12/A21

The formal birth of Costa Rican football was in 1921, although a national team was not entered into the World Cup until 1958. During the Sixties and Seventies the Costa Ricans could claim the strongest team in their region, but they were unable to convert local dominance into success on the world stage. They did not reach the finals until 1990 when they were helped by the expulsion of Mexico from the regional qualifying group.

Under the direction of Bora Milutinović the Costa Ricans shone at Italia 90. The experienced coach shook up the squad to field young talent like Ronald Gonzalez alongside more established players such as Juan Cayasso, and they defeated Scotland in their opener to become the first Central American team to win a game at the World Cup. They also beat Sweden and conceded just once to Brazil, but with talismanic keeper Luis Gabelo Conejo out of the second round through injury, Czechoslovakia hit four goals past replacement Hermidio Barrantes.

At the 2002 finals Costa Rica lost just once, but were edged out of a place in the knockout stages by Turkey, their goal difference not helped by a 5-2 defeat to Brazil. Four years later they gave the tournament a thrilling opening game but came off second best, losing 4-2 to hosts Germany. Further defeats to Ecuador and Poland left them bottom of their group. They narrowly missed out on qualification to the 2010 finals, losing 2-1 on aggregate to Uruguay in a play-off.

CÔTE D'IVORIE

Joined FIFA: 1960 **Confederation:** CAF

Finals: 2006, [2010]

Record: P3/W1/D0/L2/F6/A5

It was the French that introduced the sport of football to the Ivory Coast, and although the West African nation has one of the best-organised and richest leagues on the continent, its strength at home has not often been turned into success in the international arena. Having entered the World Cup for the first time in 1974, it was not until 2006 that the 'Elephants' reached the finals. When they did it was thanks to French coach Henri Michel and a talented generation of African stars such as Didier Drogba and Kolo Toure.

In a tough group the Ivorians acquitted themselves well in their defeats to Argentina and Holland, but once elimination from the tournament was assured they won their final game against Serbia and Montenegro, coming from two goals down to win 3-2.

They qualified for the 2010 World Cup with a game to spare after gaining a 1-1 away draw with challengers Malawi. Substitute Didier Drogba came to the rescue, equalising within two minutes of coming on the pitch.

Bonaventure Kalou, Ivory Coast v Serbia & Montenegro, 2006

Davor Suker, Croatia v Germany, 1998

CROATIA

Joined FIFA: 1992 **Confederation:** UEFA

Finals: 1998, 2002, 06

Record: P13/W6/D2/L5/F15/A11

Although Croatia did have its own league and national team under German occupation during the Second World War, for the majority of the century Croatia formed a part of Yugoslavia, and its players and clubs were among the powerhouses of Yugoslav football prior to real independence in 1991 and official FIFA recognition the following year.

Great players such as Zvonimir Boban, Robert Jarni and Robert Prosinecki had all represented Yugoslavia, but after independence they were part of a 'Golden Generation' taking Croatia to the quarter-finals of Euro 96 and the semi-finals of the 1998 World Cup in France. After beating Holland the Croatians finished third at the tournament, with Davor Suker picking up the Golden Boot as its top scorer. They had also given the competition one of its biggest shocks when they beat ten-man Germany 3-0 in the quarter-finals, before finally succumbing to France in the semis.

Despite an unbeaten qualification campaign for the 2002 World Cup, Croatia lost to both Mexico and Ecuador, and even an impressive victory over Italy, with two goals in three minutes from Ivica Olic and Milan Rapaic, wasn't enough to keep them in the competition. Four years later the Croatians should have made more of their weak group in Germany but after draws with Australia and Japan, it was the Australians who followed Brazil into the next round.

CUBA

Joined FIFA: 1932 **Confederation:** CONCACAF

Finals: 1938

Record: P3/W1/D1/L1/F5/A12

In 1938 Cuba were the first Caribbean team to make it to the World Cup finals following the withdrawal of every other nation in the qualifying group. Despite reaching the tournament unopposed, the Cubans drew 3-3 with Romania in their first round game and then caused a sensation four days later by winning the replay 2-1.

The quarter-finals proved a tougher challenge altogether and they conceded eight goals to Sweden, causing French journalist Emmanuel Gambardella to pack up his typewriter and announce, "Up to five goals is journalism, after that it becomes statistics". They have sporadically entered the competition ever since but have never managed to qualify again.

CZECHOSLOVAKIA

Joined FIFA: 1918-94 **Confederation:** UEFA

Finals*: 1934★, 38, 54, 58, 62★, 70, 82, 90

Record*: P30/W11/D5/L14/F44/A45

** Not including the records of the Czech Republic & Slovakia*

Czechoslovakia was formed after the present day territories of the Czech Republic and Slovakia declared independence from the Austro Hungarian Empire in 1918, and a Czechoslovakian national football team appeared shortly afterwards, fielding both Czech and Slovak players.

The country soon developed as a strong force in football. With the formidable forward pairing of Antonin Puc and Oldrich Nejedly, the Czechoslovakians finished runners up to Italy in the 1934 World Cup. They reached the final with a 3-1 victory over the Germans in Rome, with Nejedly netting a hat-trick. In the final against hosts Italy they took the lead

Josef Masopust scores, Czechoslovakia v Brazil, 1962 World Cup Final

through Puc in the 71st minute, but after a late equaliser the game was lost in extra-time

Four years later the Czechs reached the quarter-finals before taking part in a bruising encounter with Brazil that saw three players sent-off (two of them Brazilian) and left Oldrich Nejedly with a broken leg. The match ended 1-1 but the Czechs lost the replay.

With the country under Communist rule after 1945 the players of army team, Dukla Prague, dominated the national team. During this period Czechoslovakia finished the 1962 World Cup as runners-up to Brazil, having already shared a goalless draw with the South Americans in the group stage. A cautious, counter-attacking team, Czechoslovakia progressed to the final thanks to the heroics of Viliam Schrojf, the best goalkeeper of the tournament. He was in magnificent form in the knockout clashes with Hungary and Yugoslavia, but unfortunately Schrojf had a poor game in the final when he dropped a high ball into the path of Vavá, who stabbed home the winning goal for Brazil.

The late Seventies saw another resurgence in the fortunes of the national team, but although Czechoslovakia won the 1976 European Championship and the 1980 Olympics, the best that was achieved at the World Cup was a quarter-final appearance in 1990. Having defeated USA 5–1 in their group the Czechs claimed the runners-up spot behind Italy, comfortably beating Costa Rica 4–1 in the second round thanks to a hat-trick from Tomas Skuhravy. West Germany ended this winning run with a single goal in the quarter-final.

Czechoslovakia did not reach the 1994 finals, and by the time the qualification for France 98 got underway, the Czech Republic and Slovakia were competing as separate nations.

See also Czech Republic & Slovakia

CZECH REPUBLIC

Joined FIFA: 1907-16, 1994 **Confederation:** UEFA

Finals*: 2006

Record*: P3/W1/D0/L2/F3/A4

** Not including the record of Czechoslovakia*

From the 1993-94 season, FIFA recognised both the Czech Republic and Slovakia as the joint successors to Czechoslovakia's historic records in world football, but both have had limited success on the world stage.

The Czechs finished the 1996 European Championship as runners-up, but they have only reached the World Cup finals once, in 2006, where despite beating USA 3-0 they lost to both Ghana and Italy before exiting at the group stage. Further humiliation was heaped on them when they failed to qualify for the 2010 World Cup Finals in a group won by bitter local rivals Slovakia.

See also Czechoslovakia

DENMARK

Joined FIFA: 1904 Confederation: UEFA

Finals: 1986, 98, 2002, [2010]

Record: P13/W7/D2/L4/F24/A18

Danish football may have enjoyed a golden period in the late eighties and early Nineties, culminating in triumph at the 1992 European Championship, but little impact has been made at the World Cup. With a talented crop of players, most notably brothers Brian and Michael Laudrup, Jesper Olsen, Jan Molby, John Sivebaek and Soren Lerby, the Danes qualified for the finals for the first time in 1986. Despite being drawn in what was dubbed the 'group of death', in the early stages of the competition they appeared to be the European side best equipped to succeed in the tournament.

With Michael Laudrup in outstanding form, a 1-0 win against Scotland was merely the warm-up for an inspired 6-1 demolition of Uruguay. They pulled off another shock with their 2-0 victory over West Germany (although both teams had rested several key players), only to meet an in-form Spain in the second round, when they were roundly beaten and conceded five goals.

Though they failed to qualify for USA 94, the Danes recaptured some form at the 1998 World Cup with a run that took them to the quarter-finals, but despite taking an early lead they lost 3-2 to Brazil. They also impressed in 2002, helping to knock holders France out of the competition at the group stage with a 2-0 victory, but coming up against England in the second round they were beaten by three first-half goals. Against the odds Denmark qualified for the 2010 World Cup, forcing group favourites Portugal into the play-offs.

DUTCH EAST INDIES

See Indonesia

EAST GERMANY

Joined FIFA: 1952-90 **Confederation:** UEFA

Finals: 1974

Record: P6/W2/D2/L2/F5/A5

Along with West Germany and Saarland, East Germany was one of three post-war German teams on the world stage before reunification in 1990 brought about the fielding of a single German national team for the first time since the Second World War. After joining FIFA in 1952 the East Germans entered every World Cup until 1990, but they only managed to qualify for the finals on one occasion, ironically in West Germany in 1974, when the two Germanys were drawn in the same group. Adding to the drama surrounding the football fixture were the heightened tensions of the cold war – just weeks before the tournament West German Chancellor Willy Brandt had been forced to resign after it was revealed that one of his personal assistants was an East German spy.

When the two nations finally met in their last group game West Germany had already qualified for the next round, while after beating Australia and drawing with Chile, the East Germans needed just a point.

Despite the pre-match expectations, the West Germans struggled to break their opponents and Jürgen Sparwasser scored a late winner to take East Germany through as group winners. The victory dealt a devastating psychological blow to West Germany's manager, Helmut Schön, originally a native of East Germany who had been forced to flee from the country in 1950.

In the second group phase East Germany's run came to an end after defeats to Brazil and Holland, and a draw with Argentina.

ECUADOR

Joined FIFA: 1926 **Confederation:** CONMEBOL

Finals: 2002, 06

Record: P7/W3/D0/L4/F7/A8

Led by coach Hernan Dario Gomez, Ecuador qualified for the World Cup for the first time in 11 attempts in 2002, finishing runners-up to Argentina in the ten-strong South American group. This magnificent achievement also included a first ever-win over Brazil.

At the finals Ecuador struggled, losing their games to Italy and Mexico, before a goal from Edison Mendez secured a 1-0 consolation win in their final match against Croatia.

In 2006, under Luis Fernando Suarez, Ecuador again made it to the World Cup and their qualification campaign included another win over Brazil. At the finals in Germany goals from Carlos Tenorio and Agustín Delgado helped them to an opening win over Poland. Both players scored again in a 3-0 defeat of Costa Rica, and a place in the knockout stages was already assured by the time they were defeated 3-0 by hosts Germany. Tenorio came close to scoring again in the second round against England, before a single goal from David Beckham called time on their World Cup.

Carlos Tenorio, Ecuador v Poland, 2006

Ecuador failed to reach the 2010 finals, losing seven of 18 qualification games.

EGYPT

Joined FIFA: 1923 **Confederation:** CAF

Finals: 1934, 90

Record: P4/W0/D2/L2/F3/A6

Egypt has been Africa's most successful football nation, despite having only appeared in two World Cups. Trailblazers for African football, the Egyptians were the first team from the continent to play at the Olympics in 1920, and at the World Cup in 1934, when coached by Scotland's Jimmy McRea.

Their only game of the 1934 finals in Italy ended in a 4-2 defeat to Hungary, the nation they had beaten in the second round of the Olympic football tournament ten years earlier. The Egyptians had their chances, including a disallowed strike by captain Mahmoud Moktar, while both their goals were scored by Abdel Rahman Fawzi, who could have had a hat-trick had he made more of a solid early chance.

In 1990 the Egyptians arrived at the World Cup having beaten both Scotland and Czechoslovakia during their preparations, but few expected them to hold Holland to a draw, even if the Dutch were fielding a less than fully fit Ruud Gullit. After grinding out a second draw against the Republic Of Ireland, Egypt lost to England in a game that could have put them through to the knockout stages of the competition.

Ibrahim Hassan, Egypt v England, 1990

EL SALVADOR

Joined FIFA: 1938 **Confederation:** CONCACAF

Finals: 1970, 82

Record: P6/W0/D0/L6/F1/A22

The national team of El Salvador has qualified for the World Cup just twice, causing a war and suffering the worst defeat in World Cup finals history. In 1969 they were involved in a controversial three-game second round qualifying clash with neighbouring Honduras. Border infractions and rioting followed the first two games, and when El Salvador finally defeated Honduras 3-2 in neutral Mexico, the result inflamed an already tense border situation, causing the El Salvadorian Army to invade Honduras to protect El Salvadorian migrant workers from persecution. The action sparked war between the two countries.

At the finals in Mexico the following year, El Salvador suffered three straight defeats to Belgium, Mexico and the Soviet Union, conceding nine goals without retaliation.

Their record at the finals of 1982 was even worse, as they were thrashed 10-1 by Hungary – the biggest ever defeat at the World Cup. The win did no good for the Hungarians as they crashed out of the tournament along with El Salvador, who lost their remaining games against Belgium and Argentina, although by much narrower margins.

ENGLAND★ 2005

Joined FIFA: 1905-20, 1924-28, 1946
Confederation: UEFA
Finals: 1950, 54, 58, 62, **66**★, 70, 82, 86, 90, 98, 2002, 06, [2010]
Record: P55/W25/D17/L13/F74/A47

Although the English were the inventors of the modern game of football, a classically insular island approach, together with an overbearing sense of superiority, meant that England's Football Association repeatedly stood apart from the game's most significant developments. When FIFA began talking of a world tournament the FA declined to take part. It resigned from the federation in 1928 and did not rejoin until 1946, consistently refusing to enter the World Cup until 1950.

When the English did finally grace the tournament in Brazil they were viewed as one of the main attractions, with a side that boasted such stellar football names as Billy Wright, Tom Finney and Stan Mortensen. However, their preparations let the team down. Arriving just a few days before the tournament they left themselves no time to acclimatise, while they even based themselves in a run-of-the-mill tourist hotel on Copacabana beach rather than at a serious training facility.

In their first match the England players struggled to cope with Rio's thin air and they made hard work of Chile, but goals from Mortensen and Wilf Mannion secured a 2-0 win. However, shock defeats to the USA and Spain led to England's early and unexpected elimination from the contest.

At the 1954 finals in Switzerland the English reached the knockout stage after a 4-4 draw with Belgium and a 2-0 victory over the hosts. They should have gone further but came unstuck in the quarter-finals against Uruguay, losing 4-2 after some uncharacteristic errors by keeper Gil Merrick. "I should have saved the last one," he said after being held responsible for the defeat, "but I could not be blamed for the first three."

Four years later in Sweden they were drawn in a group with Brazil, the Soviet Union and Austria. As they had not previously lost to any of these nations they were ranked among the tournament favourites. However England weren't quite the same side that had qualified so convincingly the previous year, as the Munich air disaster had ripped the heart out of the team just four months earlier. For a period after the crash, mindful of what had happened to Manchester United, the England squad travelled to away fixtures in two planes.

England, 1966 World Cup Final

England drew the game with the Soviets, with Tom Finney equalising from the penalty spot. While injury would rule him out of the remaining matches, England went on to play out a 0-0 draw with Brazil, the first goalless result in the history of the World Cup. Another draw with Austria forced England into a play-off with the Soviet Union for a place in the next round, a game that was lost by a single goal.

For the 1962 World Cup the English were more prepared than they had ever been, and despite an early defeat to Hungary they progressed to the quarter-finals. However, they were no match for a Garrincha-inspired Brazil in their next encounter, losing 3-1, but the tournament proved a valuable learning curve for Bobby Charlton and a young Bobby Moore, two players who would make a considerable contribution to England's great years ahead.

Team manager Walter Winterbottom had led England to every World Cup since 1950 but he had never had the benefit of picking the players, a responsibility entrusted to the FA's International Selection Committee. After failure at the 1962 tournament Alf Ramsey was appointed as Winterbottom's replacement, and he set about shaking up his team's playing style and formation, and he was even allowed to select the players.

In the build up to the 1966 World Cup, hosts England were rated as outsiders by many professional analysts and critics, but Ramsey fashioned a team capable of winning, built around players who could do a job rather than selecting individual talents.

After a slow start to the tournament England progressed to the knockout rounds, winning a bruising quarter-final encounter with Argentina. The only goal of the game was scored by Geoff Hurst, a replacement for injured star striker Jimmy Greaves. In the semi-final England had Bobby Charlton to thank for the two goals that defeated Eusébio's Portugal, and in the final Ramsey's 'Wingless Wonders' lined up against West Germany, with Geoff Hurst keeping his place ahead of the fully fit Jimmy Greaves.

In a rollercoaster final the Germans

Beardsley, England v West Germany, 1990

Beckham, England v Argentina, 2002

equalised just before the end of the 90 minutes, but two goals from Hurst in extra-time completed his hat-trick and won the World Cup for England on home soil.

Despite the success, English football failed to capitalise on the resultant euphoria. Travelling to the 1970 tournament with arguably a better squad, the England team lost narrowly to eventual champions Brazil in a group game seen as a potential warm-up for the final. Progressing to the knockout round, England crashed out in a tactically disastrous quarter-final confrontation with West Germany that signified a period of upheaval from which it took years to recover.

Failing to qualify for two successive World Cups in the Seventies, the English game was hamstrung by technical shortcomings throughout the following decade. At the 1982 World Cup under manager Ron Greenwood England were determined to get it right and their campaign got off to a flying start with Bryan Robson's goal against France coming after only 27 seconds. England won the game 3-1 and qualified for the second group stage, but goalless draws against West Germany and Spain meant that it was the Germans who made it through to the semi-finals.

At the 1986 finals, with Bobby Robson in charge, England progressed to the quarter-finals after early slip-ups against Portugal and Morocco, but it had taken a Gary Lineker hat-trick against Poland to ensure qualification behind the Africans. Lineker scored twice more, and Beardsley once, as England finished off Paraguay in the second round, but it was Maradona's 'Hand Of God' goal in the quarter-final that proved their undoing, when the Argentina captain punched the ball into the net unseen by the referee. Lineker scored a consolation goal in the 2-1 defeat and would end the tournament as its top scorer.

Lineker was again the star turn of the England team that reached the semi-finals at Italia 90, only to be eliminated after losing a thrilling end-to-end contest with West Germany on penalties. The side also included Paul Gascoigne, arguably the country's greatest ever talent. Although the tournament would inspire a generation of fans, the achievement hardly heralded a new era on the pitch given the failure to qualify for the 1994 World Cup under Graham Taylor.

With Glenn Hoddle coaching the team at the 1998 tournament, England reached the second round to face Argentina once again, but a moment of madness from David Beckham resulted in a red card for the young Manchester United midfielder. England waged a formidable rearguard action, playing most of the second-half and 30 minutes of extra-time with ten men, even having an solid effort from Sol Campbell disallowed. Ultimately England's downfall was their perennial weakness in the penalty shoot-out. The end of the road came when David Batty's spot-kick was saved, but it was Beckham who was hung in effigy back home.

In 2002, as captain, Beckham gained revenge when he converted the match-winning penalty that helped England through to the second round and Argentina out of the tournament. However, this time it would be Luiz Felipe Scolari's Brazil that would bring an end to England's World Cup hopes, when a freak Ronaldinho goal, scored from 42 yards out, decided the quarter-final 2-1 in Brazil's favour.

Scolari would again be responsible for England's World Cup defeat in the quarter-finals four years later, but this time as coach of Portugal. After the penalty shoot-out defeat Beckham dramatically resigned the England captaincy and it would also be coach Sven-Göran Eriksson's last game in charge.

Under Fabio Capello, Beckham was still a member of a reinvigorated England team that qualified for the 2010 World Cup with nine wins out of ten.

WORLD CUP WONDERS

The England stars with the most appearances at the World Cup finals...

Peter Shilton
17 games

Bobby Moore
14 games

Bobby Charlton
14 games

Terry Butcher
14 Games

David Beckham
13 Games

Michael Owen
12 Games

Gary Lineker
12 Games

FEDERAL REPUBLIC OF GERMANY (FRG)

See West Germany

FRANCE☆

Joined FIFA: 1904 **Confederation:** UEFA

Finals: 1930, 34, **38**, 54, 58, 66, 78, 82, 86, **98**☆, 2002, 06☆, [2010]

Record: P51/W25/D10/L16/F95/A64

The French played a key role in the development of the World Cup but in the early days of the competition they struggled to turn their influence off the pitch into success on it. As the competition was first launched by Frenchman Jules Rimet, it was unthinkable that France would not be represented at the first World Cup.

The French were one of only four European teams to play in Uruguay in 1930. They even featured in one of the two opening games, with Lucien Laurent volleying the first World Cup goal against Mexico. At full time the French had secured a comfortable 4-1 win, but after a bruising defeat to Argentina they were left without the injured Laurent for their final group game with Chile, which they lost 1-0. Four years later they fared no better, eliminated after one game following a 3-2 defeat to second-favourites Austria.

With the storm clouds of war gathering, the French were entrusted with staging the 1938 World Cup, and although it was considered a success, the hosts suffered a 3-1 quarter-final defeat to eventual winners Italy. They qualified for the 1954 finals with 20 goals in four games, but the tournament itself kicked off with a shock on the opening day when seeded France lost to Yugoslavia and 'Les Bleus' were soon on their way home regardless of a 3-2 victory over Mexico.

Among the scorers for France in 1954 was Raymond Kopa. The biggest French star of the time, he also played a leading role at the 1958 World Cup when France reached the semi-finals, although he was overshadowed by the explosive form of his strike partner Just Fontaine, who scored a record 13 goals. That year the exuberant play of the French became known as 'Champagne football'. Fontaine even scored six goals in the group stage, including a hat trick in the 7-3 thrashing of

Zidane, 1998 World Cup Final

Paraguay. This run was brought to an end by a 5-2 defeat to Brazil in the semi-finals, but after a collision between centre-half Robert Jonquet and Vavá, France had to play much of the match with only ten fully fit players, with Jonquet exiled to the wing as a passenger.

Through the Sixties there was a steady decline in the French game and to improve football standards a national youth training programme was introduced. This system would bear fruit to such a remarkable degree in the Eighties that a new generation of French stars were dubbed the 'Blue Brazil', and inspired by the incredibly talented Michel Platini they reached the semi-finals of the 1982 World Cup. However, despite leading West Germany 3-1 in extra-time, they were pegged back and beaten on penalties.

Defeat proved hard to take, particularly as the French had watched in horror as substitute Patrick Battiston was carried from the pitch unconscious after a brutal foul by keeper Harald Schumacher.

At the 1986 finals France fielded an accomplished side, with Platini, Battiston, Maxime Bossis, Jean Tigana and Alain Giresse all still capable of performing at the highest level. They dispensed with Brazil in the quarter-finals, although they needed a penalty shoot-out to do so, and with a place in the final at stake they faced West Germany. However, their cavalier flair was once again crushed by the resilience and efficiency of their opponents, and after the 2-0 defeat 34-year-old Platini said goodbye to the World Cup by throwing his shirt to the fans as he trudged despondently off the pitch.

Platini's retirement led to a period of decline for the national side and France would not play at the finals again until hosting the tournament in 1998. For this World Cup coach Aimé Jacquet had built an efficient side around the sublime skills of playmaker Zinédine Zidane. Although little had been expected of them, even in their own country, their campaign gathered momentum and culminated in a 3-0 defeat of Brazil in the final. Zidane scored twice and the nation finally embraced this team, with more than a million supporters pouring onto the Champs-Elysées to celebrate the victory.

France had found a winning formula and although they triumphed at Euro 2000 under Roger Lemerre, their elimination at the group stages of the 2002 World Cup was the biggest shock of the tournament. Without an injured Zidane France lost the opening game to Senegal by a single goal, but even with their star back for the group decider against Denmark, the French crashed out with just one point to show from three games.

This golden generation of French stars returned to the World Cup finals in 2006. Inspired once again by Zidane, who had been encouraged out of his international retirement, they progressed to the final, but in one of the most talked about games in World Cup history, they lost on penalties to Italy. In defeat it was still Zidane who dominated the headlines. Playing in the last game of his career, he was dismissed for an off-the-ball attack on Marco Materazzi.

Qualification for the 2010 World Cup gave rise to another controversy. France secured their place in South Africa after beating the Republic Of Ireland in the play-offs, but a handball from Thierry Henry had turned the game. Although the Irish FA demanded that the tie be replayed, the result stood.

GERMAN DEMOCRATIC REPUBLIC (GDR)

See East Germany

GERMANY★★★

Joined FIFA: 1904 **Confederation:** UEFA

Finals: 1934, 38, 54★, 58, 62, 66★, 70, **74**★, 78, 82★, 86★, 90★, 94, 98, 2002★, **06**, [2010]

Record: P92/W55/D19/L18/F190/A112

One of the most successful countries in World Cup history, Germany's outstanding record in the competition is all the more remarkable given the circumstances of the rise to prominence of its national football team. The Germans enjoyed little success prior to the Second World War, after which they were cut off from international competition until 1950. Yet the Germans have earned a reputation as one of the true powerhouses of the modern game.

Their inspirational World Cup triumph in 1954 helped to instil certain qualities in the national team and through the second half of the 20th Century the Germans developed an ability to rise to the occasion, no matter what the circumstances. They have become noted for making the most of their talents, and on occasion becoming greater than the sum of their parts, building their success on a peculiar mix of skill, tactical nous and unshakeable self-belief. Three times World Cup winners, they have been finalists on four further occasions, and only the Brazilians have appeared in as many finals.

Germany first took part in the World Cup in 1934. The team arrived at the tournament having not lost a game in the previous 16 months, but were portrayed in the Italian press as one of the competition's weaker teams, largely for political reasons. In their first game they trailed Belgium at half-time but Fritz Szepan turned in a captain's performance to inspire the team to victory, helped by a second-half hat-trick scored in 20 minutes by centre-forward Edmund Conen.

Germany's run came to an end in a tightly fought semi-final against Czechoslovakia, with Dresden keeper Willi Kress taking much of the blame for the 3-1 defeat. Four days later, despite missing Sigi Haringer, who had been left out of the team by disciplinarian coach Otto Nerz for eating an orange on a station platform, the Germans outplayed a tired Austrian 'Wunderteam' to win the inaugural third place play-off 3-2, with Ernest Lehner netting the first of his two goals less than 30 seconds from the beginning of the game.

At the 1938 finals a 'Greater Germany' team fielded players from the newly annexed Austria, with coach Sepp Herberger under instructions to pick a side made up almost evenly of Germans and Austrians. However, this wasn't enough to prevent an early exit from the tournament. Despite leading 2-0 until just before half-time, the Germans lost their first round replay to a Swiss team that played part of the game with ten men.

The political split of Germany after World War II led to the creation of the Federal Republic of Germany (West Germany) and the German Democratic Republic (East Germany), but in football terms it was the West German team recognised by FIFA as the successor to Germany's pre-war heritage, while the East Germans fielded their own separate team *(see East Germany)*.

With the resumption of international football after the war, Switzerland campaigned hard for the West Germans to be readmitted to FIFA, citing "the unifying mission of sport", but they were not officially welcomed back to the world game until two months after the 1950 World Cup, paving the way for an appearance at the finals in Switzerland four years later.

Still coached by Sepp Herberger, the West Germans emerged from the post-war doldrums to achieve their first major triumph. In the final, a match that would become known as the 'Miracle Of Berne', Helmut Rahn scored twice and Max Morlock once as the West Germans beat Hungary, the outstanding team of the era, to become the surprise winners of the 1954 World Cup. This was despite having lost their group encounter

Sepp Herberger, Fritz Walter and the West German 1954 World Cup Final team

1930: The Germans are one of many European nations that don't send a team to the World Cup in Uruguay.

1934: The Germany team makes its World Cup debut, finishing in third place.

1936: Josef 'Sepp' Herberger succeeds Otto Nerz as national coach.

1938: The players give the Nazi salute but are knocked out in the first round

1945: Germany is banned from international competition.

1948: Switzerland requests that FIFA lifts the ban on Germany.

1950: The West Germans are prepared to send a team to the World Cup if asked. They are reinstated after the finals.

1954: West Germany shock the world by defeating the invincible Hungarians to win the trophy.

1958: Beaten 6-3 by France in the third place play-off match.

1962: Knocked out by Yugoslavia, it is their third consecutive quarter-final meeting.

1964: Herberger steps down as coach and is replaced by Helmut Schön.

1966: West Germany reaches the final, but loses to hosts England after a disputed goal.

1970: Gerd Müller wins the Golden Boot, having scored 10 goals as the Germans finish third.

Andreas Brehme lifts the trophy, 1990 World Cup Final

with the Hungarians by a humiliating 8-3. However, Herberger had fielded a deliberately weakened team in the earlier game, knowing that progress to the knockout rounds would be achieved by beating Turkey in a play-off.

By the 1958 tournament in Sweden, West Germany could still count on four of their world champions, Herberger staying loyal to Fritz Walter, Hans Schäfer, Horst Eckel and even Helmut Rahn, whose international career had appeared to have stalled between the two tournaments. There was also room in the team for Uwe Seeler, who made his World Cup debut and who would go on to set a competition record with 21 appearances at the finals between 1958 and 1970.

It was the goals of Helmut Rahn powering the team to a semi-final encounter with Sweden, but two strikes in the last ten minutes eliminated the West Germans, who were then roundly thumped by France in the third place play-off game.

At the 1962 World Cup, the last under Herberger, the Germans reached quarter-finals before falling to Yugoslavia, but through the remainder of the Sixties there would be a steady improvement in the national game. Partly in response to the World Cup defeat a professional league – the Bundesliga – was established in 1963, following more than half a century of regionalised leagues. Soon West Germany became a real force to in the game, reaching the final of the 1966 World Cup under coach Helmut Schön, before losing 4-2 in extra-time to hosts England. Schön had been promoted from assistant coach against the advice of Herberger, who had recommended his loyal 1954 captain Fritz Walter for the job.

With the backbone of the 1966 team still in place West Germany achieved a degree of revenge for the final defeat, knocking England out of the 1970 tournament to set up a semi-final encounter with Italy. Despite a lifeless first 90 minutes that saw the Italians score an early goal and sit back on their lead, the semi-final is remembered in both countries as one of the most thrilling games in World

1974: After defeat in the first round to the East Germans, the West Germans win the World Cup as hosts.

1978: Captain Berti Vogts scores an own-goal as the West Germans are knocked out after defeat to Austria.

1982: Led by coach Jupp Derwall, an unpopular West German team loses the final 3-1 to Italy.

1984: World Cup winning captain Franz Beckenbauer is appointed as West Germany's new coach.

1986: Despite a second-half comeback, the West Germans lose the final to Argentina 3-2.

1990: The West Germans defeat Argentina with a penalty in the final.

1994: Bulgaria beats Germany in the quarter-final.

1998: Lothar Matthaüs plays his 25th World Cup game, setting a record for the most matches.

2001: Germany defeated 5-1 at home to England in qualifying and need the play-offs to reach the World Cup.

2002: Germany reaches the final, losing to Brazil. Oliver Kahn is awarded the Golden Ball for best player.

2004: Jurgen Klinsmann is appointed national coach.

2006: As hosts the Germans finish third, but Miroslav Klose wins the Golden boot.

1974 · 1978 · 1982 · 1986 · 1990 · 1994 · 1998 · 2002 · 2006 · 2010

West Germany, 1974 World Cup Final

Cup history. Franz Beckenbauer remained a commanding presence for his team, staying on the field after dislocating his shoulder and playing from half-time with his arm strapped to his body. Karl-Heinz Schnellinger shocked the game into life when he equalised in the dying seconds of normal time, and despite losing an epic extra-time contest 4-3, the West Germans were welcomed back home by 60,000 cheering fans.

Before leaving Mexico Gerd Müller was awarded the Golden Boot for his ten goals, and although he didn't add to his tally in the third place play-off against Uruguay, just one strike from Wolfgang Overath was needed to win the game.

In 1974, as reigning European champions, the West Germans hosted the tournament. They were still able to rely on the deadliest of goalmouth poachers, Gerd Müller, and under the firm leadership of captain Franz Beckenbauer, who was the strength behind Helmut Schön's slipping authority, they triumphed over the breathtaking 'Total Football' of the Dutch to lift the trophy for a second time.

West Germany reached the final in both of the tournaments in the Eighties. Under Jupp Derwall they lost 3-1 to Italy in 1982 final when playing with a ruthlessness that won them few fans. By 1986 Franz Beckenbauer had taken over as coach, but despite having little faith in his own players, he took them to the final where they lost 3-2 to Argentina, a score much closer than the match itself.

Four years later at Italia 90, Beckenbauer exacted revenge on Argentina, when he led West Germany to a third World Cup victory. Lothar Matthäus was the midfield driving force of this team, with Jürgen Klinsmann forming a potent attacking duo with Rudi Völler. However, after defeating England on penalties in a titanic semi-final battle, by contrast the world championship decider with Argentina made a poor spectacle.

Ranked as the worst final in the history of the competition, the game was characterised by negativity and poor sportsmanship. The only goal of a shoddy contest came with just five minutes to play. Scored from the penalty spot by Andreas Brehme, the foul it was awarded for was marginal, but this was a game that no-one wanted to go to extra-time.

It was the last World Cup appearance played by the team under the name West Germany. Following the reunification of East and West Germany in 1990, a united team was sent to USA 94, but it would take some time for this new nation to hit its stride.

The Germans struggled to meet their own high expectations at a series of tournaments. However, after reaching the 2002 World Cup through the play-offs, against the odds they edged to the final thanks to the extraordinary goalkeeping of Oliver Kahn. They would contest the trophy with Brazil, the first time the two World Cup heavyweights had met in the competition's history.

Lining up with a 4-4-2 formation for the first time, the Germans ultimately lost 2-0 but Rudi Völler's side had proved the critics wrong and Kahn was voted the best player of the tournament.

In 2006 the growth of the German team continued. Playing host to the World Cup, the tournament transformed the country's feelings about itself, tapping into a level of patriotism long since suppressed by the events of the past. Jurgen Klinsmann brought his progressive coaching techniques and his love of attacking football to the national team, defying expectations by reaching the semi-finals. The team were unlucky to be knocked out by Italy with two goals in the last two minutes of extra-time, but victory in the third place play-off was wildly celebrated and Miroslav Klose ended the tournament as its highest scorer.

Klinsmann resigned after the finals and was succeeded by his assistant, the skilled tactician Joachim Löw. Under his guidance, Germany qualified for the 2010 World Cup with an unbeaten record.

WORLD CUP WONDERS The German stars with the most appearances at the World Cup finals...

Lothar Matthäus
25 games

Uwe Seeler
21 games

Berti Vogts
19 games

Karl-Heinz Rummenigge
19 games

Wolfgang Overath
19 games

Franz Beckenbauer
18 games

Thomas Berthold
18 games

Sepp Maier
18 games

GHANA

Joined FIFA: 1958 **Confederation:** CAF
Finals: 2006, [2010]
Record: P4/W2/D0/L2/F4/A6

The 'Black Stars' of Ghana were the first team to win the African Nations Cup four times and by the late Seventies they looked like their continent's most likely team to make a decent impact at the World Cup. However, Ghana's first appearance at the finals did not occur until 2006.

It took a talented generation of players such as Stephen Appiah, Samuel Kuffour and Michael Essien to finally make the difference and in their first tournament they acquitted themselves well, reaching the second round before losing 3-0 to Brazil.

Their campaign had also included group victories over the Czech Republic and USA. After waiting so long for their first World Cup appearance, Ghana made it two tournaments in a row after finishing top of their qualification group to book a place at the 2010 finals in South Africa.

Ghana v USA, 2006

GREECE

Joined FIFA: 1927 **Confederation:** UEFA
Finals: 1994, [2010]
Record: P3/W0/D0/L3/F0/A10

Greece won the 2004 European Championship in one of the biggest shocks in the history of world football. However, the Greeks have been less successful at the World Cup and have only qualified for the finals twice, despite entering all but two competitions. They even failed to qualify for the 2006 finals when they were reigning European champions.

They had an advantage when they qualified for the 1994 World Cup, as Yugoslavia were excluded from the group after a FIFA ban. At the finals coach Alketas Panagoulias kept faith with his squad of ageing players at the expense of some of the rising stars of Greek football. In the first game against Argentina, the Greeks lost 4-0 in a game notable for Diego Maradona's goal celebration. Four days later they lost to Bulgaria by the same scoreline and a 2-0 defeat to Nigeria ended their tournament.

They had played only three games and conceded ten goals, but had used all three of their keepers: Antonios Minou, Ilias Atmatzidis, and Christos Karkamanis.

With their Euro 2004 winning coach Otto Rehhagel still in charge, Greece qualified for the 2010 World Cup Finals after defeating Ukraine in the play-offs.

HAITI

Joined FIFA: 1933 **Confederation:** CONCACAF
Finals: 1974
Record: P3/W0/D0/L3/F2/A14

The Haitians first entered the World Cup in 1934 but they did not qualify for 40 years, reaching the finals at their fourth attempt in 1974. Before their opening game against Italy, the Haiti players claimed to be using voodoo as a secret weapon, and striker Emmanuel Sanon had made the audacious claim that he would score twice. He did indeed score, rounding Dino Zoff to put the ball in the net early in the second-half. But the Italian defence limited him to one goal and Haiti eventually lost 3-1.

Disturbingly, Ernst Jean-Joseph failed a drug test, was beaten up by his own officials and sent back home. With low morale in the camp the Haitians were eliminated after losing 7-0 to Poland and 4-1 to Argentina. Since then they have been eclipsed in their World Cup qualification region by the dominance of Mexico and the rise of the United States.

HOLLAND

See Netherlands

HONDURAS

Joined FIFA: 1951 **Confederation:** CONCACAF
Finals: 1982, [2010]
Record: P3/W0/D2/L1/F2/A3

First entering the World Cup in 1962, it was the early Eighties that saw the heyday of football in Honduras, with triumph in the CONCACAF Championship in 1981 and qualification for the following year's World Cup in Spain.

At the finals the Hondurans pulled off a shock as they drew with Spain after leading for over half the match. After another 1-1 draw with Northern Ireland, they missed out on qualification for the second round after conceding a Vladimir Petrovic penalty in the 87th minute against Yugoslavia.

Honduras qualified for the 2010 World Cup after finishing third to USA and Mexico in the CONCACAF qualifying table, edging out Costa Rica on goal difference.

HUNGARY

Joined FIFA: 1906 **Confederation:** UEFA
Finals: 1934, 38★, 54★, 58, 62, 66, 78, 82, 86
Record: P32/W15/D3/L14/F87/A57

Once numbering among the game's most innovative football cultures, the Hungarians wowed crowds with their marvellous attacking play in a spell that saw them dominate the game in the 1950s.

The foundations for the Hungarian style were laid down by Scottish coach Jimmy Hogan during the inter war years and it was during this period that Hungary began to display the ability and cohesion to challenge the established giants of football.

With a side spearheaded by Gyula Zsengellér and Gyorgy Sárosi, Hungary could lay claim to perhaps the most thrilling strikeforce at the 1938 World Cup, and one that proved so devastating in a 5-2 defeat of Sweden in the semi-finals. However, while strong up front, the fragile Hungarian defence was no match for Italy in the final and they lost an exciting game 4-2.

In the early Fifties Hungary created a talented team that became known as the 'Magical Magyars', built around a nucleus of stars from army club side Honvéd. With players of the calibre of Jozsef Bózsik, Sandor Kocsis, Nandor Hidegkuti and Ferenç Puskás, the Hungarians rewrote the way the game was played, and between May 1950 and February 1956 they contested 51 games and lost just once – agonisingly the 1954 World Cup final.

In that game they threw away an early 2-0 lead and ended up losing 3-2 to West Germany, who they had already beaten 8-3 in a group encounter earlier in the tournament. Hungary scored 27 goals in five games at the 1954 World Cup, including four against Brazil in a bruising encounter that became known as the 'Battle Of Berne', but it wasn't quite enough to win the biggest prize in football.

The nation's football promise ended abruptly with Soviet invasion in 1956. Many of the country's biggest stars were abroad on tour with Honvéd at the time and chose not to return. With only Bozsik, Hidegkuti and keeper Gyula Grosics remaining of the World Cup finalists, a squad of a completely different complexion represented Hungary at the 1958 tournament, one that was eliminated after finishing below Sweden and Wales in the group.

Sandor Kocsis shoots, Hungary v West Germany, 1954 World Cup Final

By the 1962 tournament Grosics was the last of the 'Magical Magyars' but a talented new side had emerged. In the group stage they knocked four past Bulgaria in the first 12 minutes of the game, winning 6-1 with a hat-trick from Flórián Albert. Their run ended in the quarter-finals after failing to beat Yugolsavia keeper Viliam Schrojf.

The Hungarians were considered to be serious contenders in 1966 but they were drawn in the toughest group, alongside Eusébio's Portugal, Bulgaria and holders Brazil. They faced the Portuguese without first choice keeper Jozsef Gelei, losing 3-1, but with him back in the side they fared better against a Brazil team minus the injured Pelé. In an outstanding victory they played with skill and flair, and Albert's performance was reminiscent of the 'Magical Magyars' of the past. It was Brazil's first World Cup defeat since the 'Battle Of Berne' in 1954 and the Hungarians looked like potential champions, but their run was ended in a robust quarter-final showdown with the Soviet Union.

It was to be Hungary's last campaign of substance at the World Cup. Despite winning Olympic gold for a second consecutive time in 1968, the Hungarians failed to qualify for the 1970 World Cup. Although they made it to all three tournaments between 1978 and 1986 they were unable to get past the group stage, which seemed particular unfortunate in 1982 when they defeated El Salvador 10-1 but were edged out by Argentina and Belgium. Having not qualified for the World Cup finals since 1986, a revival of the spirit of the 'Magical Magyars' seems a distant hope.

INDONESIA

Joined FIFA: 1952 **Confederation:** AFC
Finals: 1938
Record: P1/W0/D0/L1/F0/A6

Prior to independence in 1945, Indonesia competed as the Dutch East Indies, and it was in this guise that qualification for the World Cup was achieved in 1938, to date the country's only showing at the finals. Fielding a team largely made up of students, and with captain Achmad Nawir playing in glasses, they lost their one and only game 6-0 to Hungary. They were the first

Dutch East Indies (Indonesia) v Hungary, 1938

Asian team to qualify for the World Cup, even if they did so without kicking a ball because of the withdrawal of Japan, and they remain the only country in the history of the competition to have played just one game at the finals, a record that looks unlikely to be broken.

IRAN

Joined FIFA: 1945 **Confederation:** AFC

Finals: 1978, 98, 2006

Record: P9/W1/D2/L6/F6/A18

Iranian football rose to prominence in the Sixties and Seventies with the national team winning a hat-trick of Asian Cups and making the Olympic quarter-finals in 1976. Having first entered the World Cup in 1974 the Iranians reached the finals at their second attempt in 1978. They were comfortably beaten by Holland and Peru but succeeded in pulling off a much deserved 1-1 draw with Scotland.

Football became somewhat less of a priority for the country after the 1979 Iranian Revolution, and despite entering the 1982 competition they pulled out before the draw for qualification groups. Four years later they declined to enter in protest at being told that they would have to play their home matches on a neutral ground due to the ongoing Iran-Iraq war.

In the Nineties Iran re-emerged from a period of instability and reached the 1998 World Cup with a campaign that had opened with a 17-0 defeat of the Maldives. It was the widest margin in World Cup qualification history at the time and Karim Bagheri scored seven goals. Despite trailing Australia 2-0 in the play-offs in front of a crowd of 85,000 at the Melbourne Cricket Ground, the Iranians qualified for the World Cup on the away goals rule after Bagheri and Khodadad Azizi put them back on level terms. They recorded their first win at the finals with a much-celebrated 2-1 victory over USA, and although they didn't reach the second round, great satisfaction was taken from finishing above America in their group.

Iran qualified for the 2006 World Cup Finals in Germany, but they were already eliminated from the competition before gaining their first point with a 1-1 draw against Angola.

Bakhtiarizadeh, Iran v Angola, 2006

IRAQ

Joined FIFA: 1950 Confederation: AFC

Finals: 1986

Record: P3/W0/D0/L3/F1/A4

One of the top six sides on the Asian continent, more often than not it has been the Iraqis missing out on World Cup qualification. They did qualify for the 1986 finals but did so playing their home games on a neutral ground due to the ongoing Iran-Iraq war. Brazilian coach Evaristo de Macedo led them to the finals and they were drawn with Paraguay, Belgium and Mexico.

They lost all three of their group games, with future Asian Footballer Of The Year Ahmad Rahdi scoring their only goal of the tournament in a 2-1 defeat by Belgium. He had come close against Paraguay, but his header hit the net a fraction of a second after the half-time whistle had sounded, and despite the protests the goal was not given.

In the post-Saddam Hussein era the national team, who incredibly reached the 2004 Olympic semi-finals, continue to play home World Cup qualifiers at a neutral venue.

ISRAEL

Joined FIFA: 1929 **Confederation:** UEFA

Finals: 1970

Record: P3/W0/D2/L1/F1/A3

Before being moved into UEFA for political reasons, the Israelis were a strong force in the Asian Football Confederation, runners-up in the first two Asian Cups of 1956 and 1960 before lifting the trophy in 1964. They also qualified for the World Cup finals in 1970, losing to Uruguay but earning creditable draws with Sweden and Italy.

The AFC contrived to separate the Israelis from their Arab neighbours during qualification campaigns and grouped them with Far East opposition, such as Japan and South Korea. Arab disquiet saw Israel thrown out of the AFC in 1976, being shunted first into Europe and then Oceania, and even facing South American opposition in World Cup play-offs. As a consequence the Israelis have had the distinction of having played World Cup qualifiers on every continent. They were given a permanent football home in Europe when UEFA accepted them in 1991.

ITALY★★★★

Joined FIFA: 1905 **Confederation:** UEFA

Finals: **1934**★, 38★, 50, 54, 62, 66, 70★, 74, 78, 82★, 86, **90**, 94★, 98, 2002, 06★, [2010]

Record: P77/W44/D19/L14/F122/A69

One of the most successful nations in World Cup history, only the Brazilians have won the competition more times. Indeed, Italy was the first nation to win back-to-back tournaments, lifting the trophy in both 1934 and 1938, the first of their triumphs achieved as hosts.

Piqued at missing the opportunity to stage the first World Cup the Italians had not taken part in Uruguay in 1930, but four years later they gladly accepted the responsibility, even though FIFA insisted they would have to go through the qualification process. It would be the only time in World Cup history that the hosts would have to qualify.

The Italians were coached at the finals by Vittorio Pozzo, who had been intermittently in charge of the team since first taking the role in 1912. With Prime Minister Benito Mussolini determined that the success of the national football team should consolidate a strong nationalist feeling at home, it was a political imperative that the Italians perform well and their World Cup debut was marked with a crushing 7-1 win over the USA, with Angelo Schiavio netting a hat-trick.

Pozzo's side found Spain, their quarter-final opponents, a much tougher nut to crack. Italy had a controversial equaliser to thank for taking what had already been a bruising tie to a replay, which was duly won. After defeating Austria 1-0 in the semi-final, the *azzurri* were cheered on by Mussolini as they overcame Czechoslovakia with two late goals in the final.

Throughout the tournament there had been whispered accusations that Mussolini had handpicked the referees, but the Italians were world champions and before the end of the decade they would prove themselves worthy of the title.

Italy, 1982 World Cup Final

Pozzo led Italy to the finals again in 1938. With only two of his World Cup winners remaining, Giuseppe Meazza and Giovanni Ferrari, his new side featured several of the stars of the gold medal winning team from the 1936 Berlin Olympics, but they found opening round opponents Norway trickier than expected to beat. It took a fine display from keeper Aldo Olivieri and an extra-time winner from Silvio Piola to see Pozzo's attack-minded side win 2-1 and progress to the quarter-finals, where France were duly dispatched 3-1.

Two second-half goals saw off the Brazilian challenge in the semi, and in the final Italy beat Hungary 4-2, with Silvio Piola and Gino Colaussi scoring twice each for a historic win.

In the immediate post-war era the Italians had to endure a spell in the international wilderness, and when they were just a year away from defending their world title at the 1950 tournament, the heart was ripped out of the national side when the entire first team squad of reigning champions Torino were killed in a plane crash.

Italy failed to make it past the first round at the finals and subsequently missed out altogether in 1958. The 1962 tournament was remembered only for the infamous 'Battle Of Santiago', a battering encounter that saw nine-man Italy succumb to two late goals from Chile. They also had to endure the humiliation of losing to North Korea in 1966, a defeat that dealt such a psychological blow to the Italian game that its impact was still being felt decades later.

After a morale boosting European championship win in 1968, Italian football got itself back on track as coach Ferrucio Valcareggi took his side to the final of the 1970 World Cup. Still scarred by the defeat to the Koreans, an ultra-cautious Italy qualified from their group as leaders without conceding a goal and scoring just once. Indeed, their football was proving so dull that after the game with Uruguay, both sets of fans booed their own players off the pitch.

1930 | 1934 | 1938 | 1946 | 1950 | 1954 | 1958 | 1962 | 1966 | 1970

1930: The Italians decide against entering the first World Cup, annoyed at not being asked to host.

1934: The beginning of a golden period as the Italians beats Czechoslovakia to win the World Cup at home.

1938: Vittorio Pozzo becomes the first coach to win the World Cup twice as the Italians beat Hungary.

1949: Torino's plane crashes in the fog, killing eight of the national team a year before the World Cup.

1950: Avoiding air travel, the Italians travel to Brazil by boat but they crash out in the first round.

1954: Knocked out in the first round after a 4-1 defeat to Switzerland.

1958: After losing to Northern Ireland, Italy fail to qualify for the World Cup for the first time.

1962: Two players are sent-off as the Italians are defeated by hosts Chile in the 'Battle Of Santiago'.

1966: After being knocked out by North Korea, the players are pelted with rotten tomatoes on their return home.

1970: Victory over West Germany in one of the greatest semi-finals, but defeat to the brilliant Brazilians in the final.

Del Piero with the trophy, 2006 World Cup Final

Thankfully the campaign burst into life in the knockout phase, but despite scoring four goals in each of the games against Mexico and West Germany, the Italians were defeated 4-1 by Brazil in the final.

Under coach Enzo Bearzot Italy finished fourth at the 1978 finals in Argentina, losing the third place play-off match to Brazil. He was more successful four years later when the Italians won the World Cup for a third time. They did it the hard way, drawing all three of their first round games, before beating reigning champions Argentina and favourites Brazil in the second group phase. The latter match finished 3-2 and was memorable because of an astonishing hat-trick from 25-year-old Paolo Rossi, who had only just returned to football following a two-year ban for match-fixing. Rossi hit two more in the semi-final against Poland and was the scorer of Italy's first goal in a 3-1 triumph over West Germany in the final.

The Italians finished third when hosting the World Cup in 1990, losing to Argentina on penalties in the semi-final, a game that saw Maradona try to use his popularity in Naples to turn the local crowd against the national team.

They reached the World Cup final four years later, but were beaten on penalties again, this time by Brazil. They had the goals of Roberto Baggio to thank for powering them to the final, so it was a sad irony that in the shoot-out it should be Baggio whose missed penalty cost them the World Cup.

The curse of penalties struck again at the 1998 finals as Italy lost the quarter-final shoot-out to hosts France, but Roberto Baggio managed to score with his spot-kick this time. Four years later it was the curse of 1966 that came back to haunt Italy, when South Korean fans used their second round clash to evoke memories of the defeat to neighbours North Korea 36 years earlier, displaying messages from the crowd that read 'Again 1966' and 'Welcome To Azzurri's Tomb'.

The game went to extra time and was ultimately concluded by a 'golden goal' in South Korea's favour, leaving the Italian media to build conspiracy theories around several questionable refereeing decisions.

The 2006 campaign started under a cloud due to a match-fixing scandal that had rocked the domestic game, but Italy could boast a solid team captained by Fabio Cannavaro and coached by Marcello Lippi. However, the Italians needed all the luck they could muster to make their way past Australia in the round of 16. Playing with ten men thanks to a red card for Marco Materazzi, Italy had a controversial penalty late in injury time to thank for the victory after Fabio Grosso had fallen over Lucas Neill.

Following a 3-0 defeat of Ukraine, Italy were involved in the match of the tournament in the semi-finals, scoring twice in the last two minutes of extra-time against Germany to make it to their sixth World Cup final.

With an array of stars on the pitch, surprisingly it was the little known defender Materazzi who made the biggest impact on the 2006 final. Only in the team thanks to an injury to Alessandro Nesta, he conceded an early penalty that gave France the lead. He also headed the equaliser 12 minutes later, and in extra-time he goaded Zinédine Zidane into the head-butt that saw the France captain red-carded. Materazzi even scored one of the penalties in the shoot-out, but no-one in Italy was complaining as the *azzurri* picked up their fourth World Cup title.

1974: After finishing third to Poland and Argentina, the Italians are on their way home.

1978: Defeated by Brazil in the third place play-off after beating champions Argentina in the first round.

1980: A bribery scandal is revealed involving top Italian players and officials. Paolo Rossi is banned for two years.

1982: Paolo Rossi returns to help Italy win a third World Cup, scoring against West Germany in the final.

1986: Beaten by Michel Platini's France in the second round.

1990: Losing in the semi-final, Italy set a World Cup record after going 517 minutes without conceding a goal.

1994: Finishing runners-up to Brazil, Italy lose on penalties after Roberto Baggio shoots over.

1998: Roberto Baggio becomes the only Italian to have scored in three World Cups.

2002: Paolo Maldini bows out with a record of 2,217 minutes of World Cup pitch time.

2006: The Italians win the World Cup after beating France in a penalty shoot-out.

1974 1978 1982 1986 1990 1994 1998 2002 2006 2010

IVORY COAST

See Côte D'Ivorie

JAMAICA

Joined FIFA: 1962 **Confederation:** CONCACAF

Finals: 1998

Record: P3/W1/D0/L2/F3/A9

Although Jamaica has had a football federation since 1910, it wasn't until the late Nineties, with the rise of a generation of players known as the 'Reggae Boyz', that qualification for the World Cup was achieved.

The Jamaicans were led to the 1998 tournament in France by Brazilian coach Rene Simoes. It was the first time that they had recruited players of Jamaican descent from the English leagues, such as Frank Sinclair, Fitzroy Simpson, Robbie Earle, Marcus Gayle and Deon Burton.

After losing 3-1 to Croatia and 5-0 to Argentina, the Jamaicans enjoyed their first World Cup victory, beating Japan 2-1 in their final group game, with both goals courtesy of Theodore Whitmore.

JAPAN

Joined FIFA: 1929-45, 1950 **Confederation:** AFC

Finals: 1998, **2002**, 06, [2010]

Record: P10/W2/D2/L6/F8/A14

The Japanese first tasted success in international football at the 1968 Olympics, when they won the bronze medal, but World Cup qualification wasn't achieved until after the creation of a professional football league in Japan in 1993.

They narrowly missed the 1994 World Cup after conceding a last minute goal to Iraq in what would become known as the 'Agony of Doha'. As a result South Korea edged the final qualifying place on goal difference.

Making their World Cup debut at the 1998 tournament, the Japanese lost all three of their games to Argentina, Croatia and Jamaica, but they at least had the consolation of knowing they had already qualified for the 2002 World Cup as joint hosts.

They fared better on home soil, drawing with Belgium in their opening game before electrifying the home crowds with 2-0 victories over Russia and Tunisia. However, a strong Turkey team proved too much for them in the second round, with a headed goal from Umit Davala extinguishing their ambitions. For the Japanese, the tournament had been a steep learning curve, but their team had risen to the challenge and the players became household names in the space of just two weeks.

At the 2006 World Cup it was hoped that the team would build on the progress made in previous tournaments, but a single point earned from a draw with Croatia was all that was taken from the finals in Germany. The tournament ended with a 4-1 defeat by Brazil, although Japanese fans did experience momentary ecstasy when Keiji Tamada snatched a 34th minute lead against the reigning champions.

After beating Uzbekistan away, the Japanese were the first team other than the hosts to qualify for the 2010 World Cup, although they finished their campaign as runners-up in their group to Australia.

KOREA DPR

Joined FIFA: 1958 Confederation: AFC

Finals: 1966, [2010]

Record: P4/W1/D1/L2/F5/A9

Prior to the 1960s football in North Korea was strictly a domestic sport, with any contact at international level limited to just Communist countries. In 1966, however, the North Koreans entered the World Cup for the first time, qualifying for the finals after beating Australia in a play-off, helped to no small degree by the withdrawal of every African nation and all but two from the Asian confederation.

After losing their opening game 3-0 to the Soviet Union and drawing with Chile they astounded football with the shock defeat of Italy, with Pak Doo Ik scoring the goal that set-up a quarter-final clash with Portugal.

When faced by the Portuguese, the North Koreans took an astonishing 3-0 lead through Park Seung-Zin, Li Dong Woon and Yang Sung Kook, but they ended up losing 5-3, conceding four goals to Eusébio. They would not qualify for another World Cup until 2010, when finishing second in their group to neighbours South Korea.

North Korea v Italy, 1966

KOREA REPUBLIC

Joined FIFA: 1948 **Confederation:** AFC

Finals: 1954, 86, 90, 94, 98, **2002**, 06, [2010]

Record: P24/W4/D7/L13/F22/A53

South Korea gave Asian football a huge boost by reaching the semi-finals of the 2002 World Cup, a competition that they co-hosted with Japan. This was an amazing feat for a country that had failed to win a single match in five previous World Cup tournaments.

A consistent force in Asian football, the South Koreans qualified for their first finals in 1954, but after losing both of their games, 9-0 to Hungary and 7-0 to Turkey, it was another 32 years before they would play at the World Cup again. The creation of a professional league in 1983 accounted for the development of the domestic game and that has resulted in qualification for every World Cup from 1986 onwards.

Although they lost all three of their games at the 1986 finals, the South Koreans impressed with their industrious play, although their consistent fouling of Maradona in a 3-1 defeat drew criticism.

After three straight defeats at Italia 90, they came close to progressing to the second round in 1994. They snatched a draw against Spain when Hong Myung-Bo and Seo Jung-Won both scored in the last six minutes, while in their final group game they came from 3-0 down against the Germans to lose

South Korea v Spain, 2002

3-2; Hong Myung-Bo scoring the second with a shot from 25 yards out. If they had achieved more than the 0-0 draw against Bolivia in their second match, the South Koreans would have reached the second round for the first time. They were unable to build on this momentum in France four years later, where they had a poor tournament, conceding five goals to Holland and three to Mexico before returning home.

Joint hosts with Japan in 2002, South Korea caught the imagination of football fans around the world with a series of impressive performances. Backed by stunning home support, and coached by Dutchman Guus Hiddink, the Koreans overcame their inferiority complex and all of the pre-tournament predictions. They beat Poland 2-0, drew with USA and defeated Portugal 1-0, with the final group game estimated to have been watched on television by 75 per cent of Korean households.

A sensational second round win over Italy followed, while a tense 5-3 penalty shoot-out overcame Spain, but it was Germany who put paid to their dreams with a single goal victory in the semi-final.

In comparison South Korea were somewhat disappointing at the finals in Germany in 2006. After beating Togo and holding France to a draw, they lost their final group game 2-0 to Switzerland and failed to make it to the second round. They qualified for the 2010 World Cup as group winners along with second-placed North Korea.

KUWAIT

Joined FIFA: 1962 **Confederation:** AFC

Finals: 1982

Record: P3/W0/D1/L2/F2/A6

Prince Fahid calling his Kuwaiti national team off the field after France had 'scored' a fourth goal at the 1982 World Cup is the abiding memory of Kuwait's one appearance at the World Cup finals. Russian referee Miroslav Stupar had initially let Alain Giresse's goal stand, but in the midst of this confusion he reversed his decision and disallowed the goal. The French scored once more before the end of the match, and subsequently the Kuwait FA were fined £8,000 for Prince Fahid's interference in the game. His team finished bottom of the group after defeat to England, although they had gained one point from their opening draw with Czechoslovakia.

MEXICO

Joined FIFA: 1929 **Confederation:** CONCACAF

Finals: 1930, 50, 54, 58, 62, 66, **70**, 78, **86**, 94, 98, 2002, 06, [2010]

Record: P45/W11/D12/L22/F48/A84

The Mexicans have regularly appeared at the World Cup finals since taking part in the opening game of the very first tournament in 1930, reaching the quarter-finals on two occasions, both times as host. They were less than successful in that first competition, losing all three of their games with France, Chile and Argentina and conceding 13 goals.

They failed to qualify for the 1934 tournament, and withdrew from qualification in 1938, but they have entered ever since, qualifying for each post-war final until 1974.

It wasn't until competing in Chile in 1962 that the Mexicans recorded their first win, a 3-1 defeat of Czechoslovakia achieved despite conceding a goal in just 15 seconds. The keeper that day was the hugely experienced Antonio Carbajal, who represented Mexico at five consecutive tournaments between 1950 and 1966. He would grace the World Cup for the final time against Uruguay at the finals in England, but yet again Mexico failed to get any further than the opening round.

It was as hosts in 1970 that the Mexicans reached the knockout stages, progressing to the second round after finishing level on points with the Soviet Union. However, even home advantage didn't help them in the quarter-final against Italy, although they did manage to take an early lead. After European Player Of The Year Gianni Rivera was brought on as a half-time substitute Italy stepped up a gear and Mexico lost 4-1.

After losing all three of their games at the 1978 finals, they hosted the tournament once again in 1986, taking over from Colombia at short notice, and introducing the 'Mexican Wave' to the game, a phenomenon that was seen via the magic of television and copied by football fans the world over.

Reaching the quarter-finals under coach Bora Milutinović, it took a penalty shoot-out with eventual finalists West Germany to eliminate a team starring Hugo Sanchez, the most famous and talented Mexican player of the modern era.

Banned from all international competition after fielding an ineligible player in a youth tournament, Mexico were absent from the 1990 World Cup in Italy. Four years later a series of creditable performances saw Mexico qualify for the second round by finishing on top of the 'group of death', ahead of the Republic Of Ireland, Italy and Norway.

All four teams had finished level on both points and goal difference but Mexico had scored the most goals. A second round defeat to Bulgaria on penalties ended a good run but it was a poorly refereed match that saw each

Mexico v Republic Of Ireland, 1994

side reduced to ten men in the second-half.

In subsequent tournaments the Mexicans have consistently reached the round of 16, losing to Germany in 1998 and the USA in 2002. One of eight seeded teams at the 2006 World Cup, it was only the second time a non-hosting CONCACAF nation had been seeded. Despite beating Iran they were held to a scoreless draw by Angola and were defeated by Portugal, qualifying for the second-round as runners up before losing 2-1 to Argentina after extra-time.

While the Mexicans remain regulars at the World Cup, some critics argue that their qualification has been due to a lack of meaningful competition in the Central American region. Only in recent years, with the rise of the USA as a credible footballing force, have they experienced a serious local rival, and while it was USA that topped the table during qualification to the 2010 World Cup, Mexico also reached the finals as runners-up, along with third placed Honduras.

MOROCCO

Joined FIFA: 1959 **Confederation:** CAF

Finals: 1970, 86, 94, 98

Record: P13/W2/D4/L7/F12/A18

The Moroccans did not enter the World Cup until 1962. They reached the finals for the first time in 1970 when captained by Idriss Bamouss, who later became president of the Moroccan football association. That year they shocked Germany by taking the lead before losing 2-1. They later drew 1-1 with Bulgaria.

In 1986 they became the first African team to progress to the second round of the World Cup, after topping the group with scoreless draws against England and Poland, and a 3-1 win over Portugal. They faced West Germany in the second round, but were beaten by a last minute goal.

At the World Cup in 1994, the Moroccans lost all three group games by a single goal, while four years later, a 2-2 draw with Norway and an emphatic 3-0 win over Scotland took them to within a couple of minutes of the second round, only for a late goal for Norway against Brazil to end their competition.

NETHERLANDS

Joined FIFA: 1904 **Confederation:** UEFA

Finals: 1934, 38, 74★, 78★, 90, 94, 98, 2006, [2010]

Record: P36/W16/D10/L10/F59/A38

The architects of 'Total Football', the Dutch team have been one of the most skilful exponents of the beautiful game, yet they were late developers on the international stage, not making an impact at the World Cup until the 1970s. Since that time they have often stood on the verge of great success, but the national side has frequently been plagued by internal conflicts and uncertainties that have undermined the talents possessed by individual players.

After failing to get past the opening round in both of the pre-war World Cups staged in Europe, Holland did not enter the competition again until 1958, four years after the introduction of professionalism to the country's strictly amateur domestic game. But it was in the mid Sixties, when the concept of 'Total Football' took hold at club side Ajax, with coach Rinus Michels and the young Johan Cruyff, that world football began to take notice of the Dutch.

It was also under Michels that the national side rose to prominence at the 1974 World Cup, although he had only taken the helm on a short-term basis just three months before the tournament. It may have been their first World Cup in 36 years, but the Dutch dazzled onlookers with their scintillating brand of football. They were approaching the peak of their powers when they took on Brazil in a second group stage decider, with a place in the final at stake. The reigning champions resorted to a series of uncharacteristically brutal tackles, but two second-half goals from Cruyff and Johan Neeskens saw the Dutch through to their first World Cup final.

Contesting the trophy with hosts West Germany, Holland took the lead within two minutes of the kick-off, when Neeskens stroked in the first ever World Cup final penalty. He had scored before a German player had even touched the ball, but over-confidence proved the downfall of the Dutch as they took their foot off the accelerator in an attempt to humiliate the Germans with their pretty possession football.

With the terrier-like Berti Vogts getting the better of Cruyff, West Germany pulled themselves back into the game and held a 2-1 half-time lead until the final whistle.

This Dutch side would become known as the greatest team to never win football's biggest prize, and their defeat would inspire many theories (and one stage play) about the distractions that could have interfered with their preparations in advance of the final.

Four years later in Argentina they were once again undone by the hosts in the final,

Willy van der Kerkhof, 1974 World Cup Final

Dennis Bergkamp, Holland v Brazil, 1998

but this was a slightly different Dutch side. Doubts had persisted about whether they could mount a serious challenge without Cruyff, who had long since announced his decision not to travel. They were also without Wim Van Hanegem, their best player in the 1974 final, who had withdrawn after a dispute the night before they were due to fly to Argentina.

There had also been talk of the entire Dutch squad boycotting the competition in protest at the human rights violations being practiced by Argentina's military dictatorship, but instead they decided on registering their protest later should they reach the final.

Initially they made slow progress, edging through the second group stage as runners-up to Peru, but it was only goal difference that gave the Dutch the nod over a Scotland team that had beaten them 3-2 in their final group game. It wasn't until the next round that Holland finally exploded into life with a 5-1 destruction of Austria, and despite a 2-2 draw with West Germany, they made it to the World Cup final after defeating Italy.

In the intense atmosphere of the Estadio Monumental in Buenos Aires, it was the Dutch who conceded first, and although Dick Nanninga equalised late in the game, Argentina won the hard fought battle of extra-time, lifting the World Cup trophy as 3-1 winners. In a politically motivated gesture the Dutch boycotted the medal ceremony, but in defeat their snub to the Argentine military leadership failed to make the impact they had hoped for.

Holland would not qualify for the finals for another 12 years, but although taking a squad of world-class players such as Ruud Gullit, Marco Van Basten and Ronald Koeman to the 1990 tournament, it didn't prove to be a successful campaign. As reigning European champions, the Dutch were capable of playing thrilling, attacking football, but they only struggled out of their group as one of the best third-placed teams. A second round capitulation to West Germany proved a bitter affair, and both Frank Rijkaard and German striker Rudi Völler were sent-off.

In subsequent tournaments the Dutch have been able to boast players of international class, such as Edgar Davids, Patrick Kluivert and Dennis Bergkamp, but they have consistently failed to turn this individual talent into team success. They were knocked out by Brazil in the 1994 quarter-finals, and again in the 1998 semis. In the latter game Holland seemed to have the beating of the reigning champions but when it went to penalties both Phillip Cocu and Ronald de Boer missed.

After failing to reach the 2002 finals, the Dutch qualified for the 2006 tournament under coach Marco Van Basten, but they were knocked out in the second round by Portugal in an acrimonious contest that set a World Cup disciplinary record, with 16 yellow cards and four players sent-off.

They qualified for the 2010 World Cup with a 100 per cent record, 14 points clear of rivals Norway and Scotland.

NEW ZEALAND

Joined FIFA: 1948 **Confederation:** OFC

Finals: 1982, [2010]

Record: P3/W0/D0/L3/F2/A12

Known as the 'All Whites' to distinguish themselves from the dominant Rugby Union 'All Blacks', New Zealand's national football team made their only appearance at the World Cup finals in 1982. It took 15 qualifying games to earn their place but once in Spain they crashed out with three straight defeats, losing 5-2 to Scotland, 3-0 to the Soviet Union and 3-0 to Brazil.

New Zealand successfully qualified for the 2010 tournament having become the leading force in the Oceania region following Australia's defection to the Asian Football Confederation. Victory over Bahrain in the play-offs clinched a place at the finals.

NIGERIA

Joined FIFA: 1959 **Confederation:** CAF

Finals: 1994, 98, 2002, [2010]

Record: P11/W4/D1/L6/F14/A16

The Nigerians first entered the World Cup in 1962, although it was not until the 1980s that they had a team capable of success on the world stage. Winning the 1985 Under-16 World Cup proved to be the springboard needed for the 'Super Eagles' to reach three successive World Cups and win Olympic gold in 1996. Qualification for their first World Cup in 1994 was helped by the allocation of a third African place at the finals, following the success of Cameroon at the previous tournament.

At USA 94 the Nigerians were coached by Clemens Westerhof, a Dutchman who had helped to revitalise the national team. Although beaten by the Argentinians, Nigeria still topped the group on goal difference after a three-way tie with Bulgaria and Argentina. In the round of 16 Westerhof's team faced

Italy and took the lead midway through the first-half after Emmanuel Amunike pounced on a defensive mistake by Paolo Maldini. The Nigerians held their lead against ten men until Roberto Baggio equalised with just 90 seconds remaining. He would score again in extra-time to win the game for Italy.

At the 1998 finals in France the Nigerians topped their group once again, helped by an unexpected 3-2 win over Spain that saw the Africans twice come from behind. Their run ended in the next round after a comprehensive 4-1 defeat by Denmark, but they could take some pride from being the last of five African nations to be eliminated. In contrast, the 2002 World Cup was nothing but a disappointment as a single goalless draw with England was all they took away from the tournament.

The Nigerians qualified for the 2010 World Cup on the last day of the campaign, jumping above Tunisia in the group table after defeating bottom placed Kenya 3-2 away.

NORTH KOREA

See Korea DPR

NORTHERN IRELAND

Joined FIFA: 1911 **Confederation:** UEFA

Finals: 1958, 82, 86

Record: P13/W3/D5/L5/F13/A23

The Northern Irish did not meet non-British opposition until 1951, soon after they had stopped picking players from southern Ireland, but World Cup qualification was not achieved for the first time until 1958. When they finally reached the finals, it was with more than their fair share of luck.

Northern Ireland needed to beat Italy in Belfast to qualify, but after the FIFA-appointed referee was stranded by bad weather, the Italians would not accept a replacement and refused to play the game as a qualifier. The match went ahead as a 'friendly' and finished 2-2, but when the two teams faced each other in the restaged qualifier the following month, Northern Ireland snatched a 2-1 victory and the Italians failed to qualify for the first time in their history.

Before the finals Danny Blanchflower had comically announced, "Our tactics have

Norman Whiteside, Northern Ireland v Spain, 1986

always been to equalise before the other team scores". The team did a little better than that, but only after the Irish Football Association backed down on the rule forbidding play on the Sabbath.

After a surprise 1-0 victory over Czechoslovakia that was achieved thanks to an outstanding performance from Manchester United keeper Harry Gregg, the Irish lost to Argentina and drew with West Germany. Two goals from Aston Villa striker Peter McParland secured a play-off victory over the Czechs, but this run was ended by a 4-0 thrashing by France in the quarter-finals.

The Northern Irish did not feature at the finals again until the 1980s, when qualification for successive World Cups showcased the country's best ever team, featuring players of the calibre of Martin O'Neill, Sammy McIlroy, Gerry Armstrong, Norman Whiteside and Pat Jennings.

In 1982 the Irish drew with both Yugoslavia and Honduras, before stunning hosts Spain with a Gerry Armstrong goal that saw them qualify for the next round at the top of their group. It was an impressive feat considering they beat the hosts playing with ten men for most of the final 30 minutes following the red-carding of Mal Donaghy. They were also deeply indebted to a superb performance from keeper Pat Jennings.

In the second group stage a draw with Austria and a 4-1 defeat by France ended their campaign, although Martin O'Neill was unlucky to have an opening goal disallowed against the French. Through Norman Whiteside, however, the Northern Irish had created a little bit of World Cup history. He made his first international appearance in their opening game aged just 17 years and 41 days, becoming the youngest player to have appeared in the finals.

Despite competing with a nucleus of the same squad at the 1986 finals, Northern Ireland had less success, drawing their opening game with Algeria before losing to Spain and Brazil. They have not succeeded in qualifying for the World Cup since.

NORWAY

Joined FIFA: 1908 **Confederation:** UEFA

Finals: 1938, 94, 98

Record: P8/W2/D3/L3/F7/A8

The Norwegians made little impact on international football until the 1990s, when they qualified for successive World Cups with a generation of players that included Erik Thorstvedt, Stig Inge Bjornebye, Tore Andre Flo and Ole Gunnar Solksjaer. However, it was with an earlier generation that the 1936 Olympic bronze medallists beat Ireland over two legs to reach the 1938 World Cup.

They would play just one game at the finals, but despite facing holders Italy in their opening game, they acquitted themselves well and placed the Italians under concerted pressure for sections of the game.

Entering every tournament since 1954, it wasn't until the 1994 World Cup that the Norwegians once again qualified. Doing so was an impressive achievement as they topped their group above Holland and England, but the tournament itself proved to be a disappointment.

Achieving just a single win over Mexico, they were the only team in their group not to progress to the knockout stage, even though all four teams had finished level on points. Mexico, the Republic Of Ireland and Italy edged through thanks to superior goal difference.

They made more of an impact at the 1998 World Cup Finals in France and even managed a 2-1 win over Brazil in the group stages before losing to Italy in the second round.

PARAGUAY

Joined FIFA: 1921 **Confederation:** CONMEBOL
Finals: 1930, 50, 58, 86, 98, 2002, 06, [2010]
Record: P22/W6/D7/L9/F27/A36

One of the stronger footballing nations of South America, Paraguay remain among the poorest and least glamorous, but for a small country it can be proud of its eight World Cup campaigns, reaching the second round three times.

In 1930 the Paraguayans were among the participants of the first World Cup, but in their opening game they conceded the first ever hat-trick at the finals, scored by USA's Bert Patenaude. Luis Vargas Peña scored as they beat Belgium 1-0 in their remaining game, but it wasn't enough to keep them in the competition.

Qualifying for the 1950 competition without having to kick a ball, at the finals they drew with Sweden and lost to Italy to finish bottom of the group. Eight years later they might have hoped for a better run. Having beaten Uruguay by five goals in qualification, and boasting a prolific forward line that included Juan Bautista Agüero, Juan Romero and Florencio Amarilla, the Paraguayans arrived in Sweden as fancied outsiders but they came up against the 'Champagne football' of France in their opening game. Despite leading 3-2 early in the second-half, they crashed to a 7-3 defeat. After beating Scotland a victory over Yugoslavia would have put them into the second round, but a 3-3 draw proved not enough.

After the 1958 World Cup the departure of several key players to Spain weakened the national side and it would be Paraguay's last appearance at the finals for 28 years.

Returning to the World Cup in 1986, it was with a strong team that included the previous year's South American Player Of The Year, midfield dynamo Julio Cesar Romero, or Romerito as he was known in Brazil. He scored as Paraguay beat Iraq and drew with Mexico, while a pair from Robert Cabañas in a 2-2 draw with Belgium helped the team to the second round. However, in what was expected to be a close and physical tie, the Paraguayans proved no match for England's Beardsley-Lineker strike force, losing 3-0.

Since the expansion of the tournament to 32 teams in 1998, they have become regulars at the finals, helped by a talented generation of players that include Celso Ayala, Carlos Gamarra and José Luis Chilavert. At France 98 they progressed to the second round despite goalless draws with Spain and Bulgaria, but they were eliminated by the hosts with the first 'golden goal' in World Cup history. During their campaign Chilavert became the first goalkeeper to take a direct free-kick at a World Cup, and along with team-mate Gamarra was selected for FIFA's all-star team of the tournament.

In 2002 Paraguay once again reached the second round, edging South Africa out of the runners-up spot in their group on the number of goals scored. Although holding Germany for much of the second round tie, an 88th minute goal from Oliver Neuville resulted in defeat to the eventual finalists. It was the closest the Paraguayans have come to a place in the quarter-finals, as defeats to both Sweden and England in 2006 meant they were already certain of elimination before a consolation victory over Trinidad and Tobago.

Paraguay reached the 2010 World Cup after finishing third to Brazil and Chile in the South American qualification group.

Roberto Cabañas, Paraguay v Belgium, 1986

PERU

Joined FIFA: 1926 **Confederation:** CONMEBOL
Finals: 1930, 70, 78, 82
Record: P15/W4/D3/L8/F19/A31

Despite taking part in the first World Cup finals in 1930, when they lost both of their group games with Romania and Uruguay and saw one of their number sent-off, the Peruvians have only really been a strong force on the world stage in one era, reaching the World Cup quarter-finals in both 1970 and 1978.

At Mexico 70 Peru were the outsiders schooled in the Brazilian style by coach Didi. Having qualified at the expense of Argentina, they proved one of tournament's surprise attractions, with an outstanding strike from Teófilo Cubillas helping them to beat Bulgaria after trailing by two goals early in the second-half. Cubillas scored twice more in the victory over Morocco and once in a 3-1 defeat by West Germany, ensuring that Peru would qualify for the second round behind the West Germans. Along with Alberto Gallardo he would score again in the quarter-final, but with Brazil in unstoppable form Peru finished second best in a six-goal thriller.

Coached by Marcos Calderón, 'La Blanquirroja' qualified for the finals once again in 1978. The side that travelled to Argentina included several memorable players, such as the eccentric keeper Ramon 'El Loco' Quiroga and the rocket-like winger Juan Muñante, but Cubillas was still very much the star turn. He inspired the team through to the second phase, successfully negotiating a group that included Iran, Scotland, and eventual runners-up Holland. He was particularly impressive in the 3-1 defeat of Scotland, and although he also gave away the penalty from which the Scots opened the scoring, he found the net twice in the last 20 minutes to win the game.

Having looked so impressive early in the tournament, in the second group phase Peru lost all three of their games, with defeats to Brazil and Poland followed by a controversial 6-0 crushing by Argentina, a scoreline which took the hosts through to the final in place of Brazil. The result became the cause of much speculation and newspapers would later claim that a deal had been struck between the ruling military dictatorships of Argentina and Peru.

Peru were coached to the 1982 World Cup Finals by Elba de Pádua, better known as 'Tim', a Brazilian international who had played at the 1938 World Cup Finals in France. However, his team could do no better than draw against both Cameroon and Italy, the latter match ending their run of 493 minutes without scoring a goal, a competition record that would not be beaten for another 12 years. Even 33-year-old Cubillas, playing at his third World Cup, could not stop the slide and the Peruvians were eliminated after a 5-1 defeat to Poland. They have not managed to qualify for the finals since.

POLAND

Joined FIFA: 1923 **Confederation:** UEFA
Finals: 1938, 74, 78, 82, 86, 2002, 06
Record: P31/W15/D5/L11/F44/A40

It wasn't until the 1970s that the Polish really made an impact on the world stage, with a stylish brand of attacking play that won gold at the 1972 Olympics and provided a springboard for three excellent World Cup campaigns in the following ten years. Prior to that they had made just one appearance at the finals but their 6-5 defeat to Brazil in 1938 would prove one of the most thrilling matches in the competition's history, with striker Ernest Wilimowski becoming the first player to score four goals in a World Cup game, a record not beaten until 1994.

After the Second World War the Polish did not enter the competition again until 1958, failing to reach the finals until 1974 when they famously eliminated England in qualification. With a team coached by Kazimierz Gorski, they went on to finish third and proved to be the tournament's biggest surprise, beating Haiti 7-0 in their group and dispensing with the challenge of both Argentina and Italy.

In Grzegorz Lato they had the most prolific striker in the competition and he scored a vital second-half winner in the 2-1 victory over Yugoslavia that brought Poland face-to-face with West Germany for a place in the final. In a tight game that saw keeper Jan Tomaszewski excel, Poland were beaten by a Gerd Müller strike 14 minutes from time. Defeating Brazil in the third place play-off game was scant consolation.

Poland qualified unbeaten for the 1978 finals, dropping just a point at home to second-placed Portugal. They could rely on many of the same players as four years earlier, including Lato, Tomaszewski and Kazimierz Deyna, but the team was not in the same class, even though striker Wlodek Lubański finally made his World Cup debut having missed the 1974 tournament through injury. The Poles were further strengthened by the addition of Zbigniew Boniek, and after holding bitter rivals West Germany to a lifeless 0-0 draw in the tournament's opening game, they beat Tunisia and Mexico to finish top of the group. They were less fortunate in the second group stage, losing to Argentina and Brazil and recording their only win of the stage against an out-of-sorts Peru.

By the 1982 World Cup only Lato, Marek Kusto, Andrzej Szarmach, and Wladyslaw Zmuda remained from the squad of 1974, but with new Juventus signing Boniek approaching the peak of his powers the Poles were a fancied outside bet. After a slow start, for their final group game coach Antoni Piechniczek finally pushed Boniek into a more forward position and their campaign exploded into life with a 5-1 defeat of Peru.

They again topped the table in the second group stage, helped by a Boniek hat-trick against Belgium, but a needless booking shortly before the final whistle of their last group game against the Soviet Union ensured that the Poles were without their suspended star when they needed him most, losing to Italy in the semi-final.

Poland v Germany, 2006

By the mid-Eighties Polish football was in decline, and a poor performance at the 1986 finals saw them scrape out of their group in third place before losing 4-0 to Brazil in the second round. This would be their last appearance at the finals until 2002, when they recorded just one win against USA.

The 2006 World Cup in Germany proved little better, but after a surprise defeat to Ecuador they could at least take some pride from a fiercely contested group encounter with the hosts that was only lost in the final seconds of stoppage time.

PORTUGAL

Joined FIFA: 1923 **Confederation:** UEFA
Finals: 1966, 86, 2002, 06, [2010]
Record: P19/W11/D1/L7/F32/A21

For a nation with such a passionate footballing culture Portugal's record of reaching the World Cup has been disappointing and it has only been in the 21st Century that the Portuguese have finally established themselves at the finals.

Having entered every competition since 1934, it wasn't until 1966 that Portugal finally qualified for the finals, when Eusébio became one of the star attractions of the tournament. Drawn alongside Brazil, Hungary and Bulgaria, all four teams were considered serious contenders, yet it was the Portuguese who topped the group with maximum points.

However, for all their tantalising skills going forward, it was their ruthlessness in the tackle, aimed at eliminating the threat of Pelé, which characterised their match against Brazil. As a result, the great Brazilian was carried from the pitch and threatened to retire from international football.

Their run was almost curtailed in the quarter-finals when they came up against an unexpectedly strong challenge from the North Koreans, who exploited Portugal's defensive frailties to snatch a 3-0 lead in just 25 minutes. Inevitably it was Eusébio who kicked off a comeback with four goals, while Augusto added a fifth to save their embarrassment with a 5-3 win.

Their semi-final was altogether different, as their gifted forwards struggled to penetrate England's solid defence. Bobby Charlton

Eusébio scores, Portugal v North Korea, 1966

scored twice, while an outrageous goal line handball from his brother Jack conceded the penalty from which Eusébio pulled one back, but at the end of the game the sight of the Portuguese star leaving the pitch in tears was one of the most enduring images of the tournament. Victory over the Soviet Union in the third place play-off would see Eusébio score his ninth goal to win the Golden Boot, yet it was no consolation.

It would be 20 years before the Portuguese would make another appearance at the finals, only to fail in the first round of the 1986 World Cup, but their campaign had already been marred by poor organisation and a financial dispute that resulted in the players refusing to train. Despite exacting revenge on the English against the run of play in their opening game, they went on to lose to both Poland and Morocco.

In the Nineties Portugal developed a 'Golden Generation' of players such as Rui Costa, Paulo Sousa and Luis Figo, but the team's performances failed to outstrip expectations. When they finally qualified for the World Cup in 2002 they were heavily tipped for success, but with Figo failing to live up to his World Player Of The Year billing, Portugal were eliminated from the competition at the first hurdle after defeats to the USA and hosts South Korea.

The nation's football fortunes started to change with the appointment of Brazil's World Cup winning coach Luiz Felipe Scolari, who led the team to the 2006 World Cup where they reached the semi-finals for the first time since 1966. Drawn with Mexico, Angola and Iran, they qualified for the second round with a 100 per cent record, edging a volatile match with Holland that managed to break the World Cup record for bookings and red cards.

In the semi-finals the Portuguese lined up against France, but their petulant attitude and petty gamesmanship made them unpopular, while their young star Cristiano Ronaldo – who had played a pivotal part in engineering the sending-off of England's Wayne Rooney in the previous round – was whistled and booed throughout the match. A single penalty gave France the advantage, and on the final whistle several members of the Portuguese squad and their coaching staff had to be restrained as they tried to accost France coach Raymond Domenech.

It was an inglorious performance from a highly talented team, and defeat to Germany in the third place play-off match offered them no redemption.

Led by coach Carlos Queiroz the Portuguese came close to missing out on qualification to the 2010 World Cup, only ensuring their place at the finals after play-off victories over Bosnia and Herzegovina.

REPUBLIC OF IRELAND

Joined FIFA: 1923 **Confederation:** UEFA

Finals: 1990, 94, 2002

Record: P13/W2/D8/L3/F10/A10

The Football Association Of Ireland was founded in 1921 following the division of the country into two separate entities, and it first entered a team into the World Cup in 1934, competing as the Irish Free State. After 1936 separate 'Ireland' teams were fielded by both the FAI in the south and by the Irish Football Association in the north, each organisation claiming to represent the whole of Ireland.

Both Ireland teams contested qualification for the 1950 World Cup and both drew on players from the entire territory, including four players who represented both associations during the course of the campaign. To avoid this confusion, in 1953 FIFA ruled that the two associations should field players based on their political borders and that the FAI team should be known as the Republic Of Ireland.

While Northern Irish football experienced its heyday during the Eighties, the Republic did not really make an impact on the world stage until the following decade, when English World Cup winner Jack Charlton led the national team to consecutive World Cups. After his appointment in 1986, Charlton scoured the English divisions looking for players of Irish extraction who had not yet played at international level (the criteria was at least one Irish grandparent).

He recruited players such as John Aldridge, Kevin Sheedy and Ray Houghton, and took the Irish to their first ever World Cup finals in 1990. Reaching the second round, they beat Romania in a heart-stopping penalty shoot-out to set-up a quarter-final clash with hosts Italy, but although Charlton's team put Walter Zenga's goal under sustained attack, the tournament's top scorer, Totò Schillaci, halted their ambitions with a strike shortly before half-time.

Qualifying for the finals again in 1994 the Irish got their World Cup campaign off to an incredible start, with a well-struck Ray Houghton volley proving too much for eventual finalists Italy. A 2-1 defeat to Mexico in their second group game was notable for Jack Charlton's touchline outburst as he attempted to introduce substitute John Aldridge, who eventually scored the late consolation goal that had such vital importance to Ireland's goal difference.

With all four teams finishing level on points, it was the Irish that qualified for the second round behind Mexico, leaving the Italians to sneak through as one of the best third-placed teams. Charlton's team were beaten 2-0 by Holland in the knockout stages, with an uncharacteristic blunder from keeper Pat Bonner to blame for the second goal.

Missing out on France 98, the Republic Of Ireland qualified for the 2002 finals after negotiating a difficult group that included both Portugal and Holland, ultimately booking their place after a two-legged play-off victory over Iran. Unfortunately their tournament was completely overshadowed by the ill-tempered spat that erupted between coach Mick McCarthy and his captain, Roy Keane, who complained about the poor quality of the preparation for the tournament. As a result Keane walked out on the squad en route to the finals.

Without their biggest star, the Irish performed admirably and were inspired by a dramatic injury time goal from Robbie Keane that secured a draw with Germany. They went on to reach the tournament's second round, before being eliminated in a penalty shoot-out by Spain. Since then the Irish have failed to qualify again.

Robbie Keane, Republic Of Ireland v Germany, 2002

ROMANIA

Joined FIFA: 1923 Confederation: UEFA
Finals: 1930, 34, 38, 70, 90, 94, 98
Record: P21/W8/D5/L8/F30/A32

The Romanians played at the first three World Cups but it was not until the 1990s that they would make their biggest impact. One of only four European nations to take part in 1930, Romania had entered on the instructions of King Carol II, who also selected the squad. He gave the players three months off from their jobs with guarantees that they would be rehired on their return, a luxury not afforded to many at the competition. Starting strongly they defeated ten-man Peru 3-1, but were eliminated after losing 4-0 to the hosts.

In 1934 Romania failed to get past the first round when narrowly defeated by a strong Czechoslovakia side, despite taking an early lead through Ştefan Dobay. Four years later they qualified without kicking a ball following the withdrawal of opponents Egypt, but they fared little better once the tournament was underway. A 3-3 draw with outsiders Cuba was only achieved after an extra-time equaliser from Dobay, and in the replay the Romanians suffered the shock of the tournament, losing 2-1 despite the winning goal being flagged for offside.

The Romanians would not reach the World Cup finals again until 1970, when they shared the toughest of groups with Czechoslovakia, Brazil and England. Needing to beat the Brazilians in their final game they battled for survival, but despite goals from Florea Dumitrache and Emerich Dembrowski, they were always playing catch-up and lost 3-2.

In the Eighties European Cup winners Steaua Bucharest raised the profile of Romanian football at club level, and this helped to inspire an era of improved fortunes for the national team. With players such as Gheorghe Hagi and Ilie Dumitrescu, coach Emerich Jenei led the squad to Italia 90, where a 1-1 draw in their final group game with Argentina put them through to the knockout stages. In the round of 16 the Romanians toiled hard but were unable to break down a defensive Republic Of Ireland side, and when the game went to penalties,

Gheorghe Hagi, Romania v Switzerland, 1994

substitute Daniel Timofte saw his spot-kick – Romania's fifth – saved by Pat Bonner. David O'Leary converted Ireland's remaining penalty to eliminate the Romanians.

Coached by Anghel Iordănescu the Romanians had only just managed to qualify for the 1994 finals, but with Hagi, Dumitrescu and Florin Răducioiu all in outstanding form, they provided some of the most entertaining football of the tournament. Hagi also scored one of its finest goals against the highly fancied Colombians, hit from his position nearly 40 yards out on the left wing.

After a shock humiliation by Switzerland in the wilting indoor heat of Detroit's Pontiac Silverdome, an early Dan Petrescu goal beat hosts USA and put the Romanians through to the knockout stages where they were matched with Argentina. Their opponents may have been without the disgraced Maradona, but the Romanians hardly noticed the suspension of Răducioiu. With Dumitrescu pushed further up the pitch to compensate, he scored twice in the opening 20 minutes, and set-up Hagi for Romania's third in the 3-2 win.

It would take a penalty shoot-out defeat following a rollercoaster quarter-final with Sweden to finally end their run, with Dan Petrescu and Miodrag Belodedici failing to convert their spot-kicks.

At the 1998 finals the Romanians topped the group after goals from Viorel Moldovan and Petrescu helped them beat England, but their campaign was best remembered for the squad's decision to go entirely blond for their third group game against Tunisia at the Stade de France. It was a gesture of arrogance that almost backfired, when a late equaliser from Moldovan was needed to save their embarrassment against the group makeweights. The goal helped them to avoid Argentina in the next round, but they were eliminated by Croatia instead.

RUSSIA

Joined FIFA: 1912 **Confederation:** UEFA
Finals: 1958, 62, 66, 70, 82, 86, 90 94, 2002
Record: P37/W17/D6/L14/F64/A44

Before its break-up in 1991 the Soviet Union produced some of the finest football sides that Europe has seen, twice winning Olympic gold and also winning the inaugural European Championship in 1960. At the World Cup, however, its teams have rarely reached their full potential. After the break-up Russia was recognised by FIFA as successor to the Soviet Union, bequeathing it a controversial heritage in the game.

The Soviet Union did not enter the World Cup until 1958, by which time it had established a reputation as a formidable football nation, a pioneer of the new, scientific approach to training and preparation. Drawn in the toughest group along with Brazil, England and Austria, in their first game the Soviets led England until conceding a late penalty. After beating Austria they were finally able to call on the services of captain Igor Netto, who returned to the side following injury, but the Soviets were made to look pedestrian by Brazil, who gave tournament debuts to Pelé, Garrincha and Zito.

A 2-0 defeat pushed them into a play-off with England, which they duly won thanks to an Anatoli Ilyin strike, but less than 48 hours later a tired-looking Soviet side were outthought by Sweden coach George Raynor in the quarter-finals.

Reaching the 1962 tournament with a 100 per cent qualification record, at the finals the Soviets were surprised by a poor Colombia side that managed to claw its way back from 4-1 down, putting the ball past Yashin three times in just eight minutes. The Soviets still managed to progress to the quarter-finals, but Yashin was at fault again as they crashed out to hosts Chile.

At the 1966 finals the Soviets achieved their best World Cup finish, even fielding a reserve team in their last group game against Chile. With Yashin back in dependable form, they outmuscled Hungary in the quarter-finals, but playing with ten men following the red-carding of Igor Chislenko they crashed out of the competition in a bad tempered semi-final encounter with West Germany. They also lost the third place play-off to Eusébio's Portugal.

At Mexico 70 the Soviet Union played the hosts in the opening game, but a dull scoreless draw was notable only for the moment when Anatoli Puzach came on as the first substitute in World Cup history. Both teams made it to the quarter-finals, where the Soviets were beaten in extra-time by Uruguay.

Not taking part in the 1974 World Cup, the Soviets chose political principle over qualification, refusing to contest the away leg of a play-off with Chile at the Estadio Nacional in Santiago, a venue that had been used to house the political prisoners of General Augusto Pinochet. "Soviet sportsmen cannot play on a ground stained with the blood of Chilean patriots," announced Valentin Granatkin, the head of the Soviet football federation.

Lev Yashin, Soviet Union v England, 1958

When they next reached the World Cup finals in 1982 it was for the first time in 12 years, yet after a tame 30-yard shot from Andrei Bal somehow beat Waldir Peres, they led the elegant Brazilians in their opening game until succumbing 15 minutes from time. Losing 2-1, they reached the second group stage on goal difference at the expense of Scotland, but after a narrow victory over Belgium and a draw with Poland, they exited the competition by the same rule.

In 1986 coach Valery Lobanovsky led one of the most exciting Soviet teams to grace the World Cup, taking them to the second round after a 6-0 opening victory over Hungary. But despite their undoubted class and unrivalled fitness, in one of the most thrilling games in the competition's history they lost a seven goal rollercoaster to Belgium, having led 2-1 with just quarter of an hour to play. Igor Belanov scored a hat-trick, including a stunning 20-yard opener that helped him to win the European Player Of The Year award.

A 4-0 victory over Cameroon in their final game was the only result of note at the 1990 finals, but earlier defeats to Romania and Argentina meant the Soviet Union finished at the bottom of their group. It would be their last appearance at the finals under that name, qualifying as Russia for the 1994 World Cup, albeit with several former Soviet players of Ukrainian origin in the line-up.

It was a depleted Russian side that arrived in the USA following a dispute between coach Pavel Sadyrin and many of the squad's key players, such as Andre Kanchelskis, Sergei Kiriakov and Igor Shalimov. Without them the Russians failed to progress to the second round, and it was only after elimination was certain that they beat Cameroon 6-1, Oleg Salenko becoming the first player to score five goals in a World Cup game. He finished the tournament as its joint leading goalscorer, having reached his six-goal tally in just 215 minutes of pitch time.

After a surprise defeat to co-hosts Japan in

2002 the Russians proved to be one of the great disappointments of the tournament. They have since struggled to make an impact, and although they reached the quarter-finals of Euro 2008 under Gus Hiddink, they failed to qualify for the 2010 World Cup after losing out to Slovenia in the play-offs.

SAUDI ARABIA

Joined FIFA: 1959 **Confederation:** AFC

Finals: 1994, 98, 2002, 06

Record: P13/W2/D2/L9/F9/A32

After winning the FIFA Under-17 World Cup in 1989, Saudi Arabian football relied on the best of this generation of footballers to kick-start its future successes. Four World Cup appearances followed, but none would be more eventful than their first appearance at USA 94, when they beat Morocco in the first ever all-Arab World Cup clash. Saeed Owairan also scored the best goal of the tournament against Belgium. In the round of 16 Fahad Al-Ghesheyan hit an impressive late consolation goal but Sweden finished 3-1 winners.

The 1998 tournament proved less successful and a solitary point was all the Saudis had to take from their campaign. After a 4-0 defeat to France, they sacked manager Carlos Alberto Parreira with one game still to play. Parreira had coached Brazil to World Cup success in 1994, but now he had become Saudi Arabia's eighth managerial casualty in just four years. Prince Faisal Bin Fadh decided that assistant coach Mohamed Al-Khuraishi should take charge of the team for its final game against South Africa, where an injury time equaliser robbed them of maximum points.

On their return a committee was formed to investigate the poor showing of the players, but four years later the performance was even worse. Kicking off the finals with an 8-0 defeat to Germany, they finished as the tournament's worst team, having conceded 12 goals for no return. At the 2002 finals, a 2-2 draw with Tunisia at least allowed them to return home with a little pride, although a narrow 1-0 defeat to Spain was not without embarrassment as the Spanish had rested their entire first XI for the match.

Kenny Dalglish, Scotland v Holland, 1974

SCOTLAND

Joined FIFA: 1910-20, 1924-28, 1946

Confederation: UEFA

Finals: 1954, 58, 74, 78, 82, 86, 90, 98

Record: P23/W4/D7/L12/F25/A41

Scotland hosted the first ever international football match in 1872, but its team has often underperformed at the World Cup finals, struggling against teams that should have been easily beaten while performing heroically against far mightier opposition.

First qualifying for the World Cup finals in 1950 after finishing runners-up in the British Home Internationals tournament, the Scots chose not to attend, insisting they would only compete as British champions.

Four years later they went to the World Cup in Switzerland despite finishing second to England in their group, but they were a depleted force. Not only had Rangers refused to release its players, but the Scottish FA went into the tournament on a shoestring budget, sending just a 13-man squad including two goalkeepers. Unsurprisingly they were soon packing their bags after a 1-0 defeat by Austria and a 7-0 drubbing at the hands of Uruguay, their disillusioned manager Andy Beattie having resigned after the first game.

The Scotland team were led to the 1958 World Cup by Dawson Walker, a stand-in for manager Matt Busby, who was still recovering from injuries suffered in the Munich air disaster earlier in the year. After drawing with Yugoslavia, they lost to Paraguay and France and were eliminated from the competition. It would be their last finals for 16 years.

Willie Ormond led the Scots to the 1974 World Cup in West Germany. After putting just two goals past lowly Zaïre, they drew with Brazil and hit a late equaliser against Yugoslavia, but goal difference ruled them out of the next round, making them the first team to be eliminated from the World Cup without losing a game.

Perhaps the Scotland team that should have had the most impact was the 1978 side under Ally MacLeod, a decent outside bet crammed with talented players such as Kenny Dalglish, Graeme Souness, Archie Gemmill, Joe Jordan, Don Masson and Bruce Rioch. MacLeod recklessly promised that Scotland would bring the World Cup trophy home, a claim he would live to regret. Scotland disappointed, both on and off the field, losing to Peru and only scraping a draw with Iran before pulling off a surprise victory against well-fancied Holland. It was not quite enough to take them through to the next stage, and more embarrassingly still, winger Willie Johnston was sent home in disgrace after failing a dope test.

After a disappointing tournament in 1982 Scotland were eliminated on goal difference for a third successive tournament. Four years later they were led to the finals by Alex Ferguson, who had taken over as manager when Jock Stein died from a heart attack suffered on the touchline during the final moments of the last qualifying group game away to Wales.

Under Ferguson the Scots reached the World Cup after beating Australia in the play-offs, but despite the efforts of the dynamic Gordon Strachan they gained just a point from their three games and finished bottom of a group they had shared with Denmark, West Germany and Uruguay.

Under Andy Roxburgh they qualified for their fifth consecutive World Cup in 1990, but after defeat to Costa Rica in their first game they struggled to get a foothold and finished behind both Brazil and the Costa Ricans. At France 98 Scotland were again drawn with Brazil, but after clawing their way back into contention against the South Americans in the tournament's opening game, the Scots ultimately lost to an own goal from Tom Boyd. A humiliating defeat to Morocco ended their last World Cup campaign to date.

SENEGAL

Joined FIFA: 1962 **Confederation:** CAF

Finals: 2002

Record: P5/W2/D2/L1/F7/A6

Under French coach Bruno Metsu, Senegal caused a sensation with their first appearance at the World Cup finals in 2002, beating holders France 1-0 in the tournament's opening game. Midfielder Pape Bouba Diop beat France's galaxy of stars to score the first goal, but it was striker El Hadji Diouf who would receive the most accolades.

Nicknamed the 'Lions of Teranga', Senegal went on to draw with Denmark, and led Uruguay 3-0 before being held to another draw. They progressed to the round of 16 in second place behind the Danes, but it took a golden goal from Henri Camara, his second strike of the game, to finish off Sweden. In the quarter-finals they exited the competition in the same heartbreaking manner, with Turkey's Ilhan Mansiz scoring the golden goal that extinguished Senegal's hopes of becoming the first African nation to reach the semi-finals.

Bapa Bouba Diop, Senegal v France, 2002

SERBIA

Joined FIFA: 1919 **Confederation:** UEFA

Finals*: 1930, 50, 54, 58, 62, 74, 82, 90, 98, 2006, [2010]

Record*: P40/W16/D8/L16/F62/A56

** Includes Yugoslavia (-2003), and Serbia & Montenegro (2003-06)*

Following the break-up of Socialist Federal Republic of Yugoslavia in 1991, the present day Serbia was the footballing nation nominated by FIFA as the direct descendant of Yugoslavia's national team. The country's other constituent parts, Bosnia-Herzegovina, Croatia, Macedonia and Slovenia each formed separate international football teams, none of which lay claim to Yugoslavia's heritage in the game.

In purely footballing terms the disintegration of Yugoslavia was unfortunate, as at times in its history it could boast one of the most exciting teams in Europe. The country itself did not exist until after the First World War, and its football team was one of only four European sides to play in the first World Cup in 1930, although the country's Croatian players boycotted the team. At the finals the Yugoslavs beat both Brazil, who hadn't played a full international since 1925, and Bolivia to top their group, but a 6-1 defeat to Uruguay ended their campaign in the semi-finals.

They did not qualify again until 1950, when they found themselves once more in a pool with Brazil, who this time proved too good. Grouped together again in Switzerland in 1954, both sides progressed to the quarter-finals at the expense of France and Mexico.

Although the Yugoslavs fielded ten of their silver medallists from the 1952 Helsinki Olympics in the quarter-final, and although they could boast one of the most formidable strike forces in world football, they were unable to get on the score sheet in a 2-0 defeat to West Germany. The two teams would meet each other again in the 1958 quarter-finals, but the West Germans needed just one goal this time.

In their first game of the 1962 finals Yugoslavia faced the Soviet Union, their conquerors in the European Championship final of two years earlier. The Yugoslavs again lost 2-0 in a brutal match that saw captain Muhamed Mujić break the leg of Soviet defender Eduard Dubinsky. Although the referee did not punish him, Mujić was sent home by his own federation.

Milan Galic took over the captaincy and after beating Uruguay 3-1 and Colombia 5-0 the Yugoslavs set up a third quarter-final encounter with West Germany in as many tournaments. "I'm getting sick even thinking of having to play Germany again," said coach Ljubomir Lovric. Both sides came close, but it was Peter Radakovic, playing with his head heavily bandaged, whose shot rifled into the back of the net to win the game for Yugoslavia with five minutes remaining.

In a semi-final the Yugoslavs were defeated 3-1 by Czechoslovakia in front of a crowd of less than 6,000. The third place play-off against hosts Chile was a more passionately supported affair, but Yugoslavia lost 1-0 to a goal scored with the last kick of the game.

Not reaching the finals again until 1974, their campaign in West Germany was notable for a 9-0 victory over Zaïre that included a hat-trick from Dusan Bajevic, but despite reaching the second group stage, three straight defeats to West Germany, Poland and Sweden had them packing their bags.

In 1982 they finished a point behind group winners Northern Ireland but were edged out of a place in the second group stage by

Sasa Ilic, Serbia & Montenegro v Ivory Coast, 2006

Spain on goals scored. Preparations for the tournament had been poor, and with so many of his internationals based overseas coach Miljan Miljanic hadn't arranged an international since the previous November. They weren't helped by poor refereeing either. They were unlucky to concede a dubious penalty to Spain, and even unluckier that the spot-kick was ordered to be retaken after the first attempt had been put wide.

The Yugoslavia squad sent to Italia 90 was full of talented players, such as Dragan Stojkovic and Dejan Savicevic, but despite losing their opening game to West Germany they made it through to the quarter-finals. However, after starting brightly against Argentina they were left chasing the game following Refik Sabanadzovic's red card, and it took a penalty shoot-out to separate the teams after a goalless draw. Five spot-kicks were either missed or saved, including those of Maradona and Stojkovic, with Argentina winning the shoot-out 3-2.

It would be the last tournament for Yugoslavia in that incarnation. Against a background of civil war at home, the break up of the country resulted in the creation of new national football teams for Croatia, Bosnia-Herzegovina, Slovenia and Macedonia. Only the present day regions of Serbia and Montenegro initially agreed to continue under the name of Yugoslavia.

Before the formal break-up of the country Yugoslavia had qualified for the 1992 European Championship, but by the time the finals were due to kick-off most of the non-Serbian players had refused to take part and UEFA took the decision to expel them from the competition. They were also banned from entering USA 94, and by the time the next World Cup came about, both Yugoslavia and Croatia qualified for the finals as separate nations, the Yugoslavs doing so by beating Hungary 12-1 on aggregate in the play-offs. Reaching the second round of the tournament Yugoslavia contested a thrilling game with Holland, but lost to an injury time winner scored by Edgar Davids.

In 2003 the country of Yugoslavia changed its name to Serbia and Montenegro, fielding a football team under this name for three years. However, on the eve of the 2006 World Cup Finals, the people of Montenegro voted for independence. Although the two countries had agreed to separate, they competed at the finals as Serbia and Montenegro.

Their solid teamwork differed from the skilful play of the Yugoslav of years gone by, and although these qualities had helped them to qualify for the finals above Spain in their group, it didn't prove enough to keep them in the tournament. Losing all of their games, they were humiliated 6-0 by Argentina.

Serbia qualified for the 2010 World Cup as group winners ahead of France, securing their place with a game to spare after a 5-0 victory over Romania.

SERBIA & MONTENEGRO

See Serbia

SLOVAKIA

Joined FIFA: 1907, 1994 **Confederation:** UEFA

Finals*: [2010]

Record*: P0/W0/D0/L0/F0/A0

** Not including the record of Czechoslovakia*

Although the Slovak Republic played it's first international football match in 1939, both prior to that and after World War II, Slovak players represented the national team of Czechoslovakia, a country formed by the union of the present day territories of the Czech Republic and Slovakia. This team would represent the region until the 1993-94 season, when separate Czech Republic and Slovakia teams were formed. FIFA have recognised both as the successors to Czechoslovakia's historic records in world football, but both have had limited success on the world stage.

The Slovaks came close to qualifying for the 2006 World Cup, only to lose out to Spain in the play-offs. They qualified for the finals at their fourth attempt, topping the group ahead of Slovenia and ensuring that bitter rivals the Czech Republic would not reach the 2010 World Cup.

See also Czechoslovakia

SLOVENIA

Joined FIFA: 1992 **Confederation:** UEFA

Finals: 2002, [2010]

Record: P3/W0/D0/L3/F2/A7

The Slovenians played their first match in 1992 after the division of Yugoslavia a year earlier. They qualified for their first World Cup in 2002 after beating Romania in a play-off, but it proved to be a disappointing experience. The team returned home without a point after defeats to Spain, South Africa and Paraguay. The campaign was overshadowed by an acrimonious row between coach Srecko Katanec and the team's biggest star Zlatko Zahovic.

"I could buy you, your house and your family," Zahovic reportedly told his coach after being substituted in the opening game against Spain. The player was sent home and the coach announced that he would resign immediately after the tournament.

Slovenia would not reach the World Cup again until 2010, ironically with Zahovic as coach. They qualified for the finals after defeating Russia in the play-offs. With the aggregate score tied at 2-2, it was Slovenia that held the advantage, reaching the finals courtesy of Nejc Pecnik's away goal scored in the first leg in Moscow.

Acimovic, Slovenia v Paraguay, 2002

SOUTH AFRICA

Joined FIFA: 1952-76, 1992 **Confederation:** CAF

Finals: 1998, 2002, **[2010]**

Record: P6/W1/D3/L2/F8/A11

Football has been played in South Africa since the 1870s but the progress of the game was hindered for many years by the existence of apartheid, which resulted in a succession of FIFA suspensions and bans. In 1991 South Africa returned to international competition and with the formation of the new, multi-racial South African Football Association, was readmitted to FIFA the following year.

Nicknamed 'Bafana Bafana' (meaning 'the boys, the boys'), South Africa qualified comfortably for the 1998 World Cup. At the finals the team lacked invention but managed to beat Slovenia and take a point each off Denmark and Saudi Arabia, with Shaun Bartlett scoring a late injury time equaliser to rob the Saudis of victory.

Four years later the team performed better. An injury time penalty from Quinton Fortune salvaged a draw from their opener with Paraguay, and after beating Slovenia thanks to an early goal from Siyabonga Nomvethe, the South Africans gave themselves a chance of reaching the knockout stage.

A tightly fought game with Spain would decide their fate, and although the South Africans twice came from behind through Benni McCarthy and Lucas Radebe, a goal from Raúl made it 3-2 to Spain and ended a fine run. Although level with Paraguay on both points and goal difference, the Africans were out of the tournament having scored one goal fewer.

After controversially losing out to Germany in their attempt to stage the 2006 World Cup, South Africa benefited from FIFA's short-lived policy of rotating the tournament between the different confederations, and in May 2004 it was announced they were to be 2010 hosts, chosen from an African-only shortlist that included Morocco and Egypt.

Teboho Mokoena, South Africa v Paraguay, 2002

SOUTH KOREA

See Korea Republic

SOVIET UNION

See Russia

SPAIN

Joined FIFA: 1904 **Confederation:** UEFA

Finals: 1934, 50, 62, 66, 78, **82**, 86, 90, 94, 98, 2002, 06, [2010]

Record: P49/W22/D12/L15/F80/A57

Despite having one of strongest domestic leagues in football, the failure of the Spanish national team to make a bigger mark at the World Cup has been a surprise. Despite the abundance of world-class players to have pulled on the famous red shirt, a fourth-place finish in 1950 remains their best showing at the finals.

Making a first World Cup appearance in 1934 in Italy, the Spanish toughened up with a series of warm-up games against English club side Sunderland before comfortably dispensing with Brazil in round one. However, their campaign stuttered to a halt in the quarter-finals after facing the hosts twice in as many days.

A bruising encounter saw Spain concede a contentious equaliser that had initially been disallowed, but referee Louis Baert reversed his decision after facing a crowd of angry Italian players. In the second-half he would also disallow a Spanish goal for offside, even though Ramón de Lafuente had beaten four opponents by himself before putting the ball into the net. Injuries resulted in the Spanish making seven changes for the following day's replay but even a change of referee did them no favours as Rene Mercet disallowed two more Spanish goals in a 1-0 defeat.

As a consequence of both the Spanish Civil War and World War II, Spain would not play another competitive game until a 5-1 victory over Portugal in a World Cup qualifier in April 1950. At the finals two months later the Spanish were spearheaded by the formidable Zarra and gave a debut to keeper Antonio Ramallets, who so impressed the Brazilian crowds that he was dubbed the 'Cat of the Maracanã'. After successive wins over USA and Chile, and a famous victory over England, Spain progressed to the Final Pool, a second group stage to decide the world championship. However, a point from a physical 2-2 draw with eventual winners Uruguay was all they managed to achieve, even plunging to a 6-1 defeat to Brazil.

Spain should have been contenders at the 1962 finals. Eccentric coach Helenio Herrera took charge of a squad blessed with the adopted talents of Alfredo Di Stéfano and Ferenc Puskás. However, Di Stéfano left the World Cup without making an appearance after a training ground injury, reputedly caused by a tackle from Herrera. The Spanish finished bottom of the group after defeats to Czechoslovakia and Brazil.

They fared little better in 1966 with a team built around the players of the mighty Real Madrid side. Losing to West Germany and Argentina, they once again failed to make the second round.

There was little notable about Spain's return to the finals in 1978, while as hosts in 1982 the team failed to shine under the leadership of Uruguayan coach José Santamaría. He had constructed a team around the stars of Real Sociedad, but whereas the Spanish champions employed a highly defensive game, Santamaría didn't select Sociedad's successful backline and attempted to have his team to play like Real Madrid instead.

After a shock draw with Honduras, and a narrow victory over Yugoslavia, the Spanish suffered a 1-0 defeat to Northern Ireland. They still qualified for the second group stage but defeat to West Germany and a goalless draw with England resulted in elimination for Spain and the sack for Santamaría.

At the 1986 finals the Spanish opened their campaign with a 1–0 defeat to Brazil but they still reached the second round, where they beat Denmark 5-1 after conceding first. Emilio Butragueño scored four times, becoming the first player to do so at the finals since Eusébio in 1966. They were less prolific in the quarter-finals against Belgium, losing on penalties after Juan Antonio Señor had scored a late equaliser.

Defeat to Yugoslavia concluded Spain's 1990 campaign in the second round, while

Fernando Torres,
Spain v Tunisia, 2006

a run to the quarter-finals at USA 94 was only brought to an end after losing a thrilling match with Italy, but the Spanish should have had a penalty late in injury time after Luis Enrique was viciously assaulted by Mauro Tassotti. The Italian was not cautioned during the match but he would later receive a lengthy ban for the infraction, which provided little consolation to Spain.

While they failed to live up to the pre-tournament expectations at France 98, finishing behind Nigeria and Paraguay in their group, at the 2002 finals the Spanish were one of only two teams to progress to the second round with a 100 per cent record. After beating the Republic Of Ireland on penalties in the quarter-finals, they faced co-hosts South Korea in a tense and scoreless semi-final. Twice seeing goals disallowed, they lost the deciding penalty shoot-out after a Joaquín Sánchez spot-kick was blocked. The president of the Spanish football federation described the refereeing as a farce, whilst the Spanish media whipped up a storm of conspiracy theories.

Under Luis Aragonés, and with a stellar team including team David Villa, Xabi Alonso and Fernando Torres, the Spanish comfortably reached the second round of the 2006 World Cup. They had won all three of their group games and even rested their entire first XI against Saudi Arabia, but after taking the lead against France they slumped to a 3-1 defeat, the first time they had lost in the 25 games since Aragonés had taken charge. Sharing the FIFA Fair Play Award with Brazil hardly made up for elimination, but lifting the European Championship trophy two years later was some consolation.

The Spanish were one of the strongest sides in qualification for the 2010 World Cup, reaching the finals with a 100 per cent record, scoring nearly three goals a game.

SWEDEN

Joined FIFA: 1904 **Confederation:** UEFA

Finals: 1934, 38, 50, **58**★, 70, 74, 78, 90, 94, 2002, 06,

Record: P46/W16/D13/L17/F74/A69

There's no doubt that in football terms, Sweden has always punched above its weight on the international stage. Playing at the World Cup for the first time in 1934, the Scandinavians shocked Argentina 3-2 on the way to the quarter-finals, where they were edged out 2-1 by Germany.

They went one better in 1938, reaching the semi-finals after being given a bye to the quarter-finals due to the withdrawal of Austria. They hammered eight goals past Cuba, with hat-tricks from Harry Andersson and Gustav Wetterstöm, causing one French journalist to pack up his typewriter and announce, "Up to five goals is journalism, after that it becomes statistics".

With a place in the final at stake, they took a first-minute lead against Hungary but slumped to a 5-1 defeat. They also lost the third place play-off game 4-2, despite leading Brazil 2-0 until the final minute of the first-half.

In 1948 Englishman George Raynor was appointed national team coach, and he led the Swedes to a gold medal at the 1948 London Olympics. However, this success had its downside as several of the country's top players turned professional to play in Italy's lucrative Serie A. With strict rules barring players if they made their living abroad, Raynor had access to only two of his Olympic champions for the 1950 World Cup in Brazil, yet the newly remodelled team pulled off a major surprise by beating Italy's professional stars 3-2. Despite a crushing 7-1 defeat by Brazil in the Final Pool, the Swedes went on to pip Spain to third place.

By the time they took part in the 1958 World Cup Finals as hosts the Swedish FA had finally amended its rules and as a result Raynor was able to field what many claim to be Sweden's best ever team, with previously barred veterans such as Gunnar Gren and Nils Liedholm returning to international action. Buoyed by home advantage and a strong team spirit, they made it all the way to the final, defeating Hungary and the Soviet Union, plus ten-man West Germany in the semi-final, before being cut down to size 5-2 by Brazil in the final itself.

The Swedish did not reach the finals again until 1970 when a poor campaign ended at the group stage after they beat Uruguay by just 1-0 when a two goal advantage would have ensured progress to the next round. They met again in the deciding group game four years later, but this time a 3-0 victory saw them through to the second group stage. After twice leading hosts West Germany in a thrilling rollercoaster of a match, a 4-2 defeat ended their chances of reaching a second World Cup final.

At the 1978 tournament the Swedes were grouped with Brazil, Austria and Spain and were lucky not to lose all three of their games, salvaging a draw from their opening clash with the Brazilians thanks to the intervention of referee Clive Thomas, who blew for full time a split second before Zico's header crossed the line.

They would not make the finals again until 1990 when Brazil proved to be their opening opponents once again. Losing 2-1, defeats to Scotland and Costa Rica followed and the Swedes finished without a point.

Led to the 1994 finals by highly-regarded coach Tommy Svensson, Sweden were once again grouped with Brazil, but this time both teams made it to the second round after drawing their own game, with a fantastic Kennet Andersson volley opening the scoring. He scored twice more against Saudi Arabia and also hit the equaliser late in extra-time that took the quarter-final against Romania to penalties.

Sweden won the shoot-out thanks to two saves by Thomas Ravelli, but the only stain on an inspired team performance was the red card shown to Steffan Schwarz, who would miss the semi-final against Brazil.

Ravelli was on top of his game again in the semi, but as Sweden played with only ten men for the last 30 minutes following the expulsion of Jonas Thern, the Brazilians proved too powerful and Romario's late headed goal settled the match. In the third-

Sweden v Brazil, 1958 World Cup Final

place play-off four first-half goals gave the Swedes a comfortable win over Bulgaria.

In 2002 Sweden successfully navigated a path through the 'group of death' with England, Nigeria and Argentina, drawing with the latter thanks to a long distance free-kick from Anders Svensson. He came close to settling the round of 16 game with Senegal but after he hit the post in extra-time, Senegal nicked the game with Henri Camara's 'golden goal'.

At the 2006 finals Sweden reached the second round again after drawing with England in the group, but their campaign was ended by hosts Germany, who took an unassailable 2-0 lead in the first quarter of an hour. The Swedes had lost Teddy Lucic to a red card in the first-half, and once Henrik Larsson missed from the penalty spot the mountain was too big to climb.

SWITZERLAND

Joined FIFA: 1904 **Confederation:** UEFA

Finals: 1934, 38, 50, 54, 62, 66, 94, 2006, [2010]

Record: P26/W8/D5/L13/F37/A51

Switzerland played a significant part in the development of football in the early days of the sport. Providing a home to both the European and world governing bodies, UEFA and FIFA, the Swiss were instrumental in the formation of each organisation, and in the first half of the century they could boast a strong team. They won an Olympic silver medal in 1924 and reached the World Cup quarter-finals twice before the Second World War.

At the 1934 tournament the Swiss debuted with a defeat of seeded Holland in the first round and gave the Czechoslovakians a run for their money in the quarter-final, taking an early lead before losing 3-2.

With the clouds of war gathering, Switzerland's first opponents at the 1938 finals were the Germans, but even the opening Nazi salute did not intimidate a strong Swiss team coached by Austrian Karl Rappan, who employed his famed 'Swiss Bolt' formation, one of the first systems to use a sweeper. The game finished 1-1 after extra-time, but despite playing much of the replay with only ten fully fit men after an injury to

Switzerland v Romania, 1994

winger Georges Aeby, they shocked the so called 'Greater Germany' with three second-half goals to win 4-2. However, weakened by injuries they were out of the competition after defeat to Hungary in the quarter-final.

When the World Cup resumed in Brazil 12 years later, just Alfred Bickel remained of the team that had so impressed in 1938, but this time the Swiss were defeated 3-0 by Yugoslavia in the first World Cup match to use floodlights. They bounced back for their second group game against hosts Brazil, very nearly pulling off a shock before settling for a 2-2 draw. They were helped in their endeavours by the bizarre team selection of Brazil coach Flavio Costa, who picked a trio of São Paulo players to please local fans. The Swiss were already out of the competition when they beat Mexico 2-1.

In 1954 the Swiss hosted the tournament, although it did them few favours in the draw as they were grouped with both England and Italy. In a bad-tempered clash with the Italians they snatched a surprise 2-1 win with centre-forward Josef Hügi scoring with just 12 minutes remaining. After losing to England, the hosts finished level on points with Italy but went through to the quarter-finals after defeating the Italians 4-1 in a play-off.

Rappan's famed 'Swiss Bolt' defence capitulated in the quarter-finals as the Swiss were knocked out in the highest-scoring match in the history of World Cup finals. They lost 7-5 to Austria, despite having led the game 3-0 after 20 minutes. Hügi's hat-trick helped him to become joint second highest scorer, with six goals in just three games.

Switzerland's poor showings at the two World Cups of the Sixties illustrated how far their game had declined. Not managing a point in either tournament, on both occasions they finished bottom of groups topped by West Germany, who knocked five goals past them in 1966. On that occasion, however, the Swiss played a part in their own defeat, weakening the team by suspending Werner Leimgruber and Köbi Kuhn for breaking the squad curfew.

They would not qualify for the finals again until 1994, when coached by Englishman Roy Hodgson. Opening their campaign against USA at the Pontiac Silverdome, they secured a sweat-inducing 1-1 draw in the first ever indoor World Cup match. A 4-1 victory over Romania was followed by defeat to Colombia, but the Swiss reached the second round as group runners-up to the Romanians, where a 3-0 defeat to Spain ended their tournament.

To reach the 2006 finals Switzerland had to go two acrimonious rounds with Turkey in the play-offs before qualifying on the away goals rule. Despite having never kept a clean sheet in 22 games at the World Cup, at this tournament the Swiss goal remained impregnable. After an impressive opening draw with France, who they beat to the top of the group, Switzerland were finally knocked out of the competition in the round of 16 after a penalty shoot-out defeat to Ukraine. They became the first team to exit a World Cup without conceding a single goal.

The Swiss qualified for the 2010 World Cup as winners of a weak group that also included Greece, Latvia, Israel, Luxembourg and Moldova.

TOGO

Joined FIFA: 1962 **Confederation:** CAF

Finals: 2006

Record: P3/W0/D0/L3/F1/A6

A national holiday was called when Togo qualified for the 2006 World Cup. The West African nations were shock qualifiers from a continent where they are not considered a major player. Qualification was by far the biggest football success for 'Les Eperviers' (the Sparrow Hawks), but they went into their first ever match at the finals having just persuaded coach Otto Pfister to return to his post after walking out a few days earlier. He had been unhappy about the failure of Togo's football federation to resolve a bonus dispute. The players missed training, demanding £100,000 each to play, plus £20,000 each per win and £10,000 per draw.

When they did finally take to the pitch they took an early lead against South Korea in Frankfurt but lost the game 2-1. They also lost to Switzerland and France.

TRINIDAD AND TOBAGO

Joined FIFA: 1963 **Confederation:** CONCACAF

Finals: 2006

Record: P3/W0/D1/L2/F0/A4

With a population of 1.2 million, Trinidad and Tobago became the smallest country to qualify for the World Cup in 2006, having already come close to achieving the feat in 1974, 1990 and 2002.

At the finals coach Leo Beenhakker insisted his players ride to training on bikes to build their fitness levels, and with their most famous player and captain, Dwight Yorke, assuming a far deeper role of midfield playmaker, the 'Soca Warriors' played out of their skins to draw with Sweden.

Trinidad & Tobago v Sweden, 2006

After holding England scoreless for 83 minutes, the Trinbagonians were unlucky to concede twice in the last ten minutes, and they went on to lose their final game to Paraguay, returning home with just a point but with their reputations intact.

Unfortunately, after the tournament had ended the Trinidad and Tobago football federation ended up in a long running legal dispute with their own players over outstanding bonus payments.

TUNISIA

Joined FIFA: 1960 **Confederation:** CAF

Finals: 1978, 98, 2002, 06

Record: P12/W1/D4/L7/F8/A17

Tunisia is one of Africa's stronger footballing nations, having qualified for the World Cup on four occasions. Indeed, when first at the finals in 1978 the Tunisians were able to call on the services of one of the most impressive looking players at the tournament, African Player Of The Year Tarak Dhiab. With Tarak pulling the strings in midfield, Tunisia became the first African team to win a game at the finals, beating Mexico 3-1. Losing a closely fought tie with Poland, they drew their final game against West Germany, and although they failed to qualify for the second group stage they had acquitted themselves well.

It would be 20 years before they reached the finals again, but the team that Polish coach Henryk Kasperczak led to France in 1998 was not of the same quality. After losing to England and Colombia, Kasperczak was sacked and Ali Selmi took charge for a face-saving draw with group leaders Romania.

A series of poor results at the 2002 finals saw them take just a point from Belgium. Two years later, under European Championship winning coach Roger Lemerre, Tunisia won the African Nations Cup for the first time, but although the Frenchman led them to their third successive World Cup in 2006, it didn't end well. A red card for striker Ziad Jaziri in the final game against Ukraine hindered their slim chances of reaching the second round, which were killed off when Andriy Shevchenko knocked in a debatable penalty 20 minutes from time.

Tunisia v England, 1998

Tunisia failed to qualify for the 2010 tournament, edged out by Nigeria after a surprise defeat to Mozambique in the their final game.

TURKEY

Joined FIFA: 1923 **Confederation:** UEFA

Finals: 1954, 2002

Record: P10/W5/D1/L4/F20/A17

Until Turkey really began to establish itself on the international stage in the 1990s, its players had graced the World Cup on only one occasion, at the 1954 finals in Switzerland. The Turks had qualified for the previous tournament in Brazil at the first time of entering the competition, but had to withdraw for financial reasons. When they finally took part four years later it was as a result of a coin toss, three games having failed to separate them from Spain in the days before aggregate scores settled matters.

Having eliminated Spain the Turkish found themselves unexpectedly seeded, along with Hungary, in a group that also included West Germany and South Korea. It should have been a huge advantage, as due to the unusual format of the competition in 1954 the seeded teams would only play the non-seeded teams in the group, so Turkey avoided having to face the all conquering Hungarians, unbeaten in four years. However, their first opponents were a tough enough proposition. Although Turkey took an early lead, the West Germans were soon on level terms and won the match 4-1.

In their remaining group game the Turkish beat South Korea 7-0, with a hat-trick from Burhan Sargun. Although their goal difference was superior to that of the West Germans, who had conceded eight to Hungary, progress to the next round was settled by a play-off, which the Germans duly won 7-2, with Turkey having to field their reserve keeper Sükrü Ersoy.

Although they came close to reaching Italia 90, the Turks would have to wait until 2002 to reach their second World Cup, when they astounded fans with a run that took them to the semi-finals. In truth, the quality of Turkish football had been improving throughout the Nineties, with qualification for their first European Championship in 1996 a major turning point. By the time of the 2002 finals they could boast players of the calibre of Alpay Özalan, Hasan Sas, keeper Rüstü Reçber and their talismanic captain Hakan Sükür.

Coming through their group second to Brazil, the Turks eased past co-hosts Japan in the round of 16, before Ilhan Mansız helped them to a 'golden goal' victory over Senegal. Despite giving the Brazilians a stiff challenge in the semi-final, a magical strike from Ronaldo early in the second-half ended Turkish hopes.

Alpay Ozalan, Turkey v Senegal, 2002

Beating South Korea 3-2 in the third place play-off, Hakan Sükür netted the fastest ever World Cup goal in just 10.8 seconds. It was no mean feat considering that it had been the South Koreans who had kicked off. When the Turkish squad returned home to Istanbul they were welcomed as heroes.

UKRAINE 2007

Joined FIFA: 1992 **Confederation:** UEFA
Finals: 2006
Record: P5/W2/D1/L2/F5/A7

Until independence in 1991 Ukraine was one of the strongest football territories of the Soviet Union and its most talented players often formed the backbone of the Soviet team. However, in the early years of independence many Ukrainian stars, such as Andrei Kanchelskis and Viktor Onopko, opted to play for Russia, which had been nominated as the natural successor to the Soviet team.

Without their stars Ukraine initially struggled. Although continuing to produce players of the calibre of Sergei Rebrov and Andriy Shevchenko, they faltered in the play-offs for both the 1998 and 2002 World Cups, but their fortunes took an upturn when they became the first team to book their place at the 2006 finals, finishing above Turkey, Denmark and European champions Greece.

Despite losing their opening game to Spain, the Ukrainians progressed to the second round after beating group makeweights Saudi Arabia and Tunisia. After seeing off Switzerland on penalties, their first World Cup campaign came to an end following a 3-0 defeat to eventual champions Italy in the quarter-finals.

UNITED ARAB EMIRATES

Joined FIFA: 1972 **Confederation:** AFC
Finals: 1990
Record: P3/W0/D0/L3/F2/A11

Until the formation of the United Arab Emirates in 1971, football was not taken seriously in the region. As the sport developed, many leading coaches were enticed to the country by the generous financial rewards. England manager Don Revie and Brazil's World Cup winning coach Mario Zagallo were among the recruits, but

UAE v West Germany, 1990

it was the Brazilian ethos that was adopted. Under Zagallo the UAE qualified for the 1990 World Cup, although a place at the finals was only secured after rivals China conceded two goals in the last four minutes of their final qualifying game with Qatar.

Zagallo was sacked before the tournament after making disparaging remarks about the team's chances, and it was another Brazilian, Carlos Alberto Parreira, who would lead the team to the finals in his second spell as UAE coach. At Italia 90, however, he was unable to inspire the Emirates to rise to the challenge, losing all three games and conceding five goals to West Germany. The tournament ended on an unfortunate note when Khalil Ghanem was red-carded against Yugoslavia with just 15 minutes remaining.

UNITED STATES 2012

Joined FIFA: 1913 **Confederation:** CONCACAF
Finals: 1930, 34, 50, 90, **94**, 98, 2002, 06, [2010]
Record: P25/W6/D3/L16/F27/A51

Although it would take many years for soccer to capture the imagination of the USA, its national team has had a very long association with the World Cup. One of only 13 countries to have taken part in the very first competition in 1930, USA beat Belgium 3-0 in the first game in World Cup history, sharing the honour with the simultaneously played tie between France and Mexico. The result was something of a surprise because the Americans hadn't played an international fixture in two years. They booked their place in the semi-finals thanks to a 3-0 defeat of Uruguay, with Bert Patenaude scoring the first hat-trick in World Cup history.

Coached to the finals by Scottish-born Bob Millar and aided by Glaswegian trainer Jack Coll of Brooklyn Wanderers, the USA fielded a side that featured six British immigrants (five Scottish and one English). They defended hard and attacked with pace, using just three forwards at a time when five was the norm. A powerful team nicknamed the 'shot-putters' during the tournament, USA were found wanting when faced by Argentina in a brutal semi-final, crushed 6-1 in front of a crowd of 80,000.

Centre-half Raphael Tracy had his leg broken after just ten minutes and according to the official report written by team manager Wilfred Cummings, the dirty tricks didn't stop at fouling. "Andy Auld had his lip ripped wide open and one of the [Argentina] players... knocked the smelling salts out of trainer Coll's hand and into Andy's eyes, temporarily blinding one of the outstanding 'little stars' of the World's Series."

The Americans were late with their application for the 1934 World Cup and although Mexico had qualified once already, FIFA insisted that the two teams face each other in a play-off in Rome just three days before the tournament. The United States may have won the deciding match 4-2, with Aldo 'Buff' Donelli scoring all four goals on his international debut, but they barely registered an impact when the competition got underway, crashing out 7-1 to eventual winners Italy. USA's only goal came courtesy of Donelli, who would later become a successful American Football coach.

The Americans did not enter the 1938 World Cup, but at the 1950 finals they pulled off one of the biggest shocks in World Cup history. Coached by Scotsman Bill Jeffrey they had already shown they were capable of a spirited performance against Spain, having led 1-0 until conceding three goals in the final ten minutes. However, in their second game they beat the mighty England.

Captained for the England game by Eddie McIlvenny, a Scot who qualfied because of his intentions to take US citizenship, the Americans weathered the opening onslaught before breaking out of their own half for a 38th minute goal, scored when Haitian-born Larry Gaetjens nodded in Walter Bahr's cross. Despite the historic victory, which would inspire the 2005 Hollywood film 'The Game Of Their Lives', USA conceded five goals to Chile and finished bottom of the group.

Brad Friedel, USA v Portugal, 2002

It was another 40 years until they reached the World Cup finals again, but although defender Mike Windischmann promised a shock at Italia 90, claiming "we are the Cameroon of our group", their young and inexperienced team would lose all of its games, finishing ranked 23rd of 24 teams.

As hosts in 1994 the Americans took points from a draw with Switzerland and a victory over the highly ranked Colombians and finished third in their group, yet they still reached the second round. They came unstuck against ten-man Brazil, who had Leonardo sent-off for a vicious elbow to the face of Tab Ramos. It would take a 74th minute goal from Bebeto to end USA's tournament, but before the match was over the Americans would also lose Fernando Clavijo to a red card, at 37 the oldest player to be sent-off at a World Cup.

After a series of poor performances in 1998, the USA squad returned home as the lowest ranked team without a point from three games. They did take part in one of the most talked games of the tournament, but in a match rich in political significance, they suffered the humiliation of a 2-1 defeat to Iran and had to watch their opponents celebrate the final whistle as if they had won the World Cup itself.

Under coach Bruce Arena USA pulled off another World Cup shock in 2002, defeating the highly fancied Portuguese 3-2, having led by three goals at one point. It would be their only win of the group but results conspired to see them through to the second round, where thanks to goals from Brian McBride and Landon Donovan they progressed with a 2-0 win over Mexico. Paired with Germany in the quarter-finals the Americans were unlucky to lose to a Michael Ballack goal, especially after a goal-line handball by Torsten Fring had gone unnoticed.

It was their best finish at the finals since 1930, but rather than build on this success, four years later the Americans crashed out of the 2006 competition bottom of the group. Their only point was taken from eventual champions Italy, gained despite playing with just nine men for most of the second-half following red cards for Pablo Mastroeni and Eddie Pope. Victory over Ghana could have seen them through but in a physical game the Africans gained the upper hand. Soon after the American squad returned home Bruce Arena's contract was brought to an end after eight years as coach.

The Americans reached the 2010 World Cup under coach Bob Bradley, topping their qualification group ahead of Mexico and Honduras.

URUGUAY★★

Joined FIFA: 1923 **Confederation:** CONMEBOL

Finals: 1930★, 50★, 54, 62, 66, 70, 74, 86, 90, 2002, [2010]

Record: P40/W15/D10/L15/F65/A57

The tiny South American nation was arguably the most successful force in world football in the first half of the 20th Century, winning Olympic gold medals in 1924 and 1928, and being crowned world champion in both 1930 and 1950. Not only did they achieve a great deal, the Uruguayans were also stylish, playing imaginative pass-and-move football which stood in stark contrast to the physicality then prevalent elsewhere in the world game.

Hector Castro scores, 1930 World Cup Final

Success at the Olympics helped their selection as hosts of the first World Cup in 1930, although there were other reasons that attracted FIFA to the Uruguayan bid. Not only were they prepared to pay all the travel and accommodation expenses of the visiting teams, but they promised to build a huge new stadium in Montevideo suitable of staging such a prestigious tournament. The government of Uruguay, desperate for international recognition, had made it clear that it was prepared to underwrite the costs of staging the event, as the World Cup would coincide with the centenary of the nation's independence.

At the first tournament Uruguay beat both Peru and Romania in the group stage before dispatching Yugoslavia 6-1 in the semi-finals, a victory that was achieved despite falling behind after just four minutes. In the first World Cup final they faced neighbours and bitter rivals Argentina, the team they had beaten to win Olympic gold two years earlier. Thousands of Argentinians crossed the River Plate by boat for the game, leading to worries about security and creating a volatile atmosphere in the Centenary Stadium. On arrival at Montevideo docks, armed police searched fans for weapons and even the referee refused to officiate until assurances were given about his safety.

Uruguay took an early lead through Pablo Dorado but by half-time they were trailing 2-1. Goals from Pedro Cea and Santos Iriarte put them in front, and in the final exchanges, one-armed striker Hector Castro put the game out of Argentina's reach.

Turning down the chance to defend their world title in Italy in 1934, the Uruguayans didn't compete in the finals again until 1950. The wait proved more than worth it. They thumped their only group opponents Bolivia 8-0, with Omar Miguez scoring a hat-trick, before joining Brazil, Spain and Sweden in a Final Pool to decide the championship.

As luck would have it results conspired to turn the last fixture into an all-or-nothing showdown between Uruguay and the hosts, effectively a final, although Brazil only required a draw to top the group and win the World Cup, while Uruguay needed to win.

In front of nearly 200,000 fans packed into the Maracanã stadium Uruguay fell behind early in the second-half, but with goals from Juan Schiaffino and Alcide Ghiggia, they pulled themselves back into the game to clinch their second World Cup triumph.

Uruguay opted to defend their title this time, taking an even stronger team to Switzerland in 1954 and making it to the semi-finals. They knocked seven goals past

Scotland in the group stage and beat England 4-2 in the quarter-finals, but it took the great Hungarian team, unbeaten in four years, to end their run in one of the great matches in World Cup history.

After trailing for much of the game, a late goal from naturalised Argentinian Juan Eduardo Hohberg pulled them level. It was his second of the game, on his World Cup debut, and it forced extra-time. However, the Hungarians proved they were capable of winning without the injured Puskás, and two headed goals from Kocsis put the game beyond Uruguay's reach. Hohberg scored again in the third place play-off, but the game ended in a 3-1 defeat to Austria.

Uruguay failed to qualify for the 1958 finals and lost all three games in 1962. Although they reached the quarter-finals in 1966, negativity had replaced flair. They were eliminated after a bad-tempered 4-0 defeat to West Germany, with captain Horacio Troche and Héctor Silva both receiving their marching orders, the skipper for a kick to the stomach of Lothar Emmerich.

Uruguay's last major impact at the World Cup would come at Mexico 70. Despite the absence of captain and playmaker Pedro Rocha, who had been injured in the first game, Uruguay reached the semi-finals, but it was not without the whiff of controversy. In the run up to their group encounter against Sweden pre-match rumours suggested that Brazilian referee Antonio De Moraes had been paid to favour the Uruguayans. Nothing was proven by FIFA and the referee was switched to another game to deflect attention.

Although Uruguay were defeated in the game by a last minute goal, a draw between Italy and Israel ensured they would follow the Italians into the quarter-finals, where a dismal tie with the Soviets was settled in Uruguay's favour by Victor Espárrago.

In the semi-final Luis Cubilla gave Uruguay an early lead against Brazil, allowing them to sit back on the ball and defend, but the talented Brazilians were back in contention before half-time and two second-half goals knocked the Uruguayans out. Defeat to West Germany in the third place play-off game ended their campaign.

The Uruguayans were no longer anything like a serious football power by 1974, but on arriving in West Germany their players and coaching staff became embroiled in a serious dispute about money, refusing to give any media interviews without payment. Finishing bottom of their group, they soon proved to be of no real interest to anyone.

They would not qualify for the finals again until 1986, and although they suffered a 6-1 defeat at the hands of Denmark, draws with West Germany and Scotland saw them through to the second round as one of the best third placed teams. They were beaten 1-0 by Argentina in the knockout stage.

They made it through the group stages in the same manner at Italia 90, needing an injury time goal from substitute Daniel Fonseca to beat South Korea, but they came undone against the hosts in the round of 16.

The Uruguayans qualified for the 2002 World Cup finals after beating Australia in the play-offs, but coach Victor Pua's side failed to win any of their group games and were soon heading home.

They failed to reach the 2006 finals, losing to Australia on penalties in the play-offs, and while they reached the 2010 World Cup via the same backdoor route, it's unlikely that they will ever again be the side that once made such an impact on the game.

WALES

Joined FIFA: 1910-20, 1924-28, 1946
Confederation: UEFA
Finals: 1958
Record: P5/W1/D3/L1/F4/A4

The Welsh have only featured at the World Cup on one occasion, in 1958, but qualification was far from straightforward. After finishing second to Czechoslovakia in their group, it seemed that their chances of reaching the finals were over, but they were given a second chance. Turkey, Indonesia, Egypt and Sudan had all withdrawn from the various group stages in the Asia-Africa zone, leaving Israel alone in the group, but for the first time FIFA ruled that no country could qualify for the finals without playing a game. A draw of all the other group runners-up took place, and after Belgium refused, Wales took on Israel for a place in the finals. They won both games 2-0.

John Charles, Wales v Hungary, 1958

Arriving at the finals with a strong team that included Ivor Allchurch, Jack Kelsey, Cliff Jones and their best ever player, the imposing Juventus striker John Charles, Wales found themselves grouped with Hungary, Mexico and hosts Sweden. After drawing all of their games, Wales were tied on points with Hungary and a play-off was needed to separate the two sides. In a physical match that saw John Charles the target of some overzealous tackles, Wales won 2-1 despite having trailed at half-time.

The match took its toll on Charles, who was ruled out of the quarter-final encounter with Brazil, but for 70 minutes Wales held on as Garrincha, Didi, Mazzola and Zagallo were thwarted. Ultimately it was Pelé who knocked them out of the competition, scoring the first of his 12 World Cup goals.

The Welsh have not qualified for the World Cup since, although they came close to reaching the finals of 1994. Needing only to win their final group game at home to Romania, Paul Bodin missed a penalty when the scores were level and Romania went on to win 2–1.

WEST GERMANY

See Germany

YUGOSLAVIA

See Serbia

ZAÏRE

See Congo DR

27
48
MEXICO86
48

LEGENDS OF THE WORLD CUP

KEY

Next to the player's name at the top of each entry, a star indicates only a World Cup winner who actually played in the World Cup Final.

1990★ 1990☆ - *World Cup winner/runner-up with year and played in the final.*

1990[★] 1990[☆] - *World Cup winner/runner-up but did not make an appearance in the final*

[1990★] [1990☆] - *World Cup winner/runner-up but did not make an appearance at the tournament*

[1990] - *Did not make an appearance at the tournament*

ADEMIR

Country: Brazil **Born:** November 8, 1922
Position: Centre-forward **Finals:** 1950★
Record: P6/W4/D1/L1/F9

Son of the famous 1938 World Cup defender Domingos, Ademir Marques de Menezes made a sizeable contribution to establishing Brazil as a post-war footballing power. Most comfortable when playing either as an outside-left or at centre-forward, he had every quality required to be a world-class striker. He was exceptionally fast, immensely skilled and he could shoot with either foot.

Making his international debut in 1945 he went on to score 32 goals in 39 games for his country. His finest hour came in the 1950 World Cup when he fully deserved to be the tournament's top scorer for his total of nine goals, including four in a 7-1 defeat of Sweden (some records list his total as eight and attribute one of his goals against Spain to an own goal). The forward trio of Ademir, Zizinho and Jair is still regarded as one of Brazil's finest ever and it was said that his presence required opponents to field an extra fullback, which was the seed for Brazil's future 4-2-4 formation.

Ademir failed to find the net in the final game of the 1950 World Cup, but despite being shadowed through much of the game by Tejera and Varela, he did manage to set-up Friaça for Brazil's only goal of the final, but this was no consolation in defeat.

ALESSANDRO ALTOBELLI★

Country: Italy **Born:** November 28, 1955
Position: Centre-forward **Finals:** 1982★, 1986
Record: P7/W2/D4/L1/F5

A bit-part player through much of Italy's victorious 1982 World Cup campaign, Inter Milan's lanky striker Alessandro Altobelli only had 30 minutes of pitch time at the tournament before he was brought on in the final as an 18th minute substitute for Francesco Graziani. However, when he picked up Bruno Conti's cross late in the game and rounded Germany keeper Harald Schumacher to score Italy's third goal, he became the first substitute to score in a World Cup final. Eight minutes later, moments before the end of the game, he himself was substituted.

He would make four appearances at the finals of 1986, scoring four times in the group games, including a penalty in a 1-1 draw with Argentina. He was Italy's only real threat up front in an unsuccessful campaign.

AMARILDO★

Country: Brazil **Born:** June 29, 1939
Position: Inside-left **Finals:** 1962★
Record: P4/W4/D0/L0/F3

A striker for Botafogo and Vasco da Gama in Brazil, and for Milan, Fiorentina and Roma in Italy, Amarildo Tavares da Silveira was capped 22 times for Brazil and was a member of the 1962 World Cup winning team, scoring the opening goal of the final against Czechoslovakia and setting up Zito for the second.

Prior to the tournament he had only made substitute appearances for his country and had never scored a goal, but at the World Cup he was given his big break – and his first international start – after Pelé was ruled out with injury before Brazil's third game. He scored twice on his full debut, quickly earning the nickname the 'White Pelé', and held his place through the remainder of the competition.

After impressing at the finals he secured a high profile move to Milan and he would remain in Italy for ten years. He scored seven goals in total for his country, but although he partnered Pelé for many of the warm-up games prior to the 1966 finals in England, he won his last cap against Scotland two weeks before the tournament kicked off.

JOSÉ LEANDRO ANDRADE★

Country: Uruguay **Born:** November 22, 1901
Position: Right-half **Finals:** 1930★
Record: P4/W4/D0/L0/F0

José Leandro Andrade was among the greatest players of the early days of football. One of the mainstays of the great Uruguayan side of the late 1920s, he helped his country to win Olympic gold in Paris in 1924 and Amsterdam in 1928.

A tall and classy player, his career looked as though it would finish prematurely when injury struck in 1929, but he battled back and his experience was a vital factor when the Uruguay side lifted the inaugural World Cup on home soil in 1930.

Andrade is regarded as one of the most talented of the golden generation of Uruguayan footballers. An old-fashioned wing-half, his best years were behind him when he played at the finals of 1930, but he was still among the stars of the tournament.

The World Cup final was his very last international game. He was a guest at the final match of the 1950 World Cup and watched on as his nephew Víctor Rodríguez Andrade picked up a winners' medal.

OSVALDO ARDILES★

Country: Argentina **Born:** August 3, 1952
Position: Midfield **Finals:** 1978★, 1982
Record: P11/W6/D1/L4/F1

Although short in height, Osvaldo Ardiles was a mercurial force in the Argentina team of coach César Luis Menotti, picking up a World Cup winners' medal in 1978 with a series of impressive displays.

A slight but graceful midfield dynamo, 'Ossie' missed only the controversial second round fixture with Peru after a gashed ankle had forced him out of the previous game against Brazil at half-time.

Back in the starting line-up for the World Cup final clash with Holland, although not fully fit he still managed to skip past two players to start the move from which Mario Kempes scored Argentina's opening goal. Substituted in the 65th minute, he had

Ossie Ardiles, 1978 World Cup Final

earlier played a part in delaying the kick-off, bringing the lightweight cast on René van der Kerkhof's arm to the attention of captain Daniel Passarella, who lodged a time-consuming complaint with the referee.

Although Ardiles played at the finals of 1982, he wasn't in the same kind of form. He scored his only World Cup goal against Hungary but he made little impact on the tournament and the Argentinians were knocked out in the second group stage. He did not play for his country again.

ROBERTO BAGGIO

Country: Italy **Born:** February 18, 1967
Position: Striker **Finals:** 1990, 1994★, 1998
Record: P16/W10/D5/L1/F9

Baggio made his World Cup debut in 1990 at the age of 23. He started the tournament on the bench but when selected for Italy's final group game against Czechoslovakia he scored one of the best goals the competition had ever seen: a powerful run from the halfway line that left defenders for dead.

He scored with Italy's second penalty in the shoot-out defeat to Argentina in the semi-final, and played a vital part in the victory over England in the third place play-off game, opening the scoring after stealing the ball from right under the nose of goalkeeper Peter Shilton.

By 1994 Baggio had become the most famous player in Italy, making him the focus of his country's World Cup campaign in America. But his relationship with coach Arrigo Sacchi was strained. Like his predecessor Azeglio Vicini, Sacchi preferred to use Baggio to lead the line, rather than in his own preferred deeper positioning as a second striker. The tension wasn't helped when he was substituted after just 22 minutes against Norway to bring on a replacement keeper following the red carding of Gianluca Pagliuca. Baggio was seen to mouth the words, "This is mad".

The Italians struggled out of the group stage in third place but as the tournament progressed they relied increasingly on the 'Divine Ponytail', as he was nicknamed. He scored a last-minute equaliser and an extra-time penalty winner to eliminate Nigeria

Robert Baggio v Bulgaria, 1994

in the second round, before snatching the decider in the quarter-final against Spain.

Another two goals dispatched Bulgaria in the semis and when it came down to penalties against Brazil in the final, even though he had been carrying an injury, it seemed certain that Baggio would net the deciding spot-kick. However, he scooped his penalty – Italy's fifth – over the bar, handing victory to Brazil. He had single-handedly powered the Italians to the final, but he would also remain a symbol of their defeat.

Baggio was recalled for 1998 final and he converted a vital spot-kick against Chile to give Italy a 2-2 draw. He scored against Austria and he also converted Italy's first spot-kick in the penalty shoot-out defeat to France.

He wasn't able to make it four tournaments in a row, as Giovanni Trapattoni did not believe Baggio had fully recovered from injury and controversially omitted him from the 2002 World Cup squad. He continued to play for Italy and retired in 2004.

GORDON BANKS★

Country: England **Born:** December 30, 1937
Position: Goalkeeper **Finals:** 1966★, 1970
Record: P8/W7/D0/L1/A4

Gordon Banks was famed for his composure, agility, consistency and all-round technique, and today he is credited with developing many of the facets of modern goalkeeping. Having made his England debut in April 1963, Banks was the rock of the 1966 World Cup winning team. He conceded just one goal in reaching the final, a penalty to Eusébio, and although he was beaten twice by the West Germans in the final itself, he picked up a winners' medal in the 4-2 victory.

His finest performance came at the 1970 World Cup, the day after he was awarded an OBE. Facing Pelé for the first time in his career, he managed to scoop the Brazilian's sharp, downward header up and over the bar. It became the most replayed save of all time. But when it came to the most crucial game of the tournament Banks was unfortunately absent through illness, felled by 'Montezuma's revenge'.

Peter Bonetti took his place and conceded three goals against West Germany in the quarter-final, ending England's dream of retaining the Jules Rimet Cup in Mexico.

He would undoubtedly have played at the top for much longer had a car crash in the summer of 1972 not cost him his sight in one eye. He kept 35 clean sheets in 73 games for England and lost just nine times.

BARBOSA

Country: Brazil **Born:** March 27, 1921
Position: Goalkeeper **Finals:** 1950★
Record: P6/W4/D1/L1/A6

Regarded by some as one of the greatest Brazilian goalkeepers there ever was, for others Moacir Barbosa could not be forgiven for his perceived role in Brazil's defeat in the 'fateful final' of 1950.

With the scores level in the deciding game of the World Cup, and with Brazil only needing a draw to win the trophy, Barbosa was caught off guard by a near-post shot from Uruguay's Alcides Ghiggia, who had been given too much freedom down the right flank by the far more culpable defender, Bigode.

Despite being one of the stars of Brazil's tournament, his international career was all but over. His long and successful club career with Vasco de Gama stretched into the Sixties, but he would only make one more appearance for the national team after the World Cup, nearly three years later.

FRANCO BARESI

Country: Italy **Born:** May 8, 1960

Position: Sweeper **Finals:** [1982★], 1990, 1994★

Record: P10/W7/D2/L1/F0

The complete defender, Franco Baresi enjoyed two decades of football with his only club, Milan. A formidable stopper nicknamed 'The Steel Man', he was also comfortable on the ball and enjoyed surging out of defence to join in with the attack. As understudy to Gaetano Scirea he was a non-playing member of the Italy squad that won the 1982 World Cup in Spain, but it wasn't until five months after the tournament that he finally made his international debut.

With chances extremely limited under Enzo Bearzot, in 1984 Baresi took the decision to withdraw from international football. As a result he had to watch his brother Giuseppe make the trip to the 1986 World Cup without him. Following Bearzot's retirement Baresi made himself available for selection once more and he was a key member of Italy's backline at Italia 90. He played every game on the way to the semi-final, scoring with the opening spot-kick in the penalty shoot-out defeat to Argentina.

Four years later he captained the team to USA 94 but was at fault for the only goal of their first game, when his poor headed clearance was chested down by the Republic Of Ireland's Ray Houghton and driven into the net from 20 yards. Injury in the next game against Norway resulted in a serious knee operation but amazingly he returned to the team just 31 days later for the final itself, where he suffered heartbreak in the penalty shoot-out after spooning Italy's first spot-kick over the bar.

He played for his country 81 times, 31 of them as captain, but he would only make one more appearance for Italy after the final.

FABIEN BARTHEZ★

Country: France **Born:** June 28, 1971

Position: Goalkeeper **Finals:** 1998★, 2002, 2006★

Record: P17/W10/D5/L2/A8

Fabien Barthez played a leading role in helping France to win the World Cup on home soil in 1998. An agile and athletic shot-stopper, he was one of the most entertaining keepers of his era and he courted attention during France 98 by allowing team-mate Laurent Blanc to kiss his shaven head for good luck before the start of each match.

He conceded only two goals on the way to picking up a winners' medal, but he had the advantage of playing behind what was regarded as the best defence in the game at the time. Two years later he was a key part of the European Championship winning team, but he was also the goalkeeper for France's disastrous 2002 World Cup campaign that ended in embarrassment in the group stage without a win or a goal.

In the face of much criticism he fought off the challenge of Gregory Coupet to once again become France's first choice goalkeeper for the 2006 World Cup, although it was rumoured that his inclusion in the starting line-up was at the insistence of Zinédine Zidane, who had been talked out of international retirement.

During the 2006 World Cup Final he briefly wore the captain's armband after Zidane received a red card, but he failed to stop any of Italy's spot-kicks in the deciding shoot-out. He had conceded only three goals throughout the tournament. The final was his last international appearance.

GABRIEL BATISTUTA

Country: Argentina **Born:** February 1, 1969

Position: Striker **Finals:** 1994, 1998, 2002

Record: P12/W6/D2/L4/F10

As a youngster Gabriel Batistuta idolised Argentina's World Cup winning legend Mario Kempes but he eventually bettered his hero to become the country's top scorer with 56 goals in 78 appearances.

His achievements as a world-class marksman earned him the nickname 'Bati-Gol' and he played in three successive World Cups, scoring a hat-trick against Greece in his first game at the finals in 1994.

After the tournament Daniel Passarella became national coach and first-team chances for Batistuta became a rarity, just as they had when the two had previously worked together at River Plate. Even though Argentina struggled without him, he was left out of the majority of qualifiers for the 1998 World Cup and it seemed highly unlikely that he would play at the finals.

He was recalled just in time and scored three goals against Jamaica in Paris to become the only player to have achieved a hat-trick in more than one World Cup, although both came against poor opposition and were achieved with the help of a late penalty.

His five-goal tally at France 98 helped Argentina to the quarter-finals and placed him in joint second place in the race for the Golden Boot, one strike behind Croatia's Davor Suker. He scored once in Argentina's poor run at the 2002 World Cup and retired from international football after elimination in the first round.

BEBETO★

Country: Brazil **Born:** February 16, 1964

Position: Centre-forward **Finals:** 1990, 1994★, 1998★

Record: P15/W10/D3/L2/F6

Best known outside of Brazil for his 'cradling the baby' goal celebration that became much talked about at the 1994 World Cup, but it was his unfailing ability to find the back of the net that established his pedigree.

Making a brief substitute appearance against Costa Rica at the 1990 finals, he arrived at USA 94 as one half of an inventive forward partnership with Romario, and between them they fired a fairly ordinary Brazil team to the final. Bebeto scored three times in the early rounds but he was unable

Bebeto
v USA, 1994

to make an impact on a scoreless final and took no part in the deciding shoot-out.

After first-choice striker Romario was ruled out of the 1998 World Cup through injury, Bebeto took his place in the starting line-up alongside Ronaldo. Although publicly berated on the pitch by his captain Dunga in the match against Morocco, he scored three goals while fending off a challenge for his place from Denilson, picking up a runners-up medal after defeat to France.

Although he rarely won the headlines when partnering either Romario or Ronaldo, his 39 goals in 75 internationals leaves him fifth on Brazil's all-time scoring list.

FRANZ BECKENBAUER☆

Country: Germany **Born:** September 11, 1945

Position: Midfield/Sweeper **Finals:** 1966☆, 1970, 1974☆

Record: P18/W14/D1/L3/F5

Franz Beckenbauer was nicknamed 'Der Kaiser' for his imperious style. An unrivalled reader of the game, he was also blessed with an excellent touch, a good change of pace and flawless distribution.

Making his first international appearance in September 1965, by the time of the World Cup the following year he had established himself at the heart of the German midfield. He scored four goals, including two against Switzerland and the winner in the semi-final with Russia, but he was unable to prevent England lifting the trophy.

For the final, coach Helmut Schön took the tactical decision to use Beckenbauer to eliminate England's biggest threat by shadowing Bobby Charlton, but this robbed the German's of his creativity and is regarded as the decision that cost them victory.

At Mexico 70 Beckenbauer gained a measure of revenge in the quarter-finals. Schön once again insisted that he mark Bobby Charlton, but this time with the instruction to press forward too, dragging Charlton out of position. Beckenbauer scored the goal that pulled West Germany back into contention, and moments later, when Alf Ramsey withdrew Charlton to protect England's lead, 'Der Kaiser' was freed up to spark a startling comeback.

A sliding Franz Beckenbauer v England, 1970

The Germans may have lost in the semi-final to Italy, but the sight of Beckenbauer playing on for most of the match with his dislocated shoulder strapped to his body remains one of the defining images of the man and the tournament. He took over as captain a year later and won the European Championship in 1972. In doing so he redefined the sweeper's role, gliding out of defence to set up devastating counter-attacks.

He experienced his crowning moment as a player in 1974, captaining West Germany to World Cup victory on home soil. With Schön experiencing an emotional meltdown during the tournament, it was increasingly down to Beckenbauer to drive the team onwards. In the final, when Holland threatened to overrun the game, he marshalled his troops smartly as they overturned the odds to become world champions.

He retired from international football in 1977 after winning 103 caps. He remains the only person to have won the World Cup as both a captain and a coach.

HIDERALDO LUIZ BELLINI☆

Country: Brazil **Born:** June 7, 1930

Position: Centre-half **Finals:** 1958☆, [1962☆], 1966

Record: P8/W6/D1/L1/F0

A strong and solid central defender, Bellini was the first Brazilian to get hold of the World Cup trophy, captaining the famous 1958 side of Vavá, Garrincha and Pelé to victory in Sweden. After the final, at the request of photographers looking for a better picture of the presentation, Bellini lifted the Jules Rimet Cup above his head in celebration, the first person to do so in the World Cup.

Two years later this moment was honoured with a statue of Bellini at the entrance of the Maracanã Stadium in Río.

Replaced as both centre-half and captain by Mauro for the 1962 finals, Bellini was a non-playing member of the World Cup winning squad in Chile, but he was back as captain in England in 1966, making two appearances for an ageing Brazil team that crashed out of the tournament in the group stage.

Daniel Bertoni v Belgium, 1982

DANIEL BERTONI★

Country: Argentina **Born:** March 14, 1955
Position: Right-winger **Finals:** 1978★, 1982
Record: P11/W6/D1/L4/F4

Ricardo Daniel Bertoni made his debut for Argentina in 1974, narrowly missing out on a place in the squad for the World Cup in West Germany. A regular in the team prior to the 1978 World Cup, a pre-tournament injury saw him start the opening game on the bench, but after coming on as a 67th minute substitute for René Houseman he soon stabbed home the game's winning goal.

He got his first start in Argentina's final group defeat to Italy and he kept his place all the way to the World Cup final. He faced some bruising tackles from the Dutch in the final, but he settled the game when he burst into the box alongside Mario Kempes to score Argentina's third goal in the 25th minute of extra-time.

He would score two more World Cup goals four years later in Spain, but there would be few winners from a poor all-round Argentina performance in 1982.

ROBERTO BONINSEGNA

Country: Italy **Born:** November 13, 1943
Position: Centre-forward **Finals:** 1970★, 1974
Record: P7/W3/D2/L2/F2

A tough and combative centre-forward for Inter Milan, Roberto Boninsegna got his chance to lead the line for Italy at the 1970 World Cup after the late withdrawal of Pietro Anastasi through injury. Despite his low personal goal tally while playing in a heavily defensive Italy team, he was razor sharp and always appeared capable of finding the net.

He scored the first goal of an epic semi-final encounter with West Germany before setting up Gianni Rivera for the winner at the tail end of extra-time. In the final he hit Italy's only goal of the game, rounding Brazil keeper Felix to stroke in the equaliser. Offering his team's prime threat up front, with Italy trailing 3-1 he was unfathomably replaced in the dying minutes of the game.

He was a member of the 1974 World Cup squad, but he would only play the final 45 minutes of Italy's campaign, used as a second-half substitute in an ignominious 2-1 defeat to Poland.

JÓZSEF BOZSIK

Country: Hungary **Born:** September 28, 1929
Position: Right-half **Finals:** 1954★, 1958
Record: P8/W4/D1/L3/F1

József Bozsik was the midfield driving force of the exhilarating Hungary side that dominated football during the early 1950s, winning Olympic gold in 1952. A peerless passer of the ball, along with his childhood friend Ferenc Puskás he helped to transform the way the game was played.

Bozsik made his international debut in the 9-0 thrashing of Bulgaria in August 1947 and he was the engine of the team at the 1954 World Cup, when Hungary arrived as clear favourites to win. However, the tournament included some of the lowest moments of his career, including a shock defeat in the final to West Germany and his role in the notorious quarter-final, better known as the 'Battle Of Berne', when he captained the side in place of the injured Puskás but was sent-off for brawling with Brazil's Nílton Santos.

After FIFA's disciplinary panel failed to suspend him, Bozsik was able lead the team again in the semi-final victory over Uruguay.

He would make three appearances at the 1958 finals, twice as captain, and he scored his only World Cup goal against Wales in Hungary's opening game. The tournament would end for him after defeat to the Welsh in a group play-off.

ANDREAS BREHME★

Country: West Germany & Germany
Born: November 9, 1960
Position: Left-back **Finals:** 1986★, 1990★, 1994
Record: P16/W9/D4/L3/F4

A strong and determined defender, Andreas Brehme was always uncompromising in the tackle, though in the German tradition he was just as willing to thunder forwards too. Acknowledged as one of the best left-backs of his era, he remains most famous for converting the penalty that settled the 1990 World Cup Final.

One of the great dead ball specialists in the game, for a defender he had quite a goalscoring record. Comfortably two-footed, he was well known for taking most penalties with his right foot and free-kicks and corners with his left, believing his right to be more accurate and his left to be harder.

He first graced the world stage at the 1986 finals, racking up five appearances and collecting a runners-up medal. It proved a personal success for Brehme as not only did he convert West Germany's second penalty in the quarter-final shoot-out against Mexico but he also scored from distance early in the semi-final against France, although for the latter he had the fumbling of keeper Joël Bats to thank.

At Italia 90 he finally picked up a winners' medal. Missing only one game, he scored three times including another fortuitous

Andreas Brehme v England, 1990

semi-final goal when his free-kick deflected off onrushing England defender Paul Parker and ballooned over the stranded keeper.

His greatest moment came when the Germans were awarded a penalty in the dying minutes of the 1990 final. Lothar Matthäus was the designated penalty taker but after changing the boot on his kicking foot at half-time he felt uncomfortable with the responsibility. Brehme didn't hesitate and his carefully placed spot-kick was easily out of reach of the fully outstretched Sergio Goycochea.

He made five appearances at USA 94 but it wasn't a successful tournament for either Brehme or the Germans. He began the campaign in the starting line-up but finished on the bench, playing just the last six minutes of the quarter-final defeat to Bulgaria. It was his final international appearance.

PAUL BREITNER★

Country: West Germany **Born:** September 5, 1951

Position: Left-back **Finals:** 1974★, 1982★

Record: P14/W9/D2/L3/F4

Paul Breitner was an accomplished but controversial member of the all-conquering West Germany team of the early 1970s. Nicknamed 'Der Afro' for his distinctive hairstyle, he enjoyed success as one of the youngest members of his country's best ever team, the 1972 European Championship winners, and two years later he made his impact at the 1974 World Cup, picking up a winners' medal for his trouble.

A free-roaming left-back with a tendency to attack, Breitner scored three times at the 1974 tournament, including the equalising penalty in the final. He took the spot-kick because Uli Hoeness had missed one against Poland in an earlier round.

Only 22 at the time, Breitner had a successful tournament on the pitch but off it he made himself unpopular with the coaching staff. On the eve of the competition the players were threatening to withdraw if a bigger bonus wasn't forthcoming and coach Helmut Schön believed that Breitner, a Marxist who refused to sing the national anthem, was the ringleader. As negotiations went on into the night both Breitner and Schön had their suitcases packed ready to leave, but although a compromise was reached, the standoff wasn't forgotten. After the tournament he played just twice more for West Germany under Schön, although not until the following year, and as a consequence he retired from international football.

After nearly five years in the wilderness Breitner was talked out of retirement by coach Jupp Derwall and he was at the creative heart of West Germany's midfield at the 1982 World Cup. He converted his team's second penalty in the semi-final shoot-out victory over France, and although the Germans were outclassed in the final by Italy, he scored a late consolation goal, at the time making him only the third person to have scored in more than one World Cup final.

JOSÉ LUIS BROWN★

Country: Argentina **Born:** November 11, 1956

Position: Defender **Finals:** 1986★

Record: P7/W6/D1/L0/F1

José Luis Brown gave the 1986 World Cup its happy ending. The 29-year-old defender was without a club at the outset of the tournament, having returned home from playing in Colombia to concentrate on preparations for the World Cup. Unsigned and training for the finals alone, it was only after arriving at the tournament that he was promoted to sweeper in the first team following the withdrawal through illness of the long-serving Daniel Passarella.

A solid, dependable and well liked defender, he was the rock on which the Argentine defence was built, and in the final itself it was Brown who rose unopposed at the far post to head Jorge Burruchaga's free-kick into the back of the net for the opening goal. Running to the corner flag, he dropped to his knees and raised his hands to the heavens in a memorable celebration as his team-mates chased to congratulate him.

After dislocating his shoulder later in the game, he would leave the pitch for treatment, but without a replacement sweeper he loyally refused to be substituted and played on in discomfort until Argentina lifted the trophy. In total he would play 36 games for his country, but would only score that one goal.

Gianluigi Buffon, 2006 World Cup Final

GIANLUIGI BUFFON★

Country: Italy **Born:** January 28, 1978

Position: Goalkeeper **Finals:** [1998], 2002, 2006★

Record: P11/W6/D3/L2/A7

Gianluigi Buffon deservedly won the Lev Yashin Award for the best goalkeeper at the 2006 World Cup, coming nearly nine years after he made his international debut as a substitute for Gianluca Pagluica in a World Cup play-off against Russia. He was a non-playing member of the squad at the resulting finals in France.

In July 2001 Juventus signed him for a staggering £32.6 million from Parma and the following year he was a part of the team that suffered a shock World Cup exit at the hands of South Korea, conceding a golden goal to Ahn Jung-Hwan in the 116th minute.

At the 2006 finals he played in all seven matches as Italy won the World Cup and he was only beaten twice in the tournament – by an own goal against the USA and a penalty in the final. He didn't make a save in the penalty shoot-out that decided the fate of the trophy but Italy won because Daniel Trezeguet hit the crossbar with France's second spot-kick.

So impressive were his performances that he was runner-up in the 2006 European Player Of The Year Award.

JORGE BURRUCHAGA★

Country: Argentina **Born:** October 9, 1962
Position: Midfield **Finals:** 1986★, 1990★
Record: P14/W8/D4/L2/F3

One of the unsung heroes of Argentina's victorious 1986 World Cup campaign, Nantes midfielder Jorge Burruchaga toiled alongside his more celebrated team-mate Diego Maradona throughout the tournament, but it was in the final itself that he got the reward for all his hard work.

After setting up José Luis Brown with a well rehearsed set-piece for the opening goal, with the scores level at 2-2 and with just five minutes left on the clock he latched onto an exquisitely delivered Maradona through ball, fought off the challenge of Hans-Peter Briegel and slid the ball past Harald Schumacher to clinch the game for Argentina.

'Burru' was an ever-present member of the team at Italia 90, scoring against the Soviet Union in the group stage and having a crucial goal disallowed in the scoreless quarter-final with Yugoslavia. When the game went to penalties he converted Argentina's second spot-kick, as he did again in the semi-final decider against Italy.

He collected a runners-up medal in his second World Cup final, but was replaced by Gabriel Calderón early in the second-half.

EMILIO BUTRAGUEÑO

Country: Spain **Born:** July 22, 1963
Position: Centre-forward **Finals:** 1986, 1990
Record: P9/W5/D2/L2/F5

At his best Emilio Butragueño was a penalty box poacher without compare. 'The Vulture', as he became known, is best remembered for an extraordinary performance for Spain against a highly-fancied Denmark at the 1986 World Cup, when he became the first player to score four goals in a game at the final since Eusébio 20 years earlier.

Just 22 at the time, he failed to find a way past the strapping Belgian defence in the quarter-final as Spain crashed out following a penalty shoot-out defeat, but he would depart as the tournament's joint second highest scorer with five goals.

Captaining the side at Italia 90 Butragueño was unable to live up to expectations. Often finding himself isolated up front rather than playing the supporting role that he so enjoyed with Real Madrid, he failed to find the net in any of his four appearances at the finals in Italy. He had his chances against Yugoslavia in the second round, even heading against the woodwork, but the Spanish were knocked out in extra-time.

No-one who saw his four-goal display against Denmark in 1986 would have thought that would be the last time he would score at the World Cup.

ANTONIO CABRINI★

Country: Italy **Born:** October 8, 1957
Position: Left-back **Finals:** 1978, 1982★, 1986
Record: P18/W9/D6/L3/F1

A member of Italy's World Cup winning team of 1982, for all his numerous appearances at the tournament, Antonio Cabrini will always be remembered as the only player to miss a penalty in a World Cup final, scuffing his shot just past the post 24 minutes into the game.

Cabrini made his international debut in Italy's opening game of the 1978 World Cup in Argentina, and he played in every Italy game at three consecutive tournaments, scoring his only goal against Argentina in 1982 when he volleyed in a cutback from just outside the area. There are few players who have made more appearances at the finals.

CAFU★★

Country: Brazil **Born:** June 19, 1970
Position: Right-back **Finals:** 1994★, 1998★, 2002★, 2006
Record: P20/W16/D1/L3/F0

Marcos Evangelista de Moraes, or Cafu as he is better known, is the only person to have played in the final of three World Cups. He was a winner twice, in 1994 and 2002, captaining the side that defeated Germany 2-0 to lift the trophy in Japan.

Cafu earned his first cap against Spain in September 1990 but was just a bit-part player in the international team through the early Nineties, although he did play in the 1994 World Cup Final as a substitute for Jorginho, coming onto the pitch in the 21st minute. The final was one of three appearances he made at the tournament, all of them from the bench.

Cafu, 2002 World Cup Final

An attacking wing-back in the Brazil side that lost the final to France in 1998, for much of his international career he was to Brazil's right flank what Roberto Carlos was to the left. He missed only the semi-final on his way to a runners-up medal in France and he was appointed team captain soon afterwards.

During qualification for the 2002 tournament he was stripped of the armband, only regaining it after a late injury ruled Emerson out of the World Cup squad. He led Brazil through a successful campaign and as he raised the trophy after victory in the final he shouted a message to his wife, "Regina, I love you".

At 36 years of age he was still captain of the misfiring team defeated by France in the quarter-finals in Germany four years later. Despite protestations after the tournament that he was interested in continuing on until the 2010 World Cup, his last international game was played at the 2006 finals.

He is now regarded as Brazil's greatest ever right-back and after 143 appearances in the famous Brazil shirt, he is his country's most capped player.

FABIO CANNAVARO★

Country: Italy **Born:** September 13, 1973

Position: Central defender **Finals:** 1998, 2002, 2006★

Record: P15/W9/D5/L1/F0

Fabio Cannavaro was the captain of Italy's victorious side at the 2006 World Cup, making his 100th international appearance in the final. A stylish central defender, he makes up for what he lacks in height with an uncanny ability to read the game.

He made his Italy debut in January 1997 and was a first-team regular by the time the World Cup kicked off in France the following year. An ever-present member of the side defeated on penalties by the hosts in the quarter-final, he was one of the few Italians to come out of the tournament with an enhanced reputation. Four years later he was the glue that held the team's defence together at the 2002 finals and, tellingly, he was absent through suspension when they were eliminated by South Korea.

It seemed fitting that Cannavaro should take over the captaincy from his mentor Paolo Maldini and he led Italy with dignity throughout the 2006 tournament against a backdrop of controversy. With his club side, Juventus, mired in a match-fixing scandal that culminated in the attempted suicide of his former team-mate Gianlucca Pessotto, it was to his credit that he kept his focus. It was Cannavaro's idea to display a flag with the message 'Pessottino we are with you' at the end of the quarter-final against Ukraine, a uniting gesture that helped his team-mates express their feelings.

Whether partnering Alessandro Nesta or marshalling the inconsistent Marco Materazzi, he was a rock at the back of Italy's changing defence throughout the 2006 World Cup, and after lifting the trophy he was awarded the Silver Ball, having been voted the second best player of the tournament behind Zinédine Zidane.

Fabio Cannavaro v Germany, 2006

ANTONIO CARBAJAL

Country: Mexico **Born:** June 7, 1929

Position: Goalkeeper **Finals:** 1950, 1954, 1958, 1962, 1966

Record: P11/W1/D2/L8/A25

Antonio Carbajal carved out his legendary status by becoming the first player to appear in five World Cups. He made his international debut at the 1950 finals against hosts Brazil, and although he conceded four goals in the intimidating atmosphere of the Maracanã, his performance was applauded.

At the 1954 finals it was his understudy who faced Brazil in Mexico's opener, but after Salvador Mota shipped five goals, Carbajal returned for the remaining fixtures.

Captaining the Mexicans at the World Cups of 1958 and 1962, he was the team's outstanding player in the latter competition in Chile. His best game was against Spain and saw him weather relentless pressure for 89 minutes, keeping Puskás, Suárez and Gento at bay, but after conceding a late goal he was left in tears.

He was only once on the winning side at the finals, coincidentally on his 33rd birthday. The victory came against Czechoslovakia in 1962, but in the same game he also conceded what was for some time the quickest goal in World Cup history, scored in just 15 seconds.

He gained his only World Cup clean sheet at the 1966 finals, when playing against Uruguay in his one appearance of the tournament. In walking onto the Wembley pitch he also set a record that wouldn't be equalled until Lothar Matthäus played in a fifth tournament in 1998.

Fittingly Carbajal's first and last international games were at the World Cup.

CARLOS ALBERTO★

Country: Brazil **Born:** July 17, 1944

Position: Right-back **Finals:** 1970★

Record: P6/W6/D0/L0/F1

The career of Carlos Alberto Torres can be summed up in one sublime moment – the goal he scored in the 1970 World Cup Final against Italy. Charging onto a pass from Pelé 25 yards out, the right-back – and team captain – hammered the ball past hapless Italian goalkeeper Enrico Albertosi, proving the Brazilians had power to match their silky skills. Scored four minutes from time and sealing a glorious 4-1 victory, it became known as 'the President's goal' due to the fact that Brazil's President Médici had predicted the scoreline.

An attacking right-back most comfortable when charging forward, for all his defensive deficiencies Carlos Alberto was a vital part of this team and his biggest strength was his speed of thought on the ball. He had come close to a place in the squad for the 1966 World Cup but his inconsistency proved to be his undoing. By the time of the 1970 tournament he had grown in both stature and experience, having enjoyed considerable success at club level with Santos.

One of the senior members of Brazil's squad for Mexico 70, along with Pelé and Gérson he played a significant part in influencing coach Mario Zagallo's team selection for the tournament. Despite his success at the finals, a knee injury ruled him out of the 1974 World Cup and he played his last international in March 1977.

HECTOR CASTRO★

Country: Uruguay **Born:** November 29, 1904

Position: Forward **Finals:** 1930★

Record: P2/W2/D0/L02/F2

The last goal of the 1930 World Cup Final was scored by Uruguay centre-forward Hector Castro, who headed home a cross from Pablo Dorado to seal a 4-2 victory over Argentina. He had played just once in the build-up to the final, at inside-right in the group game against Peru. He scored Uruguay's first ever World Cup goal in the game after picking up a pass from Pedro Petrone. He was only brought into the team for the final as a late replacement for influential striker Peregrino Anselmo, who had been felled by illness.

Nicknamed 'El Manco', literally 'the one armed' because he had lost his right forearm in an accident in his teens, Castro was a brave and inventive player. He had first played for Uruguay in 1923, winning Olympic gold five years later in Amsterdam. He made his final international appearance in 1935, having played 25 games and scored 18 goals.

PEDRO CEA★

Country: Uruguay **Born:** September 1, 1900

Position: Forward **Finals:** 1930★

Record: P4/W4/D0/L0/F5

Pedro Cea was a World Cup winner with Uruguay in 1930, ending the tournament as his country's top scorer. A right-footed inside-left, he hit a hat-trick in the semi-final, opening and closing the scoring in a 6-1 victory over Yugoslavia. He also scored in the 57th minute of the final as Uruguay beat Argentina to win the World Cup.

One of Uruguay's all-conquering Olympic gold medallists of 1924 and 1928, he became known as the 'Olympic equaliser' because of his tendency to score vital goals for his country. He played his final match for Uruguay in 1932 and in 1941 he became coach of the national team for a short time.

BOBBY CHARLTON★

Country: England **Born:** October 11, 1937

Position: Midfield/Forward **Finals:** [1958], 1962, 1966★, 1970

Record: P14/W8/D0/L4/F4

Bobby Charlton went to his first World Cup tournament in 1958, just a few months after he had survived the Munich air disaster. Despite the growing clamour for him to be selected for the starting line-up, he was happy with his role as a non-playing squad member in Sweden. He eventually made his World Cup debut in 1962 playing on the left wing, where he impressed with his devastating pace and powerful shooting. His first game was a defeat to Hungary, but he would score in a 3-1 victory over Argentina.

It was at the tournament four years later that he made his biggest impact, playing as an attacking midfielder. Geoff Hurst might

Bobby Charlton v France, 1966

have stolen the headlines with his World Cup winning hat-trick, but it was Charlton who steered England to the final, kick-starting the campaign with a dazzling goal against Mexico. Running 30 yards from midfield, he blasted a drive from outside the penalty area that flew into the net, helping England to a 2-0 win. It was one of the more spectacular efforts of his 49 goals scored in an England shirt, a record that still stands.

He scored twice more in the semi-final victory over Portugal, a game that many believe to be his best in an England shirt. It was so impressive that it caused the West Germans to alter their tactics for the final and as a result Charlton had to contend with being shadowed throughout by Franz Beckenbauer. However, he picked up a winners' medal and wept openly on the Wembley pitch. He was voted Player Of The World Cup and European Footballer Of The Year.

A disappointing tournament in 1970 ended when he was substituted during a defeat to West Germany. It was his last game in an England shirt. The intention had been to rest him for the semi-final, but with Charlton off the pitch, Franz Beckenbauer was freed up to inspire a West German comeback that ended England's World Cup and Charlton's international career.

GINO COLAUSSI★

Country: Italy **Born:** March 4, 1914

Position: Outside-left **Finals:** 1938★

Record: P3/W3/D0/L0/F4

A quick and deadly left-winger for Triestina, at the 1938 World Cup Gino Colaussi did an admirable job filling the boots of one of Italy's great world champions, Raimundo Orsi. Always dangerous on the ball, Colaussi shot with the lethal precision of a marksman, scoring in all three games that he played at the 1938 tournament.

Making his international debut in October 1935, he had originally lost his place in the starting line-up on the eve of the competition. Regaining it for Italy's quarter-final against France, he scored the opening goal in just nine minutes with a lot of help from keeper Laurent Di Lorto, who let a high shot fall through his hands.

Colaussi held his position in the team until the tournament was over, scoring twice against Hungary in the final, prodding home the opening goal after just six minutes.

JOHAN CRUYFF

Country: Netherlands **Born:** April 25, 1947

Position: Striker **Finals:** 1974★

Record: P7/W5/D1/L1/F3

Johan Cruyff was easily the biggest star of the 1974 World Cup in West Germany. Hugely talented, wilful and unpredictable, he remains inextricably linked to the concept of 'Total Football' and the golden era of Dutch football, a symbol of the tournament that showcased his skills to the whole planet.

Playing his first game for his country in September 1966, Cruyff scored on his debut in a 2-2 draw with Hungary but just two months later he became the first Dutchman to be sent-off in an international. Until 1974 Holland had no presence to speak of at the World Cup, so his legend was initially built in club football, winning three consecutive European Cup finals with Ajax between 1971 and 1973, a feat mirrored by a hat-trick of European Footballer Of The Year awards.

By the time of the 1974 World Cup he was captain of a national team that had gone from perennial outsiders to hot favourites. Such was his power within the side that Cruyff

Johan Cruyff
v Argentina, 1974

actually played at the finals in a custom-made Dutch strip featuring just two stripes on his sleeve, rather than the three worn by his team-mates, insisting that as he was sponsored by a rival company he would not wear a shirt with the famous Adidas branding.

This couldn't take away from the genius of his game. Wearing his celebrated number 14 shirt at the finals, he orchestrated play with teasing skills and dazzling surges, unveiling the renowned 'Cruyff turn' to the watching millions when he turned Swedish right-back Jan Olsson inside out in the group stage. With the Holland team representing the new face of football, the shift in the balance of power was vividly demonstrated when the Dutch beat a physical Brazil side in a game notable for a sublime volley from Cruyff.

They may have been disciplined on the pitch, but off it their approach to the tournament was famously cavalier, and on the eve of the final sensationalised stories appeared in the West German press. Under the headline 'Cruyff, Champagne and Naked Girls', German tabloid newspaper *Bild Zeitung* published a story claiming that the night before the Holland-Brazil game there had been a 'naked party' in the swimming pool of their hotel, involving four unnamed Holland players and two German girls.

Whether the story was true or not, and it has been soundly denied by the Dutch team over the years, legend has it that Cruyff's wife kept him on the telephone for much of the night, and as a result he was a shadow of his best in the final. However, this may have had more to do with the fact that he was shackled by Berti Vogts during the most crucial phase of the match.

Losing to West Germany in the final did nothing to diminish his stature as a footballer of genius, although he would never appear at the World Cup again. He retired from international football in 1977 and although attempts were made to persuade him to compete at the next World Cup, Cruyff was not prepared to leave his wife and family for such a long period again, robbing football fans of one last chance to see him dazzle on the biggest stage of all.

TEÓFILO CUBILLAS

Country: Peru **Born:** March 8, 1949

Position: Midfield/Striker **Finals:** 1970, 1978, 1982

Record: P13/W4/D3/L6/F10

Peru's greatest ever player, when he was just 21 years old Teófilo Cubillas took to the 1970 World Cup Finals as a powerful shooting, fast dribbling inside-forward. Nicknamed 'El Nene', or 'the Kid', he was easily the biggest threat in a side coached by Brazilian World Cup legend Didi, scoring five goals in four games as Peru made an unexpected charge to the quarter-finals. The beautiful Brazilians proved a hurdle too far and he finished the tournament as its third highest goalscorer, behind Gerd Müller and Jairzinho.

By the time he returned to the World Cup in 1978 he had dropped into a deeper role, attacking from the midfield where he was paired with César Cueto. He shot down Scotland's World Cup hopes with two goals in a surprise 3-1 win and went on to score a hat-trick against Iran, including two penalties, taking his tally in two World Cups to ten.

He made three appearances at the 1982 finals in an insipid-looking Peru side crushed 5-1 by Poland. He failed to score and retired from international football soon after, having played 81 games and scored 26 goals for his country. He eventually became the Peruvian Minister for Sport.

ALESSANDRO DEL PIERO★

Country: Italy **Born:** November 9, 1974

Position: Striker/Midfield **Finals:** 1998, 2002, 2006★

Record: P12/W7/D4/L1/F2

Although known primarily for his creative passing play, Alessandro Del Piero has been prolific for Juventus and currently holds the club's scoring record. Although never making such a significant impact for Italy, he is still among the country's top five marksmen for the national team.

His slow recovery from a knee ligament injury limited his effectiveness at the 1998 World Cup, and although coach Giovanni Trapattoni used Del Piero only sparingly at the 2002 finals, he still came off the bench against Mexico to score a late equaliser that helped Italy qualify for the second round. He was again used largely as a substitute at the 2006 tournament, but his dramatic 121st minute goal against Germany in the semi-final set a World Cup record as the latest goal ever scored.

An 86th minute substitute in the 2006 final, he played through extra-time and converted Italy's fourth spot-kick in their 5-3 penalty shoot-out win over France.

DIDIER DESCHAMPS★

Country: France **Born:** October 15, 1968
Position: Midfield **Finals:** 1998★
Record: P6/W5/D1/L0/F0

A hard working and smart passing midfielder, Didier Deschamps first played for his country in 1989, but in a poor period for French football it wasn't until 1998 that he made his first appearance at the World Cup.

One of the few veterans to remain in a new look side after Aimé Jacquet rebuilt the national team, Deschamps captained France to World Cup victory on home soil, missing only the final group game. On the way to pick up the trophy he was congratulated by Michel Platini, a nice touch from the former national coach who had given Deschamps his international debut.

Insultingly described by Eric Cantona as a 'water carrier', he provided a platform for more creative players to perform and showed himself to be an excellent reader of the game. After success at the World Cup, Deschamps led France through a victorious European Championship campaign in 2000, before quitting international football. He won 103 caps for France and scored four goals.

DIDI★★

Country: Brazil **Born:** October 8, 1928
Position: Midfield **Finals:** 1954, 1958★, 1962★
Record: P15/W11/D3/L1/F3

Waldyr Pereira, more famously known as Didi, was the inspiration behind Brazil's successive World Cup triumphs of 1958 and 1962. Indeed, the free-flowing 4-2-4 formation employed by the Brazilians owed much to his thoughtful play and extraordinary technique, something that compensated for his lack of pace.

Didier Deschamps, 1998 World Cup Final

Such was the threat that he offered at the 1958 tournament, England's assistant manager Bill Nicholson identified Didi as the key to Brazil's success. Sweden coach George Raynor witnessed his team taken apart in the final and came to the same conclusion. "There are many people who rightly sing the praises of Garrincha, Pelé and Vavá," wrote Raynor, "but Didi was the man who commanded the middle of the field and sent through the passes which Garrincha, Vavá and Pelé converted into goals... He was masterly."

Ever-present for Brazil through three World Cup campaigns, Didi was ranked by many as pundits as the most outstanding player at the 1958 tournament, his one goal coming in the semi-final against France, a 25-yard strike hit with such power and ferocity that it gave Claude Abbes no chance.

The first of the great free-kick specialists, Didi was known to practice his set-pieces alone for hours at a time, inventing the 'banana shot', or the 'dry leaf' free-kick, so-called because it would dip and swerve unpredictably in flight like a leaf in the wind. He scored 12 of his 31 international goals from dead ball situations, although only one of his three World Cup goals came this way, his first against Mexico in 1954.

He represented his country on 85 occasions and at the beginning of his career he also had the honour of scoring the first ever goal at the famous Maracanã Stadium, playing in a game between junior representative sides from Río and Saõ Paulo shortly before the 1950 World Cup.

He later became coach of Peru and shocked South American football when he guided them to Mexico 70. He announced that his team would do well unless they came up against Brazil – which they did in the quarter-final.

PABLO DORADO★

Country: Uruguay **Born:** June 22, 1908
Position: Forward **Finals:** 1930★
Record: P3/W3/D0/L0/F2

At just 22 years of age Pablo Dorado made history when he scored the first ever goal in a World Cup final. In the 12th minute of the 1930 final he picked up a pass from Hector Castro and shot through the legs of Argentina goalkeeper Juan Botasso and past defender Juan Evaristo, who was backing up on the line. He would later supply the cross from which Castro scored Uruguay's fourth and final goal of the game.

Dorado played his club football in Uruguay for Bella Vista and was naturally a left-sided player, but after a shake-up of the forward line he gained his opportunity on the opposite flank for Uruguay's second game against Romania. He scored the opening goal of the game and held his place in the team through to the final. After the World Cup he moved to Argentina to play for River Plate.

DUNGA★

Country: Brazil **Born:** October 31, 1963
Position: Midfield **Finals:** 1990, 1994★, 1998☆
Record: P18/W12/D3/L3/F0

For a player who made 91 international appearances and captained both winning and losing World Cup final teams, Dunga's efficient and effective abilities on the pitch are little celebrated in his home country. As a player he is painfully associated with a period in the mid 1990s, referred to as the 'Dunga Era', when the national team relied more on sweat than style.

Driven and competitive, what Dunga lacked in creativity he made up for in determination, time and again proving himself to be his country's most formidable midfield enforcer. An ever-present member of all three of Brazil's World Cup campaigns in the Nineties, he made his World Cup debut at Italia 90 in a side viewed by some as the worst Brazil had ever sent to the finals.

Four years later, however, he was to lift the World Cup as captain, a responsibility he had only inherited in the knockout stages of the tournament, after the usually creative Raí, younger brother of the great Socrates, had finally been dropped from the team.

Dunga has at least been respected for his passion, while his courage to stand up and be counted for his country was evident when he successfully converted Brazil's fourth spot-kick in the shoot-outs to decide both the 1994 World Cup Final and the semi-final against France four years later. He retained the captaincy in 1998 despite playing his club football to a lower standard in Japan's J-League at the time.

His competitive nature wasn't to everyone's taste, which led to the occasional spat with team-mates – he contested an angry turf war with centre-forward Careca in 1990, and while he publicly berated Bebeto on the pitch against Morocco at France 98, he at least kept his problems with Leonardo in the dressing room after the final.

Despite no experience of coaching, Dunga took over Brazil's national side in August 2006, and en route to the 2010 World Cup he was criticised for building a team in his own image and for abandoning key Brazilian principles. "The national team is not only about skill anymore," he happily admitted, "it's about competitiveness and commitment."

His real name is Carlos Caetano Bledorn Verri, borrowing the nickname Dunga, meaning 'Dopey', from *Snow White And The Seven Dwarfs*.

STEFAN EFFENBERG

Country: Germany **Born:** August 2, 1968
Position: Midfield **Finals:** 1994
Record: P3/W2/D1/L0/F0

At his peak Stefan Effenberg was one of Europe's top players but he will probably be best remembered for being sent home from the 1994 World Cup for making an obscene gesture to the German fans after being substituted against South Korea.

It was a rash act that more or less ended his international career. Following the incident Effenberg was placed on a plane home, with the words of Berti Vogts ringing in his ears: "For as long as I'm coaching this team, Effenberg will not play for Germany again."

While Vogts eventually relented it would be another four years before Effenburg pulled on a Germany shirt. He would win just two more caps, ironically ending his international career in what would also be the last match in charge for Vogts.

EUSÉBIO

Country: Portugal **Born:** January 25, 1942
Position: Striker **Finals:** 1966
Record: P6/W5/D0/L1/F9

Eusébio Da Silva Ferreira was the undisputed star of the 1966 World Cup Finals in England. A bright and ingenious forward with a lightning turn of pace, he bewitched fans with his effortless ball control and ferocious right-foot. However, despite his talents the competition would end in bitter disappointment for the Portuguese and the sight of Eusébio being led from the Wembley pitch in tears after defeat to England gave the tournament one of its defining images.

Eusébio, Portugal v Hungary, 1966

Having scored twice against Brazil in the group stage, Eusébio's World Cup really exploded into life midway through the first half of the quarter-final. Trailing 3-0 to North Korea, he inspired his team-mates to a truly amazing comeback, scoring four goals himself, two of them from the penalty spot, as Portugal turned the game around to win 5-3.

Converting spot-kicks again in the semi-final defeat to England and in the 2-1 victory over the Soviet Union in the third place play-off, he left England as the competition's top scorer with nine goals. Such was his impact that he was nicknamed the 'European Pelé' and he even had a waxwork model erected in his honour at Madame Tussauds in London.

Although he took part in the qualifiers for the 1970 and 1974 competitions, he would only feature at the finals this once, but his performance was enough to confirm him as one of the greats of World Cup history.

GIOVANNI FERRARI ☆☆

Country: Italy **Born:** December 6, 1907
Position: Inside-left **Finals:** 1934☆, 1938☆
Record: P8/W7/D1/L0/F2

Giovanni Ferrari made his international debut in February 1930, on the same day as Giuseppe Meazza. Although he would have to wait another 12 months for his second cap, by the time of the 1934 World Cup he was a regular member of the team. He only missed one game in that campaign, the replay to a battering encounter with Spain after scoring the equaliser in the first meeting.

He was on the winning side in the victory over Czechoslovakia in the final and he picked up his second winners' medal four years later as Italy beat Hungary in Paris. Along with Meazza he is one of only two players to have taken part in both of Italy's World Cup final winning teams of 1934 and 1938, although Guido Masetti and Eraldo Monzeglio can also lay claim to being members of both squads.

Ferrari was appointed coach of the national side in 1960 and along with Paolo Mazza he was a member of the technical commission that led the team at the 1962 World Cup.

UBALDO FILLOL★

Country: Argentina **Born:** July 21, 1950
Position: Goalkeeper **Finals:** 1974, 1978★, 1982
Record: P13/W7/D2/L4/A12

When Ubaldo Fillol made his World Cup debut at the 1974 finals in West Germany it wasn't really expected, but after Daniel Carnevali had conceded 11 goals in five games, Fillol was given his chance in a meaningless game against East Germany.

There was just as much uncertainty about his chances of keeping goal at the 1978 tournament. César Luis Menotti had a straight choice to make between Fillol of River Plate and Hugo Gatti of rivals Boca Juniors, but the coach was prevaricating. When Menotti finally settled on the excellent shot stopper Fillol, his adversary pulled out with a knee injury. "It was nothing but an excuse," insisted Fillol, and the much debated incident became known as 'excusa de la rodilla', or 'the knee excuse'.

Early in the tournament Fillol looked vulnerable but he grew in stature as the tournament progressed. He even saved what could have been an equalising penalty from Poland's Kazimierz Deyna in the second round, but that would have been no surprise to the fans of Racing Club, who had seen him set an Argentine league record in 1972, saving six penalties in a season.

In the final against Holland he was in outstanding form, parrying a fantastic shot from Johnny Rep early on and making crucial saves from Rob Rensenbrink and Johan Neeskens either side of half-time. Not only did he pick up a winners' medal after the final whistle, but he was also voted the best goalkeeper of the tournament.

Known as 'El Pato', or 'the duck', Ubaldo Fillol was an ever-present member of the 1982 World Cup team, but just missed the cut for the finals in Mexico four years later. He is regarded as the best goalkeeper Argentina has produced, and strangely he never wore the number one jersey at the World Cup. With Argentina numbering their squads largely alphabetically at the time, he wore '5' in 1978 and '7' in 1982, although slightly more conventionally for a reserve keeper he wore '12' in 1974.

Just Fontaine, 1958 third place play-off

JUST FONTAINE

Country: France **Born:** August 18, 1933
Position: Centre-forward **Finals:** 1958
Record: P6/W4/D0/L2/F13

Just Fontaine made history when he scored 13 goals at the World Cup finals of 1958. It stands as the highest number of goals scored by one player in a single tournament, yet he was not even France's first choice centre-forward before the World Cup began. Only an injury to René Bliard gave him the chance to make football history.

Fontaine was born in Morocco and won his first cap for France in 1953. He was left out for nearly three years and returned to the international fold to play just four times before the World Cup in 1958. At the finals he formed a wonderful partnership with Raymond Kopa and scored six goals in the three group games, including a hat trick in the 7-3 thrashing of Paraguay.

Fontaine's assets were pace and a potent left foot, and he couldn't stop scoring, hitting two more against Northern Ireland in the quarter-final and one in the 5-2 defeat to Brazil in the semi. He scored four as France beat the West Germans in the third place play-off to take his total to 13, none of which were penalties.

To prove his World Cup exploits were no fluke, he finished as the European Cup's leading scorer in the 1958-59 season with ten goals. He had won 21 caps and scored 30 goals by the time a broken leg ended his career. In 1967 he briefly managed the French national team.

FRIAÇA

Country: Brazil **Born:** October 20, 1924
Position: Outside-right **Finals:** 1950★
Record: P4/W2/D1/L1/F1

Albino Friaça Cardoso was a nippy right winger with a strong shot who scored one of the most wildly celebrated goals of all time. Just two minutes into the second-half of the 1950 World Cup decider he received the ball from Ademir and rolled a low shot across Uruguay keeper Roque Máspoli. In front of a partisan home crowd of 198,854, the highest attended football match of all time, the goal was met by the loudest roar in sporting history, the stadium erupting in celebration. Unfortunately his legendary status evaporated with the eventual defeat.

Friaça made his international debut against Uruguay in April 1948, facing them twice in a week. He was not selected again until the World Cup warm-ups in May 1950, starting the first two games of the tournament out of position on the left wing. Missing the ties with Yugoslavia and Sweden, he was recalled in his favoured position on the right against Spain in the Final Pool, retaining his place for the final match against Uruguay.

Emotionally drained by the defeat, he would not play for Brazil again for almost two years, gaining just two more caps.

GARRINCHA★★

Country: Brazil **Born:** October 28, 1933
Position: Outside-right **Finals:** 1958★, 1962★, 1966
Record: P12/W10/D1/L1/F5

It was a miracle that Garrincha became one of Brazil's greatest players because a childhood illness had left one leg curved and the other slightly shorter. His real name was Manuel Francisco dos Santo, but he played under his nickname 'Garrincha', which meant 'little bird' or 'wren'. An exceptional dribbler and possessing a wonderful swerving 'banana shot', he was one of the outstanding stars of the Brazil side that beat Sweden 5-3 to win the 1958 World Cup.

Along with Pelé he had been forced to sit out the opening games of the tournament by coach Vicente Feola, who feared the maverick winger's style against the disciplined defences of Austria and England. He also heeded the advice of Brazil's team psychologist who had strongly advised against the inclusion of the ingenuous Garrincha, largely based on an assessment of some simplistic sketches that the winger had been asked to draw.

Before the third group game against the Soviet Union a deputation of senior players requested the inclusion of Pelé and Garrincha. Feolo acquiesced and Garrincha's wing wizardry helped to inspire Brazil's charge to the final. When Feola was asked about the influence of the psychologist just before the final, he was less than complimentary: "Senhor Feola is not saying he wished the psychologist would go to hell," explained the coach's interpreter, "but he is thinking it."

Garrincha v England, 1962

While it would be Pelé who grabbed the headlines in the final, it was Garrincha who set up Brazil's first two goals, and after the Swedes devoted two players to neutralise his threat on the right, they left themselves vulnerable to the charges of Mario Zagallo on the left, from where Brazil's remaining goals would emanate.

Four years later in Chile, with Pelé sidelined by injury, it was Garrincha who was Brazil's main inspiration. Hitting his stride in the knockout stages, he scored twice in the quarter-final win over England and then twice again in the semi-finals against the hosts Chile. Bizarrely sent-off for an innocuous offence in the closing minutes of the semi-final, FIFA didn't suspend Garrincha despite imposing one-match bans on the other five players dismissed during the tournament, allowing the winger to play in the final against Czechoslovakia and pick up his second World Cup winners' medal.

Garrincha's last game for Brazil was against Hungary at the 1966 World Cup; it was the first time in his 60 international matches that Brazil had lost with Garrincha in the side. Sadly, his wild off-the-field lifestyle caught up with him in 1983, when he died aged 49.

GÉRSON★

Country: Brazil **Born:** January 11, 1941
Position: Midfield **Finals:** 1966, 1970★
Record: P5/W4/D0/L1/F1

At the 1966 World Cup it had been hoped that Gérson de Oliveira Nunes would emerge as the natural successor to Didi as Brazil's midfield general, but he failed to assert his authority in an ageing side, making just one appearance before Brazil were eliminated in the group stage.

Four years later it was a very different story. Gérson had a superb World Cup in 1970 when most of Brazil's attacking moves were orchestrated by his fantastically potent left-foot. In the first round, against Czechoslovakia, he provided a trademark 40-yard pass from midfield for Pelé to score, and his range of distribution, together with his midfield scheming, was a consistent delight.

In the final against Italy, Gérson was arguably the man of the match and scored Brazil's second goal in the memorable 4-1 rout. He will be forever remembered as the midfield mastermind of this beautiful Brazilian side.

ALCIDES GHIGGIA★

Country: Uruguay **Born:** December 22, 1926
Position: Outside-right **Finals:** 1950★
Record: P4/W3/D1/L0/F4

For Alcides Ghiggia, the greatest moment of his career came in the final match of the 1950 World Cup, when he scored the goal that silenced the biggest crowd in football history.

Dribbling past the Brazilian left-back, exactly as he had 13 minutes earlier when he set up Juan Schiaffino to score Uruguay's equaliser, this time instead of crossing, he shot towards the near post. Keeper Moacir Barbosa was caught off guard and the ball hit the back of the net. Many years later Ghiggia would say, "Only three people have, with just one motion, silenced the Maracanã: Frank Sinatra, Pope John Paul II and me."

An agile outside-right for Peñarol and Uruguay, he scored in all of the matches he played at the 1950 finals. He later played his club football in Italy for Roma, representing his adopted country in the qualification campaign for the 1958 tournament. It was only Italy's failure to reach the finals that prevented Ghiggia from joining that rare club of players who have turned out for more than one country at the World Cup.

GILMAR★★

Country: Brazil **Born:** August 22, 1930
Position: Goalkeeper **Finals:** 1958★, 1962★, 1966
Record: P14/W11/D2/L1/A12

Born Gylmar dos Santos Neves but best known as just 'Gilmar', he is regarded as the finest goalkeeper Brazil has ever produced. With a famously calm style of play on the pitch, he was in goal when the Brazilians became world champions for the first time in 1958 and he helped them retain the title four years later, an ever-present member of both winning teams.

At the 1958 finals he didn't concede a goal until the semi-final victory over France, when he was beaten by the unstoppable Just Fontaine, and the ball only passed him three times in six matches. Agile, brave and a formidable last line of defence, he was equally impressive at the 1962 World Cup in Chile, where he made what is often cited as the best save of his career against Spain.

Although he made two appearances at the 1966 World Cup, he was one of several veterans replaced after Brazil conceded three goals to Hungry. His international career lasted until he made his final appearance in 1969, aged 39. Saving penalties was a speciality, although he never had the opportunity to face one in any of his 14 games at the World Cup.

SERGIO GOYCOCHEA

Country: Argentina **Born:** October 17, 1963

Position: Goalkeeper **Finals:** 1990★

Record: P6/W2/D3/L1/A3

Third choice keeper for Argentina on the eve of the 1990 World Cup, Sergio Goycochea was bumped up the pecking order when Luis Islas withdrew, piqued at having to understudy Nery Pumpido at the finals yet again. But when Pumpido suffered a broken leg nine minutes into Argentina's second match, Goycochea found himself in the team and on a run to the World Cup final.

Between the sticks of an uninspiring looking Argentina side, he conceded just three goals in six games and won both the quarter-final and the semi for his team, saving two spot-kicks in each of the deciding penalty shoot-outs against Yugoslavia and hosts Italy.

Although Argentina lost the final, he was beaten only by a penalty in the dying minutes and afterwards was voted the best goalkeeper of the tournament. Four years later, however, Islas finally got his chance, and despite being given the squad number '1', Goycochea watched from the bench.

HARRY GREGG

Country: Northern Ireland **Born:** October 25, 1932

Position: Goalkeeper **Finals:** 1958

Record: P4/W1/D1/L2/F9

In what was an eventful year for Manchester United keeper Harry Gregg he was voted the best goalkeeper of the 1958 World Cup, just months after pulling fellow survivors from the burning wreckage of the Munich air disaster, a tragedy that had killed so many of his club team-mates.

The award was decided by the votes of the international football press covering the tournament, and although Gregg polled nearly four times the tally of legendary keeper Lev Yashin, this was more than just a sympathy vote. Gregg had made a series of incredible saves in a 2-2 draw with West Germany, despite carrying an injury that required his fullbacks to take his goal kicks.

Although he was forced to miss the group play-off with Czechoslovakia, he took to the field for the quarter-final with France regardless of having to rely on a walking stick away from the pitch. He was left with no option but to play after his reserve had suffered a broken hand, and although he conceded four times in the defeat, he had shown his undoubted class and spirit.

Sergio Goycochea v Italy, 1990

GYULA GROSICS

Country: Hungary **Born:** February 4, 1926

Position: Goalkeeper **Finals:** 1954★, 1958, 1962

Record: P10/W5/D2/L4/A17

A member of the 'Magical Magyars' team of the 1950s, Gyula Grosics was Hungary's greatest ever goalkeeper, and along with Lev Yashin of the Soviet Union and Brazil's Gilmar, one of the best of his era.

Capable of dominating his penalty area and commanding his defence, he excelled when dealing with crosses. Quick off his line, he was even prone to dashing out of his area to intercept the ball if necessary, pioneering the role of the 'sweeper keeper' long before anyone had given it the name.

Known as the 'Black Panther' because of his distinctive black playing strip, he represented his country 86 times from 1947, winning gold at the 1952 Olympics. He played at the World Cups of 1954, 1958 and 1962, but he was turned from hero to villain in 1954 after ending up on the losing side in the World Cup final, having conceded two goals that he normally would have been expected to save.

Usually so good in the air, West Germany's equaliser came after he contested a high ball with Hans Schäfer. Missing it completely, he had to watch from the ground as Helmut Rahn stabbed the ball home.

Despite his outstanding performances throughout the tournament, he was blamed by some for the failure. On his return to Hungary he was falsely accused of spying and was kept under house arrest for 13 months. After eventually being allowed to resume his career he once again became a fixture in the national side.

Along with József Bozsik and Nándor Hidegkuti, he was one of only three of the 1954 finalists to play at the tournament four years later. He also captained Hungary to the 1962 World Cup in Chile and was unlucky not to reach the semi-finals after conceding an early goal to Czechoslovakia.

The last of the 'Magical Magyars' in the Hungary team, Grosics made three more appearances for his country after the 1962 World Cup before he called time on a 15-year international career.

HELMUT HALLER

Country: West Germany **Born:** July 21, 1939

Position: Striker **Finals:** 1962, 1966★, 1970

Record: P9/W5/D1/L2/F6

West German striker Helmut Haller certainly knew how to conform to stereotype – blond, burly and prone to theatrics. However, he was also a world-class footballer who spent the best years of his playing career in Italy, with Bologna who he helped to a first Serie A title in 33 years before taking a big money transfer to Juventus. Comfortable almost anywhere in the forward line, he was just as accomplished as a midfield playmaker.

Making three appearances at the 1962 World Cup in Chile, Haller was dropped for the deciding group match with the hosts when coach Sepp Herberger opted for a safety first approach by playing just three forwards instead of his usual five. Signing for Bologna on his return, along with other Germans playing abroad Haller found himself excluded from the national team and was not recalled until November 1964, just in time for the first of the qualifiers for the 1966 World Cup.

At the finals in England Haller would impress and irritate in equal measure. His undoubted talent could be overshadowed by his tendency to throw himself to the floor at every possible opportunity, but he finished the tournament as its second-highest goalscorer, hitting the net six times en route to the final. In West Germany's opening game against the Swiss he scored twice, and while his second was simply rifled in from the penalty spot, for his first he picked up the ball deep in his own half and sprinted the length of the pitch before slotting the ball calmly past the keeper from seven yards.

Wherever Haller was, the action followed: he attracted much of Uruguay's attention in the quarter-final, charging into the box to score the winning goal just minutes after writhing about on the floor as if his match was over; he was easily his team's best player in the semi-final victory over the Soviet Union; and he scored the opening goal of the final against England.

Haller finished the World Cup final with a runners-up medal in his hand and the match ball under his arm, although 30 years later he would be enticed to return the ball to the English after a bizarre campaign waged in the British tabloid press.

Not in the same class at the finals of 1970, he played just the first half of West Germany's opening match before being replaced by Jürgen Grabowski. Although he would continue to play club football for much of the rest of the decade, this was his last international appearance.

GEOFF HURST★

Country: England **Born:** December 8, 1941

Position: Striker **Finals:** 1966★, 1970

Record: P6/W4/D0/L2/F5

Though not England's most prolific goalscorer, Geoff Hurst will always be his nation's most celebrated for scoring the first hat-trick in a World Cup final: the three goals which made England world champions.

Although he scored 24 goals in 49 appearances for his country, he was only a fringe member of the England squad in the early stages of the 1966 World Cup. He would not have played in the final but for an injury to Jimmy Greaves earlier in the tournament. Hurst seized the opportunity, marking his World Cup debut with the winning goal in the quarter-final against Argentina. He retained his place in the team even when Greaves was declared fit before the final, scoring twice in extra-time to complete his hat-trick.

Hurst's second goal of the game was the cause of debate for decades to come. His shot cannoned down off the bar, and with the English insisting that it crossed the line and the West Germans protesting that it hadn't, referee Gottfried Dienst looked to linesman Tofik Bakhramov for the casting vote.

There was no argument about his final goal, smashed into the roof of the net so near to the end of the game that some fans had already started their pitch invasion before the ball had actually been struck.

Hurst was also a member of the unfortunate England side that crashed out of the World Cup at the quarter-final stage four years later, adding just one goal to his World Cup tally in the opener against Romania.

SANTOS IRIARTE★

Country: Uruguay **Born:** November 2, 1902

Position: Outside-left **Finals:** 1930★

Record: P4/W4/D0/L0/F2

Nicknamed 'El Canario', meaning 'the Canary', outside-left Victoriano Santos Iriarte scored Uruguay's third goal in the 1930 World Cup Final against Argentina, picking up a pass from Ernesto Mascheroni and firing a fearsome 25-yard shot past Argentina keeper Juan Botasso. He played in each one of Uruguay's four games in the tournament, also scoring in the semi-final against Yugoslavia.

Geoff Hurst, 1966 World Cup Final. His second goal

JAIRZINHO ☆

Country: Brazil **Born:** December 25, 1944
Position: Outside-right/Centre-forward
Finals: 1966, 1970☆, 1974
Record: P16/W10/D2/L4/F9

Jairzinho secured his place in World Cup history with a fantastic series of performances as Brazil won the 1970 World Cup. He had already played at the 1966 finals in England, though there was little evidence of the calibre that he would bring to the tournament four years later.

With Garrincha still hanging on to a place in the side in 1966, Jairzinho, then just 21 years old, made do with a role on the left wing of Brazil's attack and wasn't at his best. He played in all three of his team's matches, switching to the right wing for the final game, but the Brazilians were poor and they returned home after the group stage.

Four years later Jairzinho arrived at the World Cup in Mexico as a member of a very different Brazil side and he was playing as an attacking right-winger. Blessed with a direct style, scorching pace and a fierce shot, he was simply too much for opposing defenders to handle, and by the end of the tournament he had collected a winners' medal and made history by scoring in every match of the competition including the final, earning him the nickname 'hurricane of the cup'. The only other player to have achieved the feat was Alcides Ghiggia, but in 1950 Uruguay had only played four matches to win the trophy.

Jairzinho, 1970 World Cup Final

v Romania, 1970

Jairzinho started off with two goals in the first match, a 4-2 win over Czechoslovakia, the second of which was a fabulous solo effort that saw him hurdle two challenges before firing across the keeper. He also hit the winning goal in the victory over England, lauded as one of the most memorable matches of all time. The outstanding incident from that encounter has always been Gordon Banks' gravity defying save from Pelé's downward header, but it is often forgotten that it was Jairzinho's run and cross that provided the chance.

He scored in a 3-2 victory over Romania, then another in the quarter-final defeat of Peru. In the semi-final Jairzinho found the net again as Brazil beat Uruguay, memorably running to the by-line and dropping to his knees to cross himself in both thanks and celebration. He finally made it a goal in every round of the competition with the third in the 4-1 win over Italy in the final, even if the ball did roll in off his chest.

Jairzinho also played in the 1974 finals, but it wasn't just the 'afro' that made him look like a different player. A dearth of quality in the side resulted in him leading the line as centre-forward, where he had often featured for his club side, but he scored only twice as Brazil finished in fourth place, losing to Poland in the third place play-off. It effectively marked the end of his international career, although he would make one final appearance for Brazil, some eight years later and aged 37.

JAIRZINHO'S RECORD-BREAKING GOALS

In 1970 Jairzinho scored in every game of every round of the finals...

GROUP GAME 1		GROUP GAME 2	GROUP GAME 3	QUARTER-FINAL	SEMI-FINAL	FINAL
v Czechoslovakia	v Czechoslovakia	v England	v Romania	v Peru	v Uruguay	v Italy
61 mins: Puts Brazil 3-1 ahead after receiving a pass in an offside position.	**81 mins:** Beats four men to score the final goal of the game, making it 4-1.	**59 mins:** Pelé lays off a Tostão cross for Jairzinho to fire home for a 1-0 win.	**22 mins:** The second goal in a 3-2 win, Jairzinho scores from close range.	**75 mins:** Rounds the keeper to score from a tight angle, completing a 4-2 win.	**76 mins:** Scores the second goal in a 3-1 win after starting a move in his own half.	**71 mins:** Pelé nods on for Jairzinho to make history, scoring the third in 4-1 victory.

OLIVER KAHN

Country: Germany **Born:** June 15, 1969

Position: Goalkeeper **Finals:** [1994], [1998], 2002★, 2006

Record: P8/W6/D1/L1/A4

Oliver Khan was one of the greatest keepers of the modern era. He made his international debut for Germany in 1995 and although he was a non-playing squad member at the World Cups of 1994 and 1998, he was firmly the first choice keeper by the 2002 finals, when he also captained the side throughout the tournament.

He was instrumental in guiding the Germans to the World Cup final in 2002, conceding just one strike to the Republic Of Ireland's Robbie Keane before the championship decider. He had been in such stupendous form that one German newspaper described coach Rudi Völler's tactics as 'a flat back one'.

The Germans were beaten 2-0 by Brazil in the final and it was Kahn, the player who had done so much to get them there, who was at fault for the first goal. Failing to hold Rivaldo's shot, Ronaldo pounced on the rebound to fire Brazil ahead. Nevertheless, Kahn was named Player Of The Tournament, the first time a goalkeeper had received the Golden Ball award. He was also voted the best keeper of the tournament.

Before the 2006 World Cup Kahn struggled to hide his anger when asked to understudy Jens Lehmann, but in the moments before Germany's quarter-final penalty shoot-out with Argentina, the sight of Kahn approaching Lehman to shake his hand and wish him luck gave the tournament one of its most abiding memories. The feud between the two keepers had at one point threatened to overshadow German preparations for the competition, but here was the mighty Kahn putting his pride aside for the sake of national unity.

As thanks he was given his only game of the tournament as the Germans beat Portugal in the third place play-off. He retired from international football after the game, having captained the German side on 50 occasions.

Oliver Kahn v Paraguay, 2002

MARIO KEMPES★

Country: Argentina **Born:** July 15, 1954

Position: Forward **Finals:** 1974, 1978★, 1982

Record: P18/W8/D3/L7/F6

A prolific goalscorer for both club and country, only Diego Maradona is held in higher esteem among the football fans of Argentina than Mario Kempes, his lethal finishing in front of goal earning him the nickname 'El Matador', or 'The Killer'. He made his international debut aged 19, during the qualifying rounds of the 1974 World Cup, and he played every game at the finals, although he disappointingly failed to deliver on any of his great promise.

At the 1978 World Cup he was the only European-based player in César Luis Menotti's squad, having been the highest goalscorer in the Spanish league for two consecutive seasons with Valencia. However, his tournament only exploded into life when Argentina finished second in the group and had to play outside of Buenos Aires.

Kempes suddenly found himself playing all of the second round fixtures in Rosario, at the ground where he had first made his name as a professional. The change must have worked for him as he scored both goals in the victory over Poland and hit another two in the 6-0 demolition of Peru to help Argentina into the final.

Overnight Kempes became his country's biggest star, and the two goals he scored against Holland in the final confirmed his status as a national hero. For his second he beat three defenders and keeper Jan Jongbloed to slot the ball home, while he also set-up Bertoni to make it 3-1. His six goals proved enough to secure him the Golden Boot as top scorer, while he was also voted the tournament's best player.

By contrast the 1982 World Cup was a bitter disappointment for both Kempes and Argentina. He failed to score and the players were on their way home after losing to Italy and Brazil. Nevertheless, the name Kempes will always be associated with the World Cup – of his 43 international appearances, 18 were made at the finals.

LÁSZLÓ KISS

Country: Hungary **Born:** March 12, 1956

Position: Striker **Finals:** 1982

Record: P3/W1/D1/L1/F3

The Hungarians were already leading 5-0 when Vasas striker László Kiss came onto the pitch against El Salvador as a 57th minute substitute. Within 20 minutes he had set several new World Cup records, scoring the fastest hat-trick in the history of the competition and breaking the record for the most goals in a match by a substitute.

The Hungarians won 10-1, still the record for the highest scoring game at the finals, and although his three goals earned him a place in the starting line-up for both remaining fixtures, it wasn't enough to keep the team in the tournament. Kiss scored no more World Cup goals as his five-year international career lasted only until 1984.

MIROSLAV KLOSE

Country: Germany **Born:** June 9, 1978

Position: Centre-forward **Finals:** 2002★, 2006

Record: P14/W10/D2/L2/F10

Miroslav Klose has proven himself to be a prolific centre-forward on every stage, but in football terms he was something of a late developer, making the jump from German regional football to the World Cup in less than two years. Having first worked as a carpenter he didn't even make his full debut for his first professional club until he was 22, but within six months his blistering pace and lethal finishing earned him a call-up to the national team.

Miroslav Klose v Saudi Arabia, 2002

It could have all been so different. Polish-born Klose had moved to Germany with his family as a child in 1987 but although approached by the Polish national team, he declined the opportunity and held out for a call-up from Germany.

Klose opened his 2002 campaign with a hat-trick against Saudi Arabia, followed by goals against the Republic Of Ireland and Cameroon, but although he picked up a runners-up medal after defeat to Brazil in the final, he did not add to his tally in the knockout stages.

Finishing the tournament as the second highest scorer behind Ronaldo, Klose headed all five of his goals, an unrivalled achievement at the finals. He dedicated his goals to Fritz Walter, West Germany's 1954 World Cup winning captain and a legend at Klose's club Kaiserslautern, who had died four days before the quarter-final.

Klose won the Golden Boot at the 2006 finals with another five goals, scoring twice on his 28th birthday in the tournament's opening game against Costa Rica. His most vital strike came against Argentina in the quarter-final. His only headed goal of that tournament, it put the Germans back onto level terms and set up a penalty shoot-out, which they won 4–2 with Klose watching from the bench, having been substituted minutes after his goal. Defeat to Italy in the semi-final ended his World Cup.

RAYMOND KOPA

Country: France **Born:** October 13, 1931
Position: Outside-right/Centre-forward
Finals: 1954, 1958
Record: P8/W5/D0/L3/F4

Raymond Kopa, short for Kopaszewski, became the first French winner of the European Footballer Of The Year prize in 1958. Standing at just five foot six, he possessed superb balance, a phenomenal turn of pace, and an uncanny ability to find the right pass, all qualities that made him one of the game's best creators.

Starting off his career as an outside-right, he made his name as a deep-lying centre-forward, first at Reims and then as a three-time European Cup winner with Real Madrid, but is was his outstanding creativity at the 1958 World Cup that cemented his legend. He had made two appearances at the finals in Switzerland four years earlier, when playing on the right wing (and scoring a late penalty against Mexico), but in 1958 his unselfish play helped France to finish in third place. Paired in attack with Just Fontaine, he had a hand in many of his strike partner's record 13-goal tally, and he even scored three times himself, against Paraguay, Scotland and a penalty in the third place play-off against West Germany.

He played his last game for France in November 1962, but missed out on a chance of making a third World Cup that summer when France failed to qualify, although he did not feature in the side during the qualifiers. In total he scored 18 goals in 45 international appearances.

GRZEGORZ LATO

Country: Poland **Born:** April 8, 1950
Position: Right-winger **Finals:** 1974, 1978, 1982
Record: P20/W12/D4/L4/F10

Grzegorz Lato starred in three consecutive World Cups and was the tournament's top goalscorer in 1974, helping Poland to an unlikely third place finish. The Poles were blessed with attacking talent such as Robert Gadocha and Kazimierz Deyna, but it was Lato who had the biggest impact, netting seven of his team's 14 goals from his position on the right wing.

He scored twice in the opener against Argentina and grabbed another pair in the 7-0 defeat of Haiti, adding to his tally against Sweden and Yugoslavia in the second round. With a place in the final at stake the Poles did battle with West Germany in the awful rain of Frankfurt, but Lato's dashing wing play was undone by the waterlogged pitch, and a courageous point blank save from Sepp Maier kept his best chance out.

At the 1978 finals Lato scored against Tunisia and Brazil, but in the defeat to Argentina he was denied by an outrageous goal-line handball by star of the tournament Mario Kempes.

The finals of 1982 proved to be Lato's international swansong and brought him closest to success. With his blistering pace a thing of the past, he was now creating chances in a deeper midfield role. But with star striker Zbigniew Boniek suspended for the semi-final, Lato was forced to act as a makeshift centre-forward. After defeat to the Italians and a victory over France in the third place play-off, Lato picked up his second World Cup bronze medal. He retired from international football the following year.

LUCIEN LAURENT

Country: France **Born:** December 10, 1907
Position: Inside-right **Finals:** 1930
Record: P2/W1/D0/L1/F1

Lucien Laurent etched his place in football history as the scorer of the first World Cup goal. Connecting with a right wing cross from Ernest Liberati in the 19th minute, Laurent volleyed into the top of the net to put France on their way to a 4-1 victory over Mexico. "I couldn't have imagined the significance the goal would have," he recalled late in life. "We didn't even know the World Cup would last. I remember when I got home, there was just a tiny mention in one of the papers."

In the following game Laurent was injured after just ten minutes by the ferocious Argentinian defender Luis Monti but he remained on the pitch as a virtual passenger until the final whistle. It proved to be his last appearance at the World Cup.

The short but tenacious inside-right was only to play ten times for France between his debut against Portugal in February 1930 and his final game against Hungary in May 1935. Injury cruelly ruled him out of the 1934 tournament, but in honour of his achievement he was a guest at the 1998 World Cup Final, witnessing France lift the trophy for the first time.

LEÔNIDAS

Country: Brazil **Born:** November 11, 1910
Position: Centre-forward **Finals:** 1934, 1938
Record: P5/W3/D1/L1/F8

Renowned for his overhead kick, Leônidas da Silva first appeared at the World Cup in 1934, netting Brazil's only goal of the campaign against Spain. However, it was at the 1938 finals that the 'Black Diamond' really captured the public imagination, both with fans in Europe and back home in South America. He played a starring role in the best match of the tournament, scoring a hat-trick in Brazil's 6-5 defeat of Poland in the first round, although many sources incorrectly credit him with four goals.

The competition ended prematurely for Leônidas as he was rested for the semi-final against Italy, a game that Brazil lost without him. Appointed captain for the third place play-off victory over Sweden, he scored twice more to take his tally to seven, making him the tournament's top scorer.

After returning home, such was his fame that a chocolate bar and a brand of cigarettes – *Diamante Negro* – were named after him.

NILS LIEDHOLM

Country: Sweden **Born:** October 8, 1922
Position: Inside-forward/Wing-half **Finals:** 1958★
Record: P5/W4/D0/L1/F2

Nils Liedholm would become one of the most creative midfield playmakers of his generation, but his decision to move to Italy after winning Olympic gold as an amateur in 1948 was at the cost of his international career. Sweden would not select professionals for the national team and it was only the relaxation of this ruling ten years later that allowed George Raynor to recruit the versatile 35-year-old to the 1958 World Cup squad.

Possessing a knowledgeable football brain, Liedholm was also unrivalled for the accuracy of his passing and he gave Sweden several options. Starting the tournament at right-half, Raynor opted to utilise Liedholm's experience tactically as an inside-left against the threat of the Soviet Union, and so well did this plan work that he would remain in this position through the later stages of the tournament.

He captained the Swedes to the World Cup final, where they faced the impressive Brazil of Pelé and Garrincha, but it was Liedholm who scored the first goal. After first beating Orlando and then Bellini, he carefully placed a low shot inside the left-hand post, just out of the reach of the diving Gilmar. This put the Brazilians behind for the first time in the tournament and made Liedholm the oldest player to have scored in a World Cup final, a record that still stands. Over the 90 minutes Brazil proved too tough to beat, but Liedholm left the pitch with his stock high.

GARY LINEKER

Country: England **Born:** November 30, 1960
Position: Striker **Finals:** 1986, 1990
Record: P12/W5/D4/L3/F10

A deadly penalty box poacher, Gary Lineker travelled to the World Cup finals in Mexico in 1986 as England's number one goalscorer. It was a tournament that was to change the direction of his career. With Bobby Robson's team lurching towards a disastrous first round exit, Lineker forged a lethal partnership with Peter Beardsley and hit a first-half hat-trick in the must-win game against Poland. Two further goals against Paraguay, then one in the quarter-final defeat to Argentina, put Lineker on six goals – enough to win the Golden Boot and earn him a transfer to Barcelona.

At Italia 90 he notched four more World Cup goals, including two high-pressure penalties that he both earned and scored against Cameroon in the quarter-final. It was Lineker's spot-kicks that won the game for England, having trailed with only seven minutes remaining. He also scored a late equaliser that forced the epic encounter with West Germany to extra-time and penalties. He put England's first spot-kick away and after defeat, when his team-mates returned to a heroes' welcome, Lineker stayed on in Italy with Bobby Robson to pick up his team's Fair Play Award at the final.

SEPP MAIER★

Country: West Germany **Born:** February 28, 1954
Position: Goalkeeper **Finals:** [1966], 1970, 1974★, 1978
Record: P18/W11/D4/L3/A18

Sepp Maier travelled to the 1966 World Cup as understudy to Hans Tilkowski, and although the young Bayern Munich keeper didn't get a game, it was only injury that

Gary Lineker v Morocco, 1986

ruled Maier out when coach Helmut Schön considered selecting him in for the final itself against England.

By the 1970 World Cup Maier was established as his country's first choice keeper, playing in every game at the finals bar the third place play-off victory. Although West Germany only reached the semi-finals in Mexico, greater success was just around the corner. Winning the 1972 European Championship with 'Die Katze' between the posts, the West Germans went on to reach the World Cup final two years later, where they faced the 'Total Football' of the Dutch.

Although Maier had been his team's saviour against Poland in the semi-final, when he had made a series of crucial saves, in the final he conceded a first minute penalty after Uli Hoeness brought down Johan Cruyff. When he picked the ball out of the net, he became the first German to have touched the ball in the game.

The Germans forced their way back in front, and Maier weathered the relentless pressure of the Dutch as the game headed towards its conclusion, making a memorable save from a formidable Neeskens volley.

Before the 1978 World Cup, Maier was among the stars of football to sign a petition protesting against the torture of political prisoners in host country Argentina. The threatened boycott did not occur and he made six appearances at the finals, only to see West Germany knocked out by Austria.

Maradona, 1986 World Cup Final

DIEGO MARADONA★

Country: Argentina **Born:** October 30, 1960

Position: Striker **Finals:** 1982, 1986★, 1990★, 1994

Record: P21/W12/D4/L5/F8

In addition to being one of the greatest players to grace the world game, Diego Maradona is also among the most contentious and his career at the World Cup has been as controversial as it has been glorious.

At just 17 years of age he only narrowly missed out on a place in Argentina's winning squad for the 1978 World Cup Finals, cut at the last minute by coach César Luis Menotti who didn't think a player of that age could handle the immense pressure of a tournament on home soil. By the time he finally made his debut at the finals in Spain in 1982 he was the new superstar of football, having recently signed to Barcelona for a world record fee, but in his first appearance at the ground of his new club he was subdued by efficient Belgian defending.

In the following game against Hungary his campaign exploded into life and he scored twice in a 4-1 win. However, the tournament would ultimately end in disappointment and controversy. Against Italy in the second group stage Maradona was not only tightly marked, he was kicked and fouled out of the game by defender Claudio Gentile, while against the brilliant Brazilians he became frustrated and was sent-off for a high kick at João Batista with just three minutes of Argentina's World Cup remaining.

It was a very different story in Mexico at 1986, as Argentina became world champions and Maradona lived up to his reputation as the world's best but most controversial player. Fans of Pelé might argue otherwise, but never had one player made such an impact on a World Cup as Maradona did in 1986.

Coach Carlos Bilardo had constructed this Argentina team as a vehicle for Maradona, even appointing him as captain at the expense of the country's iconic World Cup winning skipper Daniel Passarella. Instilled with a new confidence Maradona took teams apart, as both England and Belgium could confirm. His second strike against Bobby Robson's side is regarded as one of greatest goals ever, while the 'Hand of God' goal that he punched past England keeper Peter Shilton remains one of the most contentious.

Although Maradona did not reach his usual dizzy heights in the 3-2 final win against West Germany, few would argue that he deserved to lift the trophy at the very peak of his career.

At Italia 90 he inspired Argentina to yet another World Cup final, but losing 1-0 to West Germany, this Argentina team not of the same vintage, while Maradona himself was carrying an ankle injury that hindered his form. He had alienated Italians during the build up to the tournament when he claimed that the World Cup was 'fixed' in their favour, but to add insult to injury, he also scored a vital spot-kick in the penalty shoot-out that knocked Italy out of the semi-final. Taking the kick was a test of his nerve, as he had seen one saved against Yugoslavia in the quarter-final shoot-out just three days earlier.

His World Cup swansong came in 1994 and he had started the competition in electric form, manically celebrating his goal against Greece by running straight at the television cameras and roaring into the lens. However, after failing a random drugs test that identified five different variants of the stimulant ephedrine in his system, he was expelled from the tournament. His World Cup career may have ended in disgrace, but only Maradona would have had the nerve to reappear to watch subsequent matches from the television commentary box.

In a bizarre twist to his World Cup story, Maradona was appointed national team coach in 2008 and after a troublesome qualifying campaign, he will lead the Argentina squad to the 2010 finals in South Africa.

JOSEF MASOPUST

Country: Czechoslovakia **Born:** February 9, 1931

Position: Midfield **Finals:** 1958, 1962★

Record: P10/W4/D2/L4/F1

Josef Masopust was an attacking left-half who scored Czechoslovakia's only goal of the 1962 World Cup Final. Known as the 'Czech Cavalier', he made his international debut in 1953 and was an ever-present member of the team during the unsuccessful 1958 World Cup campaign, which ended with elimination after defeat to Northern Ireland in a group play-off.

Four years later his skilful passing was at the heart of the team's midfield play as the Czechs progressed to the final where they contested the world championship with Brazil. He scored the goal that gave Czechoslovakia an early lead, running onto a smartly played through ball from Tomas Pospichal to fire past the onrushing Gilmar.

He collected a runners-up medal after the 3-1 defeat and his performances at the tournament saw him crowned 1962 European Footballer Of The Year. He represented his country on 63 occasions, scoring ten goals.

ROQUE MÁSPOLI★

Country: Uruguay **Born:** October 12, 1917

Position: Goalkeeper **Finals:** 1954★, 1958

Record: P9/W6/D1/L3/A14

Peñarol's Roque Máspoli was the safe pair of hands behind Uruguay's solid defence at the 1950 World Cup. A dependable and experienced keeper, he was 32 years of age when his finest hour came. Making a series of acrobatic saves in the tournament's final game, Máspoli kept the constant onslaught of the Brazilian strikers at bay, and for his efforts he collected a winners' medal and was voted the best goalkeeper at the tournament.

He played five more World Cup games at the finals of 1954 in Switzerland, but by this time he was 36 and much slower. He conceded four goals to the intimidating Hungarians in the semi-final and had to settle for fourth place.

MARCO MATERAZZI★

Country: Italy **Born:** August 19, 1973

Position: Central defender **Finals:** 2002, 2006★

Record: P5/W3/D1/L1/F2

The unexpected star of the 2006 World Cup Final, although 32-year-old Marco Materazzi had 26 caps to his name he was hardly a regular at this level, having made only one World Cup appearance as a substitute at the finals four years earlier. Coming on for the injured Alessandro Nesta in 2002, Materazzi was culpable when opponents Croatia scored twice in three minutes. He inadvertently came close to atoning in injury time, punting a harmless long ball forward from his own half that comically found its way into the net, but the goal was disallowed for an off the ball infringement.

There seemed little chance that Italy's number 23 would see much pitch time at the 2006 finals, but with Nesta again taken off through injury against the Czech Republic, Materazzi came off the bench to score with a powerful header. With Nesta still injured he retained his place, only missing the quarter-final after a harsh red card against Australia, but no-one could have imagined that the destiny of the trophy would revolve around the actions of Inter Milan's journeyman centre-half.

His foul on Florent Malouda in the World Cup final may have gifted France a penalty after seven minutes, but he made amends soon after by heading Italy's equaliser. Deep in extra-time his goading of Zinédine Zidane provoked the former World Player Of The Year into a head-butt that knocked Materazzi to the ground, leaving the French to go through the final ten minutes without their talismanic captain. Materazzi even scored from the spot as Italy triumphed in the penalty shoot-out.

Controversy raged for months about what he could have said to make Zidane snap (it eventually transpired to be an insult about the Frenchman's sister) and for a brief time Materazzi was the most talked about sportsman on the planet.

Marco Materazzi v Czech Republic, 2006

LOTHAR MATTHÄUS★

Country: West Germany/Germany

Born: March 21, 1961

Position: Midfield **Finals:** 1982[★], 1986★, 1990★, 1994, 1998

Record: P25/W15/D6/L4/F6

Lothar Matthäus holds the record for the most appearances at the finals, his 25 games stretched out over five World Cups campaigns. A powerful but arrogant and often outspoken midfielder, Matthäus made his international debut at the 1980 European Championship, and he played at his first World Cup in 1982, although his two substitute appearances didn't include the final, which Germany lost to Italy.

He would have more involvement in the tournament four years later, scoring his first World Cup goal with a curling free-kick against Morocco and also converting West Germany's third penalty in the quarter-final shoot-out against Mexico.

In the 1986 World Cup Final Matthäus was assigned the task of shadowing Maradona, stripping the Germans of his creativity going forward. Hardly a defensive midfielder, he was not able to fully suppress the talents of the Argentina captain, who had a hand in two of his side's three goals, and it was Matthäus who carelessly conceded the free-kick from which Argentina opened the scoring.

Italia 90 was a different story altogether as Matthäus was clearly a player at his peak. A commanding midfield leader capable of dominating games, he captained West Germany to another world championship showdown with Argentina. Leading by example he hit the net four times en route to the final, including two long-range goals against Yugoslavia, the second ranking among the best of the competition. Although the final itself proved to be a dismal affair, Matthäus picked up a winners' medal and throughout the tournament he had demonstrated why many regarded him among the world's greatest players.

Lothar Matthäus
v Bulgaria, 1994

Captaining an ageing side in the USA in 1994, a serious knee injury had rocked his career and to hold back the tide of time he had switched to sweeper, a position that hardly suited his style. He added just one goal to his World Cup tally, a penalty in the quarter-final defeat to Bulgaria that eliminated Germany.

Although well past his best, Matthäus made four appearances at the 1998 finals in France, the first as a substitute, and his last coming in a 3-0 defeat to Croatia in the quarter-final. Not only does he hold the record for World Cup appearances but having played 150 times for his country, he is easily the most capped German, having made 42 more appearances than second-placed Jürgen Klinsmann.

MATTHÄUS AT THE WORLD CUP

In five tournaments he has played more World Cup games than anybody else...

1982 RUNNER-UP	1986 RUNNER-UP	1990 WINNER	1994 QUARTER-FINAL	1998 QUARTER-FINAL
v **Chile** 4-1 (R1)	v **Uruguay** 1-1 (R1)	v **Yugoslavia** 4-1 (R1) ⚽⚽	v **Bolivia** 1-0 (R1)	v **Yugoslavia** 2-2 (R1)
v **Austria** 1-0 (R1)	v **Scotland** 2-1 (R1)	v **UAE** 5-1 (R1) ⚽	v **Spain** 1-1 (R1)	v **Iran** 2-0 (R1)
	v **Denmark** 0-2 (R1)	v **Colombia** 1-1 (R1)	v **South Korea** 3-2 (R1)	v **Mexico** 2-1 (R2)
	v **Morocco** 1-0 (R2) ⚽	v **Netherlands** 2-1 (R2)	v **Belgium** 3-2 (R2)	v **Croatia** 0-3 (QF)
	v **Mexico** 0-0 (QF)	v **Czechoslovakia** 1-0 (QF) ⚽	v **Bulgaria** 1-2 (QF) ⚽	
	v **France** 2-0 (SF)	v **England** 1-1 (SF)		
	v **Argentina** 2-3 (F)	v **Argentina** 1-0 (F)		

MAURO ☆

Country: Brazil **Born:** August 30, 1930

Position: Centre-half **Finals:** [1954], [1958☆], 1962☆

Record: P6/W5/D1/L0/F0

Mauro Ramos de Oliveira went to the World Cups of 1954 and 1958 without ever seeing action, but at the 1962 tournament he captained Brazil to the final and lifted the trophy after victory over Czechoslovakia.

A classy and graceful centre-back for São Paolo and Santos, he made his first international appearance in 1949 and it was only the presence of his great rival Bellini that limited his first-team chances with the national side.

LADISLAO MAZURKIEWICZ

Country: Uruguay **Born:** February 14, 1974

Position: Goalkeeper **Finals:** 1966, 1970, 1974

Record: P13/W3/D4/L6/A16

Despite being rated among the best keepers in the world, Ladislao Mazurkiewicz will always be remembered for the sucker punch that Pelé slipped him in the 1970 World Cup semi-final. Running onto a through pass from Tostão, Pelé dummied the onrushing Mazurkiewicz without even touching the ball, passing the floundering keeper on one side while the ball ran by on the other. His blushes were only spared when Pelé collected the ball and shot wide from an acute angle.

Aside from that moment of madness it had been a successful campaign for Mazurkiewicz, who had only conceded one goal before meeting the Brazilians. Despite the stiff competition from England's Gordon Banks, he was voted the best goalkeeper of the tournament.

He captained the team at the 1974 World Cup Finals but he couldn't repeat the magic of Mexico 70.

GIUSEPPE MEAZZA ☆☆

Country: Italy **Born:** August 23, 1910

Position: Inside-forward **Finals:** 1934☆, 1938☆

Record: P9/W8/D1/L0/F3

Twice a World Cup winner in the 1930s, Giuseppe Meazza was an immaculate forward blessed with speed and technique. Always lethal in front of goal, he was a generous creator too. He played much of his club football as a centre-forward, where he also featured in the first 15 of his international appearances, but after Italy coach Vittorio Pozzo switched him to inside-right to accommodate centre-forward Angelo Schiavio, he played in this position at the World Cups of both 1934 and 1938.

Nicknamed 'Peppino', he was an ever-present member of the team at the 1934 finals, forging a productive partnership with Schiavio. Meazza would score the last of Italy's seven in a defeat of the United States and the only goal of a fiercely fought quarter-final replay with Spain. Despite carrying an injury in the final, he also had a hand in Schiavio's winner against Czechoslovakia.

Of the 1934 finalists only Meazza and Giovanni Ferrari were still in the team for the World Cup in France in 1938. This time Meazza was captain and he led the team on a run that culminated in another winners' medal. He played in every match, but his only goal came from a penalty against Brazil in the semi-final, coolly taken despite having to cling onto his shorts in the run up after the elastic had snapped.

The two inside-forwards Meazza and Ferrari dominated much of the attacking play in 1938, feeding centre-forward Silvio Piola with his best chances. In the final against Hungary, Meazza set up the first three of Italy's four goals and collected the trophy with a half-hearted fascist salute.

Meazza played his last game for Italy's national side the following year. He died in 1979, shortly before the San Siro stadium, where he had played for both Inter and AC Milan, was formally renamed Stadio Giuseppe Meazza.

ROGER MILLA

Country: Cameroon **Born:** May 20, 1952

Position: Forward **Finals:** 1982, 1990, 1994

Record: P10/W3/D3/L4/F5

Dancing the *Makossa* around a corner flag, Roger Milla gave the World Cup one of its most memorable goal celebrations in 1990. A natural marksman, he scored on his international debut in 1978 and was part of the squad that returned unbeaten from the

Roger Milla v England, 1990

1982 World Cup Finals, having had a goal disallowed in the scoreless draw with Peru.

At 38 years of age he was playing on Reunion Island when the president of his country begged him to come out of retirement for Italia 90. Milla became an inspirational figure for his team, scoring four goals from the bench as Cameroon reached the quarter-finals.

At 42 he was back at USA 94 and with a goal against Russia he set a record as the oldest World Cup goalscorer, breaking his own record of four years earlier.

LUIS MONTI ☆

Country: Argentina & Italy **Born:** May 15, 1901

Position: Defender **Finals:** 1930☆ (Argentina), 1934☆ (Italy),

Record: P9/W7/D1/L1/F2

A ferocious hardman, Luis Monti experienced both victory and defeat in the World Cup final, but playing for different nations.

A key member of the Argentina team in 1930 he stamped his authority on the tournament from his first game, inflicting such a nasty injury on Lucien Laurent in just the 10th minute that it made the Frenchman a passenger for the rest of the game. Nine minutes from time he scored the winner, taking a free-kick from the edge of the penalty area that caught the French by surprise while they were still arranging their defensive wall.

He scored again in the semi-final against the United States but in the final Monti failed to live up to his ferocious reputation. Team-mate Francisco Varallo would later claim that Monti had been in a state of panic in the dressing room as a result of death threats from Uruguay fans.

He may have been on the losing side with Argentina in 1930, but four years later, after a move to Juventus, he qualified to play for the country of his parents and he helped the Italians beat Czechoslovakia 2-1 to lift the World Cup trophy, engaging in a fiercely fought battle with the Czechs' attacking centre-half Stefan Cambal in the final.

In total Monti won 16 caps for Argentina and 18 caps for Italy. He died in 1983.

BOBBY MOORE★

Country: England **Born:** April 12, 1941
Position: Centre-half **Finals:** 1962, 1966★, 1970
Record: P14/W8/D2/L4/F0

In the pantheon of English sporting heroes no footballer ranks above Bobby Moore, the only England captain to lift the World Cup. His name remains synonymous with honour, dignity and sportsmanship and for what he lacked in pace he made up for with an unrivalled reading of the game, which made him incredibly hard to beat. He was a truly world-class defender.

Moore won his first England cap against Peru en route to the 1962 World Cup finals in Chile, when deputising for the injured Bobby Robson, and he retained his place once the tournament had started, playing in all four of England's games at the finals.

At 22 he became the country's youngest ever captain when he led the team against Czechoslovakia in May 1963. Just three years later his crowning moment arrived when he lifted the Jules Rimet Cup at Wembley following the historic 4-2 win over West Germany in the final. The famous last goal was the result of Moore measuring a long pass to striker Geoff Hurst rather than listening to the entreaties of his partner Jack Charlton to put the ball over the stand.

Yet Moore's finest performance was not Wembley 66, but Mexico 70. He played the best game of his life against Brazil in the heat of Guadalajara, constantly thwarting the tide of yellow shirts that flooded towards him. When the final whistle blew, signifying a narrow 1-0 defeat, Pelé stepped past everyone, including Alan Mullery who had marked the Brazilian through the game, to swap shirts with Moore. The moment became an iconic football image.

Bobby Moore, 1966 World Cup Final

Moore would win 108 caps for England, 90 of them as captain, but his career was virtually ended by an uncharacteristic error in a World Cup qualifier away to Poland in June 1973. He made his last England appearance against Italy later that year.

MAX MORLOCK★

Country: West Germany **Born:** May 11, 1925
Position: Inside-right **Finals:** 1954★
Record: P4/W3/D1/L0/F6

The strongly-built inside-right for West Germany's World Cup winning team of 1954, 1FC Nuremberg's Max Morlock was a feisty character with a single-minded determination to win. Surprisingly good in the air despite his lack of height, he was at his best when linking defence and attack, although he was certainly capable of scoring himself, as witnessed by his six goals in just four World Cup games.

He hit a hat-trick in West Germany's 7-1 group play-off victory over Turkey, and scored one of six in the semi-final crushing of Austria, but his most important goal of all came in the World Cup final. With Hungary leading 2-0 within eight minutes of the kick-off, Morlock inspired the West German comeback by stabbing home a pass from left-winger Hans Schäfer in the tenth minute.

Although he did not make the squad for the World Cup finals of 1958, he made his last appearance for Germany a few months after the tournament, having won 26 caps and scored 21 goals.

GERD MÜLLER★

Country: West Germany **Born:** November 3, 1945
Position: Centre-forward **Finals:** 1970, 1974★
Record: P13/W11/D0/L2/F14

For 36 years Gerd Müller held a special place in World Cup history as the competition's record goalscorer, and although Ronaldo finally surpassed his 14-goal tally in 2006, Müller remains a significant part of the folklore of the finals.

The early 1970s were a golden period for West German football, forged on the

Gerd Müller in white v Poland, 1974

athleticism and unquenchable spirit that Müller typified. The ultimate poacher, he created little outside the box but his stocky build and deceptive pace made him a nightmare for defenders to handle.

He made his international debut in 1966, shortly after West Germany lost the World Cup final to England, but when the 1970 tournament arrived he was already known as one of the great strikers in the game. Despite the pressure, Müller delivered in spectacular style, hitting ten goals in six games.

Before the Germans were even out of the group stage he recorded hat-tricks against both Bulgaria and Peru, plus the winner against Morocco. He also notched the deciding goal in a quarter-final that saw West Germany come from 2-0 down to beat defending champions England. In the semi-final Müller scored twice more but West Germany bowed out of the competition after losing 4-3 to Italy.

Four years later he was less prolific but he was to prove equally lethal when it mattered most as the West Germans forged their way to a final on home soil against the more fluent Dutch. Despite going a goal down in the championship decider, the hosts persevered and it was Müller who scored the winning goal just before half-time. Turning on a loose ball in the box, he feinted to shoot through keeper Jan Jongbloed and the incoming Ruud Krol at the near post, before snapping the ball across the goal towards the unguarded far side of the net. The moment couldn't have been sweeter: not only had he achieved the greatest dream in football but he had done so in the Olympic Stadium, where he had scored so many of his goals for Bayern.

Only 28 years of age at the time, Müller retired from the international game after the 1974 final and considered quitting altogether, but instead he decided to continue playing club football with Bayern Munich.

HONG MYUNG-BO

Country: South Korea **Born:** February 12, 1969

Position: Sweeper **Finals:** 1990, 1994, 1998, 2002

Record: P16/W3/D5/L8/F2

Hong Myung-Bo was regarded as Asia's best sweeper, gaining his experience and leadership qualities playing in four successive World Cups for South Korea. An ever-present team member at each tournament, he scored twice at the 1994 finals, his goal against Spain helping salvage a late draw. He also scored against Germany, rifling past Bodo Illgner from 25 yards.

His influence on the team was most apparent when he captained South Korea's run to the semi-finals in 2002. It was Hong who inspired the win over Italy and converted the decisive penalty that knocked out Spain, although he also made the defensive error in the third place play-off that allowed Hakan Sükür to score the quickest World Cup goal of all time.

Just before his retirement Pelé and FIFA included him in their list of the 125 greatest living footballers. He was the Assistant Coach of the South Korean national team at the 2006 finals.

DICK NANNINGA

Country: Holland **Born:** January 17, 1949

Position: Midfield **Finals:** 1978★

Record: P4/W1/D2/L1/F1

Dick Nanninga might have won just 15 caps for Holland, but he will always be remembered for the goal he scored in the 1978 World Cup Final. In the week running up to the game he had to been regularly boasting to journalists that he would come on and score with ten minutes left – he was only 60 seconds out, heading the ball into the net from a René van de Kerkhof cross in the 81st minute.

Although the Dutch went on to lose the final it was Nanninga's goal that gave them a lifeline, and a few minutes later, had Rob Rensenbrink's injury time shot crept inside the post instead of ricocheting off it, things could have been so very different.

Nanninga made just four appearances at the tournament, all from the bench. He also made his own little piece of history, becoming the first substitute to be sent-off at the World Cup. He received his red card for laughing at the referee's decision to give him a yellow card, all happening just seven minutes after coming on against West Germany and one minute before the end of the match. In his brief time on the pitch he also managed to squeeze in a tremendous low shot that was saved by Sepp Maier.

JOSE NASAZZI★

Country: Uruguay **Born:** May 24, 1901
Position: Right-back **Finals:** 1930★
Record: P4/W4/D0/L0/F0

Right-back José Nasazzi was not only one of Uruguay's most famous players, but one of the great captains in the history of the game. His leadership qualities and organisational skills earned him the nickname 'the Marshall' and he captained Uruguay to Olympic gold in 1924 and 1928, as well as the Copa América in 1923, 1924 and 1926.

However, it was at the World Cup that Nasazzi etched himself into football history when he captained the first world champions, although it remains unclear whether he was actually presented with the famous Jules Rimet Cup after the 4-2 triumph over Argentina.

He was a tough player and the driving force behind the victory, urging his team-mates to do better at half-time when the Uruguayans were trailing. His voice was an important one to the players as he was captaining a side that competed without a coach as we understand the role now. When Uruguay won the World Cup it was the players who were making all of the tactical decisions and Nasazzi was the clear team leader.

JOHAN NEESKENS

Country: Holland **Born:** September 15, 1951
Position: Midfield **Finals:** 1974★, 1978★
Record: P12/W7/D2/L3/F5

Johan Neeskens was a robust playmaker blessed with terrific pace and the kind of skill and control that made him one of the greatest midfielders of the 1970s. He was an integral part of the talented Dutch teams that reached the final of both the 1974 and 1978 World Cups.

In the second minute of the 1974 world championship decider with West Germany he put the ball past Sepp Maier from the spot to set two World Cup records: it was the fastest goal in a World Cup final and it was also the first ever penalty kick in a final.

Always a fierce striker of the ball, three of his five goals at the tournament were scored from the spot, including two penalties against Bulgaria. He also scored with an impressive strike against Brazil, stretching to fire into the roof of the net after a defence-splitting one-two with Johan Cruyff.

At the 1978 tournament the Dutch were without Cruyff and they looked increasingly to Neeskens to fill the role of creator. Although he missed two second round games after an injury against Scotland, his team made the final and Neeskens collected his second World Cup runners-up medal after defeat to Argentina.

OLDRICH NEJEDLY

Country: Czechoslovakia **Born:** Dec 26, 1909
Position: Inside-left **Finals:** 1934★, 1938
Record: P6/W4/D1/L1/F7

Oldrich Nejedly finished the 1938 World Cup as its top goalscorer, but was rewarded with just a runners-up medal after losing to hosts Italy in the final. An elegant but deadly inside-left for Sparta Prague, he was capable of impressing anywhere across the forward line if needed, and at the 1934 finals he forged an imposing partnership with outside-left Antonin Puc. He hit five goals at the tournament, three of which came in a semi-final victory over Germany, but he was unable to take his chances in the title decider.

He made two appearances at the 1938 World Cup, scoring in each game and proving himself still the best forward in the Czech team. But after equalising from the penalty spot in a bruising tie with Brazil, his leg was broken and he was ruled out of the replay that he had helped to set up. Without him the Czechs were eliminated.

He made only three more appearances for his country and wound up his international career having scored 28 goals in 43 games.

RAIMUNDO ORSI★

Country: Italy **Born:** December 2, 1901
Position: Outside-left **Finals:** 1934★
Record: P5/W4/D1/L0/F3

A tremendously fast and skilful outside-left, although Raimundo Orsi is best known for scoring Italy's first goal in the 1934 World Cup Final he had already won a silver medal for his native Argentina at the 1928 Amsterdam Olympics. It was after his impressive Olympic displays in Europe that Orsi was lured to Juventus by a lucrative offer and the following year he was playing for the Italian national team, a blow for the Argentinians as he would have undoubtedly featured in their 1930 World Cup Final side.

With the Italians boycotting the first tournament, it was not until 1934 that 'Mumo' made his World Cup debut. He played in all five of Italy's games and scored three times, including his wily strike in the final. Trailing to Czechoslovakia with just nine minutes remaining, Orsi hit a freakish shot that swerved over the head of the outstretching Frantisek Plánicka. When challenged by the press the next day to replicate the shot, he tried 20 times and failed.

In total he made 35 appearances for his adoptive country and scored 13 goals, but his last international appearance was once again with Argentina, having returned to Buenos Aires to play with Independiente the year after the finals.

WOLFGANG OVERATH★

Country: West Germany **Born:** Sept 29, 1943
Position: Midfield **Finals:** 1966★, 1970, 1974★
Record: P19/W15/D1/L3/F3

When Wolfgang Overath helped West Germany to World Cup success on home soil in 1974, not only did he bring his international career to a fitting end, but he also completed a remarkable treble. Having

Wolfgang Overath v Peru, 1970

already been in the losing team in the 1966 final, he also scored the winner in the third placed play-off in 1970, so he can claim to be the only player to have finished first, second and third in the World Cup (the great Franz Beckenbauer was also in all three teams, but he didn't play in the third place play-off match in 1970).

Gifted a powerful left foot that compensated for the deficiencies with his right, he was known to strike shots with venom, such as the pile driver he hit from distance against Australia at the 1974 finals.

DANIEL PASSARELLA★

Country: Argentina **Born:** May 25, 1953
Position: Sweeper/central-defender
Finals: 1978★, 1982, [1986★]
Record: P12/W7/D1/L4/F3

Daniel Passarella was an instinctive sweeper who exuded calm, qualities that helped him when he captained Argentina to World Cup glory on home soil in 1978, aged only 25. His leadership in the face of overwhelming expectations earned him the nickname 'El Gran Capitan'.

He was an unusually skilful defender who contributed enormously in attack, scoring 22 goals in 70 internationals, three of them at the World Cup. He was particularly dangerous at set pieces and his one goal at the 1978 finals came from a penalty against France, although he did have a solid first-half chance in the final but shot over.

He would score ten penalties for Argentina in total, the last coming at the 1982 World Cup against El Salvador. Passarella was captain once again, but this time glorious moments were few and far between. He would hit a thunderous left-footed free-kick into the net from 25 yards against Italy, but it was no more than a consolation, and although keeper Dino Zoff would complain he was still arranging his wall, replays clearly show the referee, whistle in mouth. It could have been so different had Passarella's powerful header not been turned away by the stretching Zoff earlier in the game.

Four years later he was a member of the squad for the 1986 finals in Mexico but was unable to play through illness. He had already been stripped of the captaincy by coach Carlos Bilardo, who was in the process of building a new team around Diego Maradona, but 'El Gran Capitan' will always be remembered in his home country as the man who first lifted the World Cup for Argentina.

Daniel Passarella stretches for the ball. Argentina v Italy, 1982

BERT PATENAUDE

Country: USA **Born:** November 4, 1909
Position: Centre-forward **Finals:** 1930
Record: P3/W2/D0/L1/F4

For many years American striker Bertram Patenaude was at the centre of one of the great statistical discrepancies in World Cup history. Original credited by FIFA with just two goals against Paraguay at the 1930 finals, some credible historic sources listed him as having scored a hat-trick, which would have made it the first time a player had scored three goals in a game in World Cup history.

Indeed, the official report of USA team manager Wilfred Cummings, written at the end of the tournament, credited Patenaude with all three goals in the game. This report, coupled with contemporary news stories and the testimonies of several squad members years later, indicated that Patenaude had indeed scored a hat-trick, but it wasn't until 2006 that FIFA amended the record books.

Other sources, including the match report, had attributed the second goal to captain Thomas Florie, while it was sometime credited as an own-goal by Aurelio Gonzáles.

In total Patenaude played only four times for his country but he did score six goals, four of them at the World Cup.

PELÉ★★

Country: Brazil **Born:** October 23, 1940

Position: Forward **Finals:** 1958★, 1962[★], 1966, 1970★

Record: P14/W12/D1/L1/F12

Pelé, after scoring in the 1970 World Cup Final

Generally acknowledged as the greatest player the world has ever seen, Pelé's career has been inextricably linked to the World Cup, the stage for so many of his greatest performances.

Born as Édson Arantes do Nascimento, he was nicknamed Pelé so early in his life that he can't recall the reason behind it. A skilful footballer at an early age, he was given his Brazil debut in July 1957 at just 16 years of age, becoming the youngest player to score an international goal.

The early signs of his greatness were seen the following year at the World Cup in Sweden. With Brazil needing to beat the Soviet Union to be guaranteed a place in the knockout phase, Pelé made his bow in the third group game, his selection rumoured to be influenced by the pressure exerted on coach Vicente Feola by his team-mates.

He proved exceptional as Brazil won the game and he went on to score in the quarter-final against Wales – at 17 years and 239 days old it made him the youngest ever World Cup goalscorer, a record that still stands.

His pace, trickery and eye for goal ensured that he kept his place in the side and he scored a semi-final hat-trick in a 5-2 victory over France. Two more goals against Sweden in the final made sure that he was not out of the headlines and his tears at the end of the game remain an enduring World Cup memory.

Although the Brazilians successfully defended their title four years later in Chile, a pulled muscle ended Pelé's tournament after just two games, leaving his team-mates to win the trophy without him. The 1966 campaign would also end in tears and frustration. The greatest player in the world became a marked man in England and was brutally fouled in games against Bulgaria and Portugal as Brazil crashed out at the first stage. "I don't want to end my life as an invalid," moaned Pelé as he vowed to boycott the next World Cup in Mexico.

He didn't carry through with his threat and his performances in 1970 proved to be the pinnacle of an illustrious career. He was again the focal point of a Brazil side that is still regarded as the greatest team ever, and he left football fans with so many treasured memories, such as the shot from his own half against Czechoslovakia and the sublime dummy that left the Uruguay keeper floundering in the semi-final.

It was only fitting that when Pelé opened the scoring in the final it was Brazil's 100th goal at the World Cup. It was his second time on the winning side in a final.

PELÉ AT THE WORLD CUP FINALS

Twice a winner in the World Cup final, Pelé was in the winning squad three times...

1958 WINNER
- v **USSR** 2-0 (R1)
- v **Wales** 1-0 (QF) ⚽
- v **France** 5-2 (SF) ⚽⚽⚽
- v **Sweden** 5-2 (F) ⚽⚽

The youngest player at the finals, he became the youngest to score a World Cup hat-trick in the semi.

1962 SQUAD WINNER
- v **Mexico** 2-0 (R1) ⚽
- v **Czechoslovakia** 0-0 (R1)

Injury ended Pelé's tournament after two games. Brazil went on to lift the trophy without him, but years later FIFA gave winners' medals to all squad members.

1966 ROUND 1
- v **Bulgaria** 2-0 (R1) ⚽
- v **Portugal** 1-3 (R1)

Fouled throughout Brazil's opener, injury ruled Pelé out of the next game, but his premature return against Portugal was not enough to save Brazil.

1970 WINNER
- v **Czechoslovakia** 4-1 (R1) ⚽
- v **England** 1-0 (R1)
- v **Romania** 3-2 (R1) ⚽⚽
- v **Peru** 4-2 (QF)
- v **Uruguay** 3-1 (SF)
- v **Italy** 4-1 (F) ⚽

Four goals and a World Cup win.

MARTIN PETERS★

Country: England **Born:** November 8, 1943
Position: Midfield **Finals:** 1966★, 1970
Record: P9/W7/D0/L2/F2

Described by England manager Alf Ramsey in 1966 as "ten years ahead of his time", Martin Peters was one of the first modern utility players. Capable of performing almost anywhere on the pitch, he was as comfortable tackling back as going forward. In Ramsey's famous team of wingless wonders he largely featured on the left of a midfield trio alongside Bobby Charlton and Alan Ball, with Nobby Stiles perched just behind to pick up the ball and feed it forward.

Peters was the least capped player in England's side, having made his debut only two months earlier, and by the time the tournament kicked off he had gained just three caps. Coming into the team after the first game, he held his place all the way to the final, when he scored England's second goal after latching on to a poor West German defensive clearance. With only 12 minutes of normal time left, it could have been the winner had not Wolfgang Weber's last minute equaliser pushed the game into extra-time.

Four years later Peters played every game in England's 1970 World Cup campaign, but the conditions in Mexico didn't suit the intensive style of his play and on returning he faced criticism for his lacklustre performances. "I didn't feel ten years ahead of my time in Mexico," he said. His only real contribution to the tournament came when he put England 2-0 in front of West Germany in the quarter-final, and after being substituted he was even utilised to help bring the drinks out to his team-mates before extra-time.

EMMANUEL PETIT★

Country: France **Born:** September 22, 1970
Position: Midfield **Finals:** 1998★, 2002
Record: P8/W5/D2/L1/F2

When Emmanuel Petit broke down the field in injury time of the 1998 World Cup Final, not only did he score one of the most delightful goals ever to win the trophy but it also happened to be the 1000th goal for France in international competition.

Martin Peters, 1966 World Cup Final

Essentially a defensive midfielder, his classic counter-attacking goal wowed the crowd at the Stade de France and even had President Chirac on his feet in the main stand.

Earlier in the game Petit supplied the corner from which Zinédine Zidane headed the first goal. He also scored against Denmark in the first round, with a thunderous shot that rifled through a crowded 18-yard box.

Petit made two appearances at the 2002 World Cup, including the defeat to Senegal in the opening game, but France failed to reach the second round.

CARLOS PEUCELLE

Country: Argentina **Born:** September 13, 1908
Position: Outside-right **Finals:** 1930★
Record: P4/W3/D0/L1/F3

Carlos Peucelle was a highly skilful right-sided forward who starred for Argentina on the right wing in the 1930 World Cup Finals. He played in four of Argentina's five matches at the finals, only missing out on the opening game against France.

Possessing a remarkable turn of pace and the vision to carve out chances for his team-mates, one first-hand account of the semi-final against the USA described how Argentina "won the match on the right wing". Peucelle not only set up Alejandro Scopelli for Argentina's second goal, but he scored two himself in the last ten minutes.

His only other goal of the tournament came in the final. Picking up a pass from Manuel Ferreira in the 20th minute, he avoided a challenge from Fernández Gestido and silenced the huge and partisan crowd with a shot high into the far corner of the net. His equaliser inspired a period of dominance by Argentina that lasted until half-time, but after failing to stem Uruguay's second-half comeback, Peucelle and his team-mates finished the day as losers.

The year after the World Cup he caused uproar when he accepted a big money transfer to River Plate, earning himself the nickname 'El Primer Millonario', or 'the First Millionaire'. Retiring in 1941, as a coach he was credited with developing River Plate's famed team of the 1940s that became known as 'La Máquina', 'The Machine'.

SILVIO PIOLA★

Country: Italy **Born:** September 29, 1913
Position: Centre-forward **Finals:** 1938★
Record: P4/W4/D0/L0/F5

Ranking as one of the greatest goalscorers of his era, Silvio Piola was a tall and extremely imposing centre-forward recognised for his strength on the ball and his power in the air, all factors that at times made him impossible to play against.

Making his international debut in March 1935, he scored twice in a 2-0 defeat of Austria. Soon coach Vittorio Pozzo was playing Piola alongside inside-right Giuseppe Meazza, and together they made the most formidable attacking duo at the 1938 World Cup, with Piola just as much creator as goalscorer.

He scored five goals at the tournament, including two against France in the second round, and another pair in the final as Italy picked up the trophy after a 4-2 win over Hungary. In the semi-final he even got the better of Brazilian defender Domingos, forcing the best defender in the tournament to foul him, with Meazza putting away the resulting penalty to win the game.

Although Piola didn't make his final international appearance until 1950, this would be his only World Cup.

ANDREA PIRLO ☆

Country: Italy **Born:** May 19, 1979
Position: Midfield **Finals:** 2006☆
Record: P7/W5/D2/L0/F1

A creative deep-lying midfielder, ball winner and playmaker, Andrea Pirlo was an outstanding member of Italy's 2006 World Cup winning team, receiving FIFA's Bronze Ball award after the final having finished in third place behind Zinédine Zidane and Fabio Cannavaro in the Player Of The Tournament voting.

Pirlo scored one goal and set-up the other in Italy's opening game against Ghana and he was voted Man Of The Match in the semi-final win over hosts Germany, a tie regarded as the best in the tournament. He also fired in the corner from which Marco Materazzi scored Italy's only goal of the World Cup final, and in addition to collecting his World Cup winners' medal, he was also voted FIFA Man Of The Match in the final.

FRANTISEK PLÁNICKA

Country: Czechoslovakia **Born:** June 2, 1904
Position: Goalkeeper **Finals:** 1934☆, 1938
Record: P6/W4/D1/L1/A7

Goalkeeper Frantisek Plánicka was one of Czechoslovakia's most successful players and an automatic choice for the national team between 1925 and 1938, captaining the team in the World Cups in Italy and France.

At the 1934 competition his magnificent, agile performances helped the Czechs to the final where they lost to Italy in extra-time. Although Plánicka always blamed himself for conceding Raimundo Orsi's swerving equaliser late in the game, but in truth there was little he could have done about it.

Although he was voted the best goalkeeper at the 1938 tournament, it was less successful for the Czechs. In a brutal quarter-final clash with Brazil, which saw three players sent-off and fighting on the pitch, Plánicka played much of the game with a broken arm.

The match was ultimately tied and the injury he sustained ruled him out of the subsequent replay, which Czechoslovakia lost without him two days later. He had made his last international appearance after 73 game for his country.

Michel Platini v Italy, 1986

MICHEL PLATINI

Country: France **Born:** June 21, 1955
Position: Midfield **Finals:** 1978, 1982, 1986
Record: P14/W6/D4/L4/F5

With his remarkable technique, superb passing and sublime free-kicks, Michel Platini was the world's best player during the first half of the 1980s. His astonishing goalscoring record from midfield made him a match-winner at the highest level and his ability to peak on the biggest occasions set him apart from his peers.

He made his international debut against Czechoslovakia in March 1976 and he played in all three of the France games at the 1978 World Cup in Argentina, although he made little impact in the first group game against Italy as he was shadowed and hustled throughout by Marco Tardelli. He scored his only goal of the tournament against hosts Argentina, smashing the ball into the net from close range after Bernard Lacombe's chip had rebounded off the bar.

He captained France to the 1982 finals in Spain. He scored twice during the course of the tournament, on his 27th birthday against Kuwait and from the penalty spot in the semi-final against West Germany, kissing the ball before slamming it home. Following a thrilling but sometimes brutal game, the Germans won in a penalty shoot-out, with the French captain again converting from the spot. The tie took such a toll that Platini was one of seven players who did not take the field for the third place play-off defeat to Poland.

Between World Cups Platini inspired France to win the European Championship in 1984 and he was voted European Footballer Of The Year in 1983, 1984 and 1985, becoming only the second player to win the award three times (the first being Johan Cruyff).

With this majestic player at their helm the French should have performed better at the 1986 finals in Mexico, but Platini was strangely subdued. He did, however, get the better of the Italians, who had sacrificed the creativity of Antonio Di Gennaro in order to man-mark the French captain with Giuseppe Baresi, whom coach Enzo Bearzot insisted always played well against the Frenchman in Serie A. But Platini demonstrated his world class, setting up a comfortable 2-0 win with a casual chip in the 14th minute.

He scored again in the quarter-final against Brazil, but although the French won the deciding penalty shoot-out, he skied his spot-kick over the bar. After losing out to West Germany once again in the semi-final, 34-year-old Platini said goodbye to the

World Cup by throwing his shirt to the fans as he walked despondently off the field of the Jalisco Stadium in Guadalajara. It was his last appearance for France, as he again took no part in the third place play-off.

MICHEL PREUD'HOMME

Country: Belgium **Born:** January 24, 1959
Position: Goalkeeper **Finals:** 1990, 1994
Record: P8/W4/D0/L4/A8

One of the world's best goalkeepers in his day, Michel Preud'homme was unlucky to have conceded two of the best goals ever seen at the World Cup.

He made his international debut for Belgium in May 1979 at just 20, but did not establish his place in the team until the late 1980s. At his first World Cup in 1990 he pulled down Spain's Julio Salinas and was unable to save the resulting penalty. Later he kept England at bay until the last minute of extra-time, when a breathtaking David Platt volley left him with no chance.

He played the game of his life against Holland at the 1994 World Cup, making a series of fantastic saves to shut out Koeman, Rijkaard and Bergkamp as Belgium snatched an unexpected win. But in the next game he was beaten by an amazing solo goal scored by Saudi Arabia's Saeed Owairan. The 'Maradona of the Arabs' picked up the ball deep in his own half and charged through much of the Belgian midfield and defence before slotting into the net. Preud'homme was still voted the best goalkeeper of the tournament.

ANTONIN PUC

Country: Czechoslovakia **Born:** May 16, 1907
Position: Outside-left **Finals:** 1934★, 1938
Record: P5/W3/D1/L1/F2

A potent outside-left in the great Czechoslovakia side of the 1930s, 'Toni' Puc built a formidable partnership with free-scoring inside-left Oldrich Nejedly, hitting seven goals between them at the 1934 World Cup. Puc grabbed his first goal in the opening game against Romania, and helped Nejedly to a hat-trick in the semi-final against Germany, the second of which came after Puc's fiercely driven free-kick had ricocheted off the bar.

In the final against Italy his surges down the left flank offered a constant threat and in the 71st minute he scored the opening goal of the game, smartly turning on the ball and firing a low shot past Gianpiero Combi. Only moments earlier Puc had been receiving treatment on the sidelines.

He played just once at the World Cup of 1938 (although some sources list more) and featured in a testy and battering encounter with Brazil, but along with Nejedly he was judged not fit enough for the replay.

It would be the last of his 60 caps for Czechoslovakia, although after invasion by Germany in World War II, he did play one more international for what was then called Bohemia and Moravia. He was the national team's record goalscorer until the break-up of the country and the football team in 1993.

FERENC PUSKÁS

Country: Hungary & Spain **Born:** April 2, 1927
Position: Inside-left **Finals:** 1954★ (Hungary), 1962 (Spain)
Record: P6/W3/D0/L3/F4

Football had few more unlikely stars than Ferenc Puskás, the short, barrel-chested Hungarian goal machine who became known as the 'Galloping Major'. He possessed one of the most powerful and accurate left feet in the history of the game and his goalscoring record at international level was phenomenal: 84 goals in 85 matches for Hungary.

Puskás scored on his international debut against Austria in August 1945 and he captained the side to the 1954 World Cup. He scored three goals in the first two group games against South Korea and West Germany, but an injury against the Germans, the result of a late tackle by Werner Liebrich, kept him out of the side for all of the knockout games bar the final, ironically against West Germany.

Ferenc Puskás, right, 1954 World Cup Final

He played in the title decider despite claiming not to be fully fit and he had an immediate impact, opening the scoring in the sixth minute. He also had what could have been a late equaliser disallowed. "Puskás came over to me and gave me a dirty look," related linesman Mervyn Griffiths with some understatement, but even the talents of the 'Galloping Major' couldn't prevent defeat for a side that had been unbeaten in four years.

When the Soviet invasion of Hungary took place in 1956 he was abroad on a tour with Honvéd, and like many of his team-mates he did not return to his home country. He later picked up four caps as a naturalised Spaniard, three of which were at the 1962 World Cup Finals in Chile, before eventually retiring while with Real Madrid at the age of 40. In 1993 he became caretaker manager of the national side but failed to guide Hungary to the 1994 World Cup.

HELMUT RAHN★

Country: West Germany **Born:** August 16, 1929
Position: Outside-right **Finals:** 1954★, 1958
Record: P10/W5/D2/L3/F10

An outside-right with a thunderous shot, Helmut Rahn will be best remembered for the part he played in West Germany's unexpected success at the 1954 World Cup. He hadn't been expected to feature in the squad and when summoned by coach Sepp Herberger he was in South America, on the verge of signing for Nacional of Uruguay while on a tour with Rot-Weiss Essen.

Rahn was still thought to be no more than a substitute, but the coach saw something special in the player, fielding him in what was largely a reserve side to face Hungary in the second group game at the finals. Despite the thrashing they received, Herberger recalled Rahn once the knockout stages were underway and the tactical switch made all the difference to West Germany's campaign.

He proved indispensable in the World Cup final as he shot the Germans back into contention. Trailing to favourites Hungary, he hammered home the equaliser after keeper Gyula Grosics missed a high ball from a corner, and with six minutes remaining he picked up a poor headed clearance, made space to shoot, and fired past the diving Grosics to win the match.

Rahn also made an impact at the 1958 finals when his six-goal tally tied him with Pelé as the tournament's second highest goalscorer behind Just Fontaine. He netted four times in the group stage, and he also beat three Yugoslavia defenders to score the only goal of the quarter-final.

THOMAS RAVELLI

Country: Sweden **Born:** August 13, 1959
Position: Goalkeeper **Finals:** 1990, 1994
Record: P10/W3/D3/L4/A14

Thomas Ravelli was a magnificently agile keeper who helped his country to the semi-finals of the 1994 World Cup. The commanding six-footer had made three appearances at Italia 90, but his finest performance came in a tense quarter-final against Romania at USA 94. When the game went to penalties, 34-year-old Ravelli proved indispensable and saved twice from Dan Petrescu and Miodrag Belodedici to see Sweden through to the semi-final.

He was in inspired form once again against Brazil, but with Sweden playing with just ten men for the last 30 minutes, Ravelli had to settle for third place. In a 16-year international career he made 143 appearances for his country and he was the international game's most capped player until Lothar Matthäus surpassed his total.

ROB RENSENBRINK

Country: Holland **Born:** July 3, 1947
Position: Left-winger **Finals:** 1974★, 1978★
Record: P13/W8/D2/L3/F6

Rob Rensenbrink played in the final of two successive World Cups in 1974 and 1978 and took home a runners-up medal from each. An outstanding winger, he was even selected for the final in West Germany despite carrying an injury sustained in the semi against Brazil.

Rivaldo, 2002 World Cup Final

Four years later he came within a whisker of winning the final for the Dutch. With just a minute of the game remaining he chased onto a long ball lofted over the top of the defence and stabbed at it from an uncomfortable angle as keeper Ubaldo Fillol tried to close him down. The ball struck the foot of the post and bounced back into play, leaving the game to go into extra-time

Although he was never a World Cup winner, he does hold the honour of scoring the 1,000th goal in the competition's history, which came with a penalty against Scotland in 1978. Together with Teófilo Cubillas of Peru, he was the second highest goalscorer in Argentina, but four of his five came from penalties, two of which formed part of a hat-trick against Iran. He shares the record for the most penalties in a tournament with Eusébio, who scored four in 1966.

RIVALDO★

Country: Brazil **Born:** April 19, 1972
Position: Forward/Midfield **Finals:** 1998★, 2002★
Record: P14/W11/D1/L2/F8

Famous for his theatrical bicycle kicks and his left-footed pile drivers which were used to such devastating effect with Barcelona and Brazil, for a time in the late 1990s Rivaldo Vítor Borba Ferreira was rated as the best footballer in the world.

An ever-present member of the Brazil team at the 1998 World Cup when playing on the left of midfield, he scored three times in seven games, including two against Denmark, but he was on the losing side in the final when hosts France ripped his demoralised team apart. However, his personal stock remained high and he was voted FIFA World Player Of The Year in 1999.

Brilliant and selfish in equal measures, at the 2002 World Cup Rivaldo operated as playmaker, disguising the team's weaknesses through his inspired creative play. He also provided support to Ronaldo in a striking role when necessary, as he did in the final. He was Brazil's most consistent performer, scoring in each of the three group games against Turkey, China and Costa Rica, and in the knockout stages against Belgium and England. He finished as the tournament's joint second highest scorer.

In the final against Germany it was Rivaldo's shot that keeper Oliver Kahn failed to hold onto when Ronaldo nipped in to score, and it was also his dummy that gave Ronaldo the space to fire Brazil's second. However, the tournament also showcased a more unsavoury side to his character. When

Turkish defender Hakan Ünsal kicked a ball towards Rivaldo, who was waiting to take a corner, it only struck his thigh but Rivaldo dramatically fell to the ground clutching his face. The referee dismissed the Turkish player, but after FIFA reviewed the video evidence Rivaldo was fined.

ROBERTO RIVELINO★

Country: Brazil **Born:** January 1, 1946

Position: Left midfield/Forward **Finals:** 1970★, 1974, 1978

Record: P15/W10/D3/L2/F6

The arrival of Mario Zagallo as Brazil coach in the lead up to the 1970 World Cup Finals proved to be a watershed in the career of Roberto Rivelino. Under former coach João Saldanha, the Corinthians midfielder had to be content with fleeting appearances, but as the tournament got underway in Mexico, it became evident that the greatest exponent of the 'banana shot' free-kick was ready to unleash his talents on a worldwide audience.

An inside-left by preference, to accommodate all of his talented players in one thrilling line-up, Zagallo converted Rivelino to a deep-lying left-winger where he combined in perfect harmony with Pelé, Gérson, Tostão and Jairzinho to form the most potent attacking force that Brazil had ever had. The highlight of his career came against Czechoslovakia, when a swerving free-kick goal inspired his team-mates to victory. Brazil ultimately triumphed in the final, beating Italy 4-1, and with three tournament goals to his name, Rivelino had played his part.

Inheriting Pelé's number ten shirt at the 1974 finals, Rivelino still possessed the famous moustache and his thunderous shot too, as witnessed by a tremendous 25-yard goal against Zaïre and the rocket-like strike against Argentina. The old Brazilian guile was still there too: with the East Germans preparing for one of his trademark bending free-kicks, instead Rivelino hit the ball straight at the wall, allowing for Jairzinho to duck down just in time for it fly through the space where he had once stood. It was a breathtaking goal, but with a weaker team around him than the stars of 1970, Rivelino

Rivelino, 1970 World Cup Final

was unable to save Brazil's campaign alone.

Captaining the team at the beginning of the 1978 World Cup he was hardly the player of old, now clearly overweight and unfit. He was also in dispute with his coach Cláudio Coutinho and was dropped after the first game. The armband was given to keeper Emerson Leão, and although Rivelino insisted that he was injured rather than surplus to requirements, he made two further substitute appearances. The third place play-off victory over Italy was the last of his 92 international games.

GIANNI RIVERA

Country: Italy **Born:** August 18, 1943

Position: Inside-forward **Finals:** 1962, 1966, 1970★, 1974

Record: P9/W4/D3/L2/F3

Gianni Rivera was an Italian hero. Slender and graceful, he possessed superb technique, tremendous passing ability and a powerful shot, particularly from distance. However, although he was feted for his peerless skills, the World Cup never really saw the best of this intuitive inside-forward, despite his appearance at four tournaments.

Having first played in Serie A at just 15 years of age, he was billed as the rising star of Italian football, making his debut for national side at 18, just two weeks before the 1962 World Cup. Included in the team for the opening game against West Germany, he was the youngest player at the tournament but he did not appear in either of Italy's remaining fixtures, dropped before he was able to prove what he could do.

Despite this failure he was voted into third place in the European Player Of The Year Award in 1963 for his endeavours during AC Milan's European Cup winning season, and by the time of the next World Cup the Italy team was largely built around his talents. Great things were expected, but he featured just twice during a woefully short campaign, including the shock defeat by North Korea.

His performances at club level earned him the European Footballer Of The Year award in 1969 but he often had to battle for his place in the national team with Sandro Mazzola. His public displeasure at learning that he would be starting the 1970 World Cup on the bench eventually sucked the head of the Italian football federation into the debate, with coach Ferruccio Valcareggi having to reach a compromise that he christened 'staffetta', or 'relay', where Rivera and Mazzola would each play a full half of the quarter-final against Mexico and the titanic semi-final with the West Germans.

Rivera came on for the second period of each game and scored in both, kick-starting a more attacking style of play. He was at fault for West Germany's third goal in the semi. Taking up a position on the goal-line to defend a corner, he all but waved Müller's header into the net. He later claimed that he had never been in that position before and didn't know how to defend the ball.

Legend has it that the speed with which he then got himself into the opposition half to score Italy's winning goal just a minute later was an attempt to escape the fury of keeper Enrico Albertosi, who had been berating him for the error.

With the World Cup all but over he was left on the bench for most of the final against Brazil, getting on the pitch for just the last six minutes with the Italians trailing 3-0. He made two more World Cup appearances at the finals of 1974, scoring in the defeat of Haiti, but on his return he was never to wear the blue shirt of Italy again.

ROMÁRIO ★

Country: Brazil **Born:** January 29, 1966
Position: Centre-forward **Finals:** 1990, 1994★
Record: P8/W6/D0/L0/F5

At his peak in the early 1990s, Romário was arguably the world's best striker and a worthy heir to the tradition of the great Brazilian attackers of the past, but aside from his one successful campaign at the 1994 World Cup, when he was the star turn of the tournament, Romário had little luck when it came to this competition.

Making his international debut in May 1987, although he very quickly established himself as a first-team regular, he made just one appearance at Italia 90, playing 65 minutes against Scotland before getting substituted. Having broken his leg three months earlier he hadn't played for either club or country since and this really wasn't the environment for a test run. He fired his one clear-cut chance straight at goalkeeper Jim Leighton.

Things were to be so different four years later. After reconciling a dispute with coach Carlos Alberto Parreira that had forced him to miss most of the World Cup qualifiers, he was recalled when the campaign looked to be in jeopardy and he scored twice against Uruguay to book Brazil a place at the finals.

Arriving at USA 94 as Brazil's one truly exceptional player, he didn't disappoint. Forging a deadly partnership with Bebeto, he scored five goals in the tournament and although he failed to get on the scoresheet in the final itself, he was among the successful penalty takers in the deciding shoot-out. Picking up a winners' medal, he was also named World Footballer Of The Year.

Although only 28 at the time, this was to be his last World Cup. Much to his chagrin he was cut from the squad at the very last minute in 1998 because of concerns that a long-term injury might not have healed properly, and he was similarly dropped four years later when several senior players were rumoured to have asked coach Luiz Felipe Scolari not to recall the veteran striker. With Romário accorded the status of national treasure in Brazil, there was a public outcry – the player called a press conference and broke down in tears, but the coach was not for turning. Although he would continue to play for his country until April 2005, Romário's World Cup career was over.

RONALDINHO ★

Country: Brazil **Born:** March 21, 1980
Position: Forward/Midfield **Finals:** 2002★, 2006
Record: P10/W9/D0/L1/F2

One of the best players at the 2002 World Cup, Ronaldinho helped Brazil to victory in the final by forming a spectacular attacking trio with Ronaldo and Rivaldo. Scoring twice in five appearances, he made worldwide headlines after winning the quarter-final against England with an astounding free-kick goal that beat keeper David Seaman from 35 yards. Minutes later he was sent-off for a foul on Danny Mills, adding drama to the story, but he served his suspension in time to return for the final and a winners' medal.

A sublimely gifted footballer, he was named World Player Of The Year in both 2004 and 2005. Nevertheless, by his own high standard he had a poor World Cup in 2006. He started in all five of Brazil's games as part of a much-vaunted 'magic square' attack, with Ronaldinho and Kaká playing a supporting role to Adriano and Ronaldo. However, he failed to find the net and the Brazilians were eliminated by France in the quarter-finals.

RONALDO ★

Country: Brazil **Born:** September 22, 1976
Position: Striker **Finals:** [1994★], 1998★, 2002★, 2006
Record: P19/W15/D1/L3/F15

At the peak of his football powers Ronaldo demonstrated searing pace, unbelievable skill and a razor sharp finishing ability, many believing him to be the nearest thing to Pelé that Brazil had since produced. He first travelled to the World Cup at the age of 17, but he was a non-playing squad member as Brazil lifted the trophy in 1994.

He was voted World Player Of The Year in both 1996 and 1997, and at the following World Cup in France he was tipped for great success, but instead Ronaldo's world began to unravel in the face of such high expectations. The team leant heavily on him throughout the tournament but he managed only four goals. On the morning of the final he suffered a fit, which led to his name being struck-off the team sheet in the hour leading up to the kick-off. However, when the Brazilians took to the pitch he had been reinstated in the line-up, though patently out of sorts. Brazil lost the game amid much acrimony.

Wear and tear after years of playing top-level football from a young age resulted in a serious knee injury in November 1999. Many wrote off his chances of returning to football but he fought back after extensive rehabilitation to prove his fitness in time for the 2002 World Cup Finals.

The competition proved his redemption as he picked up a winners' medal. He scored eight goals, including two in the final against Germany, and was awarded the Golden Boot as the tournament's top scorer. He was also named FIFA World Player Of The Year for the third time.

At the 2006 finals in Germany he appeared out of shape and both his physique and his performances were criticised. Even the president of Brazil poked fun at his bloated appearance on a live television link with the training camp, but he nevertheless

Ronaldo, 2002 World Cup Final

netted three goals. The last of which came five minutes into the second round defeat of Ghana, when he ran onto Kaka's through ball and rounded the keeper. That made him the competition's all-time top scorer with 15 World Cup goals, breaking Gerd Müller's record that had stood since 1974.

PAOLO ROSSI★

Country: Italy **Born:** September 23, 1956
Position: Centre-forward **Finals:** 1978, 1982★
Record: P14/W8/D4/L2/F9

A small and skilful centre-forward, Paolo Rossi travelled to the 1978 World Cup with no real certainty of playing. He had only won two caps since his debut the previous December, but once in Argentina his outstanding form in training games saw him elevated above Torino striker Francesco Graziani in the pecking order.

He was selected for the first game against France, and playing in a flexible forward line with Franco Causio and Roberto Bettega, he scrambled his first international goal just before the half-hour mark. He would also score against Hungary and Austria and held his place right through to the third place play-off game, which Italy lost to Brazil.

He had confirmed his potential at the tournament and demonstrated why he had been given a £3m price tag by his club side Lanerossi Vicenza, but in a surprising turn of events, by the following year it seemed highly unlikely that he would play in another World Cup.

He was accused of taking a bribe while playing on loan for Perugia in December 1979. Despite protesting his innocence he was suspended from football for three years, later reduced on appeal to two. Not returning to first-team football until six weeks before the 1982 World Cup, he received a surprise late call up for the Italian squad, and it was at the finals in Spain that his ailing reputation enjoyed an extraordinary resurrection.

He looked off the pace in the early stages of the competition, but he had the perseverance of coach Enzo Bearzot to thank for his continued selection, and he repaid that loyalty in full when he scored six goals in the last three games, including a hat-trick

Paolo Rossi v Brazil 1982

against Brazil and the opening goal of the final against West Germany. Italy ended the tournament as world champions and Rossi was named European Player Of The Year.

Injuries blighted his later career and he would not grace the World Cup again, retiring at 29, but he would always be remembered for his wonderful performances in the latter stages of the 1982 World Cup.

KARL-HEINZ RUMMENIGGE

Country: West Germany **Born:** Sept 25, 1955
Position: Forward **Finals:** 1978, 1982★, 1986★
Record: P19/W7/D7/L5/F9

One of the true greats of the German game, Karl-Heinz Rummenigge was a prolific goalscorer who represented his country at three World Cups and played in the final twice, collecting a runners-up medal on each occasion and scoring in the 1986 final.

First playing for the national side in 1976, coach Helmut Schön took Rummenigge to the 1978 finals as one of the few younger players in a side that was well past its best, and the Bayern forward made his World Cup debut against Mexico in West Germany's second game. Scoring twice in the 6-0 win, his first strike came at the end of a galloping solo dribble from deep inside his own half. It was enough to earn him his place in the team until Germany's campaign ended in the second group stage.

After the tournament Rummenigge's career really took flight and he was twice voted European Footballer Of The Year before he returned to the World Cup in 1982, when he captained the side to the final. He scored in West Germany's opener, a shock defeat to Algeria, but compensated with a hat-trick against Chile in the next game.

A slight injury saw him start the semi-final against France as a substitute, but he came off the bench in extra-time to score as the Germans turned around a 3-1 deficit to reach the final on penalties. It was the Italians that won the trophy but his performances throughout the tournament inspired the cult hit single 'Rummenigge', with the frighteningly catchy chorus, "Karl-Heinz Rummenigge, he's so strong, Rummenigge, Rummenigge, all night long".

Four years later and by now playing for Inter Milan, Rummenigge arrived at the World Cup beset by injuries and was used judiciously in the first round, coming on for the last 20 minutes of each game. With the team struggling he returned to the starting line-up from the knockout stages onwards, reclaiming the captain's armband from keeper Harald Schumacher. Once again he led the team to the final and although defeated by Argentina, Rummenigge sidefooted Germany's first goal from close range, his only strike of the tournament

He made just one more international appearance after returning home from Mexico. He had scored 45 goals in 95 games.

OLEG SALENKO

Country: Russia **Born:** October 25, 1969

Position: Centre-forward **Finals:** 1994

Record: P3/W1/D0/L2/F6

Oleg Salenko is a World Cup legend for just one game. He began the 1994 finals as a substitute, coming on as a 55th minute replacement for Sergei Yurin in Russia's 2-0 defeat to Brazil. He started the remaining games, scoring from the spot against Sweden, but with Russia already eliminated he scored five times against an ageing Cameroon side to break a 56-year-old tournament record.

Becoming the first player to score five goals in a World Cup, he also finished as the competition's highest scorer, sharing the Golden Boot with Hristo Stoichkov. Despite this performance, Salenko played only nine international matches in his career, one of them for Ukraine, and he didn't score a goal for either country outside of USA 94.

Oleg Salenko, right, v Sweden, 1994

LEONEL SÁNCHEZ

Country: Chile **Born:** April 25, 1936

Position: Outside-left **Finals:** 1962, 1966

Record: P9/W4/D1/L4/F4

Leonel Sánchez was the star of the Chilean team that finished third as hosts in the 1962 World Cup. Raiding from the left-wing in direct fashion, Sánchez ended the tournament as joint top scorer with four goals, a distinction he shared with five others.

He is also remembered for his part in the infamous 'Battle Of Santiago' between Chile and Italy. After being repeatedly kicked by Mario David, Sanchez knocked the Italian defender to the floor with a powerful left hook. Soon after David retaliated and was sent-off for a flying neck high kick aimed at Sánchez. The son of a boxer, Sánchez also broke the nose of Italian captain Humberto Maschio in front of the linesman, but again he avoided any sanction himself.

Four years later he was a member of a disappointing Chile side that crashed out of the World Cup in the first round. He captained two of the games in England.

JOSÉ SANTAMARÎA

Country: Uruguay & Spain **Born:** July 31, 1929

Position: Centre-half **Finals:** 1954 (Uruguay), 1962 (Spain)

Record: P7/W4/D0/L3/F0

The hard-as-nails Uruguayan centre-back was the defensive lynchpin of the all-conquering Nacional de Montevideo and Real Madrid teams of the 1950s and 1960s. He is one of five players to have represented two countries at the finals of the World Cup.

He missed out on a chance to win the World Cup in 1954 after his team Nacional refused to let him join the Uruguay squad, insisting that he was a defender rather than an inside-forward, the position he had been selected to fill. Four years later he was one of the stars of the tournament, playing in the centre of defence as Uruguay finished fourth, knocked out by Hungary and losing the third place play-off to Austria.

His impressive performances at the World Cup caught the attention of Real Madrid and he soon transferred to Spain. At the finals of 1962 he was to be found in Spanish colours, playing only twice in a side that also included Puskás. He won 17 caps for his adopted country and he was later the coach of a disappointing Spain side during the 1982 World Cup Finals.

DJALMA SANTOS★★

Country: Brazil **Born:** February 27, 1929

Position: Right-back **Finals:** 1954, 1958★, 1962★, 1966

Record: P12/W8/D2/L2/F1

An ever reliable right-back in the groundbreaking Brazil sides of the 1950s and the early 1960s, Djalma Pereira Dias dos Santos was a key member of the national squad for 16 years, making an impressive 93 appearances for his country. Although only three people have represented Brazil on more occasions, strangely he played just 12 times at the World Cup, a measly tally considering he appeared at four consecutive tournaments and played in the final twice, a winner on both occasions.

Making his international debut in April 1952 in a scoreless draw with Peru, Santos played in all three of Brazil's games at the finals two years later, mirroring on the right flank what his namesake Nílton Santos was doing on the left. He scored his one World Cup goal in the quarter-final of this tournament, converting from the penalty spot against Hungary after Jeno Buzánszky had brought down Índio.

Four years later coach Vicente Feola largely used Djalma Santos as an understudy for Newton De Sordi, who held the right fullback's slot through most of the competition. However, when faced with the threat of Sweden in the final, Feolo made a ruthless tactical switch to bring back the more experienced Santos for his only game of the tournament. Effectively neutralising the threat of winger Lennart Skoglund, Santos picked up his first World Cup winners' medal after the game.

An ever present member of the 1962 team, Djalma Santos formed a terrific understanding with star of the tournament Garrincha on the right flank. Not only did he collect another winners' medal, but he also set up Brazil's third goal of the final. With 12 minutes remaining and with the Brazilians holding a 2-1 lead, Santos hooked a high ball into the box from the right flank and the outstanding Czech keeper Viliam Schrojf let it drop through his hands, leaving Vavá to tap into an empty net.

Santos was 37 when he played at his fourth World Cup but the 1966 tournament was not a happy experience, and after just two games he was one of several veterans dropped following defeat to Hungary. He would make just one more appearance for Brazil, some two years later and aged 39.

NÍLTON SANTOS★★

Country: Brazil **Born:** May 16, 1925
Position: Left-back **Finals:** [1950★], 1954, 1958★, 1962★
Record: P15/W11/D3/L1/F1

Nílton dos Santos was described as a fullback, but in Brazil's revolutionary 4-2-4 formation of the late 1950s he was much more like a modern wing-back. He was at his best on overlapping runs up the left flank to support the strikers, but having started his career as a forward himself this was familiar territory.

Santos represented Brazil for 14-years, a spell that included two World Cup winning campaigns and 75 international appearances. He made his debut in April 1949 and although he embarked upon Brazil's ill-fated World Cup campaign the following year, he failed to make it onto the pitch and had to watch defeat in the final game from the sidelines of the Maracanã.

In 1954 Brazil fared slightly better in reaching the quarter-finals, but for Santos the tournament would have an embarrassing conclusion, as he was sent-off for brawling with Hungary's József Bozsik in the notorious 'Battle Of Berne'. Referee Arthur Ellis dismissed both of them and later commented, "Never before had I sent a player off in an international game, but never before had a player had the audacity to mix boxing with his soccer."

Santos did, however, score his one World Cup goal at the tournament. Finding himself high up the pitch in a one-on-one with the Austrian keeper, he gently lifted the ball over the diving Rudi Szanwald and into the net.

Nílton Santos and Bozsik, the 'Battle Of Berne', 1954

Four years later at the finals of 1958 Santos was an ever-present member of the Brazil side that became the first team to win the World Cup outside of its own continent. At 37 years of age, he also played in every game of Brazil's campaign in Chile in 1962, collecting his second winners' medal. The victorious World Cup final was his last game for his country.

GYÖRGY SÁROSI

Country: Hungary **Born:** September 12, 1912
Position: Centre-forward **Finals:** 1934, 1938★
Record: P5/W3/D0/L2/F6

A skilful and cultured forward, György Sárosi may have been a prolific goalscorer for his country but he was just as comfortable as a creator. One of the game's great players between the wars, he debuted for Hungary in May 1931 and made just one appearance at the 1934 finals, scoring a penalty in the quarter-final defeat to Austria.

In 1937 he scored seven goals in one game against Czechoslovakia and a year later he captained Hungary to the 1938 World Cup, leading the team to the final. In doing so he forged an exciting attacking partnership with Gyula Zsengellér and they proved devastating against Sweden in the semi-final. He scored five goals at the tournament, including Hungary's second in the final, but his team was soundly beaten by the Italians when it really mattered.

Holding a law degree, he was nicknamed 'The Doctor' and he also represented Hungary at other sports.

JUAN SCHIAFFINO★

Country: Uruguay **Born:** July 28, 1925
Position: Inside-forward **Finals:** 1950★, 1954
Record: P9/W6/D1/L2/F5

Small but lethal, Schiaffino was a lightning fast forward in the Uruguay team which won the 1950 World Cup in Brazil, stroking home a cross from Alcides Ghiggia to open the scoring in a 2-1 win over the hosts in the final game. It was his third goal of the tournament, having scored twice in Uruguay's 8-0 defeat of Bolivia.

He played again at the 1954 finals and was his country's most dynamic performer, having shifted into a more commanding midfield role. He scored twice as Uruguay reached the semi-finals, helping to see off the challenges of Czechoslovakia and England. However, with a place in the final in sight, this ageing Uruguay team lost out to the magnificent, undefeated Hungarians.

After losing to Austria in the third place play-off Schiaffino had done more than enough at the tournament to land himself a transfer to AC Milan for a then world record fee of £72,000. He later played four times for Italy, twice in the qualifiers for the 1958 World Cup, but after defeat to Northern Ireland the Italians failed to reach the finals.

ANGELO SCHIAVIO★

Country: Italy **Born:** October 15, 1905
Position: Centre-forward **Finals:** 1934★
Record: P4/W3/D1/L0/F4

Angelo Schiavio scored four goals at the 1934 World Cup, but the most important was the extra-time strike that won the final. He did so with a little help from the touchline, as Vittorio Pozzo was barking instructions to winger Enrique Guaita to keep switching positions with centre-forward Schiavio, as they had done on occasion earlier in the competition.

The ploy worked and although exhausted, Schiavio rounded a defender and beat the Czechoslovakia keeper. He had earlier scored a hat-trick in Italy's opening game against the United States. The World Cup final would be his last international.

SALVATORE SCHILLACI

Country: Italy **Born:** December 1, 1964

Position: Centre-forward **Finals:** 1990

Record: P7/W6/D1/L0/F6

Lasting less than a year and a half after his debut against Switzerland in March 1990, 'Totò' Schillaci's international career was nothing if not short. However, his place in World Cup history is assured thanks to the six goals he netted at the 1990 finals.

The Juventus striker had only gained two caps before Italia 90 but his goals proved pivotal throughout the competition. He came off the bench in Italy's opening game against Austria and scored after just four minutes on the pitch. He also hit the vital winning goal against the Republic Of Ireland in the quarter-final, and put Italy ahead in their semi-final clash with Argentina, only to see Diego Maradona's team come back to win on penalties. In the third place play-off he accepted a generous offer from Roberto Baggio and stepped up to score from the spot, winning the Golden Boot.

Totò Schillaci v Argentina, 1990

Despite his heroics, Schillaci played just eight more games for his country after the finals ended and scored just one more goal.

VILIAM SCHROJF

Country: Czechoslovakia **Born:** August 2, 1931

Position: Goalkeeper **Finals:** [1954], [1958], 1962★

Record: P6/W3/D1/L2/A7

The outstanding goalkeeper of the 1962 World Cup, Viliam Schrojf was the rock at the back of the highly defensive Czechoslovakia side that finished the tournament as runners-up. That the Czechs reached the final was largely down to the outstanding performances of Schrojf, who was in magnificent form in their quarter-final and semi-final clashes with Hungary and Yugoslavia, making a series of magnificent saves that kept the opponents at bay in both games.

It was unfortunate that against Brazil in the final Schrojf had a poor game by comparison and he was culpable when a high ball from Djalma Santos fell through his hands for Vavá to poke into an open net. Brazil won the game 3-1, but he was still voted the best keeper of the tournament.

He had been the only one of three Czechoslovakia keepers not to get a game at the 1954 World Cup, and he was a non-playing squad member again at the finals in Sweden in 1958.

HARALD SCHUMACHER

Country: West Germany **Born:** March 6, 1954

Position: Goalkeeper **Finals:** 1982★, 1986★

Record: P14/W6/D4/L4/A17

Instead of being remembered for all of his great performances in a seven-year career with the West German national team, Harald 'Toni' Schumacher will always be associated with one moment of madness in the 1982 World Cup semi-final against France. Dashing to the edge of his box to break up an attack, he leapt into the air, turning his upper body as he charged to protect himself from the impact, and clattered into Patrick Battiston, knocking the Frenchman unconscious.

In the minutes after the incident it was his callous attitude to Battiston's ever more serious looking treatment that caused outrage, waving the lifeless Frenchman and physios away as he waited impatiently to take a goal kick. Although Schumacher would win the game with two saves in the penalty shoot-out, in one action he had summed up the problem that many people, German fans included, had with the single-minded approach of Jupp Derwall's team of that time.

Four years later the World Cup saw a different side to Schumacher as he proved to be one of the stars of the tournament and he was voted its best goalkeeper, despite his team crashing to a shock defeat to Algeria in their first game. He put in a series of inspired performances to help a decidedly below par West Germany team reach the World Cup final, saving two penalties in the quarter-final shoot-out with Mexico. It was only in the final against Argentina that he failed, unable to get anywhere near the incoming high ball that José Luis Brown headed into the net for Argentina's opening goal.

After collecting his second World Cup runners-up medal, Schumacher would only play twice more for West Germany. For better or for worse he had made his mark on the World Cup – and on Patrick Battiston.

UWE SEELER

Country: West Germany **Born:** November 5, 1936

Position: Centre-forward **Finals:** 1958, 1962, 1966★, 1970

Record: P21/W13/D4/L4/F9

A small and sturdy centre-forward, Uwe Seeler was revered in German football for his fighting qualities and his never say die spirit, and he was known for his spectacular goals for the national team. His career took him to four World Cups, reaching one final, two semi-finals and one quarter-final. He scored in each tournament, an achievement matched only by Pelé, and his 21 appearances at the finals was a record that stood for 28 years.

Seeler made his international debut in October 1954, aged just 17, but it wasn't until the World Cup four years later that he really established himself, having made only four appearances prior to the finals. He scored

Uwe Seeler, right, v England, 1970

on his World Cup debut, which was his first game for West Germany in over two years, and he put the ball in the net once more before the campaign ended with defeat in the third place play-off.

He played in every game of the run to the quarter-finals in 1962, scoring twice, and four years later he skippered the West Germans at the 1966 World Cup, although his appearance at the tournament was something of a medical miracle. After a career-threatening injury he underwent a successful operation to fit an artificial Achilles tendon in 1965, and although not fully fit he returned to action six months later in time to score the winner against Sweden that took West Germany to the World Cup.

At the tournament Seeler was an ever-present member of the team, scoring twice as he led the Germans in the final game, where they lost to England after extra-time.

Seeler had dropped back into a deeper attacking midfield role by 1970 as he turned creator for Gerd Müller, who was to succeed him as Germany's most prolific striker, but it was Seeler whose looping backwards header equalised against England and pushed the quarter-final into extra-time. West Germany won the game but he had to settle for third place after losing to Italy in the semi-final and beating Uruguay in the third place play-off.

He played one more game for West Germany at home to Hungary after the finals. He scored 43 goals in 72 appearances and had been voted Germany's Player Of The Year on three occasions. He played his club football with Hamburg for his entire career.

PETER SHILTON

Country: England **Born:** September 18, 1949

Position: Goalkeeper **Finals:** 1982, 1986, 1990

Record: P17/W8/D6/L3/A10

Peter Shilton is England's most capped player with 125 international appearances, yet his final tally could have been higher. For years he vied with Ray Clemence for the goalkeeper's jersey, playing alternate games for quite a while, and it wasn't until his early thirties that he emerged as England's regular shot stopper. When Ron Greenwood selected Shilton as his first choice keeper for the 1982 World Cup it signalled the end of the Shilton-Clemence rivalry and after that he became England's dependable first choice for the remainder of the decade.

He made his international debut under Alf Ramsey in November 1970, but he first appeared at the finals in 1982, when he conceded just one goal in five games as England went out in the second round.

He appeared at the next two tournaments and in total kept ten clean sheets in 17 World Cup matches, at one point holding the record for the most minutes played without conceding a goal. However, for all his saves he is still remembered for the two goals that Diego Maradona put past him in the 1986 quarter-final: the first was an outrageous handball while the second was one of the greatest goals ever seen at the finals.

He quit the international game after helping England to fourth place in the World Cup in Italy in 1990.

AGNE SIMONSSON

Country: Sweden **Born:** October 19, 1935

Position: Centre-forward **Finals:** 1958

Record: P5/W4/D0/L1/F4

For a tall centre-forward Agne Simonsson was remarkably comfortable on the ball and he was also a fine creator of goals for those around him. He only played at one World Cup, in 1958, but he made his mark, scoring four times in five games. He missed just the group match with Wales, when he was replaced by Henry Kallgren and rested after Sweden had already qualified for the quarter-finals with a game to spare.

One of Sweden's most impressive looking players in a successful tournament, he was the scorer of a late goal in the World Cup final, but after a 5-2 defeat to Brazil it was a runners-up medal that he collected.

GUILLERMO STÁBILE

Country: Argentina **Born:** January 17, 1905

Position: Forward **Finals:** 1930★

Record: P4/W3/D0/L1/F8

A fast and prolific centre-forward, for many years Guillermo Stábile had his name in the history books as the first player to score a World Cup hat-trick, until in 2006 FIFA finally accepted the USA's claim on behalf of Bert Patenaude.

Stábile's hat-trick came on his international debut in Argentina's second game of the 1930 finals, a 6-3 defeat of Mexico. He had only got his break in the side by chance, as captain Manuel Ferreira had to miss the game to sit a law exam, and when Ferreira returned a space was made in the side for both of them.

Stábile proved he was no one-hit wonder, scoring twice more against Chile. He hit both the back of the net and the woodwork in the final, but although he was on the losing side he ended the campaign as the tournament's highest scorer. It would prove to be his last appearance for Argentina. Stábile, whose game was based on blistering pace, went on to play his club football in Europe, in both Italy and France. He would later coach the Argentina national side, occupying the post between 1939 and 1960.

HRISTO STOICHKOV

Country: Bulgaria **Born:** August 2, 1966

Position: Striker **Finals:** 1994, 1998

Record: P10/W3/D2/L5/F6

A lethal left-footed striker with a blistering turn of pace, Hristo Stoichkov was one of the world's best players when he helped unfancied Bulgaria to the semi-final of the 1994 World Cup. In doing so the Barcelona star finished the tournament as its highest scorer, an honour that he shared with Russia's Oleg Salenko.

The most important of his goals came in the 75th minute of the quarter-final against Germany, when he equalised with a 25-yard free-kick that was hit with such power that it left keeper Bodo Illgner rooted to the spot. He would later recall the goal as the best moment of his career, but the memories were no doubt enhanced by a match-winning header from Yordan Lechkov three minutes later.

In total Stoichkov scored six times at the tournament, three of which came from the penalty spot, two in a 4-0 victory over Greece and one a consolation in the semi-final defeat to Italy. Bulgaria had to settle for fourth after losing to Sweden in the third place play-off, one of only two games at the finals where Stoichkov failed to find the net.

He was also a member of the Bulgarian side eliminated in the first round of the 1998 World Cup, and he was appointed coach of the national team in 2004. He failed to take them to the 2006 World Cup and resigned the following year.

DAVOR SUKER

Country: Croatia **Born:** January 1, 1968
Position: Striker **Finals:** 1998, 2002
Record: P8/W5/D0/L3/F6

The star player of Croatia's run to the semi-finals of the 1998 World Cup in France, Davor Suker proved that he was worth more than a space on the Real Madrid substitutes' bench by scoring six goals in seven games, including a memorable late strike that capped a 3-0 win over Germany in the quarter-final.

He finished the tournament as its leading goalscorer, winning the Golden Boot, and he also collected the Silver Ball award after the world's media voted him the second-best player of the competition behind Ronaldo.

Davor Suker, v Romania, 1998

On the eve of the 2002 tournament 34-year-old Suker declared that he wanted to win the Golden Boot again, but he played just once at the finals, captaining the team for its first game before being substituted in the 67th minute and subsequently dropped. It was his last international appearance.

HAKAN SÜKÜR

Country: Turkey **Born:** September 1, 1971
Position: Forward **Finals:** 2002
Record: P7/W4/D1/L2/F1

A legend of the Turkish game, Hakan Sükur might not have been on his best form during his only World Cup, but he made a lasting mark when he set a new record for the quickest goal in the competition's history, beating a time that had stood since 1962.

Coming just 10.8 seconds into the third place play-off game against South Korea, Ilhan Mansiz capitalised on a defensive blunder by Hong Myung-Bo just outside the edge of the penalty area, and when the ball fell to Sükür he stabbed it home from 17 yards. The feat was all the more amazing considering it was the South Koreans who had kicked off.

MARCO TARDELLI★

Country: Italy **Born:** September 24, 1954
Position: Midfield **Finals:** 1978, 1982★, [1986]
Record: P13/W8/D4/L1/F0

Of all of his achievements in football, and they include five Italian league titles and a European Cup win, Marco Tardelli is most famous for the goal he scored in the 1982 World Cup Final and for the celebration that accompanied it.

Making his international debut in April 1976, he played the majority of Italy's campaign at the 1978 finals and missed only the third place play-off through suspension. He scored his first World Cup goal four years later against Argentina in the second group stage. Starting a sprint in his own half, he finally received the ball at the end of his dash and scored with a low cross shot from just inside the area. He ran up the flank in celebration but that was nothing compared to the moment of uncontrolled joy that accompanied his goal in that year's final.

Sweeping home a long-range shot that put Italy 2-0 in front and on course to winning the trophy, Tardelli went into ecstasy, running hands outstretched as if he would never stop and screaming at the top of his voice. This passionate celebration has become iconic in Italian culture and is known as 'Tardelli's scream'. "It was the pinnacle of joy," he would later say. "My kids give me joy but there's nothing like that one moment. In sport or in life, nothing compares to that moment."

Although he made the last of his 81 international appearances in September 1985, he was a member of the Italian World Cup squad in Mexico the following year and was among the named substitutes for three of Italy's four games at the finals.

PÁL TITKOS

Country: Hungary **Born:** August 1, 1908
Position: Outside-left **Finals:** 1938★
Record: P2/W1/D0/L1/F2

A powerful attacking left-winger with club side MTK Hungária, he made 48 international appearances for Hungary and scored 12 goals, the most important of which came after just seven minutes of the 1938 World Cup Final against Italy. The goal put the Hungarians back on level terms, and although he finished on the losing side, Titkos had scored twice in as many games, having only come into the team for the semi.

JAN TOMASZEWSKI

Country: Poland **Born:** January 9, 1948
Position: Goalkeeper **Finals:** 1974, 1978
Record: P11/W8/D1/L2/A8

Brian Clough dubbed him "a clown" on television in 1973, but after the Polish keeper pulled off a string of improbable saves that helped Poland reach the World Cup at England's expense, no-one was laughing.

Tomaszewski made his international debut in 1971 but really made his mark at the 1974 World Cup. He conceded just five goals in seven games on the way to third place and he also became the first player to save two penalties in the same finals, shutting out Sweden's Staffan Tapper and

West Germany's Uli Hoeness. For his outstanding performances he was voted the best goalkeeper of the tournament.

Two years later he won a silver medal at the 1976 Olympics and he also represented Poland at the 1978 World Cup, although his campaign would be abruptly brought to an end after conceding two goals to Argentina in the second round. He was replaced for the two remaining games by Zygmunt Kukla.

MARCELO TROBBIANI☆

Country: Argentina **Born:** February 17, 1955
Position: Midfield **Finals:** 1986☆
Record: P1/W1/D0/L0/F0

Marcelo Trobbiani can boast just about the shortest ever World Cup career. Coach Carlos Bilardo rewarded Trobbiani for his tireless work for the squad during training with one full minute of 1986 World Cup Final. It was his only appearance of the tournament and his only touch of the ball was a back-heeled pass – for that he was able to pick up a World Cup winners' medal.

JORGE VALDANO☆

Country: Argentina **Born:** October 4, 1955
Position: Striker **Finals:** 1982, 1986☆
Record: P9/W7/D1/L1/F4

Jorge Valdano made just 22 international appearances and scored seven goals for his country, four of them at the 1986 World Cup, but none were more important than the second goal of the final, which he slotted majestically past West German keeper Harald Schumacher after breaking down the pitch with a clear run on goal.

Partnering Maradona up front in 1986, Valdano was a tall and graceful centre-forward plying his trade with Real Madrid at the time, and the only overseas-based player selected by Carlos Bilardo for his home grown squad. He scored three goals en route to collecting his World Cup winners' medal, two against South Korea and a header against Bulgaria.

Nicknamed the 'Philosopher Of Football' for his intelligence both on and off the pitch, Valdano also made two appearances at the 1982 finals in Spain but missed the remainder of the tournament after sustaining an injury against Hungary.

Jorge Valdano v Italy, 1986

WIM VAN HANEGEM

Country: Holland **Born:** February 20, 1944
Position: Midfield **Finals:** 1974☆
Record: P7/W5/D1/L1/F0

Holland's best player at the 1974 World Cup wasn't any of its fine exponents of 'Total Football', but a footballer straight out of the old school. Wim Van Hanegem was a gifted left-footer who commanded the midfield with vision, precision and power. Tall, skilful and intelligent on the ball, he made his lack of pace seem like an asset.

Having lost much of his family to the war, the final against West Germany held an added significance for him and in defeat he famously left the pitch in tears.

Four years later he was named in the squad for the World Cup in Argentina, but he pulled out the before they were due to fly. His absence was attributed to a dispute with manager Ernst Happel over his place in the starting line-up, but in reality he was annoyed that the players preferred to keep individual sponsorship and advertising revenues for themselves, rather than pay everything into a central players' pool to be divided out among the whole squad.

Van Hanegem quit the team in disgust and sat out the tournament on a beach in Spain. He would tune in to the coverage for just one game: the final.

OBDULIO VARELA☆

Country: Uruguay **Born:** September 20, 1917
Position: Centre-half **Finals:** 1950☆, 1954
Record: P7/W6/D1/L0/F2

A gifted attacking centre-half, Obdulio Varela was the inspiration behind Uruguay's 1950 World Cup triumph, both on and off the pitch. Before the deciding game he rallied his players with a motivational team-talk, firing them up ahead of entering the intimidating Maracanã to face hosts Brazil. Out on the park he magnificently held the defence firm against relentless Brazilian attacks and after the break he drove his team forward.

Even after conceding a goal to Brazil he took the ball to the centre circle for the restart and shouted to his team, "Now, it's time to win". Uruguay scored two late goals and won the Jules Rimet Cup.

Varela was captain again for his swansong four years later when Uruguay finished third, but he was injured shortly after scoring in the quarter-final victory over England and missed the semi-final defeat to Hungary and the third place play-off. He made his last international appearance at the finals but he was able to look back with satisfaction, having never been on the losing side at the World Cup.

VAVÁ☆☆

Country: Brazil **Born:** November 12, 1934
Position: Centre-forward **Finals:** 1958☆, 1962☆
Record: P10/W8/D2/L0/F9

Real name Edvaldo Izidio Neto, Vavá wasn't certain to play at the 1958 World Cup, but was brought into the team to partner Mazzola for the second game of the tournament against England. Holding his place alongside World Cup debutants Pelé, Garrincha and Zito in a refreshed line-up for the pivotal clash with the Soviet Union, he scored twice as the Brazilians really came alive. Indeed, the game's opening moments, culminating in Vavá's first goal, are considered to be the best three minutes of Brazilian football ever played.

Dropped for the quarter-final against Wales, it became apparent how important Vavá was to the team and he replaced Mazzola for the remaining games, scoring twice in the World Cup final victory over Sweden.

Vavá, 1962 World Cup Final. After Brazil's third goal

In the years immediately after the tournament he played his club football in Spain, but after returning to Brazil in 1961 it seemed unlikely that he would do any more than understudy Coutinho and Pelé at the following year's World Cup in Chile.

It was a shock when he was selected as centre-forward, starting the tournament between Pelé and Garrincha, but he more than justified the decision with four goals, including a 78th minute tap-in that made him the first person to have scored in the final of two World Cups. His relationship with Garrincha on the pitch was the cause of much of the team's success and it blossomed after injury ruled Pelé out of the tournament following the second game.

Despite his success at the World Cup, he was curiously underused by the national team, his 20 international games and 15 goals spread over a decade.

FRITZ WALTER★

Country: West Germany **Born:** October 31, 1920

Position: Midfield/Forward **Finals:** 1954★, 1958

Record: P11/W7/D2/L2/F3

In his day Fritz Walter was the biggest star of German football. The captain of the 1954 World Cup winning team, his skill and creativity as a goal scoring midfielder was unrivalled in the immediate post-war era, and only Franz Beckenbauer could make a claim to outrank him in the list of German football legends, although Walter is held in far more affection by the country's football fans.

Playing for hometown club Kaiserslautern throughout his career, Walter made his international debut in 1940, scoring a hat-trick against Romania. After being drafted into the armed services, it was only when a Hungarian guard recognised him at a POW camp towards the end of the war that he narrowly escaped being sent away to the Soviet gulags.

In 1948 he returned to football, now alongside his brother Ottmar. At the age of 33, national team coach Sepp Herberger made him captain of the West German team for the 1954 World Cup in Switzerland. Although Walter might have been a fine captain, as a man he was prone to self-doubt and rather than pair him with his brother, Herberger had him sharing a room with the effervescent winger Helmut Rahn. The motivational policy worked and the German captain was inspirational throughout the campaign.

He scored three goals at the tournament as the West Germans bounced back from a heavy defeat to Hungary in the group stage to beat them in the final, in a match that would become known as the 'Miracle Of Berne'. In doing so Fritz and Ottmar Walter became the first siblings to win a World Cup.

Although not the captain of the West Germany team at the 1958 finals in Sweden, Herberger recruited Walter for his valuable experience and he made another five World Cup appearances as the Germans reached the semi-finals. It would be his last international game after 61 matches and 33 goals. He could have come out of retirement to play at the finals in Chile in 1962 had he listened to Herberger's entreaties, but aged 41 he declined the opportunity, having given up the game three years earlier.

In his last days it had been his dream for World Cup football to be played in Kaiserslautern, but his death during the 2002 World Cup meant he would never see this happen. However, on the fourth anniversary of his death, when Italy lined up to play the United States at the 2006 finals in Germany, the Fritz Walter Stadium fell silent to honour the memory of a true football legend.

WOLFGANG WEBER

Country: West Germany **Born:** June 26, 1944

Position: Centre-half **Finals:** 1966★, 1970

Record: P8/W6/D1/L1/F1

Wolfgang Weber certainly picked the right time to score his first international goal. With West Germany trailing England 2-1 and with only 15 seconds of the 1966 World Cup Final remaining, he capitalised on a goalmouth scramble to poke the ball into the net from close range, lifting it just over the stretching Gordon Banks and Ray Wilson. However, his efforts proved in vain after two extra-time goals settled the game in England's favour.

A tough and formidable central defender at club side Köln, with whom he spent his entire 16-year career, he made his international debut in April 1964 against Czechoslovakia and was a regular in the team by the time of the World Cup.

Weber made just two appearances at the 1970 finals. Coming on as a late substitute for Franz Beckenbauer against Bulgaria, he also started the third place play-off game. He played his last international against Spain in February 1974 and was not selected for the 1974 World Cup squad. He played 53 times for West Germany and scored twice.

ERNEST WILIMOWSKI

Country: Poland **Born:** June 23, 1916

Position: Inside-left **Finals:** 1938

Record: P1/W0/D0/L1/F4

No player in World Cup history has a better goals-per-game ratio than Ernest Wilimowski. Proving himself to be one of the most dangerous forwards in Europe at the time, in Poland's only match of the 1938 finals the 21-year-old scored four times, but the feat was eclipsed in a 6-5 defeat to Brazil. His World Cup record of four goals was often equalled but was not beaten until 1994, when Russia's Oleg Salenko scored five times against Cameroon.

A tall, flame-haired striker with six toes on his right foot, 'Ezi' made his international debut in May 1934 at just 17. He scored 21 goals in 22 appearances for Poland, but he missed out on the opportunity to impress at the 1936 Olympics, suspended for a year as a result of his fast-living lifestyle.

After the World Cup his international football career was shaped by world events. He was born in Katowice, Upper Silesia, when the province was in Germany (it would later become a part of Poland). During the war Wilimowski retook his German citizenship and played for the German national side, scoring 13 goals in eight games.

After the war the Polish government treated him as a traitor and he was not allowed to return home. He settled in Germany, where he continued his playing career, finally retiring aged 43 in 1959. He is said to have been disappointed that he was not selected for West Germany's squad for the 1954 World Cup, even though he was 37 at the time.

Years later he was reported to have wanted to visit the Polish team during the 1974 World Cup, but was refused permission.

LEV YASHIN

Country: Soviet Union **Born:** October 22, 1929

Position: Goalkeeper **Finals:** 1958, 1962, 1966, [1970]

Record: P13/W6/D2/L5/A18

Lev Yashin is regarded by many as the greatest goalkeeper in the history of the game. Extremely vocal, he kept his defence constantly on its toes and was one of the earliest keepers to venture out of his area to kick the ball away. His huge throws helped to launch rapid counter-attacks and he was also a penalty specialist, saving 150 in his career, including one from Hans Buzek of Austria at the 1958 World Cup.

Making his international debut in 1954, he was instrumental in taking the Soviet Union to the quarter-finals of the World Cups of 1958 and 1962, although the Soviets were eliminated by the hosts on both occasions. He was blamed for both goals against Chile in the 1962 quarter-final but he bounced back to win the European Player Of The Year award in 1963.

Along with Puskás and Pelé he was one of the big star attractions of the 1966 World Cup in England as his side reached the semi-finals, losing narrowly to West Germany with ten men. He also captained the Soviet Union to defeat in the third place play-off game against Portugal. Named in the squad for the 1970 World Cup in Mexico, he travelled to the tournament as third-choice keeper but didn't make an appearance.

Lev Yashin v Italy 1966

To commemorate his achievements in the game, in 1994 FIFA introduced the Lev Yashin Award for the best goalkeeper at the World Cup. Its recipients so far have included Michel Preud'Homme, Fabien Barthez, Oliver Kahn and Gianluigi Buffon.

MARIO ZAGALLO★★

Country: Brazil **Born:** August 9, 1931

Position: Outside-left **Finals:** 1958★, 1962★

Record: P12/W10/D2/L0/F2

Mario Zagallo's name is synonymous with the World Cup, although famously he allowed it to be spelt 'Zagalo' as a player and 'Zagallo', its correct spelling, as a manager.

He is the most successful individual in the history of the tournament, having won it on four occasions with Brazil in various roles, twice as a player in 1958 and 1962, once as a coach in 1970, and once as an assistant coach in 1994. He was also in charge of the team when the Brazilians were runners-up in 1998, which gives him an unrivalled track record at the tournament.

An intelligent outside-left renowned for his high work rate, it was this industry on the pitch that earned him the nickname the 'Little Ant'. He was an ever present member of the team's campaign in 1958, but he was rather fortuitous to get his place in the side.

Only debuting for Brazil the month before the tournament, he was third in the pecking order for the left-wing position, but following injuries to both Pepe and his reserve Canhoteiro, Zagallo came into the side and the tactics were adjusted to suit his less forceful style. Yet whatever he lacked in a physical presence on the pitch, Zagallo made up for with his tireless commitment to the team and you could always be certain that he would be the first back to defend if the team lost the ball.

He kept his place in the starting line-up throughout the tournament and he was at his best in the final against Sweden, heading off the line in the first-half . After the break he scored his team's fourth goal and then created Pelé's second of the match as Brazil claimed a 5-2 victory.

He picked up another winners' medal in 1962, having dropped back to a left midfield role, but again he had only reclaimed his place after a serious injury ruled out Pepe the month before the finals. Ultimately it was Zagallo's versatility that helped convert Brazil's attacking 4-2-4 formation to their trademark 4-3-3 playing style.

He made his last international appearance in 1964, having played 33 games and scored five goals. He hung up his boots a year later.

RICARDO ZAMORA

Country: Spain **Born:** January 21, 1901

Position: Goalkeeper **Finals:** 1934

Record: P2/W1/D1/L0/A2

Ricardo Zamora was the first huge star of Spanish football and also became the first goalkeeper to save a World Cup penalty, a 62nd minute stop from Brito against Brazil at the 1934 tournament.

He was inspirational in the bruising quarter-final against Italy, but was impeded by Schiavio for Italy's equaliser and so badly fouled that he was unable to play in the following day's replay, which Spain lost.

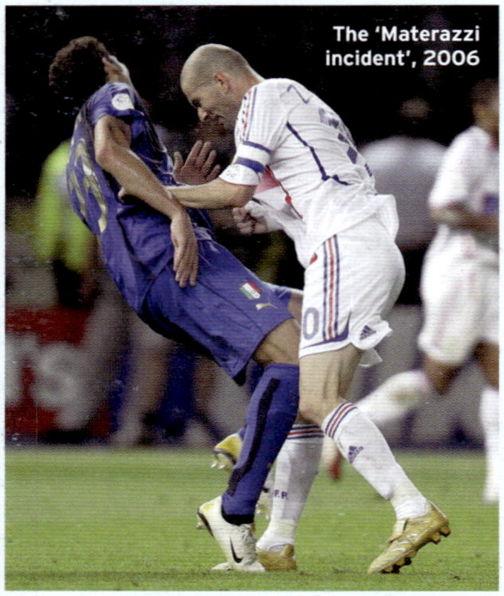

The 'Materazzi incident', 2006

Zinédine Zidane, 1998 World Cup Final. Celebrating his second goal

ZINÉDINE ZIDANE★

Country: France **Born:** June 23, 1972
Position: Midfield **Finals:** 1998★, 2002, 2006★
Record: P12/W7/D4/L1/F5

Zinédine Zidane's awareness on the ball, his sublime skill, peerless touch, and his unmatched big-game mentality marked him out as a genuine footballing superstar.

Consecutive Champions League finals with Juventus underlined his exceptional talent, but at the 1998 World Cup he bettered that, inspiring his country to victory for the first time. 'Zizou' ran rings around the world's best players and he scored the two goals that killed off Brazil in the final.

His triumph wasn't without controversy. He had been sent-off for violent misconduct earlier in the tournament, suspended for two games after senselessly stamping on Amin Fuad-Anwar. However, such was his talent that the game often overlooked his transgressions, and he was soon voted FIFA's World Player Of The Year, an honour that he was accorded once more in 2000.

Injury prevented him from rescuing France's 2002 World Cup campaign from disaster and he appeared only for the final group game against Denmark, although he was clearly not fully fit. He retired from international football after a disappointing 2004 European Championships, but the following year he was encouraged to make a comeback when the French were struggling with their World Cup qualification.

Captaining the side to the 2006 finals, he had made it clear that he was hanging up his boots after the tournament, but it was to be a sad ending to an illustrious career. In the World Cup final against Italy he converted a seventh minute penalty to put France in front, and by half-time the world's press had voted him the tournament's best player. However, after the game went to extra-time he was sent-off for violent conduct, goaded into butting Italian defender Marco Materazzi in the chest. Minutes after the game saw the last of Zidane, France lost the World Cup on penalties.

ZIDANE AT THE WORLD CUP

A winner and a loser in the World Cup Final, he was also a hero and a villain...

FRANCE 1998

ROUND 1 – ROUND 2 – QUARTER-FINAL – SEMI-FINAL – FINAL

Round 1: In only his second game at the finals, Zidane is suspended for two games after stamping on a Saudi Arabia player with France leading 2-0.

Quarter-final: Zidane returns to the team for the quarter-final with Italy and scores France's first penalty in the deciding shoot-out.

Final: He scores two first-half goals to help France to a 3-0 win over Brazil in the World Cup final.

JAPAN/SOUTH KOREA 2002

ROUND 1

Round 1: Injury rules him out of the first two games. Not fully fit he returns to face Denmark, but the team are eliminated.

GERMANY 2006

ROUND 1 – ROUND 2 – QUARTER-FINAL – SEMI-FINAL – FINAL

Round 1: After two yellow cards in two games he misses the group fixture with Togo.

Round 2: Back for the second round he is booked again but scores in a 3-1 defeat of Spain.

Quarter-final: He is voted Man Of The Match in the quarter-final victory over Brazil.

Semi-final: He scores the only goal of the semi-final against Portugal.

Final: After putting France ahead in the final, he is sent-off. It is his last ever game.

ZITO★★

Country: Brazil **Born:** August 8, 1932
Position: Midfield **Finals:** 1958★, 1962★
Record: P10/W9/D1/L0/F1

Born José Ely de Miranda, the player better known as Zito was on the winning side in two World Cup finals for Brazil, playing as half-back alongside Didi to form the pivotal midfield engine room on which Brazil's successes were built. More defensive by tendency and less inclined to run with the ball when an accurate pass could do the job, Zito was the perfect foil for his midfield partner.

Making his international debut in November 1955, he wasn't a first team regular at the start of the 1958 World Cup, but in the same shake-up that introduced Garrincha and Pelé to the team for Brazil's third game, Zito also got his chance. He supplanted Dino and held his place right through to the final.

He faced a stiff challenge for the position from Zequinha before the 1962 World Cup, but was ultimately selected because of the understanding he had already built with Brazil's lynchpin, Didi. He justified his selection in the final when his 69th minute headed goal gave Brazil the advantage.

Despite not having made an appearance for Brazil since May 1963, Zito was brought back into the squad for the 1966 World Cup, and although he played in many of the warm-up games and travelled to England, injury prevented him appearing in a disastrous campaign for the Brazilians.

A perfectionist who always liked to ensure things were performed efficiently, he later went into club management, gaining valuable experience while sidelined in 1966 by throwing himself into helping with the organisation of the squad.

ZIZINHO

Country: Brazil **Born:** October 14, 1921
Position: Inside-right **Finals:** 1950★
Record: P4/W3/D0/L1/F2

A marvellous player who lit up the 1950 World Cup to such a degree that reports in Italy's *Gazzetta Dello Sport* described him as Leonardo da Vinci, "creating works of art with his feet on the immense canvas of the Maracanã pitch". He formed a potent strikeforce with Ademir and Jair, and it was only due to the devastating impact of the defeat that Brazil suffered in the final game of the World Cup that his reputation has become somewhat eclipsed.

Pelé has often described Zizinho as the greatest player he ever saw, but for all his talents, as with other members of the losing team he was tainted by the defeat. He did not play again for Brazil until 1953. He made his last international appearance in April 1957 and was again overlooked for the World Cup squad the following year.

DINO ZOFF★

Country: Italy **Born:** February 28, 1942
Position: Goalkeeper **Finals:** [1970★], 1974, 1978, 1982★
Record: P17/W9/D5/L3/A16

One of the finest goalkeepers of all-time, Dino Zoff's career was packed with honours and memories, but none greater than the moment that he lifted the World Cup as Italy's captain in 1982. It was an achievement that had its own place in the history of the tournament: at 40 years and 133 days old he was the oldest player to have featured in a World Cup final.

Zoff made his debut for Italy in a European Championship quarter-final match against Bulgaria in April 1968, and he retained his place in the team as the Italians went on to win the tournament. At the 1970 World Cup he was supplanted by Enrico Albertosi and Zoff had to watch from the sidelines as a non-playing reserve.

Between October 1972 and June 1974 he went 1,142 minutes without conceding an international goal, setting a record that still stands. However, it took the unlikely Emmanuel Sanon of Haiti to end the run in Italy's first game of the 1974 World Cup. It didn't bode well and the Italians crashed out in the first round.

As captain Zoff led the Italians to the second group stage of the 1978 finals, but they were eliminated after defeat to Holland. Four years later he shepherded the team through difficult times. The players embarked on a media boycott after being unfairly pilloried by the Italian media, and the responsibility of facing the press fell to the taciturn Zoff.

After beating West Germany in the final all the rancour was forgotten for a moment. "For me personally, being captain and 40 years old, it wasn't a small thing. The happiness was extraordinary," he would later recall .

He retired from playing at the end of the 1982-83 season, having played 112 games for Italy, 59 of them as captain. He went on to coach the Italians to the final of Euro 2000, and despite his team leading until the last minute, they were beaten by France in extra-time, provoking his immediate resignation.

Dino Zoff, Italy v Haiti, 1974

Index

EVERYTHING YOU NEED TO KNOW

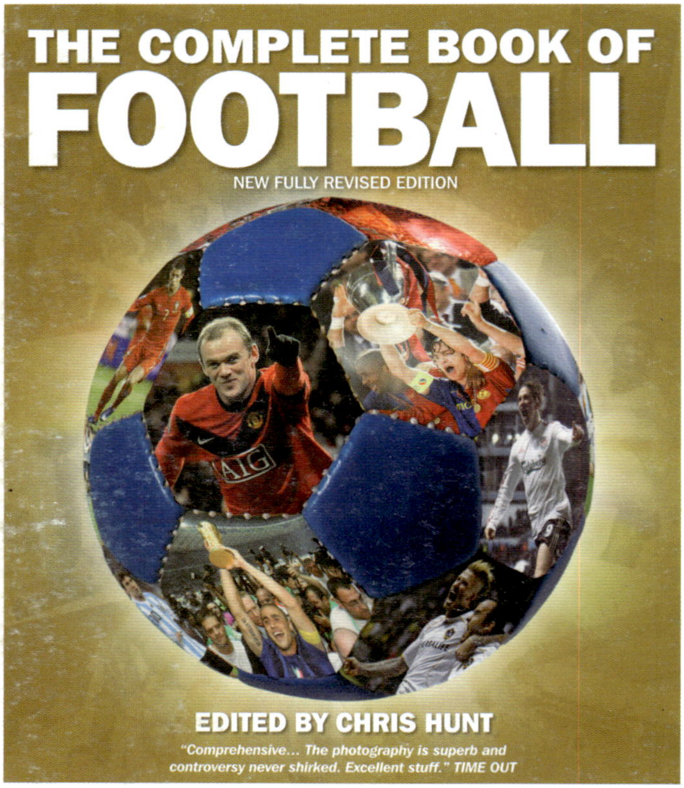

COMPANION TO
THE COMPACT BOOK OF THE WORLD CUP

ABOUT THE AUTHOR

A magazine editor and journalist, Chris Hunt has written about football and rock music for many years. He is the author of *World Cup Stories: The History Of The FIFA World Cup*, published to accompany a BBC TV series, while his experiences in Japan for the World Cup in 2002 were documented in another BBC television programme, *Beckham For Breakfast*. His football encyclopedia *The Complete Book Of Football* has been published around the world in many languages and is the companion publication to this book.

For more information: www.ChrisHunt.biz